Employment Relations in a Changing World Economy

Employment Relations in a Changing World Economy

edited by
Richard Locke
Thomas Kochan
Michael Piore

The MIT Press
Cambridge, Massachusetts
London, England

1995 Massachusetts Institute of Technology

This book was set in Palatino by Compset Inc. and was printed and bound in the United
States of America.

Library of Congress Cataloging-in-Publication Data

Employment relations in a changing world economy / edited by Richard
  Locke, Thomas Kochan, Michael Piore.
    p.   cm.
  Includes bibliographical references and index.
  ISBN 0-262-12191-3 (hc : alk. paper). — ISBN 0-262-62098-7 (pb :
alk. paper)
    1. Comparative industrial relations. 2. Employment (Economic
theory) 3. Labor economics—Case studies. 4. Human capital.
I. Locke, Richard M., 1959–   . II. Kochan, Thomas A. III. Piore,
Michael J.
HD6971. E554   1995   95-22499
331—dc20   CIP

to our students

Contents

List of Contributors   ix

Preface   xi

Introduction: Employment Relations in a Changing World Economy   xiii

Richard Locke, Michael Piore, and Thomas Kochan

1 **The Limits of Diffusion: Recent Developments in Industrial Relations and Human Resource Practices**   1

Marc Weinstein and Thomas Kochan

2 **Change and Continuity in British Industrial Relations: "Strategic Choice" or Muddling Through"?**   33

Keith Sisson

3 **Managed Decentralization? Recent Trends in Australian Industrial Relations and Human Resource Policies**   59

Russell Lansbury and John Niland

4 **Developments in Industrial Relations and Human Resource Practices in Canada: An Update from the 1980s**   91

Noah Meltz and Anil Verma

5 **Between Voluntarism and Industrialization: Industrial Relations and Human Resource Practices in Italy**   131

Ida Regalia and Marino Regini

6   Inertial Choices: An Overview of Spanish Human Resources,
    Practices and Policies   165
    Víctor Pérez-Díaz and Juan Carlos Rodríguez

7   Industrial Relations and Human Resources in France   197
    Jean Saglio

8   Continuity and Change in the "German Model" of
    Industrial Relations   231
    Martin Baethge and Harald Wolf

9   The Swedish Model: Demise or Reconfiguration?   263
    Andrew Martin

10 A Social Democratic Order under Pressure: Norwegian
    Employment Relations in the Eighties   297
    Karl Henrik Sivesind, Ragnvald Kalleberg, Svein Hovde, and
    Arvid Fennefoss

11 Developments in Industrial Relations and Human Resource
    Practices in Japan   325
    Keisuke Nakamura and Michio Nitta

12 Conclusion: The Transformation of Industrial Relations?
    A Cross-National Review of the Evidence   359
    Richard Locke and Thomas Kochan

    Index   385

List of Contributors

Martin Baethge
Georg-August University-
Göttingen
Soziologischesforschungs
Institut (SOFI)
Germany

Víctor Pérez-Díaz
University of Madrid
Spain

Arvid Fennefoss
University of Oslo
Norway

Svein Anton Hovde
University of Oslo
Norway

Ragnvald Kalleberg
University of Oslo
Norway

Thomas Kochan
Massachusetts Institute of
Technology
United States

Russell Lansbury
University of Sydney
Australia

Richard Locke
Massachusetts Institute
of Technology
United States

Andrew Martin
Harvard University
United States

Noah Meltz
University of Toronto
Canada

Keisuke Nakamura
Musashi University
Japan

John Niland
University of New South Wales
Australia

Michio Nitta
University of Tokyo
Japan

Michael J. Piore
Massachusetts Institute of
Technology
United States

Ida Regalia
Istituto di Ricerche Economiche e
Sociale (FRES)
Italy

Marino Regini
Istituto di Ricerche Economiche e
Sociale and University of Trento
Italy

Juan Carlos Rodríguez
University of Madrid
Spain

Jean Saglio
Centre National de la Recherche
Scientifique and University
of Lyon
France

Keith Sisson
University of Warwick
United Kingdom

Karl Henrik Sivesind
University of Oslo
Norway

Marc Weinstein
Massachusetts Institute
of Technology
United States

Harald Wolf
Soziologischesforschungs
Institut (SOFI)
Germany

Preface

This book is the product of an international network of researchers that has been meeting periodically since 1991 to debate changes in employment practices in industrialized countries. The initial meetings were held at the OECD headquarters in Paris, and subsequent meetings were held in conjunction with the ninth and tenth World Congresses of the International Industrial Relations Association.

The objectives of this network, and a sister group studying changing employment practices in Asian countries, are to help revive and reconceptualize comparative analysis in the field of employment relations and to do so by engaging scholars from different countries in collaborative projects that employ a common set of analytical concepts and methods. But at the same time we stress the need to engage in open debate to surface differences in perspectives and interpretation of events. Out of this dialogue we hope will emerge important theoretical advances and insights on how to respond to the challenges facing employment policies and institutions in our various countries.

We also hope that the range of participants in our research networks both broadens and deepens as our work progresses to its second phase, the study of changing practices across countries within specific industries. Our goal is to build a new cohort of researchers who work together in joint research projects, come together frequently at international meetings and conferences, and continue their dialogue via the modern information technologies now available to support global communications. If a new paradigm for the field of industrial relations (or employment relations as we call it here) is to emerge, it is likely to build on the ideas and data generated by networks such as this.

Support for this work was provided by the MIT Industrial Performance Center with funds provided by the Alfred P. Sloan Foundation.

Support for the two conferences in Paris was provided by the OECD. While working on this project, Richard Locke was supported by a Younger U.S. Scholars Fellowship from The German Marshall Fund of the United States. The publication of this book was aided by the diligent research assistance of MIT industrial relations students Brenda Lautsch, Lucio Baccaro, and Philip Hirschsohn. Susan Wright and Karen Boyajian provided the administrative support required to coordinate a group of highly individualistic colleagues spread across the world. We appreciate all the good work of our MIT team. Finally, we express our appreciation to each of our contributors for their perseverance through long hours of debate, consideration and reconsideration of different ways to organize ideas, and the long editing process required to see this project to completion. To our colleagues, we say, hopefully, this is only the beginning of better things yet to come!

Richard Locke, Thomas Kochan, and Michael Piore

Introduction: Employment Relations in a Changing World Economy

Richard Locke
Michael Piore
Thomas Kochan

Industrial relations emerged as a distinctive field of study and a locus of public policy in the aftermath of the Great Depression and the Second World War. Its focus was upon the organization of workers through trade unions and the way in which those organized workers operated to structure the economy, and through the economy, the society in which they lived. It tried to understand how that process could be channeled and controlled through public policy.

In recent years, however, industrial relations has been out of fashion. Unions have become passive actors, responding to economic pressures and social forces, seemingly without independent capacity to shape events or determine outcomes. Policy and scholarship have increasingly been dominated by neoliberal social thought. The belief that the structures that the economy requires to operate effectively are self-generating has become pervasive. Constraints imposed upon the operation of the market by government policy or through agreements negotiated among the social actors have come to be blamed for unemployment, inflation, and economic stagnation. Aggressive policies of deregulation and decontrol have spread from Thatcher in England and Reagan in the United States throughout the Western Hemisphere. Industrial relations research itself has retreated from national economic policy to niches in schools of business where, rechristened as human resource management, it has begun to prescribe strategies for individual enterprises.

The influence of neoliberalism upon public policy reached its apogee with the collapse of the Soviet Empire, and then of the Soviet Union itself, and the rush of the former communist countries to dismantle the structures of state control in order to let the natural market emerge beneath it. But the collapse of state communism has also marked the limits of the neoliberal resurgence. The transition of the old communist regimes has made it increasingly apparent that there is no such thing as the natural market. Capitalism, these counties are learning, operates within an institutional framework. That framework does not emerge spontaneously; it must be deliberately created through law and its operation motivated and directed by public policy. Economic theory, however much it may explain market economies already in operation, has not proved to be very helpful in creating effective and efficient market systems from scratch. And the search for guidance in the practices of operating capitalist economies has revealed a bewildering variety of different institutions and approaches. It is clear that there are several distinct models of how a reasonably successful capitalist economy might operate. In choosing among these models, indeed in even specifying what they are, the kind of economics that underlies neoliberal thought must be complemented by other social sciences.

The rediscovery of the institutional and social foundations of a capitalist economy has operated to reinforce a certain residual anxiety about the role of labor in industrial society. Nobody entirely understands why spontaneous worker protest and organized labor agitation, which were such central features of industrial society virtually from its inception, have suddenly declined or even disappeared. There is thus a lingering sense that it might suddenly reemerge and that, in the vacuum created by the atrophy and disintegration of the institutions through which it was channeled, we will be faced with the kind of chaos and anarchy that it regularly produced in industry throughout the nineteenth century and in Western Europe in the late 1960s. Apprehension is heightened in the United States by the recognition that the decline of the labor movement has been accompanied by a dramatic increase in income and other social disparities, a development that, as the separate chapters of this volume make clear, is by no means unique to this country. The centrality of organized labor in many of the dramatic regime changes of recent times—in Poland and in South Africa, for example—serve to heighten this sense of uneasiness and create a nostalgia for the insights and perspective that industrial relations scholarship was once able to provide.

But it is clear that to address contemporary issues, industrial relations as a field of study will have to take an increasing international and comparative dimension. It is not simply that the emergent regimes in Eastern Europe and the former Soviet Union need to understand the impact of the alternative institutional structures in the countries that serve as models for their own economic reforms. Developments in the capitalist world itself have brought compatibility, or lack there of, of institutional arrangements in different countries increasingly to the fore. Even in the narrow domain of human resource management to which industrial relations as a field of study has been progressively reduced, the globalization of markets has forced individual companies to operate with ever greater frequency in a variety of different national contexts where they must reconcile—or at least justify differences in—labor policies across national boundaries. Similar forces are bringing national economies increasingly in competition with each other, creating a need for them to identify the distinctive features of their own national systems and evaluate their impact upon economic performance. The movement toward economic integration in Western Europe, and now in North America, is also underscoring differences among national laws and institutions and creating insistent pressures for reconciliation. Increased liberalization of trade under the World Trade Organization (WTO) is creating these pressures on a global scale.

We have thus entered into a form of international competition/cooperation that requires us to separate out legitimate differences in structures, institutions, and social values from hidden subsidies and unfair competition. In neoliberal theory these differences can be conveniently made to go away through deregulation, but when economic activity requires an institutional framework for its operation, deregulation cannot proceed indefinitely without the eventual disintegration of the economy itself. As we begin to reach those limits, we must ultimately decide what parts of the remaining structures to preserve and/or recast. And in the international economy toward which we are moving, this will have to be done with references to the institutions and structures of other nations, including the institutions' governing employment relations. The emergent debate about international labor standards is thus symptomatic of the basic problem that this new trading regime poses for public policy and for research. This volume represents the first phase in a project directed toward clarifying these issues and contributing to this debate.

Existing Theory and Its Limits

The last major attempt to develop a comprehensive framework for thinking about national differences in industrial relations was the

Ford Foundation's interuniversity study, a project initiated in the late 1950s. This work was heavily influenced by John T. Dunlop's *Industrial Relations Systems* (1958). Dunlop advanced the notion of industrial relations as a distinct sphere of socioeconomic activity, in the sense that politics and economics are separate spheres of activity and, like politics and economics, understandable in terms of distinctive national systems. In his analytical schema, industrial relations systems had an *output* in the sense that the economy has an output of goods and services and politics has an output of legislation. For industrial relations, he argued, that output were the rules of the workplace.

The perspective that emerged in the interuniversity study was synthesized by Clark Kerr, John Dunlop, Fredrick Harbison, and Charles Myers in *Industrialism and Industrial Man* (1960). Looking back upon that synthesis from the perspective of contemporary social science, it can be characterized as excessively functionalist, technologically deterministic, and ethnocentric. It was functionalist in that it sought to understand and explain practices by reference to their contribution to economic efficiency and social stability. It was technologically deterministic in that the evolution of industrial relations was driven by a singular technological dynamic. It reflected the ethnocentrism pervasive in American social science of the period in that the United States was seen as the technological leader and its institutions and its practices were presented as the "best practice" model for other nations to emulate. Patterns in other countries were viewed as derivative of, or deviations from, the U.S. model. The view was reinforced in industrial relations scholarship more broadly by the many European industrial relations scholars who had studied in the United States.

The major competing schools of labor studies were heavily influenced by Marxian scholarship (Hyman 1975). Work in this tradition embodied a much more acute sense of class conflict and of the role of ideology, and it had a different idea of the system's historical trajectory, though it too explained outcomes in terms of the functions they perform for interested actors. Its functionalism was embedded in a different but equally deterministic view of technology's role in the evolution of industrial society; and Marxists were, if anything, even less inclined to recognize and highlight distinctly different national patterns.

Both events and scholarship have undermined the perspectives that dominated industrial relations in the early postwar decades. Particularly influential in this regard was the wave of labor protest that broke over Western Europe in the late 1960s, the growing recognition among European scholars that it could not be adequately captured within the framework developed by their American colleagues, and the emergence of distinct European strands of non-Marxist industrial relations scholarship. More recently the emergence of Japan, with its distinct labor practices, as a competitive power in world markets has further challenged the preeminence of the American model and the ideas about efficiency and the historical evolution of national practices with which it is associated. Finally, the changes in practice in the 1980s called into question that model even within the United States itself.

Most of the new scholarship, however, has focused upon individual countries, often in the context of particular national debates. It has thus produced a heightened awareness of national peculiarities, without generating a framework through which different national practices could be compared and evaluated. Several genuine international comparisons have focused on pairs of countries. Of these the most influential and important are undoubtedly Ronald Dore's (1973) study of Britain and Japan and the Aix-en-Provence study of France and Germany (Maurice, Sellier, and Silvestre 1986). Together these studies suggest differences among countries that are both more profound and more enduring than is consistent with the spirit, if not the letter of Kerr, Dunlop, Harbison, and Myers. More important, the framework of U.S. industrial relations theory is obviously inadequate for capturing these differences.

In a sense these two studies present different approaches. Dore follows the earlier tradition in seeking to establish the relative efficiency of the two systems and predict, on that basis, the historical evolution of practices in other countries. The novelty of his argument is that Japan, not Great Britain, and by extension, not the United States, has emerged as the best practice model. The Aix-en-Provence group, by contrast, presents two completely different but equally effective approaches to labor organization and management and traces them to factors rooted so deeply within national culture and history that convergence seems to be virtually precluded.

Both Dore and the Aix team have made efforts to extend their work to other countries but with no clear results. Dore studied a group of developing countries, looking for (but failing to find) a tendency for late developers to follow the Japanese pattern in a determinate fashion. The Aix approach has been extended by various researchers to

Japan, Great Britain, and Italy in a way that seems to reinforce the lesson that each national pattern is peculiar but does not really address the question that seems critical to the practical problems posed by the competition among countries and enterprises, namely what can be learned from other experiences.

One lesson that the Aix studies make clear, and that is also implicit in Dore's work as well, is that industrial relations alone is not a self-contained domain of activity. It has to be understood in terms of related activities and broader social and cultural structures. These include the systems of education and training and of government labor market regulation. In the United States a significant portion of what in other countries is provided by the social security system is also generated by industrial relations, and hence in comparative work we must look at welfare state provisions as well in order to compare our employment relations to those in other countries. A recognition of these interrelationships raises analytical questions that extend well beyond comparative research to the analytical framework of industrial relations itself. Changes in practice, especially in the United States, also pose a series of challenges to the analytical framework, for they have been directed, as much as anything else, at the use of explicit work rules in the governance of the workplace (which Dunlop took as the output of industrial relations systems and hence as the end point that the analytical framework was constructed to explain).

Growing dissatisfaction with traditional frameworks and interpretations has stimulated researchers to reexamine developments within their individual national settings in search of a better explanation and understanding of the changes under way (Edwards and Sisson 1990; Shirai 1983; Streeck 1991; Chaykowski and Verma 1992; Piore and Sabel 1984; Kern and Schumann 1984; Kochan, Katz, and McKersie 1986; Locke 1995; Osterman 1988; Mathews 1989). Yet to date, little effort (for an exception to this, see the Industrial Democracy in Europe Committee, 1980, 1981) has been made to look across countries to update our perspectives on comparative industrial relations and human resource policy questions. That is the task which this book begins to undertake.

The Present Project

The essays that constitute the core of this volume employ a common framework to examine changes in the employment relations and work structures in eleven OECD countries: The United States, United Kingdom, Canada, France, Germany, Italy, Spain, Norway, Sweden, Australia, and Japan. They constitute the first phase of a longer-term project centered at the Center for Industrial Performance at MIT. The support to launch this project was provided through the Center with the aid of the Sloan Foundation and the OECD, but each of the individual studies received additional support from within their own countries. Through the sponsoring agencies, this project on work and employment relations is linked to a broader research program whose aim is to enrich our understanding of industrial competitiveness in a global economy. It is in this sense an integral part of an ongoing effort to update and, in the process, to reconceptualize our analytical model and conceptual categories so as to better understand and interpret the changing face of employment relations. The hope is that this, in turn, will enable the scholarly community to provide the analytical tools and the substantive knowledge required to reconfigure the social foundations of national economic activity in a fashion consistent with the emergent globalization of production, distribution and exchange.

The Conceptual Framework

From the beginning this project was based on the belief that significant advances in theory and policy analysis can best be achieved if carried out by scholars who possess a deep knowledge and understanding of the culture, institutions, and policy issues of the country they are studying. Thus each chapter in this volume is written by national scholars. The authors agreed at the outset to adopt a common framework that allowed considerable latitude for individual researchers to incorporate their own insights and to pursue the particular directions toward which those insights may point. The project was initially conceived of and organized by the Industrial Relations Section of the MIT Sloan School of Management, and the hypotheses of that group were the starting point for discussion and debate among the researchers represented in this volume. In that sense these hypotheses provided the initial direction for the project, so it might be helpful to readers to have a minimal understanding of these ideas as they have evolved.

The initial hypotheses were developed in three texts: *The Second Industrial Divide* by Michael Piore and Charles Sabel, *The Transformation of American Industrial Relations* by Thomas Kochan, Harry Katz, and

Robert McKersie, and *Employment Futures* by Paul Osterman. Each of these books presents a distinct series of arguments, and they are not wholly consistent with each other but do suggest a single, relatively coherent story about the recent evolution of the institutional and labor market structures of the American economy. The relevant part of that story for the domain of this project may be summarized as follows:

In the early postwar period the United States became committed to a distinct approach to industrial relations, human resource development, and social welfare policy. The key element in that approach was a process of collective bargaining between large employers and national industrial unions in key manufacturing industries. The unions were rooted in the shop, where they sought to control not only wages and working conditions but also specific work practices and career opportunities. The framework for shop-level and company agreements was developed, *de facto* or *de jure*, at the industry level and effectively took wages and working conditions out of competition. There was no interindustry collective bargaining, but the labor movement managed to impose, through the political process, a set of minimum wages and labor standards as well as a base level of old-age and unemployment insurance. And there were relatively strong patterns of imitation in collective bargaining across industries that caused wages and employment conditions to move, more or less, in tandem throughout the economy. Particularly important in postwar wage movements was a commitment in the automobile industry to a general wage-setting formula consisting of an annual improvement factor (AIF) of 3 percent plus an allowance for changes in the cost of living (COLA). The collective bargaining structure was anchored in the shop by a list of meticulously defined *jobs*, each assigned to a particular worker. The rules governing the allocation of employment opportunities, wage rates, and work practices were specified in terms of these job definitions, and it was thus through these jobs that the collective bargaining agreement controlled work practices. But apart from the negotiation and administration of these rules, the union played an essentially passive role. Indeed a clearly demarcated division of labor between workers and their union, on the one hand, and management, on the other—comparable to the sharp delineation of job assignments among workers—was established. This division of labor was such that within the framework of the collective agreement, management ran the shop and labor grieved.

This labor relations system appears to have grown up around and been predicated upon an underlying commitment of U.S. business to mass production as a competitive strategy, that is, the production of long runs of standardized products for a large mass market. The American approach to mass production involved the specialization of productive resources through the use of dedicated machinery and narrowly trained, semiskilled workers. The standardization of the product and the consequent stability of the product design and the equipment with which it was produced lent itself to the job definitions around which collective bargaining arrangements were built. Indeed such job definitions were thought to be central to efficient management and had been introduced in the leading sectors of American industry with the initial development of mass production, long before industrial unions emerged in the late 1930s. Other aspects of the postwar system—the wage floor imposed by legislation and the auto industry wage formula which served as a general pattern for the economy as a whole—were conducive to macroeconomic stability in a productive system where highly specialized resources made it difficult for price variation to stabilize the economy.

This industrial union model of collective bargaining essentially replaced an earlier tradition of labor relations associated with craft unions. The craft tradition was one in which the union played a much more active role in the training and allocation of labor and was often involved with management in the organization of the production process itself. The craft tradition was at one time strong even in the manufacturing sector, but modern industry had emerged in the United States by and large by breaking the craft unions and introducing productive techniques that minimized the dependence on craft skills. Craft unions continued in the postwar period, but as an important force largely outside the manufacturing sector. Within manufacturing only vestiges remained incorporated within industrial unions or operating as appendages to industrial collective bargaining.

Because the American system of collective bargaining, and of production more generally, is tied to narrow, semiskilled jobs, it operated independent of education, training, and human resource development. The necessary training for semiskilled labor was provided by the employer on the job and placed virtually no reliance upon prior education and experience. The skilled work force was generated on an ad hoc basis through arrangements with vestigial craft unions, by recruitment from the construction industry where craft unions remained strong, by particular arrangements with local schools, and through the periodic recruitment of skilled migrants from elsewhere in the country.

In the 1970s these arrangements came under increasing strain and began to break down. A variety of factors appear to be responsible for the breakdown of the old structure: heightened competition due to the increasing internationalization of economic activity and the deregulation of American industry; the increasing instability and uncertainty of the business environment associated with fluctuating energy prices, exchange rates, inflation, and the like; new, more flexible productive techniques growing out of advancements in information technology and telecommunications; a shift in competitive strategy toward differentiated, high-value-added products; and a shift from blue- to white-collar jobs and from manufacturing to service industries. Piore and Sabel argue that all of these factors are associated with a shift away from mass production to a technological trajectory driven by "flexible specialization" which employs more general resources capable of responding rapidly to changes in business conditions and market demand.

The new labor relations models introduced in response to these changes seem to have first originated in the late 1960s and early 1970s in experiments in non-union companies and/or the non-union plants of otherwise organized firms, but they have been highly influenced as well by various patterns and practices observed in Japan. Relative to the industrial union model of the postwar period, they are characterized by (1) much more flexible work assignments and less easily defined and clearly demarcated jobs, (2) a greater involvement of the work force in production decisions and a consequent blurring of authority between labor and management, (3) compensation systems detached from jobs and more tightly linked to individual characteristics such as skill level or performance evaluation, (4) overall wage levels detached from the old automobile formula and often including profit-sharing and/or lump-sum bonuses as opposed to regular annual increases in the basic wage rate, and (5) enhanced employment security arrangements in which some or all of those currently employed are given protection from layoff in return for a greater commitment to the company and greater flexibility in work assignments. As noted earlier, this model was developed originally in the non-union sector. Kochan, Katz, and McKersie had argued that when these arrangements were adopted by unionized establishments, the focus of collective bargaining had to shift from the negotiation and enforcement of rules and constraints upon managerial action to more substantive business objectives. Unions gained increased control not by imposing and policing rules but by participating in strategic company planning through arrangements like seats on board of directors and/or employee stock ownership plans (ESOP). All of this implies a weakening of collective bargaining and control at the industry level and a change (which the rank-and-file often perceive as a weakening as well) in the mode of control on the shop floor.

Companies often conceive of these new arrangements in terms of a core-periphery model, in which the new participatory arrangements and associated employment guarantees (profit-sharing systems, etc.) extend only to a portion of the labor force. Flexibility to adjust to uncertainty is then reintroduced through a peripheral labor force that has no strong company ties and can be easily hired and fired. Generally, the new arrangements are associated with an increase in skill requirements, better education, and broader training at least for the core labor force. Employment security arrangements and new compensation systems are often seen as binding this labor force to the firm and permitting greater company investment in skill development.

The new model, however, has not proved to be as compatible with unionization as the old. It has been introduced largely in non-union facilities and, even there, has not diffused as rapidly or extensively within the United States as, say, in Japan, or, even among certain European nations. The non-union bias and the rate of diffusion was one of the issues that we were anxious to explore through comparative international research.

Comparative Research—The Original Propositions

Based on the U.S. experience, the MIT team developed four broad propositions to guide the research of the various country teams. First, we argued that labor and human resource policy in today's environment cannot be understood using the narrow terms of traditional industrial relations theory or what has come to be defined as human resource management.

Second, we claimed that employment policies, procedures, and institutions had to be conceived of as fitting into *systems* of interlocking and mutually reinforcing elements: The individual components of such systems cannot be understood in isolation or changed piecemeal. This is as true of the personnel practices of single enterprises as it is for the broader institutions that structure the roles of labor, management, and government interactions at the local, industry, and national levels.

Third, we claimed that in all countries, employment policies must be studied in combination with business (competitive) and production strategies at the enterprise level. Indeed in a number of countries, interactions at the enterprise level appear to be taking on greater importance as firms restructure their operations in light of changing markets, technological opportunities, and new conceptions of the relationship between production and human activities. But it is also clear that in some countries the choices of competitive strategies and employment policies are determined outside the boundaries of individual firms. To be sure, the levels at which these choices are made and the roles of business, labor, and government in shaping these choices pose an important intellectual and policy puzzle, one that will feature prominently in the discussion to follow.

For example, much of the U.S. research tends to emphasize two basic competitive strategies firms make that are expected to be tightly coupled with employment practices: (1) cost-driven mass production strategies based on low wages, low skill levels, and arm's-length or adversarial labor management relations and (2) strategies emphasizing product quality, innovation, and differentiation, production flexibility, and well-paid, well-trained, highly skilled workers and cooperative labor-management relations. But in countries where state policies, strong institutions for worker representation, and/or more centralized structures exist, the choice of competitive strategies and/or the ability to vary employment practices according to the strategy adopted may be constrained. Thus understanding what linkages exist (if any) between these different competitive and production strategies and human resource practices in different industries or segments of industries, and what role (if any) industry associations and government policy play in strengthening and diffusing one set of linked practices over another emerged as a key issue and a hotly debated topic as our research progressed.

In connection with the last point is a fourth proposition that was introduced in the initial discussion of this framework but evolved and deepened as our work progressed. This proposition is that corporate governance arrangements have important and systematic effects on employment policies and practices. There appears to be considerable cross-national variation in the importance firms accord to human resource issues depending on the norms and legal doctrines that shape the conceptions and obligations of corporations in different societies and on the nature of their capital markets and institutions (Aoki 1988). Exploring further the role of public policy and legal regimes in defining particular patterns of corporate finance, governance, and their relationships to employment practices is another important goal of this study.

To discuss these initial propositions, researchers from the eleven countries covered in this study met first in 1991 and then again in 1992 at the OECD headquarters in Paris. As one might well imagine, the debates that took place at these meetings were lively, since the group mixed together scholars from different cultures, disciplines (sociology, political science, economics, industrial relations, and law), and individuals identified with different intellectual paradigms and methodological approaches to the study of employment issues.

Thus, although these four propositions provided the starting point for our analysis, they were subjected to considerable questioning and debate. This is important to keep in mind when reading the chapters that follow, for some of these critiques will surface again. For example, some questioned whether the original conception of the project was still too attached to John Dunlop's (1958) industrial relations systems model or to the strategic choice approach advocated by those of us from MIT. Questions were raised over whether we would adequately capture the differences in the roles and definitions of the different levels of interaction above the level of the firm. Others questioned whether the new, growing white-collar occupations, service industries, and nontraditional employment relationships were adequately captured in the framework. Still other questions were raised about just how much change actually had occurred in traditional practices in different countries and wondered whether the amount and fundamental nature of the changes emphasized in so much of the U.S. literature reflected the historical exceptionalism of the U.S. situation or differences in research methodologies employed in studying change (Marginson et al. 1988; Sisson 1990; Wood 1990). Readers of this volume will eventually have to judge for themselves whether these critiques are valid or not. We raise them here to urge others to join us in these debates in the hope of stimulating more critical thinking about how to best conceptualize and study employment issues in a comparative context.

Out of these initial discussions emerged a consensus over a two-phase research strategy and framework to guide our analysis. Phase 1 would consist of country papers prepared to apply and test the fit of the general framework to recent events in employment relations in the various countries. Phase 2 would then move to more micro analyses of practices followed within specific industries and enterprises. This book reports on the results of phase 1, and in the last chapter we highlight questions our work to date poses for future and more micro investigation in the second phase.

The Common Framework

Figure I.1 summarizes the general concepts and the structure guiding the organization of the analysis contained in the country chapters that follow. The framework focuses on four common firm-level employment practices:

1. Changes in the organization and scheduling of work due to new technologies and altered competitive strategies (decentralization, flexible working times, etc.). Linked to this are shifts in work rules and changing patterns of employee participation within the firm.

2. New compensation schemes affecting the level, structure, and forms of compensation for both blue- and white-collar workers.

3. Changing patterns of skill formation and training to match the altered needs of firms. Related to this is another set of questions regarding the shifting balance between the public and private provision of not just education and training but a whole array of other social welfare benefits and services.

4. Issues of staffing, employment security, and job mobility. How are entry and exit regulated in the various nations? How do individual firms and industries adjust their labor force when faced with cyclical and long-term or structural declines in product demand?

This does not obviously constitute an exhaustive list of employment practices. We rather hope that these four practices serve as a window on the behavior and developments in employment relations in a given country. Moreover, although the above list focuses primarily on enterprise-level practices, we are in fact interested in learning which actors (management, labor, or government) shape these practices and at what level (national, industry, region, or firm).

In summary, we decided to begin our study by examining a representative set of observable employment practices and outcomes and

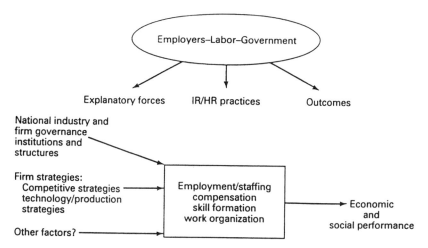

Figure I.1
Initial framework for organizing the comparative IR/HRM research project (suggested by H. Druke and Russell Lansbury). Within any country IR/HR practices may vary across industries, firms, and over time, and all the variables in the model may be shaped by different employer, labor, and government influences.

to structure the research so that these practices and outcomes could be understood as they have unfolded or changed in different national and industrial settings. This permitted us to search for an understanding of the forces responsible for these changes. By beginning with the employment practices and working our way backward, we were able to assess the degree of change in practices and outcomes that had occurred in recent years and to determine for each nation who the relevant actors promoting/regulating these changes were, at what level of the national political economy these debates/decisions were taking place. The framework was designed to address whether a focus on the competitive strategies of firms or one that emphasizes the role of public policy and legal institutional arrangements (or some combination of these two approaches) best explains recent shifts in employment relations.

It is only after these intermediate questions about the institutional structures and analytical categories and about the causal factors promoting change have been answered, that further questions about the nature and consequences of the changes themselves can begin to be addressed. The country studies that follow seek to address these questions as well as to push the analytical categories in an effort to further the debate over how to relaunch the study of work and employment relations.

Industrial relations has always been a field in which researchers are in close contact with labor, management, and government professions. Given that practice in our field must now have a global perspective, we hope that this book provides both students of labor and professionals with not only accurate information on recent developments in advanced industrial nations but also a framework for comparing these developments to their own experiences. In this way we hope our effort here and in the work to follow at the industry and enterprise levels will support the type of informed, "adaptive learning" process (Westney 1987; Cole 1989) that is an important part of the process of institutional innovation in our increasingly more global world.

References

Aoki, Mashahiko. 1988. *Information, Incentives and Bargaining in the Japanese Economy.* New York: Cambridge University Press.

Cole, Robert E. 1989. *Strategies for Learning: Small-Group Activities in American, Japanese, and Swedish Industry.* Berkeley: University of California Press.

Chaykowski, Richard, and Anil Verma, eds. 1992. *Industrial Relations in Canadian Industry.* Toronto: Holt Reinhart and Winston.

Dunlop, John T. 1958. *Industrial Relations Systems.* New York: Holt, 1958.

Dore, Ronald. 1973. *British Factory Japanese Factory.* Berkeley: University of California Press.

Edwards, Paul K. and Keith Sisson. 1990. Industrial relations in the UK: Change in the 1980s. ESRC Research Briefing. University of Warwick.

Hyman, Richard. 1975. *Industrial Relations: A Marxist Introduction.* London: Macmillian.

Industrial Democracy in Europe Committee. 1981. *Industrial Democracy in Europe.* Oxford: Oxford University Press.

Industrial Democracy in Europe Committee. 1980. *European Industrial Relations.* Oxford: Oxford University Press.

Kerr, Clark, John T. Dunlop, Frederick Harbison, and Charles Meyers. 1960. *Industrialism and Industrial Man.* Cambridge: Harvard University Press.

Kern, Horst and Michael Schumann. 1984. *Das Ende der Arbeitseilung?* Frankfurt: Campus Verlag.

Kochan, Thomas A., Harry Katz, and Robert B. McKersie. 1986. *The Transformation of American Industrial Relations.* New York: Basic Books.

Locke, Richard. 1995. *Remaking the Italian Economy.* Ithaca: Cornell University Press.

Marginson, Paul, et al. 1988. *Beyond the Workplace: Managing Industrial Relations in the Multi-establishment Enterprise*. London: Basil Blackwell.

Mathews, John. 1989. *Tools of Change*. Sydney: Pluto Press.

Maurice, Marc, Francois Sellier, and Jean-Jacques Silvestre. 1986. *The Social Foundations of Industrial Power*. Cambridge: MIT Press.

Osterman, Paul. 1988. *Employment Futures*. New York: Oxford University Press.

Piore, Michael and Charles Sabel. 1984. *The Second Industrial Divide*. New York: Basic Books.

Shirai, Taishiro, ed. 1983. *Contemporary Industrial Relations in Japan*. Madison: University of Wisconsin Press.

Sisson, Keith. 1990. Strategy, structure and choice in industrial relations: A comparison of U.S. and U.K. research and its implications. Working Paper. Industrial Research Unit, University of Warwick.

Streeck, Wolfgang. 1991. The Federal Republic of Germany. In John Niland and Oliver Clarke, eds., *Agenda for Change*. Sydney: Allen and Unwin.

Westney, D. Eleanor. 1987. *Imitation and Innovation: The Transfer of Western Organizational Patterns to Meiji Japan*. Cambridge: Harvard University Press.

Wood, Stephen. 1990. Comparing survey and case study interpretations of change in industrial relations. Draft manuscript. London School of Economics.

Employment Relations in a Changing World Economy

1

The Limits of Diffusion: Recent Developments in Industrial Relations and Human Resource Practices in the United States

Marc Weinstein
Thomas Kochan

The persistence of economic pressures that first challenged American industry in the 1970s reflects fundamental changes in the competitive environment of firms. Globalization of markets, rapid technological advances, shorter product life cycles, and shifts in consumer preferences have undermined the competitiveness of the American mass production strategy and its traditional industrial relations and human resource practices. Prompted by these challenges, a growing number of U.S. firms have experimented with alternative production and IR/HR strategies. By the mid 1980s the apparent economic superiority of these innovations suggested that they might diffuse throughout the American economy. Indeed, in our own work (Piore and Sabel 1984; Kochan, Katz, and McKersie 1986; Osterman 1988) we identified what we believed to be the outlines of a new system of employment relations at the enterprise level that appeared to be emerging out of these private experiments. But American industry has been slow to innovate and in a number of firms where alternative strategies have been pioneered, innovations have been difficult to maintain.

1.1 Distinctive Features of the U.S. Industrial Relations System

The key features of the traditional IR/HR system have their origins in the rise of mass production and the matrix of American institutions and legal traditions that constrained the choices of capital and labor in shaping human resource practices. Trade unions with competing strategies were defeated or co-opted, and managerial perspectives were influenced by state policy and the practices of lead firms (Fligstein 1990). These features were later formalized in the National Labor Relations Act (NLRA) in 1935 and were reinforced by the subsequent growth in private sector unionism from 10 to 35 percent of the work force in the fifteen years following the enactment of the NLRA. Although trade unions, even at their peak, only represented a minority of the U.S. work force, their influence extended considerably beyond the unionized sector of the economy. To reduce the incentives for their workers to organize, large- and medium-sized nonunion firms developed personnel policies and in some cases wage levels that either matched or were close to practices in unionized firms. Moreover, the IR/HR practices that became associated with the management of blue-collar industrial workers in some respects were mirrored in the human resource management of nonprofessional white-collar employees.

The central feature of this system was the role of collective bargaining as the key institutional mechanism to resolve labor-management conflict. With the passage of the NLRA, the federal government formally endorsed the right of workers to collectively negotiate the terms and conditions of employment. Although the NLRA incorporated the principles of earlier government commissions and built on the practices that were first developed in industries such as clothing (Fraser 1983), its provisions were nevertheless a significant milestone in U.S. labor relations. The NLRA created a regulatory framework that enabled labor to organize significant portions of the industrial work force and established institutional structures to promote stability and permanency in union-management relations.

The centrality of the collective bargaining process was strengthened by a second distinctive feature of the New Deal industrial relations system: exclusive managerial prerogative at the strategic level of the firm. By law and tradition, American management has enjoyed the sole right to determine the strategic direction of the firm, while labor has been traditionally confined to negotiate the impact of these policies through the collective bargaining process. Labor and management's mutual acceptance of this fundamental principle has deep roots and has been reinforced by American labor's tradition of business unionism whose core premise implicitly rejects the notion that the effective representation of worker interests requires worker control or ownership of enterprises.

American labor's aggressive pursuit of "job control" unionism has constituted the third distinctive feature of U.S. industrial relations. Whereas labor traditionally has acknowledged the exclusive rights of management at the strategic level of the firm, it has attempted to codify rules governing the deployment of labor on the shopfloor. In the unionized sector of the economy, an elaborate set of local rules have been formulated through the collective bargaining process that precisely specify the rights and obligations attached to each job. Strict lines of demarcation separate jobs within and across the bargaining unit and an elaborate seniority system determines which workers have the first right to these specific jobs.

These distinctive features of the U.S. industrial relations system produced particular patterns in firm-level governance and, subsequently, in the IR/HR practices of firms. Specifically, in the United States, both blue- and white-collar employees have neither *de jure* nor *de facto* stakeholder rights by virtue of their employment with the firm. Underpinning this traditional conception is the distinctly American notion that the firm is a bundle of tradable assets owned by shareholders whose sole agents are the managers and officers of the enterprise. In the United States, employers have neither the juridical nor socially expected responsibility to involve employees in the daily or strategic decisions of the firm. In the unionized sector of the economy, industrial democracy has been reduced to industrial jurisprudence. Through the collective bargaining process, trade unions and management negotiate the complex set of rules governing the deployment of labor, promotions, and layoffs, and in cases of dispute, well-defined and formalized arbitration procedures ensure that these local rules are applied equally to all workers. In nonunionized firms, even this limited notion of industrial democracy is rarely institutionalized.

A number of factors explain the institutionalization and diffusion of this model of firm governance and the pattern of IR/HR practices it has generated. Collective bargaining meshed well with the American political and social ethos favoring limited government intervention in substantive decision making, the protection of property rights, and the freedom to contract. Furthermore the combination of business and job control unionism provided a set of compensating mechanisms that fostered its acceptance by labor and capital. Labor's implicit recognition of managerial prerogative and private property ameliorated the business community's resistance to NLRA provisions. At the same time job control unionism provided some compensation to organized labor by enhancing labor control over the rules determining layoffs and promotions. The New Deal industrial relations system also created the necessary preconditions for the macro and micro modes of regulation for mass production. At the macro level the organization of labor raised aggregate income and subsequently demand for mass produced goods. At the micro level, collective bargaining provided the stability and permanency needed for the smooth operation of mass production. Finally, the state's promotion of the New Deal system at a formative moment in its development, particularly the activity of the War Labor Board during World War II, contributed to its institutionalization and diffusion.

While the distinctive features of the New Deal industrial relations system helped diffuse a common set of IR/HR practices across U.S. firms, there is some diversity across and within individual firms in the U.S. economy. Noting this variation among firms, Osterman (1987) has identified four "employment subsystems" with distinctive patterns in their internal labor market structures and IR/HR practices. And even within those firms that pioneered mass production techniques and traditional IR/HR practices there are often distinctive employment subsystems for unskilled blue-collar, craft, nonprofessional white-collar, and professional white-collar workers. What has been notable about the innovations in IR/HR practices is that related changes can frequently be found in a firm's multiple employment subsystems.

Many of the innovations were initiated in the 1960s when IBM, Digital Equipment, Hewlett Packard, Texas Instruments, TRW, Motorola, and other high-technology firms consciously departed from traditional human resource practices. Since more capital was going into these new predominantly nonunionized industries and since the lion's share of new investment in partially unionized industries went to new nonunion work sites rather than to older, higher-cost union facilities (Verma 1985), innovative human resource practices became almost synonymous with nonunion systems (Foulkes 1980). Although in some key unionized relationships, particularly in the telecommunications and automotive industries, important steps were taken to introduce experiments with employee participation under the general heading of "quality of working life" (QWL), this pattern continued through the 1970s. Partly because of the identification of these newer practices with their nonunion origins, organized labor tended to perceive such efforts as union avoidance or "union busting," and it was not until the 1980s that these efforts gained acceptance in some unionized environments. Thus, while new HR practices began to spread in the growing non-union industries of computers, electronics, and communications, the same was not true in traditional lower wage and declining industries such as textiles and apparel or in the quasi-public health care sector.

By the beginning of the 1980s unionized sectors faced a widened labor cost gap with nonunion competitors, (the union/nonunion wage differential increased from approximately 15 percent in the 1960s to 25 percent in the late 1970s; Freeman 1986) due to older plants and a labor-management system that was reluctant to entertain significant ideas for change. The confluence of the election of a popular conservative president in 1980, the deep recession instigated by the Federal Reserve Bank's attempt to reduce inflation, increasing trade deficits resulting in part from the rapid rise of the dollar, and the accumulated impact of labor cost gaps between union and nonunion alternatives produced an unprecedented flurry of change in IR/HR practices in union and nonunion settings in the early 1980s.

In what follows, we assess the extent to which U.S. firms have adopted new human resource strategies by examining the diffusion of new IR/HR practices and systemic change throughout the economy and selected industries. Since the U.S. lacks a reliable national data base for measuring the current state of IR/HR practices our assessments must be based on various *ad hoc* surveys and case studies. Although these data are incomplete, our tentative conclusion is that new IR/HR practices are only partially diffused throughout the U.S. economy. Thus, given our earlier arguments that a mismatch exists between the traditional industrial relations system and the new competitive environment, we need to ask: Why has the diffusion of transformed human resource systems been so limited, and what differentiates between employment relationships that have continued to evolve toward a new model and those that have not?

1.2   IR/HR Practices: Traditional Practices, Change, and Diffusion

Work Organization

The traditional organization of work in U.S. firms is characterized by narrowly defined semiskilled jobs to optimize long production runs of standardized goods. Over the years organized labor has adapted these categories and codified them into a system of job classifications that have become a central element of industrial jurisprudence. In traditional human resource systems, managers are responsible for determining how work is organized and how tasks are performed, but the terms of the contract specify the criteria by which individual workers can be assigned to specific jobs. In this way, job control unionism has preserved the tight division of labor once considered by management to be an essential element of efficient production, and that provided labor with a contractual safeguard against managerial favoritism that could be utilized to divide the work force.

In an environment in which flexible production techniques are perceived as critical, the rigidities intrinsic in the codification of narrow job categories and the strict division of labor have become particularly problematic. In response, firms have introduced new production systems based on the flexible deployment of labor, broad job categories, teamwork, and worker self-regulation of quality control. In unionized plants the move to consolidate job categories frequently has followed innovations at old nonunionized or greenfield plants, and in nearly all cases reductions in job classifications have been linked to broader efforts to reorganize production. For instance, when retrofitting older unionized plants, Corning reorganized work flows and reduced the number of job classifications (Osterman 1992). Similar reductions in job classifications have been introduced in a number of innovative production arrangements in the automobile industry (Katz 1985), and numerous other unionized (Cutcher-Gershenfeld 1988; Kochan and Cutcher-Gershenfeld 1988) and nonunionized firms (Kochan, Katz, and McKersie 1986).

Our best data on the extent of innovations in employee participation and work redesign are found in a recent nationally representative survey of establishments conducted by Paul Osterman (Osterman 1994). He examined both the extent of innovations in individual practices such as employee problem-solving groups, work teams, total quality management (TQM) practices, and job rotation as well as various combinations of these practices. He found that 64 percent of the establishments reported that at least half of their core employees (those engaged in the direct production or delivery of the products or services of the firm) were covered by one or more of these workplace innovations. But only 5 percent indicated that half or more of their employees were covered by all of these innovations. Using a rather liberal measure of the extent of adoption of workplace innovations (i.e., whether half or more of the establishment's core employees were covered by two or more of these innovations), Osterman estimates that approximately one-third of American workplaces are significant adopters of innovative practices. Of these approximately 15 percent have had these innovations in place five years or longer. These data therefore suggest that a substantial number of American firms have experimented with various workplace innovations in recent years, about one-third have implemented more than one form of workplace innovation, and a small minority (less than 20 percent) have demonstrated a deep enough commitment to these innovations to have sustained them for five or more years. Thus, taken together, these data paint a picture of an economy where substantial workplace innovation has been introduced, but one where these practices are only partially diffused within and across firms and where their staying power is still being tested.

Given the broad array of white-collar jobs, we must be somewhat cautious about formulating generalizations about the traditional work design of these occupations. We can note, however, that they have been prone to the same type of criticisms leveled against the structure of blue-collar work. American firms have difficulty in achieving effective cross-functional integration. This, in part, results from the strength of traditional disciplines and the prevalent notion that narrow specialization fosters expertise.

In reaction to these traditional views, we can see a set of changes in the structuring of white-collar jobs that parallel those found in blue-collar work. Indeed, Osterman's survey found that teams and TQM techniques are more widely used in structuring white-collar (professional and technical, sales, clerical, and service) jobs than in blue-collar work. Advances in information technologies have led to the elimination of many low-skilled white-collar jobs. In their place have emerged new job designs that involve more service and sales activities and often incorporate some functions that have traditionally been the domain of professional and managerial workers. This "para-professionalization" of many nonprofessional white-collar jobs has been noted in insurance, banking, telecommunications, and business services (Baran and Gold 1988; Noyelle 1987). The expanded responsibilities of these new job designs lend themselves to the utilization of TQM techniques in which workers in coordination with their supervisors formulate their own job descriptions. Importantly, technological innovation alone is not responsible for the broadening of job requirements; rather, the paraprofessionalization of traditionally semiskilled white-collar work is the result of a conscious managerial strategy to improve efficiency and offer new higher-quality products. But with the introduction of these changes come the same debates as experienced with blue-collar work redesign. Barley and Bechky's (1994) ethnographic studies of technicians in scientific laboratories documented deep tensions and conflicts among different supervisors and technicians over the distribution of power and control over decision making that in the past would have been more highly centralized or focused within specific disciplines. Ancona (1992) documented the effects of greater diversity found within new product teams that include representatives of multiple functions (often referred to as cross-functional teams). The greater diversity increases the potential for conflict both within the team and with groups outside the team's boundaries. Unless these conflicts are well managed, these teams do not result in improved performance. Thus there is considerable experimentation with cross-functional and other types of teams in white-collar work in the United States. Whether it becomes a permanent feature of the structure of white-collar work or another passing managerial fad will depend, in part, on the ability of the parties to manage both the internal and organizationwide processes of conflict management, consensus building, and redistribution of power and decision-making authority that are critical to these new arrangements.

Before moving on to other workplace issues, we should note that historically the high rates of experimentation with new forms of participation and work organization experienced in the United States have been matched by an equally high rate of abandonment. This has been the long history of labor-management cooperation dating back as far as the 1920s and continuing through the job enlargement-job rotation movement in the 1960s. The same track record of high rates of attrition can be seen in the current period of experimentation, as witnessed by the Osterman finding that the vast majority of workplace innovations reported in his survey were begun within the past five years. Earlier studies have also found high attrition rates. Lawler and Mohrman (1985) estimate that the majority of quality circles have been disbanded. Similarly Drago (1988) found that the survival rate for Quality Circles two years after implementation was only about 30 percent. The high failure rate of employee involvement programs is frequently related to their isolation from other organizational transformations since more frequently than other human resource practices employee involvement initiatives have been introduced as stand-alone programs. While the introduction of such programs may lead to other important organizational changes, more often they are abandoned because they fail to produce sufficient returns to productivity or product quality to sustain managerial commitment. Thus, we expect that the durability of employee participation and work reorganization is highly dependent on the extent to which these innovations are matched or reinforced by appropriate modifications of the other human resource and organizational practices discussed below.

Skill Formation and Development

In traditional job structures in manufacturing, the semiskilled jobs generated by mass production strategies, require little, if any, reliance on prior education or experience. What skills are needed are firm specific and can be learned on the job, usually from other workers. Firms are able to rely upon experienced workers to provide on-the-job training because seniority provisions eliminate potential threats to job security resulting from junior employees learning these skills. Furthermore the specificity of skills ties workers to the firm because the skills have value to employees only so long as they remain with the firm. For the same reason enterprises have little incentive to lure workers from competing firms. When skilled workers are needed they are acquired on an ad hoc basis through arrangements with craft unions, through particular arrangements with outside schools, and through recruitment on the external labor market. Since the limited skills needed to perform narrow tasks could be acquired on the job without formal training, issues concerning education, training, and human resource development are generally not an integral part of the collective bargaining process in firms with traditional human resource systems.

Although nonprofessional white-collar jobs normally require higher levels of general skills than blue-collar manufacturing positions, the essential dynamics of skill formation and development have traditionally been the same for both. Thus most skill upgrading for these employees have been provided on the job as white-collar employees learn new firm-specific skills demanded to perform higher-paid jobs within the firm. Until the recent transformation of nonprofessional white-collar work, even jobs in the banking and insurance industries consisted of idiosyncratic practices with very limited transferability across firms (Baran and Gold 1988).

But as work systems in manufacturing are redesigned to break down traditional specializations and lines of demarcation, they require significantly higher skill training. This training includes both technical and behavioral components and a heavy dose of computer skills. Work in these new production systems requires employees to have cross-functional competency, familiarity with quality control methods, and problem-solving skills. Moreover, since employees are unlikely to have obtained these skills through on-the-job training or in the public education system, firms committed to alternative human resource and production strategies must make continued and significant investments in employee training. Indeed, the Osterman survey found a very strong positive correlation between the use of teams, participation, and other measures of work redesign discussed above and investments in technical, analytical, and problem-solving training.

Similarly, in nonprofessional white-collar occupations, the creation of new job categories requires employees to attain skills that senior employees do not have. Under these circumstances the traditional reliance on on-the-job training is insufficient to meet the new needs of redesigned white-collar occupations. This, combined with the universalization or homogenization of skills in many new service-oriented jobs (Noyelle 1987), has both increased the importance of on-the-job training and training provided off the job in vocational education institutions and community colleges.

For both blue-collar and nonprofessional white-collar occupations, it is difficult to interpret data on the overall extent of firm-level training provided by U.S. firms. While there appears to have been increased levels of expenditures on employee training, these increases have been highly uneven across occupational categories. In a 1985 survey of Fortune 500 firms, the Conference Board found that 60 percent of the sample ($n=218$) provided formal training to managers, while 11 percent provided formal training to blue-collar workers. Lynch's (1990) analysis of data from the National Longitudinal Survey of young people found that 14.7 percent of those surveyed had received off-the-job training, 4.2 percent had received company training, and 1.8 percent received apprenticeship training. With respect to trends over the last five years, 72 percent of the firms reported an increase in training expenditures for first-line supervisors, 63 percent reported an increase for technical professionals, and 34 percent reported an increase for craft workers. Despite these increased expenditures, Lawler, Mohrman, and Ledford (1992) found that in 90 percent of the firms in their Fortune 1000 sample, most employees had not received general skills training in the previous three years.

Interpretation of these results is complex since national surveys do not reveal the motivation behind these increased expenditures. In many instances the gap between the skills demanded by new jobs and those provided to workers through the educational system has prompted industry concern with upgrading the skill levels of their current work forces. Less frequently, however, it appears that these efforts are broadly linked to a more general and deep commitment to human resource development. For instance, in their study of high-technology firms in Massachusetts, Kochan and Osterman (1991) found that training budgets were the first to be reduced when firms encountered economic hard times and that these training programs were not part of a broad human resource strategy. Research in the service sector confirms an increased reliance on the external labor market to fill redesigned nonprofessional white-collar jobs (Appelbaum 1985; Noyelle 1990) and reveal the limited commitment of firms to the skill enhancement of their current employees.

One measure of the extent of diffusion of training is a relative one: Are U.S. firms investing in training at a level that is equivalent to their strongest international competitors? Studies of the auto industry suggest American firms are not doing so. MacDuffie and Kochan (1991) found, for example, that training in U.S. auto plants lagged that of Japan and Europe largely because U.S. firms were slower in adopting other transformed human resource practices than the Japanese and lacked the national infrastructure that promoted investments in training found in most European countries. Kochan and Osterman (1991) concluded that, in general, the U.S. economy suffers from an under-investment in human resources when this comparative standard is used. Why this is the case is still subject to considerable debate; however, we suspect that U.S. firms' hesitancy to invest in training reflects the short time horizons and weakness of human resources and employee interests in the strategic decision-making process and governance structures of American corporations, an issue to which we will return in a later section.

An important question remains as to whether there has been any shift to general from firm-specific training that might be linked to broader changes in human resource practices. On this point there are conflicting data. On the one hand, there is evidence that mangers recognize that blue-collar and nonprofessional white-collar workers need more general training, but, on the other hand, this recognition is not always matched by a commitment to raise the skills of the current work force. Thus, in unionized manufacturing firms with transformed systems, jointly administered training funds ensure a continued commitment to firm-specific as well as general technical and interpersonal skills training. Broad commitment to general training has also been observed in the absence of joint programs in the banking, insurance, and telecommunications industries where Baran and Gold (1988) found expanded training efforts in virtually all the firms they studied. Stanback (1990) even observed that part-time employees in the retail sector received general interpersonal skills training. However, as with the level of training, the type of training appears to vary by occupational category. Such was the case in high-technology firms in Massachusetts where it was found that formal in-house training for blue-collar technicians tended to be limited and job specific, though nearly all these firms reported high usage of their tuition assistance programs which, for the most part, could be used for general education (Kochan and Osterman 1991).

Levels, Form, and Structure of Compensation

The organization of mass production and the New Deal industrial relations system have combined to produce matching compensation practices in manufacturing firms. Wages in the traditional system are attached to jobs rather than individuals. Through a combination of community wage surveys and job evaluations, a specific rate is assigned to each of the narrowly demarcated work tasks in the production process. Since these jobs are allocated on the basis of seniority bumping, wages of employees are largely determined by their tenure with the firm. After the rates for each job classification are initially established, they generally move in tandem on the basis of a widely emulated formula first introduced in the automobile industry which, until the wave of concessionary bargaining in the 1980s, guaranteed workers an annual cost-of-living adjustment in addition to an annual improvement factor (typically in the range of 3 percent). Similarly nonprofessional white-collar workers have traditionally been paid a straight hourly wage attached to a particular job.

The consolidation of job categories and emphasis on skill enhancement has led to new compensation practices. Whereas in traditional human resource systems wages are tied to jobs, in transformed manufacturing systems the move has been to detach compensation from specific tasks and to tie wages more tightly to individual skill levels. In a growing number of firms, production workers are paid a salary based on attained competency. Although the number of firms in which production workers have been moved to a salary system is still relatively small, Lawler, Mohrman, and Ledford (1992) report that 21 percent of the firms in their survey plan to shift to an all salaried pay system, and 53 percent plan to increase knowledge and skill-based pay.

Additionally firms have experimented with various forms of gain sharing, profit sharing, and small group and individual incentives in efforts to link compensation and performance. In the 1980s an increasing number of hourly employees had some portion of their pay become contingent on individual, group, or firm performance. A 1989 Bureau of Labor Statistics survey estimated, for example, that only 16 percent of the labor force was covered by some form of profit sharing, and the vast majority of those covered were managers and professionals through deferred compensation plans (Coates 1991). Based on the responses of 1,592 firms, the American Productivity Center found that 32 percent of sampled firms had profit-sharing arrangements, 28 percent had some form of individual incentives, 14 percent had small group incentives, and 13 percent had gain sharing (Mitchell, Lewin, and Lawler 1990). In this last group are included Scanlon, Rucker, and Improshare programs, though Mitchell et al. note that most gain-sharing schemes are customized. Consistent with this, Kaufman (1992) has been only able to identify 273 firms that have an Improshare program. In any event, these ad hoc surveys most likely oversampled large and more innovative firms. Clearly we lack complete data needed to specifically estimate the extent of diffusion.

Although the data are somewhat fragmentary, changes in compensation for nonprofessional white-collar employees has also followed changes in work design. In the banking industry, for instance, tellers are now given bonuses for opening new accounts, and in the telecommunications industry commissions for hourly personnel are becoming more common (Baran and Gold 1988). Noyelle (1987) notes the greater reliance on group incentives for hourly employees and, in many instances, the replacement of hourly compensation by flat salaries combined with incentive bonuses.

One of the largest areas of growth in new compensation arrangements seems to be in the number of firms that adopted employee stock ownership plans (ESOPs). Blasi and Kruse (1991) report that 10.8 million U.S. workers, 12.5 percent of the private work force, are participating in employee-ownership plans in 10,000 companies. The rapid growth of ESOPs is expected to continue, and Blasi and Kruse estimate that by the year 2000 more than a quarter of companies traded on the three major U.S. stock exchanges will be more than 15 percent owned by their employees. However, these authors also point out that the majority of these ESOP plans do not provide any meaningful role for employees in the governance of the firm. Instead, the primary motivation for the growth in ESOPs appears to have been the defense against hostile takeover bids and/or the desire to reduce labor costs. The latter was particularly true in the trucking and airline industries following deregulation in the early 1980s. While the Teamsters Union negotiated *quid pro quos* in the form of board representation in these companies, most did not follow through with efforts to transform the rest of the company's IR/HR practices in ways that complemented representation at the top (Hunter 1992). Instead, most remained focused on the challenge of surviving in the deregulated environment. By the end of the 1980s most of these companies had either merged or gone out of business, and the experiments in board membership, with a few notable exceptions in the steel industry, had largely disappeared. A new wave of ownership and board representation emerged again in the airlines and steel industry in 1993. Employees and their unions at Northwest, TWA, and United Airlines traded concessions for ownership and board seats. The United Steelworkers Union negotiated a package of employee participation and work organization reforms, including board representation with each of the major unionized companies in the steel industry. These should prove to be interesting developments to watch in the years ahead.

While these developments in compensation structure are potentially important for the long-run performance of the economy, by far the most significant compensation developments of the 1980s were the stagnant and declining real wage position of the majority of American workers and the rapid growth of nonwage compensation, particularly the escalation of health care costs. Both have grown sufficiently large to become significant political issues. Between 1978 and 1989 real average hourly wages of production workers have declined 9 percent (U.S. Department of Labor 1991). Thus, whereas in 1980 compensation costs for manufacturing workers was higher in the United States than in all OECD countries excepting Sweden and Germany, by 1990 Canada, France, Germany, Italy, and Sweden all had higher compensations costs for production workers than U.S. manufacturing firms.

Declining real wages of U.S. workers were further eroded by the rising cost of health care and the increasing proclivity of firms to shift the burden of these costs to employees. A recent survey of 4,000 companies by Business and Legal Reports, Inc. (1991) confirmed a continuing shift of health care costs to employees. In 1991, 31 percent of the companies surveyed reported that they raised employees' share of health insurance premiums and 23 percent reported that they raised the deduction in the last year. The same researchers reported that whereas in 1989, 56 percent of employers reported paying full health premiums, in 1991 only 48 percent of the surveyed companies paid the full cost of health insurance for their employees. Even these figures may understate the burden of health care costs, since the growing number of temporary and part-time workers do not receive health insurance from their employers.

Finally, there was an important change in the distribution of earnings in the United States over the course of the past decade. Katz (1993) reports that between 1979 and 1989 the incomes of families in top twentieth percentile bracket increased 20 percent, while the income of the families in the bottom fortieth percentile remained the same. During this period Katz also notes that the returns to college education compared to high school education increased from 32 to 55 percent. Also contributing to the increased inequality in the income distribution in the United States was the rapid escalation of salaries of top executives and professionals. Both groups experienced real wage improvements over the 1980s and early 1990s.

Employment Security and Staffing Arrangements

Traditional compensation patterns and reverse seniority layoff procedures encourage long-term attachment to firms. Despite the fact that American employers have no obligation, contractual or otherwise, to provide employment security, internal labor market rules governing wages and dismissals provide workers with strong incentives to remain with one employer. Absent such formal job security, it is in the interest of workers to have precisely specified their job classifications and the intricate rules concerning job ladders and seniority. Although long-term attachment to firms resulting from formal security arrangements may lead to employer flexibility in the deployment of labor, relative job security secured through high tenure leads to inflexibility.

While highly specified job classifications in nonprofessional white-collar employees have never rivaled those of blue-collar employees, internal labor markets for these workers have nevertheless been important in determining career paths. The port of entry for these white-collar employees traditionally has required a high school diploma. Though not strictly allocated on the basis of seniority, promotions into higher positions have normally corresponded to employee tenure with the firm. Unlike blue-collar promotion paths, however, many nonprofessional white-collar job ladders have not led to supervisory and managerial positions.

In manufacturing firms, efforts to enhance job security for blue-collar workers often accompanied the introduction of transformed human resource systems. Once again, this practice complements other features of the transformed system. It is not surprising, for example, that many of the recognized leaders in the introduction of innovative HR practices (IBM, DEC, and Hewlett-Packard) were also known for their commitment to employment security throughout the 1970s and 1980s. The decoupling of wages and jobs dramatically reduces the importance of seniority in determining promotions, wages, and layoffs and thus poses a potentially divisive resistance point in introducing a transformed human resource system. In this context increased commitment to job security represents a distinct advantage to low-seniority workers without undermining the position of high-tenure employees. Similarly efforts to enhance productivity through the reorganization of work and employee involvement programs have little chance of succeeding unless employees are assured that they will not lose their jobs because of the productivity gains resulting from these programs. Therefore it is not surprising that formal no-layoff guarantees are often the *quid pro quo* for acceptance of transformed human resource practices in unionized settings and are equally common in transformed systems in non-unionized settings.

Enhanced job security for the core labor force, however, is in many cases sustainable only through increased use of contingent workers. By employing core workers at levels that are sufficient to meet production at the stable portion of demand, firms can increase production during periods of high demand by increasing the number of contingent workers; during periods of relatively slack demand firms can reduce the number of these noncore employees. Moreover, it has proved difficult, if not impossible, for most firms to maintain their commitments to employment security over the long run. By the early 1990s most of the U.S. firms best known for their no-layoff commitments (IBM, Digital Equipment Corporation, Delta Airlines, etc.) had undergone significant downsizing and layoffs of both blue-collar and white-collar workers. The issue of employment security clearly poses a significant paradox to employers and employees alike. It is clear that greater security is critical to gaining acceptance of internal labor market flexibility and work reorganization but individual firms are generally incapable of credibly committing to strong employment security promises. A solution to this paradox may require broader public commitment to labor market policies that support greater employment security and easier transferability across employers.

In contrast to the enhanced job security often offered to blue-collar workers in transformed human resource systems, a number of observers (Noyelle 1987, 1990; Appelbaum 1985, 1987; Christopherson 1990) have argued that the introduction of new jobs with expanded responsibility has contributed to the breakdown of nonprofessional white-collar internal labor markets. In this view the paraprofessionalization of work has made internal promotion too expensive both in terms of actual training costs and in terms of the time required to train current employees. As a result firms have turned increasingly to the external market to fill these new jobs. Further evidence of reduced employment security for white-collar and middle management employees came with the wave of corporate downsizing in the early 1990s. While hard evidence is still difficult to find, there has been some discussion that these layoffs were the result of the decentralization of responsibility to lower-level employees and have reflected the delayed returns to expanded use of information technologies.

Consistent with these trends is the increased used of nonpermanent employees. Although national data are sparse, the three most common forms of contingent work—part-time, temporary, and contract work—all appeared to increase in the 1980s. In the last two decades the number of part-time workers as a percentage of the work force has steadily increased from 15.5 percent in 1969 to 18.1 in 1989. During this same period the percentage of men aged between 22 and 64 employed in part-time positions rose from 3.7 to 6.7 percent (Tilly 1991). The growth in the use of temporary workers is even more dramatic. One survey of the use of temporary workers estimated that temporary workers increased at an annual rate of 11 percent between 1975 and 1986 (Abraham 1991). The National Association of Temporary Services, Inc. also reported that the payroll of temporary agencies doubled from $3.0 billion in 1980 to $6.0 billion in 1985, and Hartmann and Lapidus (1989) report that the constant dollar pay of temporary firms grew 236 percent in the 1980s, after a 754 percent increase in the 1970s. The only known survey of trends in the use of contract workers explained their use for maintenance and renovation work in the oil and chemical industries. They found that use of contract workers increased over the course of the 1980s and resulted in increased labor-management tension and conflict and possibly increased the probability of injuries and accidents, and reduced the investment in training and human resource development (Wells, Kochan, and Smith 1991; Rebitzer 1991). Without further data on the extent to which contingent workers are being used to bolster the job security of hourly workers, it is not possible to discern whether the move to greater reliance on contingent workers signals a more general trend to increased job security of the core work force or simply to a greater use of contingent employees. However, it is probably safe to conclude that the net result of these developments has been to increase the inequality in wages, benefits, human resource development, and job security in the American economy. The real question, however, is the magnitude of these effects and whether this trend will continue to grow, peak, or reverse itself in the next decade.

Industry Developments

Of all the industrial sectors the U.S. automotive industry has seen the most innovation. GM, Ford, and Chrysler working with the United Automobile Workers (UAW) accelerated their efforts to spread QWL and later various experiments in team concept work systems to a larger number of facilities. This is not surprising given the pressures from international competition in general, and from Japan in particular. More specifically, progress on employee participation and work organization continues to be made incrementally. It appears to be generally accepted that new work sites should be designed with more flexible work systems that encourage teamwork and employee participation in problem solving and quality management. All the new auto plants opened or significantly retrofitted in the past decade moved in this direction regardless of whether they were union or non-union or U.S. or Japanese managed. These firms have also made important advances in training and human resource investments for blue-collar workers. The UAW has negotiated training funds jointly administered by the unions and the companies and funded by a negotiated amount per work hour. More ambitious are the training targets at GM's new Saturn division. Before production even started, operating technicians at Saturn received 300 hours of training and skilled trade workers received between 450 and 700 hours of training. Additionally, during the course of normal production, all employees at Saturn are scheduled to spend at least 5 percent of their work hours in training, and detailed training histories are kept on each employee to ensure that this target is met. Contingent compensation has been introduced in the form of profit sharing in the major auto companies and pay-for-skills plans are found in perhaps as many as half of those plants that have adopted team concept systems of work organization. The sharp decline in employment levels in the industry in the 1980s was accompanied by enhanced income security protection for displaced workers and employment security protection for those who have remained.

Despite these developments only in isolated cases is there evidence that IR/HR considerations have been elevated significantly to the strategic level of decision making or have influenced corporate governance. At Saturn, shared governance was built into the original design of the corporation and is in place. But this is the exception. Indeed, as shareholders have escalated their attempts to increase their influence over top management of GM and other large companies, employees as stakeholders may have found a strong opponent to gaining influence. Thus the industry treated in most accounts as the leading edge of innovation in IR/HR concepts in the 1980s finds itself partially transformed. It recognizes on the management side that further or complete transformation (except for the issue of governance) is needed but faces short-term pressures for cost control and restructuring that may destroy the trust needed either to sustain the process of change or to reap the benefits of the more flexible work systems and leaner staffing arrangements that are associated with this alternative strategy.

The computer and telecommunications facilities opened in the 1980s also sought to emphasize flexibility and total quality management concepts. However, here we have to be rather cautious in our conclusions, since our data are limited and some of the plants that received the most publicity for their innovative features have been closed as the industry pared its work force in the past several years. The best available data comes from a survey conducted by Ernst and Young. The results of this survey indicate that in the computer industry the level of employee participation, investment in training, and utilization of total quality management programs cover a smaller percentage of the work force than in the automotive industry (Kochan, Hoffer-Gittel, and Lautsch 1993). Nevertheless, the leading firms in the computer and telecommunications industries expanded their investments in training in the 1980s; indeed, firms such as IBM, Motorola, Hewlett Packard, Polaroid, DEC, AT&T, and the various regional telephone companies (e.g., Bell South, Ameritech, NYNEX) may be among the leaders in the amount of resources devoted to training on their own and, in the telecommunications industry, jointly with their unions. By 1980 these accelerated efforts were particularly visible in the union sector of telecommunications, namely at AT&T and the Bell System working with the Communication Workers of America (CWA). This effort dissipated, however, in the first years following divestiture. It was not until the late 1980s, when union employment in the former Bell system was reduced more than 50 percent in response to automation and the loss of market share to new nonunion telecommunication companies such as Sprint and MCI, that efforts to initiate joint labor-management participation reappeared. At the present, joint union management programs promoting participation and related workplace innovations are once again expanding within both AT&T and the regional telephone companies that were formerly part of the Bell System. At AT&T these efforts have expanded to include a significant joint governance arrangement called the "Workplace of the Future" in which union-management committees consult on both workplace issues and broader human resource strategies.

Whether this level of investment in training and employee participation generalizes to the smaller companies in the information industries is rather questionable; however, we again lack the widespread data needed to assess this fully. Other major firms in telecommunications and computers also experienced drastic employment reductions in the past decade, and most of them used various alternatives to layoffs for significant number of these reductions. At the same time nearly all were forced to turn to some form of layoff or substitute involuntary reduction method. Finally, none of these firms, with the exception of IBM which historically had a very influential human resource department, have demonstrated that HR or IR plays a strong role in the strategic decision making or governance of the firm when key decisions such as restructuring, mergers, and acquisitions, and/ or new competitive strategies are concerned. And this may even be changing at IBM which has recently reduced the role and influence of its corporate human resource staff by creating a separate contracting firm from which business units can purchase personnel services previously supplied in house. Many interpret this change as a signal that human resources will play a less strategic role in corporate and business unit decision making in the future.

The clothing industry has been much slower to move away from piecework and adopt other innovations in HR practices largely because it has continued to lose jobs and market share to lower-wage foreign producers, to non-union producers in the United States, and to up-scale, European high-fashion designers and marketers. Combined employment in the apparel and textile industries declined 24 percent from 1973 to 1988 from 2.4 million to 1.8 million as a result of technological innovation, increased international competition, and the easing of import restrictions in the 1980s. Unionization has also declined in this sector over this time period as a result of a continued flow of new immigrants that provided opportunities for non-union firms to operate at below union rates and the general decline in employment resulting from international competition. The slow innovation in this industry has been documented by Dunlop and Weil (1992) who found that less than 10 percent of apparel firms have changed from the traditional bundle system to modular production and its attendant innovations in human resource practices (e.g., teamwork, multiskilling). Given these developments it is not surprising that relative wages of workers in the apparel and textile industries declined from 72.4 percent of average hourly wages in manufacturing in 1969 to 60.1 percent in 1989 (Monthly Labor Reports).

Again we have a number of exceptions. Companies such as the Gap, Levi-Strauss, and other firms that enjoyed increasing market share and growth in the 1980s and early 1990s appear to be investing in more efforts to involve employees and move to team-based production systems. These efforts are being done largely with union cooperation but are led by management. The one exception to the management-initiated innovation is found in the men's tailored suit industry where a joint labor-management committee has sought to encourage innovations in individual firms and served as the most visible champion for innovation in that industry (National Clothing Industry Labor-Management Committee 1992).

In the financial services industry, what we know comes from a relatively narrow set of case studies. Nevertheless, some important patterns are emerging. After growing rapidly in the financial boom years of the 1980s, portions of the industry dramatically contracted when the take over and junk bond markets collapsed following the failed effort to take over United Airlines in 1990. Even prior to this, firms had sought expansion by entering new product markets which together with the paraprofessionalization of traditionally semiskilled white-collar occupations increased firms' reliance on external labor markets to meet the changing human resources requirements demanded by new product market strategies. In business services, employers have dramatically reduced the ratio of clerical workers to financial service professionals. Among the former, the tendency has been to hire individuals with four years of college education, and among the latter, traditional promotion patterns have been disrupted as senior associates have been hired directly from the external market (Noyelle 1990). Despite these shifts in product markets, one recent study has estimated that less than 20 percent of all employees in this industry receive continual customer relations training (Kochan, Hoffer-Gittel, and Lautsch 1993). Nevertheless, this figure is expected to grow dramatically in the coming years and the same study reports that non-management training is growing faster than management training. Still relatively little is known about the actual work practices or other human resource policies governing the large numbers of clerical, office, and technical workers in this industry. We do know that the financial and business service industries invested heavily in information technology in the 1980s and did not get a significant return on its high rate of capital investment (Roach 1987).

Health care grew in employment throughout the 1980s and into the early 1990s as demand for its services expanded. The real question is whether a contraction will come in the 1990s as concerns for health care cost containment intensify or whether demand will continue to grow as the equally strong concern for the expanded health care coverage to those who fall outside of the private insurance systems be included in some type of public system. Unions held their own in this sector, although they have not increased their market share in the past decade. All other human resource and industrial relations issues seem to have taken on a lower priority and profile in this industry. This is reflected in a recent survey that indicates that the service sector in general, and the health sector in particular, utilize gain sharing at much lower rates than the manufacturing sector of the economy (Markham et al. 1992).

Although our analysis of changes in IR/HR management practices has considered specific IR/HR practices separately, some have reasoned that optimally functioning employment systems will consist of internally cohesive practices (Kochan, Katz, and McKersie 1986; Osterman 1987, 1988). For instance, pay-for-performance schemes are more likely to yield desired outcomes when they are complemented by job security. Conversely, in firms where there is no formal job security, employees will have a disincentive to cooperate in efforts to restructure work in ways that may increase productivity and subsequently could lead to firmwide employment reductions. For this reason we need to consider the evidence that particular IR/HR practices cluster.

In one of the few empirical attempts to measure the distribution and clustering of human resource practices across U.S. firms, Ichniowski (1990) classified firms into nine clusters according to bundles of human resource practices. At one end of the transformed/traditional human resource system continuum, 13 percent of the sample were grouped in a transformed cluster characterized by broad job classifications, high levels of training, and employee involvement programs. At the other end of the continuum, 13 percent of the sample were in the traditional cluster distinguished by strict seniority procedures and narrow job classifications. Forty-six percent of the sample were distributed across the middle seven clusters, and 28 percent were unclassifiable. On their own, these cross-sectional data reveal little about the extent to which human resource practices in U.S. firms have been transformed in the last decade. Yet, when combined with earlier research documenting the shift away from the New Deal industrial relations system, they paint a picture of transition. Nevertheless, only a relatively small number of firms can be unambiguously categorized as transformed, and we still do not have data as to whether the transformation process is continuing, stalled, or reversed.

Three studies—one of work groups at Xerox Corporation (Cutcher-Gershenfeld 1991), another of automobile assembly plants (MacDuffie 1992), and a third of steel plants (Ichniowski, Shaw, and Pernusshi 1993)—have shown that systemic bundles of transformed human resource practices both exist and produce higher levels of productivity and quality than traditional practices. This is a small but rapidly growing avenue of research, one that we expect to see expand considerably in the future as more industry specific studies of human resource and industrial relations practices are completed. If the early results are any indication, they promise to shed considerable light on the potential economic payoffs to systemic approaches to workplace transformations for firms and unions or employees that are able to take this broad systemic approach.

1.3   Summary: Current State of Diffusion of Innovative Practices

Our best qualitative judgments on the current state of diffusion of alternative IR/HR practices in the key industries of interest remain tentative. As was stated earlier, they are based only on the cumulative findings and evidence from various industry and firm-specific studies and reports and a few national surveys. Nevertheless, the overriding conclusion based on available evidence is that innovations are only partially diffused across these industries and across the economy. Innovations are more widely diffused in (1) greenfield sites than in existing facilities, (2) in larger firms than in midsize and smaller firms, and (3) in high value-added industries such as autos, telecommunications, and computers than in clothing, finance, and health care. Moreover, although the available evidence suggests that leading non-union firms began the process of moving their human resource management practices away from the New Deal model earlier than their union counterparts, by 1990 union enterprises had largely caught up. The most recent surveys of Lawler, Mohrman, and Ledford (1992) and Osterman (1994) found no significant differences in the rates of adoption of workplace innovations between union and non-union establishments. In a few cases, especially pertaining to employment security, skill development, and consultation in corporate governance, management-union programs have gone beyond their counterparts in non-union firms. These surveys also indicate that workplace innovations are most prevalent in firms managed by executives whose values are supportive of employee participation, firms that adopt competitive strategies that stress product quality and innovation over cost competition, firms most heavily exposed to pressures of international competition and especially competition from Japan, and firms where human resource professionals have significant influence in strategic decision making and corporate governance.

At present, however, only a relatively small minority of American firms fit this profile. The economic success of the organizations that have taken a systemic approach to transforming their human resource practices might be expected to spur the diffusion of innovations in IR/HR practices throughout the U.S. economy, but the experience of U.S. firms in the 1980s suggests that this has not been the case. One plausible set of explanations for this limited diffusion turns on the costs and benefits to any individual firm of investing in these organizational changes. Simply put, the costs incurred by reorganizing production, upgrading the skill base of the current work force, and restructuring other employment practices may exceed the returns on these investments, particularly during a period of recession and sluggish economic growth.

Though plausible, arguments that attribute the limited diffusion of alternative IR/HR systems to the performance of these systems are not entirely convincing. Whatever the gaps in our data about the outcomes of these new systems, we do have sufficient evidence to state that traditional IR/HR strategies of U.S. firms have performed poorly in the competitive international environment. Even in the event that traditional systems are found to perform better than transformed systems as they exist in U.S. firms, something must explain the failure of U.S. firms to formulate more profitable alternative systems. This is all the more true given the relatively strong performance of many Japanese and western European firms that appear to have derived some measure of competitive advantage from alternative human resource practices. Moreover the durability of these practices outside the United States in recessionary periods underscores that they are not merely fair-weather systems whose sustainability is derived exclusively from high growth rates.

Another approach in explaining the limited diffusion of alternative IR/HR strategies would be to look at micro and macro environment in which they have been implemented. At the level of the firm, innovative human resource practices are frequently initiated on a piecemeal basis, either because practitioners fail to perceive the interdependence of different programs or because human resource professionals have only marginal influence at the strategic level of the firm. And in many instances when holistic systemic change has been introduced with the full support of senior management, middle-level managers and supervisors have not been involved. In other instances change has been forced upon nonmanagement employees through hard bargaining. While these tactics may initially be successful in persuading workers to accede to work rule changes, they rarely succeed in prompting enduring behavioral change necessary for the success of other elements of the system, and they have the adverse consequence of solidifying opposition to new human resource policies among labor leaders whose support is ultimately needed for the diffusion of these systems to unionized firms. Finally, the governance structure of U.S. firms in which employees, union leaders, or human resource professionals do not have voice at the strategic level of the firm and in which stockholders are frequently concerned with short-term returns on equity diminishes the probability of a firm embarking upon a IR/HR strategy that requires sustained investment for long-term profitability. This last point is confirmed by Lawler, Mohrman, and Ledford (1992) who report that nearly half of the firms in their sample cite short-term performance pressure as a barrier to further innovation.

At the macro level U.S. firms embarking on a strategic approach to transforming IR/HR practices have done so in an hostile environment. The shortcomings of the public education system and the paucity of publicly funded training programs have forced firms either to fully internalize the costs of skill upgrading or to turn to the external market to meet their new labor requirements. Both approaches are nonoptimal, since in the former case, the costs to the firm may be too high to sustain the support of stockholders, and in the latter, the firm must implicitly reject its commitment to employment security. And even when firms have made employment security commitments to their current work forces, the absence of flexible employment adjustment programs has also made alternative strategies difficult to sustain in an economic environment that frequently requires restructuring and downsizing of firms. Finally, the failures of American labor law to protect workers' rights to organize and the anti-union posture of many firms have made it increasingly difficult for labor to support innovative IR/HR programs.

While there is no compelling force that produces systemic cohesion between the micro policies of the firm and the macro policies of the state, the policies of the state can foster experimentation and sustainability of transformed IR/HR systems. There are a number of education or labor market programs that can lower the cost to firms that wish to pursue high value-added product strategies, flexible production techniques, and innovative human resource practices. Likewise policy or statutory changes that provide stakeholder rights may expand the time horizons of firms that, in turn, may change the cost calculus for transforming production and IR/HR practices. With the election of the Clinton administration in 1992, a new debate and analysis of labor law and policy with respect to workplace innovations began. At this point the outcome of these deliberations is not yet known. It is clear, however, that the future rate of diffusion of innovations will depend in part on the future of American labor policy and the extent to which the American labor movement becomes a more visible champion of these changes.

1.4 Implications for IR/HR Theory

The framework used to guide this project grew out of the American experience, so this chapter is the least qualified to assess its adequacy for explaining the dynamics of IR/HR practice. Yet several points can be made. Experimentation with new IR/HR practices was clearly a firm-level phenomenon throughout the past decade. The combination of changed market and technological conditions did lead firms to reconsider their competitive strategies and their employment practices to reduce costs as well as to improve productivity, quality, and flexibility. Government played an important role by weakening its enforcement of labor and employment laws and by allowing (some would argue encouraging) a harder line by management in its resistance to unions. But the biggest effects of government policy came in its deregulation of key industries such as transportation, communications, and banking and its macroeconomic policies that produced the deepest recession since the 1930s and prolonged recession from 1990 to 1992.

The result is that compared to a decade ago American IR/HR practices and outcomes are more diverse and unequal. Innovations are partly diffused. Wage and income disparities, employment security, and exposure to training and career development opportunities are more unequal. At the same time labor-management relations are both more cooperative and expansive in scope in selected relationships and more hostile and rigid in others where the parties have engaged in protracted and increasingly violent strikes that are not simply extensions of traditional collective bargaining but potentially fights over the survival of the union and/or the company (e.g., Eastern Airlines, Greyhound Bus, Phelps Dodge Metals, Hormel Meatpacking, Caterpillar Tractor, International Paper).

What this implies is that the absence of government support for a transformed IR/HR system produces greater variation, inequality, and partial diffusion. Whether pressures to reduce these inequalities and support broader diffusion occurs will depend on the political process and the future of government policy. Thus the role of the state has been the real "invisible hand" in the dynamics of American IR/HR practice in the past decade. What is clear to us is that the traditional system is not likely to perform any better in the future than it did in the past, and without greater diffusion of alternative IR/HR strategies there will no dramatic increase in U.S. macroeconomic performance. Whether the state takes a more visible and firm grasp on this aspect of the economy will depend on the political choices and social pressures the American public displays in the remaining years of this century.

References

Abraham, Katharine. 1991. Restructuring the employment relationship: The growth of market mediated arrangements. In Katharine Abraham and Robert McKersie, eds., *New Developments in the Labor Market: Toward a New Institutional Paradigm.* Cambridge: MIT Press.

Ancona, Deborah, and David Caldwell. 1992. Demography and design: Predictors of new product team performance. *Organization Science* 3:321–40.

Appelbaum, Eileen. 1985. Alternative work schedules of women. Working Paper. Department of Economics, Temple University, Philadelphia.

Appelbaum, Eileen. 1987. Restructuring work: Temporary, part-time, and at-home employment. In Heidi Hartmann, ed., *Computer Chips and Paper Clips: Technology and Women's Employment*, vol. 2. National Academy Press: Washington, DC.

Baran, Barbara, and Jana Gold. 1988. New markets and new technologies: Work reorganization and changing skill patterns in three white collar service industries. Berkeley Roundtable on the International Economy, Berkeley, CA.

Blasi, Joseph, and Douglas Kruse. 1991. *The New Owners.* New York: Harper Business Press.

Barley, Stephen, and Deth Bechky. 1994. In the back rooms of science: The work of technicians in science labs. *Work and Occupations* 21:85–103.

Business and Legal Reports Inc. 1991. Survey of fringe benefits. Madison, CT.

Christopherson, Susan. 1990. Emerging patterns of work. In Thierry Noyelle, ed., *Skills, Wages, and Productivity in the Service Sector.* Boulder, CO: Westview Press.

Coates, Edward. 1991. Profit sharing today: Plans and provisions. *Monthly Labor Review* 114:14–25.

Cutcher-Gershenfeld, Joel. 1988. *Tracing a Transformation in Industrial Relations.* U.S. Department of Labor: Washington, DC.

Drago, R. 1988. Quality circle survival. *Industrial Relations* 27:336–51.

Dunlop, John, and David Weil. 1992. Human resource innovations in the apparel industry: The industrial relations system in perspective. Mimeo. Harvard University and Boston University.

Fligstein, Neil. 1990. *The Transformation of Corporate Control.* Cambridge: Harvard University Press.

Foulkes, Fred. 1980. *Personnel Policies in Large Nonunion Companies.* Englewood Cliffs, NJ: Prentice-Hall.

Fraser, Steve. 1983. Dress rehearsal for the New Deal: Shop-floor insurgents, political elites, and industrial democracy in the amalgamated clothing workers. In Michael Frisch and Daniel Walkowitz, eds., *Working-Class America: Essays on Labor Community and American Society.* Urbana: University of Illinois Press.

Freeman, Richard. 1986. The effect of the union wage differential on management opposition and organizing success. *American Economic Review* 76:92–96.

Hartman, Heidi, and June Lapidus. 1989. Temporary work. In Commission on Work Force Quality, *Investing in People*, U.S. Department of Labor: Washington, DC.

Hunter, Larry. 1992. Union representation on the corporate board: A new forum for governance. Mimeo.

Ichniowski, Casey. 1990. Human resource management systems and the performance of U.S. manufacturing business. NBER Working Paper 3449.

Ichniowski, Casey, D. Lewin, and J. Delaney. 1989. The new human resource management at the workplace. *Relations Industrielles* 44:97–123.

Ichniowski, Casey, Katherine Shaw, and Giovanna Pernusshi. 1993. The effects of HR practices on productivity. Unpublished manuscript.

Katz, Harry. 1985. *Shifting Gears: Changing Labor Relations in the U.S. Automobile Industry.* Cambridge: MIT Press.

Katz, Lawrence. 1993. Understanding recent changes in wage structure. National Bureau of Economic Research: Cambridge, MA.

Kaufman, Roger. 1992. The effects of IMPROSHARE on productivity. *Industrial and Labor Relations Review* 45:311–23.

Kochan, Thomas, and Joel Cutcher-Gershenfeld. 1988. *Institutionalizing and Diffusing Innovations in Industrial Relations.* U.S. Department of Labor: Washington, DC.

Kochan, Thomas, Harry Katz, and Robert McKersie. 1986. *The Transformation of American Industrial Relations.* New York: Basic Books.

Kochan, Thomas, and Paul Osterman. 1991. Human resource development: Does the United States do too little? Paper prepared for the American Council on Competitiveness.

Kochan, Thomas, Jody Hoffer-Gittel, and Brenda Lautsch. 1993. Adoption, institutionalization, and sustainability of total quality management practices. Working Paper. Sloan School of Management, Massachusetts Institute of Technology.

Lawler, E. E., and S. A. Mohrman. 1985. Quality circles after the fad. *Harvard Business Review* 63: 65–71.

Lawler, Edward., Susan Mohrman, and Gerald Ledford. 1992. *Employee Involvement and Total Quality Management: Processes and Results in Fortune 1000 Companies.* San Francisco: Jossey-Bass.

Lynch, Lisa. 1990. The private sector and skill formation in the United States: A survey. Working Paper 3125–90-BPS. Massachusetts Institute of Technology: Cambridge, MA.

MacDuffie, John Paul, and John Krafcik. 1992. Integrating technology and human resources for high performance manufacturing: Evidence from the international auto industry. In Thomas Kochan and Michael Useem, eds., *Transforming Organizations*. Oxford: Oxford University Press.

MacDuffie, John Paul, and Thomas Kochan. 1991. Determinants of training: A cross national comparison in the auto industry. Paper presented at the 1991 meetings of the Academy of Management.

MacDuffie, John Paul. 1991. Beyond mass production: Flexible production systems and manufacturing performance in the world auto industry. Ph.D. dissertation. Massachusetts Institute of Technology.

Markham, Steven, et al. 1992. Gain sharing experiments in health care. *Compensation and Benefits Review* 24:57–64.

Mitchell, Daniel, David Lewin, and Edward Lawler. 1990. Alternative pay systems, firm performance, and productivity. In Alan Blinder, ed., *Paying For Productivity*. Brookings Institution: Washington, DC.

National Clothing Industry Labor-Management Committee. 1991. *A Strategy for Innovation: A Report of the ACTWU/CMA*. National Clothing Industry Labor-Management Committee. New York.

Noyelle, Thierry. 1987. *Beyond Industrial Dualism: Market and Job Segmentation in the New Economy*. Boulder, CO: Westview Press.

Noyelle, Thierry. 1990. Toward a new labor market segmentation. In Thierry Noyelle, ed., *Skills, Wages, and Productivity in the Service Sector*. Boulder, CO: Westview Press.

Osterman, Paul. 1987. Choice of employment systems in internal labor markets. *Industrial Relations* 26:46–67.

Osterman, Paul. 1988. *Employment Futures: Reorganization, Dislocation, and Public Policy*. Oxford: Oxford University Press.

Osterman, Paul. 1992. Internal labor markets. In Clark Kerr and Paul Staudohar, eds., *Labor Economics, Institutions, and Markets*, Stanford: Stanford University Press.

Osterman, Paul. 1994. How common is workplace transformation and how can we explain who adopts it? Results from a national survey. *Industrial and Labor Relations Review* (January): 175–88.

Piore, Michael, and Charles Sabel. 1984. *The Second Industrial Divide: Possibilities for Prosperity*. New York: Basic Books.

Rebitzer, James. 1991. Contract workers and workplace safety: The case of the petrochemical industry. Mimeo. Massachusetts Institute of Technology.

Roach, S. 1987. *America's Technology Dilemma: A Profile of the Information Economy*. Morgan Stanley Special Economic Study, New York.

Stanback, Thomas. 1990. The changing face of retailing. In Thierry Noyelle, ed., *Skills, Wages, and Productivity in the Service Sector*. Boulder, CO: Westview Press.

Tilly, Chris. 1991. Continuing growth of part-time employment. *Monthly Labor Review* 114:10–18.

U.S Department of Labor. 1969–1989. *Monthly Labor Report*. U.S. Washington, DC: GPO.

U.S. Department of Labor. 1991. *Employment Hours, and Earnings, United States, 1909–90.* vol. 1. Washington, DC: GPO.

Verma, Anil. 1985. The relative flow of capital to union and non-union plants within a firm. *Industrial Relations* 24:395–405.

Wells, John, Thomas Kochan, and Michael Smith. 1991. *Managing Workplace Safety and Health: The Case of Contract Labor in the U.S. Petrochemical Industry.* John Gray Institute, Beaumont,TX.

2 Change and Continuity in British Industrial Relations: "Strategic Choice" or "Muddling Through"?

Keith Sisson

Views about what has been happening to employment relations in the United Kingdom in recent years depend upon two separate but related issues. One is the choice of cases. It is perfectly possible, for example, to focus on a number of greenfield workplaces such as Continental Can, Nissan, and Sony and come to a similar conclusion to that reached by Kochan, Katz, and McKersie (1986) for the United States, namely that employment relations in the United Kingdom are being transformed. U.K. employment arrangements, although varied from case to case, have typically involved such novel features as the exclusive recognition of a single union, flexibility of working, single statue, a joint consultative council, "no strike" provisions that rule out industrial action even as a last resort, and pendulum arbitration (for further details, see Bassett 1986; Trevor 1988; Wickens 1987). Or the focus could be on the "brownfield" workplaces of mainstream companies and public sector organizations, in which case a much more cautious conclusion is appropriate (e.g., see Storey 1992). The second issue concerns whether to put the emphasis on change or continuity or change *and* continuity in employment relations. Here a range of positions is possible. One commentator (MacInnes 1987), for example, has argued that very little of substance has changed that cannot be explained in terms of an economic and political climate exceptionally hostile to trade unions.

In the circumstances it is proper at the outset that the author make known his own opinions about these matters. They are, first, that the focus should be on mainstream rather than the state-of-the-art workplaces and, second, that the emphasis should be on change *and* continuity rather than one or the other. The reason for the first is that while state-of-the-art workplaces are important in formulating hypotheses about possible future directions, in the United Kingdom a very false impression would be gained from concentrating on them; the so-called new style agreements (Advisory Conciliation and Arbitration Service 1987) touched on above remain very rare, and they affect relatively small numbers of workers. The reason for the second will be clear from the conclusion to a much lengthier and wider ranging analysis of IR recently written with other IRRU colleagues:

During the 1980s they (industrial relations) altered dramatically, while retaining many features from the past. The fact that change has been complex and uneven reflects one key aspect of continuity, namely, that neither employers nor unions, nor for that matter the state have been able to press through a coherent strategy of renewal and rationalization. All parties still labor under a legacy of the past. (Edwards et al. 1992)

This chapter is divided into four sections. Section 2.1 describes some of the distinctive features of the U.K. situation needed to understand developments in recent years. The second discusses change and continuity in the four designated areas of employment relations practice in mainstream companies and public sector organizations. The third considers, in particular, why managements seem to be muddling through rather than developing a strategic approach. The fourth summarizes the implications of the discussion for the theoretical debates and goals of the broader, more comparative project.

2.1 Distinctive Features of U.K. Industrial Relations

The legal framework is one obvious feature that sets the United Kingdom apart from most other countries. Notwithstanding the welter of employment acts in the 1980s, there is relatively little direct legal regulation of the employment relationship in the United Kingdom. Unlike in other countries, where a series of positive rights was established, in the U.K. legislation took the form of a series of immunities from common law liabilities. There is, for example, no legal right to strike. Uniquely, the relationship between management and trade unions was allowed to develop its own informal logic. Thus collective bargaining is built on procedural rules, whereas in most other countries it rests on a code of substantive rules that are intended to exhaust negotiations for a specified period. Also these procedural rules, along with the substantive rules to which they give rise in collective bargaining, are deemed to be gentlemen's agreements binding in honor only rather than legally enforceable contracts (for further details of this and other points in this introduction, see Edwards et al. 1992).

Perhaps the only area where so-called voluntarism has not been dominant has been social security. Here statutory provision was made for a minimum framework of state pensions as early as 1909; provision for health care followed in 1948. In both cases the provisions are funded by national insurance payments deducted at source by employers and passed on to government.

A second distinguishing feature is a highly complex and diverse structure of representation. As of December 1990, the latest date for which comparable data are available, there were 287 trade unions listed by the Department of Employment; of these 70 were affiliated to the Trades Union Congress. There were 456 employers' organization of which 134 were members of the Confederation of British Industry.

It is not just the sheer number of trade unions and employers' organizations that is important, however. Many trade unions and, in particular, the larger ones are "general" in coverage and have members in a wide range of occupations and sectors. Other unions, such as the engineers and electricians amalgamation, focus on particular occupations that are common to virtually every sector. A third group, such as the banking and finance union or the teachers unions, restrict their activities to particular occupations in particular sectors. The result is that it is not unusual for there to be half a dozen unions represented not just in the same sector but even the same organization.

A further complication is that the membership of employers' organizations, such as it is, is also highly fragmented. In some industries, such as may be covered by one or two employers' organizations as in France or Germany, there may be several. Construction is a prime example. Often the membership is overlapping, and there is competition for members.

A third distinguishing feature of U.K. industrial relations is the structure of collective bargaining. Superficially the multi-employer bargaining system that developed at the national level after 1918 was very similar to that in other European countries; the Donovan Commission described it as a "formal" system of industrial relations as recently as 1968. Unlike in the other countries, however, multi-employer bargaining in the United Kingdom never succeeded in neutralizing the workplace, and it has been in decline for several decades. In many industries multi-employer agreements set minimum terms directly affecting only a minority of employees. In others, including engineering, multi-employer agreements have been terminated altogether. Significantly, too, many of the large auto manufacturers (Ford, Peugeot-Talbot, and Vauxhall [General Motors]) are not members of their employers' organization in the United Kingdom. Many large chemical companies, such as ICI, are "nonconfirming" members: They belong to the employers' organization but do not follow the terms of the multi-employer agreement. Only in industries such as clothing, where there is a large number of small and highly competitive companies, is multi-employer bargaining significant; even here the soon-to-be-abolished statutory wages council has been an important consideration.

The United Kingdom does not therefore have a dual system of industrial relations in the sense that most other European countries have. There is no clear-cut distinction between collective bargaining and the role which trade unions in other countries play outside the workplace and the joint consultation and employee-based systems of representation which take place inside the workplace. In some sectors, such as the public services, the vestiges of such a dual system remain; employee councils are also a feature of some of the Japanese-owned subsidiaries (for further details, see IDS 1988). In the great majority of cases where trade unions are recognized, however, management deals directly with lay trade union representatives or shop stewards, and there is little distinction between the processes of joint regulation, joint consultation and communications.

The explanation for these features is deeply rooted in a continuity of experience, which itself might be said to be another distinctive feature of U.K. industrial relations. Thus the relatively protracted nature of industrialization in the nineteenth century, coupled with the continued need for skilled craftsmen due to the demand for nonstandard goods in export market, meant that in key sectors such as engineering, U.K. employers were confronted by the challenge of craft unions rather than semi- and unskilled workers. The resort to "procedural" as opposed to "substantive" rules recognized that district and workplace negotiations had already given rise to a very considerable and complex body of practices and rules.

Equally important, the relative success of the compromises struck—notably in engineering in 1898—reinforced the ranks of those who favored "voluntarism" as opposed to "compulsion" in collective bargaining matters. This shaped the form and status of collective bargaining more generally, when it spread its net out of the craft-based industries to manufacturing industries in the period at the end of and immediately following World War I. The form and status of collective bargaining, in turn, are key considerations in developments in the structure of collective bargaining; multi-employer agreements never enjoyed the authority they have in other European countries and gave British employers little or no support in the event of management decisions being challenged in the workplace.

A fourth feature may or may not be as permanent as the others and yet is very important for understanding recent developments in employment relations. It is the conjuncture of a political and economic context exceptionally hostile to trade unions. Since 1979 trade unions in the United Kingdom have not only had to contend with the impact of two worldwide recessions, both of which have brought about major employment shifts away from their traditional heartland, but also with a radical shift in the political climate. The coming to power of the first of what has now become four Conservative governments led to a fundamental rejection of the policies that had dominated the approach of governments since World War II: Keynesian demand management and support for collective bargaining. Moreover, as well as passing a number of acts designed to limit the powers of trade unions, the government has taken steps to deregulate the labor market in pursuit of an "enterprise" economy. It has also privatized many of the public enterprises and abandoned the traditional role or the "good" or "model" employer in the remaining public services in favor of a more contingent approach in the hands of local managers (for further details, see Sisson 1989).

Some of the implications of this conjuncture are only now becoming apparent. Whatever the verdict on the range of practices discussed later in the chapter, there have certainly been major, and most probably irreversible, changes in the institutions of collective bargaining over the period. In the words of the team responsible for the third Workplace Industrial Relations Survey (WIRS) (Millward et al. 1992), "all the indicators of trade union presence and strength showed a marked decline." Fewer employers recognized trade unions for the purposes of collective bargaining over pay; trade union density was down from 58 to 48 percent over the period 1984 to 1990 in workplaces with more than 25 employees. In the workplaces that continued to recognize trade unions, there was a decline in the number with shop stewards from 81 to 71 percent in the same period. Cases of industrial action were down by about a half, and over the decade there was an even more dramatic fall in the coverage of the closed shop, from 5 million workers in 1980 to just a half a million in 1990.

Parallelling the long-running shift from multi-employer to single-employer bargaining touched on above, there have also been considerable changes in the level at which collective bargaining takes place in the large multi-establishments that dominate employment in the United Kingdom. Decentralization to individual business units is a near-universal trend in these larger companies (IRRI 1986b; 1990). In some cases (e.g., British Steel and Pilkingtons) it has meant a move from company-level negotiations; in others (e.g., GEC) it has meant the breakup of site negotiations. Similar changes are also under way in the public services. The Post Office, for example, has been split into a number of separate businesses; national bargaining is also under threat in the civil service with the hiving off of "executive agencies," in the National Health Service with the introduction of semi-independent "trusts," and in education with the provision for opting-out of schools from local authority control. Only in the relatively few organizations with integrated operations—for example, the auto manufacturers and clearing banks—are negotiations held at the multi-establishment level.

2.2 Employment Relations Practices: Dominant Patterns, Changes, Diffusion

Even though the multi-establishment organizational context gives rise to massive if not infinite variety, three generalizations are possible so far as the four areas of practice are concerned. The main one, which echoes the overall argument of the chapter, is that most of the very considerable change taking place seems to be piecemeal rather than strategic. The second and third are that any strategic, as opposed to piecemeal, change seems to be associated with companies that are foreign-owned and/or have single-business integrated structures rather than the dominant multidivisional form (Purcell et al. 1987; Marginson et al. 1988).

In the interest of presentation, the emphasis throughout this section is on the first of these generalizations. The second and third will be taken for granted for the moment; their significance will emerge in the following section.

Work Organization

The absence of a framework of law and collective bargaining defining the rights and obligations of the parties is especially important in understanding the "traditional" pattern of work organization in the United Kingdom. In the words of Edwards et al. (1992):

> The rules of employment were settled on a day-to-day basis within the workplace. A major source of authority was 'custom and practice': the unwritten norms and understandings which established in a particular workplace the rules of work (Clegg 1972, 4–6). Workplaces developed their own sets of custom and practice rules, which naturally had some family resemblance with each other but which stemmed from negotiation at the point of production and not from any higher level authority.

Taylorism and Fordism, it must also be remembered, were never as dominant in the United Kingdom as it has been claimed they were in the United States. Thus it was only in the 1970s that work study and job evaluation became widely prevalent. As for recent changes, the third WIRS distinguishes between three main types of change (Millward et al. 1992):

1. Advanced technical change (involving microprocessors).

2. Conventional technical change (not involving microprocessors).

3. Organizational change (not involving new equipment).

It was found that more than one-half of manual and two-thirds of nonmanual workplaces with more than 25 employees had experienced one or other of the forms of change. In all but simple technical change in nonmanual workplaces, the incidence of change reported was above that reported in 1984. Especially significant was the increase in organizational change—for example, there was a doubling in the number of nonmanual workplaces reporting such change (Millward et al. 1992, 13–16). Other surveys and case study collections confirm that there have been considerable changes in work organization due to new technologies and altered competitive strategies, as will be discussed further below. In the case of task or functional flexibility, these include the combination of jobs—with elimination of differences within and between crafts, team working involving interchangeability and flexibility between jobs, "balanced labor force" techniques designed to deal with surpluses and shortages, the ending

of trade supervision under which craftsmen would accept instruc-
tions only from a first-line manager who had completed an apprenticeship in the same trade, and the breaking down of the distinction
between manual and nonmanual jobs (NEDO 1986; ACAS 1988; Cross
1988). In the case of time flexibility, there have been considerable developments in hours of work including the adoption of annual hours
systems that guarantee annual salaries in return for the freedom to
vary the number of hours worked each week (IRRR 1991a).

Three points need to be made about these changes. First, there is a
great deal of continuity with earlier phases of productivity bargaining
in the 1960s (e.g., see the argument in Elger 1991) and with what has
been described as the "reconstruction" of workplace industrial relations (Purcell and Sisson 1983) in the 1970s. Significantly the team
working that has received so much attention in the MIT studies is
very much the exception than the rule; survey evidence suggests only
a fraction of workplaces (Millward et al. 1992, 178; ACAS 1988, 15;
Marginson et al. 1988) have autonomous working groups. Second, it
is a moot point whether these changes have gone as far as they at first
appear. For example, many of the much heralded changes in task flexibility turn out to be not what they seem (Cross 1988); major alterations in job content have been rare as has the amalgamation of
production and maintenance jobs. Third, the main preoccupation, as
with earlier attempts, seems to have been "financially driven cost reductions" (Jones 1991, 245) rather than a change in thinking. Even
team working appears to have more to do with the implications of the
delayering of management than with a commitment to new theories
of working arrangements (Geary 1992).

There have been two major developments in involvement and participation that parallel the changes in work organization. One is the
growth in face-to-face communications systems such as team briefing
(Townley 1989). The survey evidence suggests that these affect as
many as two-thirds of large companies with 1,000 plus employees
(Marginson et al. 1988) and about one-half of workplaces with more
than 25 employees (Millward et al. 1992, 166). The other is the introduction of problem-solving groups such as quality circles (Dale and
Collard 1989). Although the number of companies with quality circles
is much smaller—probably no more than 2 percent of establishments
with more than 25 workers (Millward et al. 1992, 166) and one-fifth of
large companies have them (Marginson et al. 1988)—the number is up
from a handful in the late 1970s.

Team briefing and quality circles, it must be emphasized, have not only been introduced to involve individual employees in the affairs of the business. Both practices, as with many of the changes in work organization, are seen as helping to assert or reassert the authority of first-line managers more generally (Townley 1989; Dale and Collard 1989).

By comparison, with the exception of the "new style" agreements discussed above, there have been few initiatives in arrangements for collective involvement and participation. Thus, although unions have been involved in negotiations over changes in working practices, their role in the introduction of new technologies that frequently pave the way for these changes has at best been consultative. As with much else, management's approach to the introduction of new technology has been essentially opportunistic, consulting with unions where it felt constrained to do so but not otherwise. Much depends on the tradition of workplace trade union organization rather than structural features. Unions, for their part, appear to have been most concerned to negotiate over the impact on pay and employment rather than the design or the wider implications of new technology (Daniel 1987).

In terms of outcomes there was a considerable increase in productivity in manufacturing in the 1980s—both in labor productivity and total factor productivity (see the discussion of OECD statistics in Nolan 1989)—which reflects the shakeout in employment. There has been no major improvement in unit costs, however (Ray 1990). There are two explanations for this: First, earnings in the United Kingdom rose faster than in competitor countries (see below), and second, there was no substantial investment in new technology—capital spending per employee between 1980 and 1989 was considerably less than in other competitor economies (e.g., see the calculation based on OECD data of the Confederation of British Industry [CBI] 1992).

Skill Formation and Development

Education, training, and development in the United Kingdom, like so many other aspects of employment relations, have been massively influenced by the voluntarism touched on earlier. Responsibility for education was highly decentralized in the hands of "semi-autonomous educational institutions, a multiplicity of local education authorities, often at odds with central government; and a profusion of examining and validating bodies" (Keep 1989, 189). Until recently, for example, there was no national curriculum in schools. Vocational education and training was assumed to be the responsibility of individual employers and employees, and for practical purposes, vocational training was synonymous with a distinctive form of exclusive craft apprenticeship system. The government intervened from time to time, most notably in the form of the 1964 Industrial Training Act, but there were no fundamental changes to the underlying principles and practices of the United Kingdom's training system.

Concerns about the effects of these arrangements, which date back to the last century, have intensified in recent years. In the case of compulsory education, there have been growing concerns about declining standards (National Foundation for Educational Research 1992). In the case of postcompulsory education, it was the relatively low staying-on rate that has come in for comment (OECD 1991) and the generally low levels of attainment achieved in comparison with other countries (for a compendium of the reports of the National Institute for Economic and Social Research on this matter, see Prais 1991). Other influential reports complained about the relatively low priority given to training and development at work (Coopers and Lybrand Associates 1985; Industrial Society 1985; Manpower Services Commission 1985). Yet another group focused on the comparatively little provision being made for the training and development of the managers who might have been seen as the key to the successful implementation of change (Mangham and Silver 1986; Constable and McCormick 1987; Handy et al. 1987).

In the 1980s the government, while refusing to depart from its commitment to a market system, did take a number of major initiatives. In education, it introduced a core curriculum into schools, together with compulsory testing, and made provisions for an expansion in the number of students in universities and polytechnics. In training, it replaced the Manpower Services Commission with an employer-led structure, the centerpiece of which is the locally based Training and Enterprise Councils; these are charged with responsibility for administering existing schemes for the unemployed, persuading companies to undertake more training, and stimulating local enterprise and economic growth (Keep 1992).

Management too have begun to take training and development more seriously. In a number of industries, including chemicals and engineering (which covers autos), there has been a radical overhaul of the apprenticeship system involving standards-based training (IRRR

1985). Provision for adult training has also increased—the number of workers benefiting from job-related training was reported to be up from around 9 percent in 1984 to 15 percent in 1990 (Training Skills 1990). A number of companies, including BP and Shell in chemicals, have introduced payment for skills. There has also been a big increase in management education. The output of MBA programs, for example, has quadrupled from 1,000 to 4,000. Expenditure on training has also increased, the CBI says (1991), and is holding up well during the recession.

It is not only technical training that has been involved. There has been a number of examples of managements using training to bring about significant attitudinal changes. In the first half of the 1980s, it was the "customer care" and "customer first" campaigns associated with major organizations such as British Airways and British Rail, which caught the eye (e.g., see Sacker 1987). In the second half of the 1980s, total quality management (TQM) programs became more prominent. British Airways, British Telecom, BP, ICI, National Westminster Bank, Philips Electronics, and Shell are all notable examples (IFF Research 1991).

Finally, it is important to note that there have been significant developments in "open" and "distance" learning that are not immediately job related. In autos, for example, Jaguar and Rover launched major initiatives in "open" or "distance" learning in the 1980s (Muller 1991; Williams 1990); British Telecom and Lucas (aerospace and auto components) were also in the forefront of such developments (Keep 1989). In 1989 Ford UK launched its Employee Development and Assistance Program, which allows employees to qualify for grants of up to £200 per annum for personal development activities (Hougham et al. 1991).

Clearly, then, there have been significant developments. Many commentators nevertheless remain unconvinced that U.K. companies are devoting anything like the time and resources to training and development—despite recent attempts by the government and the CBI to argue to the contrary. The United Kingdom, it has been argued (e.g., see Finegold and Soskice 1988) is trapped in a "low-skills equilibrium" from which escape will not be easy. In this the link with business strategies is seen to be critical.

. . . the UK's training problems do not simply stem from difficulties with the supply of training and skills. They also reflect the fact that, because of their product market strategies, demand for skills from many employers is weak.

The lack of a sufficiently strong demand for skills in the economy limits not only the efficiency of the training supply system, but also the incentives available to individuals to get trained. (Keep 1992)

Compensation: Forms, Structures, and Levels

Compensation was very much a status issue in the United Kingdom. A typical manual worker was paid each week in cash for a standard number of hours plus overtime, whereas the typical nonmanual worker was paid a salary each month by bank transfer without payment for overtime. The manual worker would more likely have had a proportion of pay related to results; the nonmanual would more likely have received annual increments. Appraisal and individual performance pay were largely restricted to management grades; the same goes for profit sharing and share ownership. The status divide was also reflected in nonpay items; there were significant differences in holidays, sick pay, occupational pensions supplementary to the state system, and so on (for further details, see Price 1989).

In recent years the status divide has closed. There has been some harmonization of terms and conditions such as sick pay and pensions (Price 1989). Many of the developments discussed below, such as the extension of profit sharing and share ownership, are also common. Even so, single-status arrangements covering a company's entire labor force remain rare—it has been estimated, for example, that only one in eight organizations have "integrated" job evaluation schemes involving most groups of workers (ACAS 1988, 7)—as does "single-table" bargaining involving manual and nonmanual workers (Marginson and Sisson 1991).

In the case of payment systems, there have been two major changes. One is the growth in individual performance pay. In the case of manual workers, although the "rate for the job" remains dominant, there is evidence of the extension of appraisal and merit pay. The Institute of Personnel Management, for example, found a phenomenal increase in the appraisal of skilled manual workers—up from 2 percent in 1976 to 26 percent ten years later (Long 1986)—and the third WIRS suggested that one-fifth of this group were now in receipt of some form of merit pay (Millward et al. 1992). In the case of nonmanual workers, appraisal and merit pay are becoming widespread in both the public and the private sector (ACAS 1988). In financial services, for example, they are increasingly replacing automatic annual pay increases and increments (for further details, see Blisset and Sisson 1989). Significant groups of managers, notable in the public services and the recently privatized public enterprises, have been taken out of collective bargaining and put on individual performance-related contracts.

The second major change is the growth in the coverage of group performance-related systems. These include work group schemes, plant and enterprise schemes, and profit sharing. In its survey of 667 workplaces in 1988, for example, ACAS found that the numbers covered by such arrangements were 30 percent, 13 percent, and 37 percent, respectively. The third WIRS suggested a lesser overall coverage, which is explained by the lower threshold of workplace size, but found a marked increase in the proportion of workplaces with some form of profit sharing—up from 18 percent in 1984 to 43 percent in 1990 (Millward et al. 1992, 264).

A key structural change has been the further decentralization of pay bargaining referred to earlier. In the private sector, the shift from multi-employer to single-employer bargaining has been accompanied by moves from multi-establishment to single-establishment bargaining. In the public sector, the government has promoted similar developments in the Post Office, the civil service, the National Health Service, and education.

In terms of general trends in pay, three main conclusions suggests themselves. First, earnings rose faster than prices throughout the decade, despite high levels of unemployment mentioned below—there was no year, for example, in which average earnings in manufacturing did not rise by more than 7.5 percent (New Earnings Survey quoted in IRRR 1991b). Second, there was a considerable widening of the distribution—managers in particular did very much better than the rest (Renumeration Economics/British Institute of Management Survey quoted in IRRR 1991b). Third, notwithstanding these developments, the United Kingdom remained a relatively low-pay economy; not only did pay remain low but also nonpay labor costs (Ray 1987, 1990); this helps explain the attraction of the United Kingdom in the 1980s to inward investors able to set up greenfield operations.

Employment Security

In the United Kingdom, employment security has been a sector as well as a status issue. Manual workers in the private sector enjoyed little if any security—they could be dismissed with a week's notice. Nonmanual workers in the private sector enjoyed greater security. In the public sector both groups enjoyed greater security. De facto they enjoyed lifelong employment if they wanted it.

Thus the third WIRS found that more than one-half of workplaces in manufacturing and one-third in private services had used compulsory redundancy as a means of reducing the size of their labor force. By contrast, only 4 percent of workplaces in the public sector had done so. Early retirement and voluntary redundancy were the main methods used to achieve reductions (Millward et al. 1992, 321).

Employment in the 1980s and early 1990s has become less secure as is evidenced by the very high levels of unemployment. Few manual workers, as already indicated, enjoy single-status conditions; examples of the package deals involving greater security negotiated in the United States are rarer still—one such case, involving Rover in autos, has recently been negotiated (Lorenz 1992). Any advance that manual workers have made also has to be offset against the much more precarious position of nonmanual workers. Thus there have been considerable reductions in employment due to delaying of administrative and managerial posts; British Telecom, BP, and the major clearing banks are prime examples. Similarly there is much less security in the public sector as a result of privatization, the contracting out of services, the tightening of cash limits on public expenditure (for further details of developments in public enterprises, see Ferner 1988; for public services, i.e., civil service and National Health Service, see Fairbrother 1991; Bach 1989).

Social plans for the management of redundancies have also been the exception rather than the rule. There are long-standing examples in public enterprises such as coal (for details of the most recent arrangements, see IRRR, 1992) and electricity (now privatized). In the private sector some of the big companies, for example, IBM, have introduced special measures (Peach 1992).

So far as contingent or nonstandard forms of employment are concerned, the 1980s saw considerable growth, which also helps to explain the overall increase in employment. According to Casey's (1991) analysis of the Labour Force Survey, between 1979 and 1987 there was an increase from 1.75 million (7.3 percent) to 3.0 million (12.4 percent) in the number of self-employed and an increase from 4.4 million (18.3 percent) to 5.4 million (22.4 percent) in the number of part-time workers. The number of temporary workers, contrary to expectations, showed little increase.

It is questionable, however, how far these developments reflect an explicit strategy of distinguishing between a core of full-time permanent employees and a periphery of part-time, temporary and subcontract workers as some have argued (e.g., see Atkinson 1984). A fair amount of the increase is attributable to structural shifts—a decline in manufacturing and an increase in services (see Pollert 1987)—and a response to the fall in the number of young people coming into the labor market in the late 1980s. Examples of increases in the subcontracting of mainstream activities are comparatively rare (Marginson et al. 1988, 88–90); the fashionable idea of networking or teleworking is even rarer—a recent survey of 477 organizations by the National Computing Center suggested that 13 percent used some form of teleworking and that the workers in only about half of these spent more than 50 percent of their time at home (Moore et al. 1992). Even those who were originally responsible for suggesting that a core and periphery approach might be developing have stressed that many companies have not made the stark distinction between the two groups and that they have often reacted to events in an ad hoc fashion (Atkinson and Meager 1986; see also Wood and Smith 1989).

Conclusions

There have certainly been major changes in employment relations in the United Kingdom in recent years. Management has responded to pressures from the marketplace and the opportunities presented by new technology to introduce practices that would have been unthinkable a decade or two ago. Especially noteworthy is what John Storey (1992, 28), after a detailed study of 15 mainstream organizations, has termed the "remarkable take-up" by large British companies of initiatives that are in the style of the human resource management model. The state, out of a deep commitment to free market principles, has played an important role in bringing about change in its roles of legislator and economic manger; it has been directly involved in sponsoring many of the changes in the public sector. Trade unions, for their part, have been on the defensive; they have been able to do little to shape the agenda or apply pressure for the developments they would like.

It is important not to get carried away, however. Fundamental though the changes have been, there has not been a transformation of U.K. employment relations. Indeed, there are good reasons for suggesting that employment relations have been characterized by continuity as much as change. Many organizations remain more or less untouched by the changes discussed above; the number with quality circles, for example, is very small and the number with autonomous working groups even smaller. There must also be question marks about the depth and the permanency of many of the changes; some revised working arrangements turn out to be relatively superficial on close inspection; some practices, such as team briefings, have fallen into disuse. As Storey's (1992) study confirms, the initiatives associated with HRM, where they are practiced, rarely seem to add up to an integrated approach; there are also major inconsistencies—an emphasis on team working, for example, and yet an insistence on having individual performance pay, with the different forms of participation and involvement being seen as alternatives rather than complementary. Few companies, moreover, have sought to articulate their initiatives toward individual employees with their approach to trade unions; very often HR and IR are the responsibility of two separate departments (Storey 1992).

In brief, what has been happening is best seen as essentially ad hoc or piecemeal reactions by U.K. management to the economic and political context. Sir John Cassels, formerly secretary of the Donovan Commission and recently retired as director-general of the National Economic Development Organization, offers a fitting overall conclusion in discussing U.K. management's preparedness to deal with the implications of the "demographic time bomb" facing the United Kingdom:

The disappointing results . . . indicate that we are in for a bout of "muddling through," British-style . . . many companies are chucking money at the problem and assuming that will do the trick. Given that level of complacency, can hysteria be personnel matters (because labour is so cheap?), most employers live hand-to-mouth and the idea of taking a strategic view and of doing so at board level is quite alien. (Cassels 1989, 6)

2.3   Corporate Governance: The Legacy of History

In seeking to account for the state of organizational affairs in the United Kingdom, two views can be found. The first is associated with much of the prescriptive management literature; if there is a problem, it is largely one of will and the need for enlightenment. The second, to which the author subscribes, stresses the importance of a number of structural conditions that are deeply embedded in historical experience. Significantly, in view of the framework in chapter 1, these go far beyond the traditional bounds of industrial relations and can most appropriately be discussed under the heading of corporate governance.

Short-Termism

Several conditions might be said to contribute to a tendency to short-term thinking in employment relations, and in management practice more generally. Each is important in its own right, but it is the mutual reinforcement that gives them their true significance. Briefly, one is the relatively poor education and training of British managers already referred to above. Relatively few British managers are likely to have been exposed to any serious discussion of the opportunities involved in the formal processes of planning, where planning, for reasons that will become clearer below, is budgeting. A second is the composition of British management. Not only do the functional divisions within management go very deep, the dominance of the finance function, of accountancy logic, and of accountancy-driven managerial control systems is overwhelming (Armstrong 1984, 1987); it has hindered the development of both general and strategic human resource management. Probably no more than one-third of companies with over 1,000 employees has a specialist director in the area (Marginson et al. 1988). A third is the business strategies and organization structures of U.K. companies. There has been overreliance on domestic and defense markets, and in the past two decades, within major companies there has been considerable diversification, divisionalization, and devolution, coupled with a tradition of corporate head offices emphasizing control rather than development. This has reinforced the emphasis on "numbers-driven" rather than "issue-driven" planning (McKinsey and Co. Inc. 1988). The fourth is the patterns of institutional investment and the relationship between industry and the financial markets (the "city"). The overriding importance of such institutional investors as investment trusts and pension funds, plus the threat of takeover in the form of the large conglomerate (e.g., BTR and Hanson) anxious to maintain the price-earnings ratio of its shares, has put considerable pressure on delivering short-term financial results (Dore 1986; Keep 1989). In short, the wider organizational context in which British managers have to work is not conducive to the development of a strategic approach.

. . . managerial performance horizons are adjusted to meet annual, half-year, and even quarterly reporting schedules. The exigencies of this regime place a premium on behaviors and investments which have an immediate pay-back. This, up to a point, may act as a useful discipline. But, a consequential effect is to discourage, and even penalize, actions which are geared to a beneficial return over a longer time horizon. Many HRM initiatives would fall into this latter category—most notably those which relate to training and development and investments of time and resources in winning commitment.

   . . . short-term reporting periods tend to put pressure on managers to have recourse to opportunistic quick-fix agreements; firefighting solutions; and Tayloristic job design methods which are built on command and control rather than the more time-consuming consensus-seeking methods. Little wonder then that these are the managerial devices and methods which have come to be so characteristic of the British scene. (Storey and Sisson 1995)

The Absence of Countervailing Pressures

There are a few, if any, countervailing pressures to offset the tendency to short-termism. It is in this context that some of the distinctive features of U.K. industrial relations discussed earlier take on a particular significance.

Voluntarism

The voluntarism, which permeates virtually every area of U.K. employment relations, is critical. The United Kingdom lacks the framework of rights and obligations to be found in most developed economies that requires management to have a higher regard for employment relations issues. This is true of both individual and collective rights. Especially important, however, is the lack of any statutory provisions for participation and involvement allowing labor a collective voice in the key policy decisions of U.K. companies.

   Much has been made of the impact of state policies in the 1980s. In many respects, it is true, these policies have had a significant impact. The state has done nothing, however, to offset the short-term pressures on British management. Indeed, the publicity material produced by the Department of Trade and Industry for potential inward investors makes a positive virtue of the voluntary nature of employment relations practice—"quality people at low cost" is the message:

Unlike most continental European countries, employment regulations are largely on a voluntary basis with no requirements for works councils and no mandatory union agreements, while single-union agreements are relatively easy to negotiate. (Quoted in the *Guardian*, 9 April, 1992)

Similarly, despite the widely held view that the highly fragmented structure of pay bargaining contributes to wage inflation (e.g., see IRRR 1991), the state has arguably made things worse by encouraging further decentralization. Under these circumstances there are strong grounds for arguing that in its pursuit of an enterprise-based economy, the state has reinforced the ad hoc*ery* and opportunism of U.K. management. Ironically, then, the 1980s may will go down in history as contributing more to continuity than change in U.K. industrial relations.

Trade Unions and the Structure of Collective Bargaining
In the changed political and economic circumstances of the 1980s and 1990s, some of the inherent weaknesses of unionism in the United Kingdom have been fully exposed. Trade unions have been unable to provide a substitute for legal enactment as they have done in the past. Trade unions, especially at the national level, are relatively weak and ineffective; recent mergers are largely a defensive measure. Developments such as the "new style agreements" pioneered by the electricians union in the 1980s attracted a great deal of publicity. Not only were they relatively rare, but their significance is open to question, and in some cases—Nissan is an example—it has been necessary for the management to seek to stimulate union membership.

The widespread decentralization of collective bargaining that has been described in an earlier section is also fundamentally important in understanding the relative weakness of U.K. unions. Unlike their western European counterparts, U.K. unions lack the framework of national multi-employer bargaining to establish and develop standards for entire sectors. The ability of trade unions to mount industrywide campaigns has been further undermined by the prohibition on secondary industrial action; in 1989–90 the engineering unions, for example, were obliged to wage their campaign for reduction in the working week, workplace by workplace rather than across the industry. The decentralization of negotiations within organizations is also putting unions at a disadvantage. Management finds it relatively easy to coordinate the outcome. Trade unions, by contrast, have found coordination much more difficult because they lack effective company (as opposed to workplace) organization. Decentralized negotiations, moreover, exaggerate the focus on workplace issues at the expense of occupational comparisons or notions of the "going rate."

2.4   Implications

Implications for Policy

Although they are not the main concern here, the policy implications
that flow from this analysis are very similar to the propositions put
forward by Kochan and Dyer (1992) with respect to the United States.
The inability of any individual management to initiate and sustain
employment relations innovations on its own is central to debates
about the need for a statutory framework for training; "poaching" is
seen as a major barrier to investment in human capital (Keep 1992).
The "insufficiency" of top management commitment for transforming employment relations practices is accepted by many managers
themselves. For example, Sir John Harvey-Jones, a former chairman
of ICI, has recently argued:

> . . . Everyone knows the short-term pressures on British business, yet time af-
> ter time they are denied. The pressures to pay dividends that should not be
> paid. The threat of takeover, and the fear that the smallest slip in short-term
> performance will lead to predation, is ever present in the UK. Yet time and
> again we are told that these are irrational fears in the minds of managers who
> are concerned only for their own futures and wellbeing. (*Observer*, 1 March
> 1992)

Many would further accept that a coalition of stakeholders is required if there is to be genuine change. Particularly crucial is the role
of the state; this lies at the heart of the debate over the pros and cons
of industrial policy and over whether the United Kingdom should
commit itself to the European Community's social charter. Finally,
there is a growing recognition on the part of managers of the need to
learn from international sources—the example of the Japanese transplants has been particularly important here—and to secure hard information that helps to prove that employment relations change is
worthwhile.

Appendix: Some Propositions to Be Tested in Management
Industrial Relations Research

• Management in industries with high capital-labor ratios, such as
chemicals/pharmaceuticals, is more likely to follow a quality strategy, whereas management in industries with low capital-labor ratios,
such as clothing, is more likely to pursue a low-cost strategy;

• Management in companies that have "stuck to their knitting" (to borrow from Peters and Waterman 1982) is more likely to follow a quality strategy, whereas management that is diversified or has become part of diversified companies is more likely to pursue a low-cost strategy.

• Management in companies that practice strategic planning or strategic control from headquarters is more likely to follow a quality strategy, whereas management that relies on financial control is more likely to pursue a low-cost strategy.

• Management in companies belonging to Porter's (1990) successful clusters of internationally competitive industries is more likely to follow a quality strategy, whereas management in stand-alone companies or companies not part of a successful cluster is more likely to pursue a low-cost strategy.

• Management in industries where there is multi-employer bargaining is unlikely to be in the vanguard of change, but the average is more likely to nearer the quality strategy than where there is single-employer bargaining.

• Management in general is more likely to be under pressure to adopt a quality strategy in countries where there is a highly centralized trade union movement than where bargaining is decentralized and the power rests in the workplace.

• Management in general is more likely to adopt a quality strategy in countries where there is a high measure of state regulation, especially in the training of workers (e.g., Germany and France), whereas management in relatively unregulated countries such as the United Kingdom and the United States is more likely to follow a low-cost strategy.

• Management in general is more likely to adopt a quality strategy in countries where there is a protected environment (e.g., Germany, France, and Japan), whereas management in countries with a stock market—which puts greater emphasis on short-term profitability and encourages predatorial behavior (e.g., the United States and the United Kingdom)—is more likely to follow a low-cost strategy.

References

Advisory, Conciliation and Arbitration Service. 1987. *Annual Report.* London: Her Majesty's Stationary Office.

Advisory, Conciliation and Arbitration Service. 1988. *Labour Flexibility in Britain: The 1987 ACAS Survey*. Occasional Paper 45. London: ACAS.

Atkinson, J. 1984. Manpower strategies for flexible organizations. *Personnel Management* (August):28–31.

Bach, S. 1989. Too high a price to pay? *Warwick Papers in Industrial Relations* 25. Coventry: Industrial Relations Research Unit.

Bassett, P. 1986. *Strike Free: New Industrial Relations in Britain*. London: Macmillan.

Blissett, E., and K. Sisson. 1989. *Pay System Practices Labour Flexibility in the UK*. Paper prepared for the International Labour Office. Coventry: University of Warwick, Industrial Relations Research Unit. Mimeo.

Casey, B. 1991. Survey evidence on trends in "non-standard" employment. In A. Pollert, ed., *Farewell to Flexibility*. Oxford: Blackwell, pp. 179–99.

Cassels, J. 1989. Facing the demographic challenge. *Personnel Management* (November): 6.

Clegg, H. A. 1979. *The System of Industrial Relations in Great Britain*. Oxford: Blackwell.

Commission on Industrial Relations. 1974. *The Role of Management in Industrial Relations*. Report 34. London: Her Majesty's Stationary Office.

Confederation of British Industry. 1992. *Competing with the World's Best: The Report of the CBI Manufacturing Advisory Group*. London: CBI.

Constable, R., and R. J. McCormick. 1987. *The Making of British Managers: A Report for the BIM and CBI into Management Training, Education and Development*. London: British Institute of Management.

Coopers and Lybrand. 1985. *A Challenge to Complacency: Changing Attitudes to Training*. London: Coopers and Lybrand.

Cross, M. 1988. Changes in working practices in UK manufacturing, 1981–88. *Industrial Relations Review and Report* 414:2–10.

Dale, B., and R. Collard. 1989. Quality circles. In K. Sisson, ed., *Personnel Management in Britain*. Oxford: Blackwell, pp. 356–77.

Daniel, W. W. 1987. *Workplace Industrial Relations and Technical Change*. London: Pinter.

Donovan, Lord. 1968. *Report of the Royal Commission on Trades Unions and Employers' Associations*. London: Her Majesty's Stationary Office.

Dore, R. 1985. Financial structures and the long-term view. Part I. *Policy Studies* 6 (July).

Edwards, Paul, Mark Hall, Richard Hyman, Paul Marginson, Keith Sisson, Jeremy Waddington, and David Winchester. 1992. Great Britain: Still muddling through? In A. Ferner and R. Hyman, eds. , *Industrial Relations in the New Europe*. Oxford: Blackwell.

Elger, T. 1991. Task flexibility and the intensification of labour in UK manufacturing in the 1980s. In A. Pollert, ed., *Farewell to Flexibility*. Oxford: Blackwell, pp. 46–66.

Fairbrother, P. 1991. In a state of change: Flexibility in the civil service. In A. Pollert, ed., *Farewell to Flexibility*. Oxford: Blackwell, pp. 69–83.

Ferner, A. 1989. Ten years of Thatcherism: Changing industrial relations in British public enterprises. In *Warwick Papers in Industrial Relations No. 27.* Coventry: University of Warwick, Industrial Relations Research Unit.

Finegold, D., and Soskice, D. 1988. The failure of training in Great Britain: Analysis and prescription. *Oxford Review of Economic Policy* 4:21–53.

Geary, J. 1993. Team working: Employee participation enabled or constrained. In K. Sisson, ed., *Personnel Management in Britain.* 2d ed. Oxford: Blackwell.

Goldthorpe, J. H., D. Lockwood, F. Bechhofer, and J. Platt. 1968. *The Affluent Worker: Industrial Attitudes and Behaviour.* Cambridge: Cambridge University Press.

Goold, M., and A. Campbell. 1987. *Strategies and Styles: the Role of the Centre in Managing Diversified Corporations.* Oxford: Blackwell.

Gregory, M. 1986. The no-strike deal in action. *Personnel Management.*(December):30–33.

Handy, C., et al. 1987. *The Making of Managers: A Report on Management Education, Training and Development in the United States, West Germany, France, Japan and the UK.* London: National Economic Development Office.

Hougham, J., J. Thomas, and K. Sisson. Ford's EDAP scheme: A roundtable discussion. *Human Resource Management Journal* 1:77–91.

IFF Research. 1991. *Total Quality Management.* London: IFF Research Ltd.

Incomes Data Services. 1988. *Company Councils.* Study 437, July.

Incomes Data Services. 1991. Focus. *Performance Pay.* London: IDS.

Industrial Relations Review and Report. 1985. Apprentice training. Report 354, October.

Industrial Relations Review and Report. 1989a. Single union deals. Report 442, June.

Industrial Relations Review and Report. 1989b. Decentralised bargaining in practice: 1. Report 454, December.

Industrial Relations Review and Report. 1990. Decentralised bargaining in practice: 2. Report 457, February.

Industrial Relations Review and Report. 1991a. Annualised hours: The concept of the flexible year. Report 488, May.

Industrial Relations Review and Report. 1991b. Long-term earnings trends 1971–91. Report 500, November.

Jones, B. 1991. Technological convergence and the limits to management control: Flexible manufacturing systems in Britain, the USA and Japan. In S. Tollidat and J. Zeitlin, eds., *The Power to Manage: Employers and Industrial Relations in Comparative-Historical Perspective.* London: Routledge, pp. 231–55.

Keep, E. 1992. Missing: Presumed skilled; Training policy in the UK. Coventry: University of Warwick, Industrial Relations Research Unit. Mimeo.

Kinnie, N, 1985a. Local managers' control over industrial relations: Myth and reality. *Personnel Review* 14:2–10.

Kinnie, N. 1985b. Changing management strategies in industrial relations. *Industrial Relations Journal* 16:17–24.

Kochan, T. A., H. Katz, and R. B. McKersie. 1986. *The Transformation of American Industrial Relations*. New York: Basic Books.

Kochan, T. A., and L. Dyer. 1992. Managing transformational change: The role of human resource professionals. Paper for the Conference of the International Industrial Relations Association. Sydney.

Lorenze, A. 1992. Rover drives for Japanese working practices. *Sunday Times*. April 5.

Long, P. 1986. *Performance Appraisal Revisited*. London: Institute of Personnel Management.

MacInnes, J. 1987. *Thatcherism at Work*. Milton Keynes: Open University Press.

McKinsey and Co. Inc. 1988. *Strengthening Competitiveness in Electronics*. London: NEDO.

Mangham, I. L., and M. S. Silver. 1986. Management training: Context and practice. School of Management, University of Bath.

Manpower Services Commission/National Economic Development Office. 1987. *People: The Key to Success*. London: NEDO.

Marginson, P., P. K. Edwards, R. Martin, K. Sisson, and J. Purcell. 1988. *Beyond the Workplace: Managing Industrial Relations in Multi-Establishment Enterprises*. Oxford: Blackwell.

Marginson, P., and K. Sisson. 1990. Single-table talk. *Personnel Management* (May): 46–49.

Marsden, D., and M. Thompson. 1990. Flexibility agreements and their significance in the increase in productivity in British manufacturing since 1980. *Work, Employment and Society* 4:83–104.

Miller, W., et al. 1992. *Teleworking in the UK: An Analysis of the NCC Teleworking Survey*. Manchester: National Computing Centre.

Millward, N., M. Tevens, D. Smart, and W. R. Hawes. 1992. *British Workplace Industrial Relations in Transition*. Aldershot: Gower.

Müller, F. 1991. A new engine of change in employee relations. *Personnel Management*. (July):30–34.

National Economic Development Office. 1986. *Changing Working Patterns: How Companies Achieve Flexibility to Meet New Needs*. London: NEDO.

National Foundation for Educational Research. 1992. *TVEI and the Management of Change: An Overview*. Slough: NFER.

Nolan, P. 1989. The productivity miracle? In F. Green, ed., *The Restructuring of the UK Economy*. Hemel Hempstead: Harvester Wheatsheaf, pp.101–21.

Organization for Economic Cooperation and Development. 1991. *OECD Economic Surveys: UK*. Paris: OECD.

Peach, L. 1992. Parting by mutual agreement: IBM's transition to manpower cuts. *Personnel Management* (March):40–44.

Porter, M. E. 1990. *The Competitive Advantage of Nations*. London: Macmillan.

Prais, S., ed. 1990. *Productivity, Education and Training.* London: National Institute for Economic and Social Research.

Price, R. J. 1989. The decline and fall of the status divide? In K. Sisson, ed., *Personnel Management in Britain.* Oxford: Blackwell, pp. 271–95.

Purcell, J., and K. Sisson. 1983. Strategies and practice in the management of industrial relations. In G.S. Bain, ed., *Industrial Relations in Britain.* Oxford: Blackwell, pp. 95–120.

Ray, G. F. 1987. Labour costs in manufacturing. *National Institute Economic Review* 120 (May):71–74.

Ray, G. F. 1990. International labour costs in manufacturing 1960–88. *National Institute Economic Review* 132:71–76.

Sacker, F. 1987. Customer service training in context. *Personnel Management* (March): 34–37.

Sisson, K. 1989. Personnel management in transition? In K. Sisson, ed., *Personnel Management in Britain.* Oxford: Blackwell, pp. 22–52.

Sisson, K. 1990. *Strategy, Structure and Choice in Industrial Relations: A Comparison of US and UK Research and Its Implications.* Coventry: University of Warwick: Industrial Relations Research Unit.

Smythe Dorward Lambert. 1991. *The Power of the Open Company.* London: Smythe Dorward Lambert.

Storey, J. 1992. HRM in action: The truth is out at last. *Personnel Management* (April): 28–31.

Storey, J., and K. Sisson. 1989. Limits to transformation: Human resource management in the British context. *Industrial Relations Journal* 20 (1):60–65.

Storey, J., and K. Sisson. 1993. *Managing Human Resources and Industrial Relations.* Milton Keynes: Open University Press.

Terry, M., and P. K. Edwards, eds. 1988. *Shopfloor Politics and Job Controls.* Oxford: Blackwell.

Terry, M. 1989. Recontextualizing shopfloor industrial relations. In S. Tailby and C. Whitston, eds., *Manufacturing Change.* Oxford: Blackwell.

Thurley, K., and S. Wood, eds. 1983. *Industrial Relations and Management Strategy.* Cambridge: Cambridge University Press.

Townley, B. 1989. Employee communications programmes. In K. Sisson, ed., *Personnel Management in Britain.* Oxford: Blackwell, pp. 329–55.

Training Statistics. 1991. London: Her Majesty's Stationary Office.

Trevor, M. 1988. *Toshiba's New British Company.* London: Policy Studies Institute.

Wickens, P. 1987. *The Road to Nissan: Flexibility, Quality Team Working.* London: Macmillan.

Williams, M. 1990. Learning to win. *Transition* (June).

Wood, D., and P. Smith. 1989. *Employers' labour use strategies: First report on the 1987 survey.* Department of Employment Research Paper 63.

3

Managed Decentralization? Recent Trends in Australian Industrial Relations and Human Resource Policies

Russell Lansbury
John Niland

Australia has traditionally been viewed as having a rather centralized system of industrial relations. Yet, in common with most industrialized countries, Australia has been subject to strong economic, social, and political influences in recent years that have had a marked impact on traditional structures, policies, and practices. Pressures for change have focused particularly on industrial relations, and significant measures have been taken to encourage greater flexibility at the enterprise level, albeit within a predominantly regulated system. Unlike many other market economies during the past decade or so, Australia has maintained a form of incomes policy through an agreement between the federal Labor government and the trade union movement, known as the Accord (Lansbury 1985). At the same time, however, the industrial relations system has become more decentralized without the degree of labor market deregulation that has characterized many other industrialized countries.

The argument advanced in this chapter is that the Australian system of industrial relations is in transition toward a less centralized approach and that, as might be expected, developments are uneven across various sectors of the economy. The system cannot be described, at this stage of the transition process, as having undergone a complete transformation, although the past five years have witnessed significant changes. As in many comparable countries, Australia has faced increasing international competition that has exposed serious structural weaknesses in the economy. A decline in the nation's terms of trade, a growing current account deficit, and chronic foreign debt have acted as catalysts to wide-ranging reforms. Deregulation of the financial markets and other areas of economic activity has drawn attention to perceived rigidities in the labor market and other aspects of the industrial relations system. Yet, until recently, the labor market institutions have proved to be remarkably resilient despite widespread criticisms of their operations. However, recent trends toward greater enterprise bargaining by employers and unions, reinforced by legislative changes by the Australian government, may yet result in a profound transformation of the system.

3.1 Distinctive Features of the Australian Industrial Relations System

The centralized character of Australian industrial relations is perhaps one of its most distinctive features. This has been achieved through a network of arbitration tribunals, which exist at the federal level and in all six states of the Commonwealth and which have quasi-judicial status. Since 1904, when the federal tribunal (now known as the Australian Industrial Relations Commission) was established, the predominant forms of dispute settlement and wage determination have been conciliation and arbitration. More than 80 percent of the Australian work force is covered by awards of arbitral tribunals which set out the terms and conditions of employment. Yet collective bargaining, of a particular Australian variety, does occur within the conciliation and arbitration system to quite a degree. This has caused some observers to remark that the Australian system might more accurately be described as a hybrid of arbitration and bargaining.

Another feature of Australian industrial relations is the relatively high level of unionization. The establishment of the federal arbitration system in the early years of this century encouraged the rapid growth of unions and employers" associations. By 1921 approximately 50 percent of the Australian labor force were unionized and a peak of 65 percent was achieved in 1953. However, union density has suffered a decline in recent years and had fallen to 41 percent (45 percent of males and 35 percent of females) by 1990. In the private sector, unionization is now less than 30 percent. The deterioration in union coverage has sparked a vigorous debate on reform of the labor movement, and the current strategy pursued by the ACTU is to create fewer but larger unions, organized along industry lines (ACTU 1987). Union organization in Australia, however, continues to be comparatively weak at the workplace level, reflecting the reliance of many unions on the arbitration system to achieve their objectives (Lansbury and Macdonald 1992). While the ACTU have pursued a strategy to merge existing unions to approximately twenty large industrywide bodies, opposition parties and employer associations have advocated the formation of enterprise-based unions (BCA 1989, 1993).

Employers were initially hostile to the establishment of the (then) Commonwealth Court of Conciliation and Arbitration in 1904, since it forced them to recognize trade unions registered under the relevant Act of Parliament. Despite their initial opposition to the system, however, employers subsequently discovered that they could use the arbitration procedures to their advantage (see Mcintyre and Mitchell 1989). However, it has been argued that the employers and their associations "vacated center stage to unions in determining the structure of awards and the patterns of bargaining" during this early period because their energies were directed mainly at opposing arbitration rather than shaping the structures that emerged from it (Plowman and Rimmer 1992, 134).

The Australian situation thus became one in which the state imposed union recognition on employers but limited the role of unions to seeking improvements in "industrial" matters. This has largely remained the case until the present time, in that reform of industrial relations structures has been initiated by the state rather than by the bargaining partners. Under the past decade of federal Labor governments, however, the ACTU has played a dominant role in recent legislative reforms. Although various employer organizations have expressed views about the directions for change, they have lacked a single unified voice to match the ACTU and have thereby proved less influential in achieving their desired reforms.

The continued weakness of employer organizations can be seen in the inability of the peak organization, the Confederation of Australian Industry (CAI) to develop a strategy acceptable to its heterogeneous constituents. Since it rejected tripartism, it was excluded from the economic policy deliberations. However, the farming, construction, and engineering employers'[70] associations resigned from the CAI. With the emergence of the Business Council of Australia (BCA), the New Right Australian Federation of Employers, the Australian Chamber of Manufacturers, and the Australian Employers' Federation, employer representation has become even more fragmented, thereby perpetuating a lack of concerted action beyond the enterprise level. The BCA has been a persistent and effective advocate of an increased role for enterprise-based bargaining and a diminution in the powers of the industrial tribunals (BCA 1989, 1993).

In 1992 a series of mergers involving the CAI, the Australian Chamber of Commerce, and amalgamations of employer bodies at the state level led to the establishment of the Australian Chamber of Commerce and Industry. Although it represents the most complete integration of employer interests in two decades (MacIntosh 1992), it has yet to make an impact on the national agenda.

The past decade has been a period of significant change in industrial relations and human resources policies and practices in Australia. There was considerable economic turbulence during the 1980s with uneven progress in attempts to reduce high levels of inflation and unemployment. Australia elected a Labor government in 1983, which is still in office, as the longest serving Labor government at the national level since federation in 1901.[1] Strong economic growth from the mid to the late 1980s enabled the labor market to expand, and unemployment was reduced. However, deteriorating economic circumstances, including severe balance-of-payments deficits, caused the consumer price index to rise to 8 percent in 1989–90. During the early 1990s the government reacted by tightening fiscal policy, thereby achieving very low levels of inflation but, in turn, creating a sharp downturn in the economy, causing real wages to decline and unemployment to rise above 11 percent. Both the rate of wage increases and days lost through industrial disputes continued to decline, the latter being the lowest for several decades (Beggs and Chapman 1987).

Economic outcomes were strongly influenced throughout the past decade by an Accord on wages and prices, signed by the Australia Labor Party (ALP) and the ACTU just before the federal election of March 1983. The original Accord envisaged the Labor government's support for full wage indexation in return for the union movement pledging to make "no extra claims" for wage increases. Although the Accord has been modified a number of times since 1983, as a result of negotiations between the ACTU and the Labor government, the terms of the agreement have been honored by the unions. There has been little movement in wages beyond the national pay rates determined by the Australian Industrial Relations Commission. Following a severe economic crisis in 1985–86, which saw a dramatic fall in the exchange rate of the Australian dollar and an accompanying stimulus to

---

1. The ALP was led to victory by R. J. L. Hawke in the federal election on March 5, 1983. Hawke ceased to be prime minister on December 20, 1991, when he was replaced by P. J. Keating. The ALP was reelected in a historic fifth consecutive victory in the federal election on March 13, 1993, under the leadership of Keating.

inflation, the ACTU agreed to abandon its demands for full wage indexation. This ushered in a new era in which a "two-tier" wages system was introduced by the Australian Industrial Relations Commission in the National Wage Decision of March 1987.

Following a lengthy national wage case, the commission promulgated a new set of wage determination guidelines that ended the indexation system. The new guidelines provided for wage increases in two tiers. The first tier provided a $10 wage increase for all affected workers and the possibility of a further 1.5 percent increase in October 1987. The second tier, with an increase of up to 4 percent, was conditional on improvements in work practices to achieve greater efficiency and productivity. The significance of the March 1987 decision was that it promoted a productivity bargaining element that was based on unions and employers agreeing to minimize costs through the removal of inefficient and restrictive work practices. According to Niland and Spooner, an important component of the decision was the understanding that "such efficiency (had to) be sought at a decentralized industry and enterprise level" (Niland and Spooner 1991, 153).

The National Wage Case Decision of August 1988 continued the process of reform. It introduced the Structural Efficiency Principle whereby wage increases were granted only if unions and employers pursued "restructuring and efficiency." The decision provided for a 3 percent wage increase to be paid not earlier than September 1, 1988 and for a further $10 a week no earlier than six months after the receipt of the 3 percent. The granting of these increases was made conditional upon unions making a commitment to formal reviews and/or restructuring of their awards, taking into consideration such issues as skill-related career paths, wage relativities, flexibility, and any cases where award provisions discriminated against sections of the work force. The decision reinforced the central role of the commission while also supporting moves toward the establishment of enterprise agreements between employers and unions.

In the next major National Wage Case Decision of August 1989, the commission reviewed progress under the Structural Efficiency Principle. The commission made it clear that the second installment of the structural efficiency adjustment would only be available if it was satisfied that the principle had been properly implemented. The commission also reaffirmed that in restructuring their awards, unions and employers would be required to "improve the efficiency of industry

Table 3.1
National Wage Case Decision and price movements, 1983–91

Quarters by years	Percentage change in the cpi	Increases granted by National Wage Case Decisions (%)	Dates from which wage increases were operational
1983 March–June	4.3	4.3	September 1983
September–December	4.0	4.1	April 1984
1984 March–June	−0.2	—	—
September–December	2.7	2.6	April 1985
1985 March–June	3.8	3.8	November 1985
September–December	4.3	4.3	July 1986
1986 March–June	4.0		
September–December	5.5		
1987 March–June	3.5	$10.00	
September–December	3.4	$6.00[a]	February 1988
		(4.0)	Varied
1988 March–June	3.5		
September–December	4.0	3.0	From September
		($10.00)	1988[b]
1989 March–June	4.0		
September–December	4.2	3.0	From August
			1989[c]
1990 March–June	3.3	3.0	
September–December	3.4		
1991 March–June	−0.1	2.5	
September–December	0.6		From April 1991

Sources: Australian Bureau of statistics, Consumer Price Index, Cat. No. 6401.0 and National Wage Case Decisions 1983–91.
a. Taking the $10.00 and $6.00 together, this represented a 3.6 percent increase for full-time adult males.
b. The date for the initial 3 percent payment depended on the finalization of agreement between employers and unions, on structural efficiency. The $10.00 was to be paid as a second instalment at least six months later.
c. The Commission determined that again there should be a six month interval between installments.

and provide workers with access to more varied, fulfilling and better paid jobs" (Macken 1989, 142).

In the National Wage Case Decision of October 1991, the commission further refashioned the principles governing wage policy to encourage enterprise bargaining. This was another major change in the direction of a more decentralized approach to industrial relations. The Federal Minister for Industrial Relations explained the government's support for enterprise bargaining, despite previous caution on this matter, as follows: "Encouraging and facilitating more bargaining at the workplace level is a logical extension of (the) reform process . . . Such bargaining must be done freely and jointly, however, and in ways which do not damage the public interest." (Cook 1991)

Although the commission had earlier expressed reservations about the ability and maturity of the parties to effectively engage in enterprise bargaining, it reluctantly agreed to such a development occurring and issued a series of principles to be followed. In the words of the National Wage Case Decision of October 1991: "In all the circumstances confronting us, we are prepared, on balance, to determine an enterprise bargaining principle. In deciding the best way to proceed, we have taken account of views of the parties and the need to limit the risks inherent in the approach chosen." (National Wage Case Decision 1991b, 6)

Currently Australia appears to be in transition from an industrial relations system that was one of the more centralized of the market economies to one of a dualistic character. While the majority of unions and employers remain in the more highly regulated area of arbitrated awards, an increasing minority are moving toward a more decentralized bargaining approach at the enterprise level. According to the federal government, over 720 workplaces and over 30 percent of employees covered by federal awards are now covered by workplace agreements (ILR).

In keeping with its Accord commitments, the federal government has ensured that all enterprise-based agreements continue to be subject to some scrutiny by the commission, although special amendments to the Industrial Relations Act in 1992 weakened the commission's vetting role. It is expected that the parties will pursue an increasingly independent approach to enterprise bargaining, with minimal intervention by the Australian Industrial Relations Commission. The most recent version of the Accord (known as Mark VII) was released in March 1993, immediately before the federal election. It was based on an understanding by the government that it would help to create 500,000 new jobs over the next three years. While confirming support for more decentralized enterprise bargaining, Accord Mark VII also provided for a "safety net" wage increase for lower-paid employees and for union members in workplaces where no agreement had been concluded. The reality, however, is that enterprise bargaining has not expanded as rapidly as both the ACTU and the government had hoped. The government is therefore considering further legislative amendments to make the process of enterprise bargaining easier and faster.

The impact of the Accord on Australia's traditionally conflictual industrial relations pattern is subject to debate. In the 1970s days lost through industrial stoppages continued to be high. The strike level fell markedly after 1981 and has maintained a low level thereafter (Frenkel and Peetz 1990). Between 1983 and 1985 working days lost to strikes declined to 40 percent of the levels experienced during the previous ten years. The proportion attributable to wages fell from 42 percent (1980–82) to 19 percent (1983–85). Frenkel and Peetz suggest that this can be attributed partially to union goodwill following the election of a Labor government. Although some analysts attribute much of the decline in strikes to the Accords, others suggest that it reflects a decline in union power and employer unwillingness to pursue provocative strategies in the face of uncertain demand conditions and intensified competition (Frenkel and Peetz 1990, 135).

Although there is evidence of a small annual decline in real earnings, and a redistribution of national income to profits and managerial employees, Frenkel and Peetz suggest that most union leaders are convinced that they and their members have been better off under the Accords than they would have been under a decentralized bargaining system as found in the United Kingdom and the United States. As a result of the centralized nature of the negotiations, the ACTU acquired a growing share of union resources in the 1980s, thereby increasing its influence relative to its affiliates.

Frenkel and Peetz (1990) suggest that the industrial relations structures shaped by the government and the unions, with support from the Federal Conciliation and Arbitration Commission, has limited labor cost increases and demonstrated the unions' capacity for restraint. Despite employer weakness at the national level the Accords were conducive to growth, favored capital accumulation, and enabled management to reorganize production and improve workplace relations.

3.2   Proposals for Change

Since the mid-1980s three different proposals have been advanced to change Australia's industrial relations arrangements. The first has advocated the maintenance of the centralized system. The second has proposed radical decentralization. The third has argued for greater decentralization within a centralized framework, or "managed decentralism." The argument for retaining and consolidating the existing system, albeit with certain modifications, was put forth by the Committee of Review into Australian Industrial Relations Law and Systems (known as the Hancock Report) in 1985. This committee was commissioned by the Labor government soon after it assumed office in 1983. At the heart of the Hancock Report was a conviction that the relatively centralized system in Australia facilitated the enforcement of incomes policies. This was seen to be an important factor in achieving the wider objective of reducing both unemployment and inflation. The Hancock Report was unconvinced that dismantling the existing system and placing greater reliance on collective bargaining would be of long-term benefit to the economy, and described it as a "leap in the dark." The findings of the Hancock Report were supported by the ACTU two years later in *Australia Reconstructed* (ACTU/TDC 1987), which advocated the retention of a centralized wages system but also argued that wages policy should be linked to taxation and social welfare policies. Furthermore the ACTU was concerned that wages policy should take into account the necessity of achieving greater skills development, productivity, and international competitiveness as a means to achieving greater wealth creation and equity. The ACTU has since shifted its position on centralized wage determination to become a significant advocate of greater decentralization and is seeking to develop more effective enterprise bargaining strategies among its affiliated unions.

A leading advocate of more radical change to the current system toward enterprise-based bargaining has been the Business Council of Australia (BCA). The BCA consists of the chief executive officers of Australia's largest business organizations. It was established in 1983 partly as a result of dissatisfaction with adherence by the Confederation of Australian Industry (CAI) to the centralized approach of the arbitration system. The BCA has argued that the key to improved competitiveness is a shift to enterprise-based agreements that emphasize the mutuality of employee-management interests and enhance flexibility (BCA 1989). In recent years the CAI has moved closer to the BCA position, although it still sees a role for the Australian Industrial Relations Commission. The view presented by the CAI is that there must be "greater cooperation between management and employees (together with) a greater degree of negotiation in the workplace" (CAI 1991, 30). The CAI became the Australian Chamber of Commerce.[2] There has also been some academic support for this position. In a far-reaching report on industrial relations reform for the state government of New South Wales, Niland argued for the need to "lower the centre of gravity" in industrial relations decision making through more enterprise bargaining (Niland 1989). A number of the provisions advocated by Niland have subsequently been adopted by the federal government, both in policies and legislation.

Although some of the more extreme arguments for enterprise bargaining have been criticized for seeking to reduce or eliminate the role of trade unions (Dabscheck 1990; Easson and Shaw 1991; Frenkel and Peetz 1990), the mainstream of reform has moved toward greater decentralization within a centralized framework. The Australian government's position, expressed by the Minister for Industrial Relations (October 17, 1991) is that "there is a place for bargaining beyond the existing conciliation and arbitration framework for those who are able to do so responsibly . . . Encouraging and facilitating more bargaining at the workplace level is a logical extension of this reform process" (Cook 1991, 6, 8). The ACTU has also advocated a form of enterprise bargaining "designed to create more interesting and financially rewarding jobs, by stimulating greater worker involvement in all aspects of the way their industry and workplace operates, thereby driving enterprise reform and pushing up productivity levels" (Kelty 1991, 1). In April 1993, however, Prime Minister Keating announced a review of existing federal legislation to facilitate more rapid development of decentralized bargaining at the enterprise level. Keating argued that in the long term, enterprise-level agree-

2. The ACCI has recently called for a radical overhaul of state and federal laws on enterprise bargaining which includes the removal of the need for small work places to create an "industrial dispute" to register an agreement. It also seeks the removal of the requirement that unions be party to agreements, and it wants the introduction of laws to recognize autonomous branches of unions at the enterprise level (see Bolt 1993).

ments would eventually replace the award system. After some unions objected to this statement, the prime minister "clarified" his position and emphasized that the existing award would continue to provide a "safety net" of minimum wages and conditions, especially for those employees in a weak bargaining position. However, the government has been critical of the commission for constraining enterprise bargaining. It has considered alternative measures that may be needed to provide non-unionized employees with easier access to enterprise agreements. This latter issue has created tensions with the ACTU, which is seeking to preserve a union monopoly in negotiating enterprise agreements.

One of the strongest advocates of a "middle way" was the Metal Trades Industry Association (MTIA), which sought to retain the advantages of a centralized framework provided by the commission in order to broaden the scope for direct bargaining between the parties. The MTIA, however, has cautioned its members to beware that enterprise agreements can be inflexible if arrangements entered into are rigid and untried (MTIA 1991). The "managed decentralism" approach of the MTIA gained widespread support, as reflected in the National Wage Case Decision of October 1991 when the commission endorsed movement toward a more devolved system and issued a series of enterprise bargaining principles. This led commentators to remark that the latter months of 1991 were "the most dramatic in modern times (in Australia) for shifting industrial relations policy" (Niland et al. 1991, 2). However, the MTIA has been under subsequent pressure to adopt more fully decentralized approaches, in line with the policies of the ACCI (Norrington 1993).

The push toward decentralization has been reinforced by reforms initiated in the Victoria state legislature. Mass public demonstrations and considerable national media attention accompanied the passage of the Employee Relations Act 1992. The Act brings an end to compulsory arbitration and the central role of the Accord in the determination of conditions of employment in Victoria as new awards can only be made with the consent of all employers and all employees concerned.

Unlike the federal legislation, this state-level legislation permits the conclusion of agreements that do not require the approval of the third party. Employees and employers may enter into individual or collective agreements, but unions, as third parties, cannot be party to an agreement. The Victoria government believes that this will allow agreements suited to local needs to be concluded at the industry, enterprise, or occupation level (ILR).

Employees will be permitted to conclude an individual employment agreement that overrides a collective agreement, provided that it does not undercut the base award rate and the minimum annual leave, sick leave, and parental leave provisions. Macintosh (1993) suggests that the details of the legislation were almost obscured by the public demonstrations and the provocative stance of ministers, who adopted a "take it or leave it" approach. "It is apparent that the legislation strikes a blow at the existence of an effective union movement, while individual rights and protections have been quite significantly reduced" (p. 57).

Because this legislation directly challenged the federal government's policy, the federal government facilitated the transfer of Victorian employees to federal awards as all awards in Victoria ended on March 1, 1993. The compatibility of the Victorian legislation with federal law will soon be tested by the High Court, which has been asked to rule on the jurisdiction of the Industrial Relations Commission (ILR).

3.3   Industrial Relations/Human Resource Policies and Practices: Dominant Patterns, Changes, and Diffusion

In order to gain a general perspective on the ways in which key IR/HR policies and practices have changed since the mid-1980s, data were gathered from nine large Australian organizations. Interviews were conducted with senior IR/HR managers at the corporate level and, in some cases, also at the plant level. The nine organizations were drawn from both the private and public sectors in the following industries: automobiles, chemicals, food, communications, financial services, airlines, white goods, and water supply. The cases were selected on the basis that they represented organizations and industries that had played key roles in shaping IR/HR policies and practices in Australia during the past decade. The interviews focused on the five IR/HR practices identified in chapter 1 but also included some additional questions that reflected current concerns in Australia, particularly in regard to productivity and enterprise bargaining. The relationship between the five IR/HR practices and broader variables are outlined in figure 3.1. However, these organizations should not be seen as representative of Australian industry as a whole. For this rea-

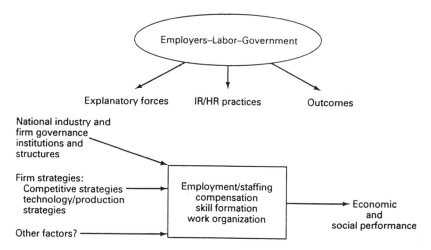

Figure 3.1
Initial framework for organizing the comparative IR/HRM research project. Within any country IR/HR practices may vary across industries, firms, and over time, and all the variables in the model may be shaped by different employer, labor, and government influences.

son reference is also made to data from the Australian Workplace Industrial Relations Survey which examined more than 2,000 workplaces with 20 or more employees in 1989–90 (Callus et al. 1991).

While it is acknowledged that IR/HR activities cannot be treated in isolation from the broader issues, such as the economic environment in which the firm or industry operates, it was necessary to examine specific policies separately in order to gain an overall perspective. It was clearly apparent, however, that many of the individual IR/HR components are interrelated (e.g., work organization and skill formation) and are influenced by other policies (e.g., business strategies) developed in other areas of the enterprise.

Work Organization

Work organization in Australia, as in the United Kingdom and the United States, was traditionally characterized by an extremely large number of job classifications. The system has traditionally inhibited flexibility and the acquisition and upgrading of a broader range of skills. For example, 700 job classifications are detailed in the awards covering the clothing, footwear and textile industries. The metal industry has 348 job classifications, including many that are obsolete.

During the past decade, however, there has been a general movement away from rigid and closely defined job specifications to
broader and more flexible forms of work design. This has been
assisted by the process of award restructuring, referred to at the beginning of this chapter, which has reduced the number of job classifications in many areas and broadened the range of activities
undertaken by particular categories of workers (see Mathews 1989).
For example, greater emphasis is being placed on the need for employees to be multi-skilled in order to undertake a wider variety of
tasks and assume a wider range of responsibilities. Significant progress has been made in this regard in many of the so-called blue-collar
areas, particularly in the manufacturing sector. As the chemical company in our survey explained "we now define jobs on the basis of
skills rather than tasks . . . ."

Several organizations in our survey claimed that they had moved
away from general duty descriptions toward defining the outputs required from the work area or work group. According to one of the automobile companies surveyed, "we now focus on outputs and the
quality requirements of the job rather than being concerned about
specific job content." However, other firms also noted that many jobs
had been so poorly or inaccurately defined in the past that individual
employees had been uncertain about what was required of them. This
had exacerbated demarcation disputes as workers sought to defend
the boundaries of their jobs and to preserve their job security. Most of
the organizations in our survey, however, reported fewer demarcation disputes as a result of award restructuring and work redesign.

Although demarcation problems persisted between some trades
or craft areas, new areas of friction have developed between blue-
and white-collar workers, especially as the scope of blue- collar jobs
expanded to absorb tasks previously performed by clerical, supervisory, and even professional staff. As one manufacturing company
noted, "While blue-collar jobs are becoming more flexible, white-
collar and supervisory jobs have remained rather rigid . . . supervisors feel threatened as blue-collar workers are able to manage their
own areas."

The role of the first line manager or supervisor was perceived as
undergoing significant change as organizational structures became
flatter and the number of managerial levels were reduced. The role
of the supervisor was also changing from a traditional custodial,
policing function to more of a team leader or facilitator, especially as

team-oriented approaches became more common. This is not a new phenomenon (see Gilmour and Lansbury 1984). However, some organizations mentioned difficulties that they had encountered in seeking to implement such changes. According to one banking representative, "The banks are still very hierarchical, even though the levels have been reduced and the boundaries have become blurred . . . ." Other organizations reported uneven progress: "The supervisor issue is often the last to be tackled . . .; it is just too hard . . . there are still major status differences between supervisors and workers." One automobile manufacturer noted that the recession had set back reform of the supervisory function, for it had caused greater reliance on supervisors who had to undertake increased work loads.

The general view, however, was that the role of the supervisor was irrevocably changing as organizations became more decentralized and important decisions were increasingly undertaken by work groups. As one chemical company representative noted: "Up to one-third of the supervisors in our major plant have been removed and ultimately the teams will manage themselves."

Although teamwork was a major objective or strategy, in almost all of the organizations surveyed, progress was uneven. Teamwork was well advanced in certain areas, such as the engine and plastics plants in both of the automobile manufacturers, but it had encountered difficulties in other areas, particularly where continuous process operations were involved. In some cases there was resistance to teamwork on the ground that it undermined existing work practices. In other cases, however, the concept of teamwork was simply not understood by those who were required to implement the new strategies. Not infrequently these were designed by management who were often located beyond the relevant workplace.

Management has increasingly sought changes in work organization by means of improved communication and participation structures. Consultative arrangements or direct forms of participation such as quality circles and productivity improvement groups appear to have increased (Frenkel and Peetz 1990).

Employee involvement in decision making appeared to be most advanced where there was extensive teamwork, requiring workers to be well informed and equipped to make decisions. Consultative committees were used in most of the organizations surveyed and were often required under provisions of award restructuring. Yet the effectiveness of these committees varied. Not surprisingly, successful consultative committees tended to be correlated with high levels of employee involvement, although some organizations commented that they had moved beyond consultation toward greater direct involvement in decision making by their employees. Several respondents noted that success in this area required strong commitment by management to genuine forms of consultation and employee involvement. It is interesting to note that the Australian Workplace Industrial Relations Survey found that only 14 percent of workplaces, covering 40 percent of the total work force, had formed consultative arrangements (Callus et al. 1991, 135).

Frenkel and Peetz (1990) question whether these structures will persist where management has little commitment to power sharing and unions remain weak on the shop floor. Management has also stressed the importance of line management responsibility and a formalization of disputes, dismissals, and redundancy procedures.

There appeared to have been few major changes in working hours since the mid-1980s, when a shorter working week was introduced. Several companies had introduced twelve-hour shifts as a result of award restructuring, thereby expanding the span of hours. However, the recession of the early 1990s meant that some organizations followed a survival strategy of placing their work force on shorter working weeks for less pay. In the automobile industry, for example, employees were asked to take unpaid leave to reduce the levels of production during periods of low demand. This had generally been voluntarily agreed upon between management and the unions in order to assist the companies through difficult economic times.

Skill Formation

The expansion of training opportunities to promote greater skill formation has been a major priority of the Australian government and a key element in award restructuring during recent years. Various government inquiries have identified low percentages of young people undertaking post-secondary education and low levels of spending on training at the industry and enterprise levels as major impediments to Australia's economic growth and competitive advantage (Carmichael 1992). While there have been significant improvements in the proportion of young people completing twelve years of schooling (rising from approximately 40 percent in 1981 to 71 percent in 1991), Australia is still well short of the target of 90 percent set by the federal government by the year 2001. Expenditure on training has also increased since the government established a compulsory levy on companies, rising to 1.5 percent of gross wages by the end of 1992. However, a national survey in 1989 found that while the average employer spent 2.2 percent of gross wages on training, there was a wide discrepancy between employers according to size and industry sector. The OECD Economic Outlook Report on Australia for 1992 also claimed that "Australia's system of education and training (has) not been capable of keeping up with increases in educational attainment overseas and (has) been biased against vocational skills—producing too few skilled workers and training them too narrowly" (Australian Financial Review, May 15, 1992, 16).

Employers in our survey indicated that until recently most skills were still acquired by experience on the job, without a planned program of skills training and development. In general, however, industry was now demanding higher levels of education and skills before a job was offered. Once hired, an employee was now likely to be required to undertake formal training on the job to acquire necessary competencies. Progress within an enterprise or industry was increasingly based on skills acquired and demonstrated levels of competency. This trend had been enhanced by award restructuring, which placed greater emphasis on skills-related wage systems. It may also have been enhanced by the economic recession when employers have had a wider range of employees from which to choose.

In some industries, such as automobiles and chemicals, specific industry certificates have been introduced, with the support of both management and the unions, to formalize the training process and recognize skills acquired. It is anticipated that progression by individuals to higher levels within industry will ultimately depend on having passed stages of the certificate courses (e.g., the Vehicle Industry Certificate). Several organizations in the survey commented, however, that these requirements had been applied only to the blue-collar work force at this stage and that white-collar employees lagged behind in this regard.

Since embarking on more extensive formal training at the workplace level, several companies reported that they had discovered significant problems of literacy and numeracy among their work force. This required extensive remedial education programs to raise the level of basic education before skills development programs could be introduced. Even when this had been undertaken, there were residual groups of employees who simply could not cope with the learning demands that were placed on them.

It was also noted that despite the efforts being made to upgrade skills, progress was not keeping pace with increased requirements, particularly as new technologies introduced higher levels of complexity. While some companies felt that they were keeping pace in the blue-collar areas, they were having to "buy in" more highly qualified professional and managerial employees from the external labor market.

The increased emphasis on skills formation has exposed weaknesses in other organizational aspects. One manufacturer commented:

We have realized that we are not a good learning organisation. . . . We have found that we need to revise our skills acquisition program every twelve months. . . . We have also had to change our work organisation to ensure that new skills are fully utilized.

Compensation

During the latter part of the 1980s, the wage system in Australia moved away from a relatively centralized approach toward a greater emphasis on enterprise-level bargaining, albeit still within the framework of arbitration. It is widely believed that from 1983, when wage indexation was reintroduced as part of the Accord, until the latter 1980s, pay differentials became progressively compressed. However, according to respondents in our survey, with the introduction of the two-tier approach to wages in 1987, pay differentials appeared to widen again.

Gregory (1992) has argued, however, that the widening gulf between higher and lower wage earners has been occurring in Australian over the past fifteen years. Since 1975, the number of male middle-income earners has fallen by 25 percent, relative to the size of the population, while the ranks of the low-paid workers have expanded by 15 percent. In the past, argues Gregory, Australia was able to create a more egalitarian society by increasing the lowest wages, maintaining full employment, and making transfer payments. In recent years, however, rising levels of unemployment have caused the lowest wages to fall, and pressure on government budgets have reduced the amount of welfare income redistribution. Gregory also describes the surge in real wages during the mid-1970s, early retirement, and structural changes associated with manufacturing.

Considerable international debate has occurred in recent years concerning the desirability of performance-related pay and other variable or contingent forms of compensation (see Milkovich and Wigdor 1991). The Australian Workplace Industrial Relations Survey reported that 39 percent of workplaces with five or more employees, covering 34 percent of the Australian labor force, had performance-related pay schemes operating for nonmanagerial employees. The highest proportion of workplaces with such schemes were in the wholesale and retail sectors, while less than 1 percent of workplaces in public administration provided performance related pay. The most common schemes were those in which pay was explicitly linked to measured output, such as payment by results (Callus et al. 1991, 44).

While elements of performance-related pay have been introduced at senior executive levels in most of the organizations in our Australian survey, this did not extend very far down the organizational hierarchy. Among senior managerial and professional employees, in both the private and public sectors, there has been a trend toward employment contracts, whereby complex compensation packages are negotiated for a fixed term of years and their renewal depends upon a number of factors, including the achievement of agreed performance targets (Lansbury and Quince 1989). However, this approach has not been applied to the unionized work force.

In many organizations the number of levels between senior management and the worker at the shop floor has been reduced. In several companies in our survey, for example, the number of levels in the organizational hierarchy had been significantly reduced. This has not translated into a reduction in salary differentials. In some cases, however, there has been a change in the way compensation is paid in order to reduce the differences between managerial and nonmanagerial employees. In the chemical company, for example, annualized salaries were introduced for all production employees. Among former weekly paid workers, the movement to annualized salaries also involved the absorption of overtime and other penalty rates. This was part of the company's philosophy to move toward "single-status" employment for all. This approach to compensation has not yet been followed by many other companies, although it was under consideration by several participants in our survey.

Although various nonwage benefits were common among managerial employees, such as the provision of a company car, a fringe benefits tax introduced by the federal government in the mid-1980s curtailed the spread of such benefits to other types of employees. The extension of occupational superannuation has increased significantly during the past decade due to trade union demands and federal government pressures.

Profit-sharing and other share ownership schemes have not been widely used within Australian organizations. The Australian Industrial Relations Workplace Survey (Callus et al. 1990, 244) indicated that in workplaces with twenty or more employees, 8 percent of workplaces covering 7 percent of employees, had profit-sharing schemes. Share ownership schemes were somewhat more popular, being present in 13 percent of workplaces and covering 17 percent of employees. These schemes were most prevalent in the finance and related sectors where they were present in 19 percent of enterprises covering 21 percent of employees. Furthermore a quarter of all large firms with 200 or more employers operated either profit-sharing or share ownership schemes. Only two of the organizations in our survey, however, operated such schemes and these were introduced during the past five years.

However, Callus (1992) has argued that the degree to which the wage system in Australia is regulated has been overstated. He points out that while 85 percent of wage earners are covered by awards, the award rates and conditions, particularly in the private sector, only specify the minimum requirements. Earnings are often supplemented by overaward rates and incentive bonuses. Drawing on the results of the Australian Workplace Industrial Relations Survey, Callus has shown that overaward payments applied to 68 percent of all Australian workplaces with five or more employees. These were highest in manufacturing where they covered 88 percent of all workplaces. Similarly incentive payment systems were found in 61 percent of all Australian workplaces, the highest coverage being in the wholesale and retail sectors, followed by financial and business services. Callus argued that extensive use of overaward and incentive payment systems were largely outside the control of the tribunals (or regulated system). They were generally paid in response to product and labor market conditions or for management reasons, rather than as a result of workplace bargaining, even though they were introduced "under the shadow" of the arbitration system.

3.4 Employment Security and Staffing Arrangements

The rise in unemployment to more than 11 percent by 1992 has placed concern about job security high on the IR/HR agenda. Most of the organizations in our survey had shed employees during the past five years. Following the experience of widespread redundancies during previous economic recessions, particularly in the mid-1970s and early 1980s, most unions negotiated redundancy agreements and had clauses inserted in their awards by the industrial relations tribunals. As part of its commitment to the Accord with the trade union movement, the federal government supported the ACTU in a lengthy test case before the Australian Industrial Relations Commission to expand employee rights to information and consultation over technological change that could result in loss of jobs. Under the terms of the Termination, Change and Redundancy Decision of 1984 by the commission, employers were required to consult with their employees and unions before introducing major changes to production methods or to organizational structures. In addition, where redundancies were contemplated, the length of the required advance notice was increased. While many employers were opposed to the commission's decision as impinging on their managerial prerogatives, it did help to more firmly establish employee rights in regard to redundancies (see Deery 1987). It did not, however, stem the rising tide of redundancies during the early 1990s.

In all of the organizations surveyed, voluntary redundancy programs were used where labor force reductions were undertaken. In most cases unions accepted the rights of the employer to implement a redundancy program as long as natural attrition was used, where possible, and the process was voluntary. The focus of union action was mainly on ensuring that agreed-upon procedures were followed and that redundancy payments agreed under the award were adhered to by employers.

A variety of procedures were used by employers to adjust labor requirements to a decline in demand for goods and services during the recession, including shorter working hours and longer holidays, with commensurate reductions in pay. In some cases managerial and other non-unionized staff were requested to work without pay on their rostered days off. Extensive job transfers and redeployment of staff were also used to fill positions vacated by former employees. Employers noted that cooperation by unions in these matters was much greater in recent years than had been the case previously. Union representatives commented that this was due, in part, to the willingness of their members to take the redundancy payments rather than risk losing their jobs without compensation at a later stage, should their employers close down entirely. There was little enthusiasm among employees for resisting redundancies as long as the programs were voluntary and there was adequate compensation. Most companies in our survey conducted their redundancy programs in cooperation with the unions, followed the agreed award provisions, but sought to avoid arbitration if possible.

There has been a steady increase in the number of part-time, casual and temporary workers in the Australian labor market in the past decade (see Bray and Taylor 1991). In 1992 approximately 23 percent of the Australian labor force worked less that 37 hours per week (which is defined as full-time employment). This represents an increase of 25 percent over the past five years. The impact of increased numbers of part-time and casual employees has helped to reduce the average working week to 31.6 hours. The shift away from full-time employment was exacerbated by the mini-economic boom of the mid-1980s when increasing numbers of women with children returned to the work force, often on a part-time basis. Between 1983 and 1990 the number of part-time jobs increased by 55 percent compared with an increase of 20 percent in full-time jobs. In 1991 women accounted for 75 percent of all part-time workers, and 42 percent of the female work force was engaged in part-time work, compared with 10 percent of the male work force. Total part-time workers can be further divided into 66 percent casual part-time and 34 percent permanent part-time (Affirmative Action Agency 1992).

In most of the organizations in our survey, however, more than 90 percent of the work force was classified as regular, full-time employees. The main exception to this situation was the bank which had negotiated a change to its award to permit 17 percent of its work force to be employed on a part-time basis. The bank was also using casual employees on a trial basis. Most of the organizations surveyed indicated that a small but increasing range of jobs was being "contracted out" and that they were seeking to have these arrangement included in enterprise awards. Although only a few percent of current positions were classified in this way, they included office services, catering, accounting, sales, and various engineering and technical activities. Several companies noted that they were investigating which "noncore" functions of their businesses could be assigned to contractors.

Corporate Governance

The election of the Hawke Labor government in 1983 revived interest in the issue of industrial democracy and employee participation in management, which had briefly flourished in the early 1970s and then declined as the result of political and economic changes (see Lansbury and Davis 1991). The mid-1980s witnessed the creation of a more favorable framework than had existed previously. The Accord stated that there must be "continuous consultation and cooperation between the parties involved over economic, industrial and social matters." It also noted that "consultation is a key factor in bringing about change in industry. This consultation will be extended to industry, company and workplace level" (ALP/ACTU 1983, 9). By the late 1980s these statements had been endorsed by the main national employers body. The Confederation of Australian Industry had joined with the ACTU in issuing a Joint Statement on Participative Practices (CAI/ACTU 1988).

At the enterprise level, however, progress on industrial democracy and employee participation has been less encouraging. The Australian Workplace Industrial Relations Survey reported that consultation appeared patchy and sporadic. With the exception of committees on occupational health and safety, less than 20 percent of private sector workplaces engaged in joint consultation, task-force committees, quality circles, or employee representation at the board level. The situation was more positive in public sector workplaces, where more than 40 percent of workplaces engaged in some form of participation. Yet the survey concluded that "in nearly three quarters of workplaces, unions were not consulted or even informed about organizational changes which would affect employees" (Callus et al. 1991, 135).

A more detailed analysis of the results of the Australian Workplace Industrial Relations Survey by Marchington (1992) revealed that while only 14 percent of workplaces operated joint consultative committees. These covered 30 percent of employees, indicating the greater propensity to establish formal schemes in larger workplaces. Furthermore the proportion of workplaces with formal consultative committees nearly doubled in the five years prior to the survey. However, only 7 percent of workplaces reported that they had worker representatives on their board of directors.

Among the organizations in our survey, unions played little or no role in strategic decisions. With the exception of one of the public sector firms, there were no employee or union representatives on boards of directors. Some of the organizations claimed that senior union officials were consulted on major decisions, which had implications for the work force; this occurred only when management chose to do so. There were no formal mechanisms, in the private sector organizations, for consulting unions or their representatives on strategic decisions. Other stakeholders, such as banks with a major financial interest in the company and significant shareholders, were more likely to be consulted about strategically important issues than were employees or their unions.

Although a number of commentators have noted that the status and influence of the IR/HR function has risen within both the private and public sectors in recent years, conclusive evidence of this has been difficult to establish. The Australian Workplace Industrial Relations Survey, however, revealed that approximately 34 percent of all organizations surveyed had a specialist manager for industrial relations. This rose to 87 percent for organizations with 500 or more employees. The survey also sought to gauge the influence of the IR/HR function within the workplace. Managers at workplaces where there was at least one person with specialist IR/HR responsibilities were asked: "If a major new product line or service was introduced at the workplace, involving a change in the way that work was organized, what role would the industrial relations area at that workplace play?" In total, 16 percent of workplaces had an industrial relations area or department. Of these workplaces, 55 percent claimed they would be consulted before the decision was made, a further 30 percent indicated that consultation would take place before the product change was introduced, and in 12 percent of the cases the IR/HR area would be involved only when there was a problem. This led the authors of the survey to conclude that "these results indicate that a workplace with a clearly defined area of industrial relations expertise used it for more than 'fire fighting' . . . it was actively involved in the process of change" (Callus et al. 1991, 89). While such workplaces are still in the minority, it would appear that the IR/HR function is enlarging its range of influence and expertise, particularly in larger organizations.

The organizations in our survey generally argued that the influence and status of the IR/HR function had increased in recent years, although the most senior IR/HR manager was a member of the board in only half of the companies surveyed. In most cases, however, the executive committees responsible for day-to-day management of the organizations included a senior IR/HR manager. The influence of the IR/HR function was regarded as having waned in some of the organizations surveyed as a result of devolution and decentralization, whereby line managers had become more accountable and responsible for industrial relations matters. In several other cases the most senior IR/HR managers commented that although they were members of the executive committee, other functions such as finance and production had more influence over major strategic decisions. It was also noted that the role played by the IR/HR function in the management hierarchy depended a great deal on the influence wielded by the individuals who occupied the most senior IR/HR position.

3.5   Factors Influencing the Degree of Stability or Change in IR/HR Policies and Practices

A major concern expressed by economic commentators, politicians, business executives, and trade union leaders in recent years has been the decline in productivity levels and competitiveness of Australian industry compared with its trading partners. While there has been a significant slow-down in the growth of labor productivity throughout OECD countries since the 1960s, Australia's relative position has steadily deteriorated (except for a brief period from 1973 to 1979) and stood at just over 60 percent of the OECD average by the end of the 1980s (OECD 1989). Furthermore the growth in Australia's total factor productivity has been persistently less than the OECD European average and far below the best performers (see Blandy and Brummitt 1990).

The Australian Workplace Industrial Relations survey reported that despite the considerable debate about productivity, half of the workplaces surveyed did not measure productivity in a quantifiable manner, while more than one-third indicated that they did not monitor productivity at all (Callus et al. 1991, 94). Another survey by Hilmer (1992) reported that the most common labor productivity measure used by Australian firms were productivity schedules, which rarely captured aspects of value and time. This and a variety of other studies indicate that the value added per employee (i.e., labor productivity) in manufacturing is low compared with the other countries shown. Although there was some improvement between 1980 and 1987, this was not in relation to other countries' performances. Furthermore the competitiveness of the Australian manufacturing sector has been falling.

All of the organizations in our survey used some measure of productivity and most claimed that their productivity levels had risen in the past decade. Yet most also expressed dissatisfaction with the productivity indicators which were used. They were particularly critical of measures used at the enterprise or workplace level on the grounds that such measures were often not well understood by the work force. Some also commented that much of the recent increase in productivity was attributable to work force reductions and it would be difficult to make future gains in this area. There was also a need to use more international benchmarks to compare their performance with best practice overseas and that Australia had long been too inward looking in this regard.

New technologies were regarded as having been very significant in the late 1970s and early 1980s when their impact had been all pervasive, but it was felt that quantum increases in productivity had not generally been as great as anticipated. In some cases, however, new technology had enabled organizations to overcome their competitors' advantage based on cheaper labor costs.

Some of the manufacturers in our survey were critical of the Australian government's plans to significantly reduce the level of tariffs during the coming decade. This had unleashed competitive pressures on many Australian companies which had long been protected by high tariff barriers. Several organizations, however, were seeking to expand their production and to develop niche markets with the objective of exporting to other parts of the world. Increased competition and deregulation had caused some of the companies in our survey to reduce the range of their products and services to concentrate on fewer core businesses, after diversifying during the 1980s and encountering financial difficulties in the 1990s. They were now seeking to enter more specialized and differentiated markets in which they had a comparative advantage.

Although some aspects of IR/HR policies were regarded as playing a significant role in improving the levels of productivity and competitiveness, many respondents to our survey focused on other factors such as international competition and government regulations as the major determinants of their future success. This was somewhat surprising given the emphasis that has been placed on microeconomic reform in recent years and the significant changes that have occurred at the workplace level. This is supported by the Australian Workplace Industrial Relations Survey which reported that 84 percent of workplaces had experienced some form of change in the previous twelve months. Among the most significant changes were reorganization of management structures, the restructuring of workplaces and the introduction of new technology (Callus et al. 1991, 186–87). It would seem that the IR/HR function has generally taken the role of reacting to changes from external sources rather than initiating change from within organizations. Thus, rather than engaging in strategic approaches to HRM or industrial relations, the IR/HR function in many Australian organizations has tended to be reactive to changes in the wider environment.

3.6 Conclusions

The key objectives of this paper were, first, to analyze the extent to which the five IR/HR practices listed in chapter 1 changed over the course of the past decade; second, to determine the factors that have been driving or causing the degree of change in these practices; and third, to assess the economic and social impacts of these changes.

Within the literature, two alternative visions of how to understand recent changes in IR/HR policies and practices have emerged (see Kochan et al. 1991). One view has focused on the changing competitive environment and new technologies that are causing firms to experiment with a variety of new production systems and IR/HR practices. The second view has emphasized the roles of national institutional arrangements and public policies in defining new patterns of IR/HR practices, in particular national contexts. These two approaches have provided useful competing explanatory hypotheses. In summary, the first hypothesis argues that competitive strategies pursued by firms in key sectors determine changes in IR/HR policies and practices; the second hypothesis assigns the dominant role in creating changes in these areas to public policy and legal-institutional arrangements.

The Australian experience, as outlined in this chapter, has shown that the degree of change in the IR/HR practices has varied considerably between different organizations and industries during the past decade. The factors driving the changes have been far from uniform and quite uneven in their impact on different organizations. For example, the reduction by the Australian government of tariff protection for manufacturing industries has meant that many firms have been forced to undertake immediate and drastic changes to their IR/HR policies. Other firms, however, that are still sheltered from competition, have seen little need to implement significant reforms.

The survey of Australian organizations presented in this chapter suggests that neither competitive strategy pursued by firms or industries acting to protect or enhance their positions in the marketplace, nor changes to legal-institutional arrangements created by governments can alone explain why IR/HR policies and practices have changed in the past decade. In most cases it has been a combination of actions at the enterprise, industry, and national levels, including both government and private firms, that has led to significant changes in IR/HR practices in Australia during recent years.

As outlined at the beginning of this chapter, the election of the Federal Labor Government in 1983 ushered in the era of the Accord between the trade unions and the government that initially strengthened the centralized wages system. Yet changes in the international economy, which undermined Australia's trading position, caused both the federal government and the trade union movement to reconsider their commitment to full wage indexation. Furthermore the determination of the Business Council of Australia, representing large firms in key sectors of the economy, to pursue enterprise-based bargaining was influential in persuading the ACTU, the federal government, and other leading employer bodies to modify their positions on the centralized approach to wage determination. Indeed the Keating government is currently seeking to increase the speed and volume of enterprise agreements by further restricting the role of the commission in the process.

It should be noted, however, that during the latter 1980s the Australian system of industrial relations achieved an unusual combination of flexibility and decentralization in wage determination while maintaining a largely centralized framework. This was made possible by the Accord, which proved to be remarkably durable despite fluctuations in the economy, as well as by the agility exhibited by the commission which generally achieved an accommodation between the often conflicting demands of the employers, unions, and governments. The commission has also displayed a capacity for policy modification when pressures have built up to do so, as in the National Wage Case of October 1991.

The process of "managed decentralism," which was pursued during the late 1980s and early 1990s by the major unions, employer groups, and federal government, is currently under pressure for being too slow to achieve change. The major conservative opposition political parties, and some significant employers, have indicated that they wish to implement a far more radical deregulated approach. Some trade unions would also like to move away from the centralized system, which they feel has hampered their freedom to bargain directly with employers and the extract higher wages and improved conditions. The Australian Industrial Relations Commission has found itself at odds with all of the parties at various times in recent years and has reluctantly consented to enterprise bargaining in the National Wage Case Decision of October 1991, on the ground that the parties adhere to a set of principles governing this area. Recent pronouncements by the federal government indicate that the commission's role in the wage determination system is likely to be further restricted in an effort to promote greater enterprise bargaining.

Due to the wide variations, it is difficult to summarize the dominant patterns that are emerging in IR/HR practices at the enterprise and industry level. Work organization appears to be undergoing significant change as companies move away from formerly rigid job definitions to more flexible approaches to work design and increasingly utilize teamwork. Similarly skill formation is an issue of major importance in all of the organizations surveyed, and it had been assisted by the process of award restructuring. However, greater progress has occurred among blue-collar employees, who have been more the focus of workplace reform, than among white-collar workers.

Although there has been a transition from a relatively centralized system of wage determination to one that is related more closely to productivity levels, progress at both the industry and enterprise level is still uneven. Performance-related pay is confined mainly to senior management, and there is little evidence of gain sharing or similar programs being implemented. The rise of unemployment has meant that considerable attention has been devoted to implementing redundancy schemes, especially in the early 1990s. There has been some growth in nonregular forms of work contracts, and an expansion in casual and part-time work, but these have yet to make a major impact on mainstream IR/HR practices.

Finally, although the Accord provided a framework for consultation between unions and the government at the national level, and a number of tripartite advisory bodies were established in the 1980s, consultation and employee involvement at the workplace level has remained sporadic. A key determinant in the degree to which change has been successfully introduced appears to have been the degree to which employers have emphasized a "cost minimisation approach" or a "productivity enhancement approach" (Curtain and Mathews 1990). The latter has been a longer-term strategy that has necessitated involvement and commitment by all the parties, while the former has stressed short-term gains for management. Furthermore, despite a great deal of workplace reform, the IR/HR function still does not appear to play a major role in strategic decisions at the level of the enterprise.

The framework outlined in figure 3.1 has been useful in providing a map of the forces that have had significant impact on IR/HR practices in the past decade. Our survey has indicated that, in the Australian context, public policy and institutional arrangements have interacted with strategies pursued by firms seeking improved levels of productivity and competitiveness within a turbulent economic environment. The resilience of the industrial relations institutions in Australia, particularly the Commission, has meant that their influence had been maintained until the early 1990s. However, the government has exhibited increasing frustration at the relatively slow pace of change toward enterprise level bargaining. Although the peak employer and union organizations have also expressed criticisms of the Commission for inhibiting the flow of enterprise agreements, it is clear that a number of individual employers and unions are less enthusiastic about totally abandoning the system of centralized awards. Hence the transformation of Australian industrial relations may take longer, and a somewhat different form than many advocates of more radical change anticipated.

References

Affirmative Action Agency. 1992. Integration of permanent part-time workers. Workshift Information Service No. 3. Melbourne.

Australian Council of Trade Unions. 1987. *Future Strategies for the Trade Union Movement*. Melbourne: ACTU.

Australian Council of Trade Unions and the Trade Development Council. 1987. *Australia Reconstructed*. Report of the ACTU and TDC Mission to Western Europe. Canberra: Australian Government Publishing Service.

Australian Financial Review. 1992. The importance of a skilled work force. Editorial. May 15.

Australian Labour Party and the Australian Council of Trade Unions. 1983. *Statement of Accord by the ALP and ACTU Regarding Economic Policy*. ALP and ACTU, Melbourne.

Beggs, J. J., and B. J. Chapman. 1987. Australian strike activity in an international context. *Journal of Industrial Relation* 29:137–49.

Blandy, R., and W. Brummitt. 1990. *Labour Productivity and Living Standards*. Sydney: Allen and Unwin.

Bray, M., and V. Taylor, eds. 1991. *The Other Side of Flexibility: Unions and Marginal Workers in Australia*. ACIRRT Monograph 3. University of Sydney.

Business Council of Australia. 1989. Enterprise based bargaining units: A better way of working. Report to the BCA by the Industrial Relations Study Commission. Melbourne.

Business Council of Australia. 1993. *Working Relations: A Fresh Start for Australian Enterprises*. Melbourne: BCA.

Callus, R. 1992. Current approaches to wage determination: Implications for the future. *Proceedings of a Conference on National Wages Policy and Workplace Wage Determination*. Australian Centre for Industrial Relations Research and Teaching, University of Sydney.

Callus, R., A. Moorehead, M. Cully, and J. Buchanan. 1991. *Industrial Relations at Work*. Canberra: Australian Government Publishing Service.

Carmichael, L. 1992. The Australian vocational certificate training system: Report by the Employment and *Skills Formation Council*. National Board of Employment, Education and Training, Canberra.

Committee of Review into Australian Industrial Relations Law and Systems (The Hancock Report). 1985. *Report*. Canberra: Australian Government Publishing Service,

Confederation of Australian Industry and the Australian Council of Trade Unions. 1988. *Joint Statement on Participative Practices*. Canberra: Australian Government Publishing Service.

Confederation of Australian Industry. 1991. *A New Industrial Relations System for Australia*. Melbourne: CAI.

Cook, P. 1991. *Ministerial Statement on Industrial Relations to the Senate*. Canberra: Office of the Minister for Industrial Relations.

Curtain, R., and J. Mathews. 1990. Two models of award restructuring in Australia. *Labour and Industry* 3:58–75.

Dabscheck, B. 1990. The BCA's plan to Americanise Australian industrial relations. *Journal of Industrial Relations* 29:425–49.

Deery, S. 1987. Redundancy, employment protection and the law. In G. W. Ford, J. M. Hearn, and R. D. Lansbury, eds., *Australian Labour Relations: Readings*. Melbourne: Macmillan, pp. 318–42.

Easson, M., and J. Shaw, eds. 1990. *Transforming Industrial Relations*. Sydney: Pluto Press.

Evans, A. C. 1989. Managed decentralism in Australia's industrial relations. *Eleventh Sir Richard Kirby Lecture at the University of Wollongong*. Sydney: Metal Trades Industry Association.

Frenkel, S., and D. Peetz. 1990. Enterprise bargaining: The BCA's report on industrial relations reform. *Journal of Industrial Relations* 32: 69–99.

Gilmour, P., and R. D. Lansbury. 1984. *Marginal Manager: The Changing Role of Supervisors in Australia*. St. Lucia: University of Queensland Press.

Gregory, R. 1992. Quoted by P. Cleary, "The end of the old Aussie dream." *Sydney Morning Herald*. May 26, 1992, p.11.

Hilmer, F. 1992. Coming to grips with competitiveness and productivity. *EPAC Discussion Paper*. Economic Planning and Advisory Council, Canberra.

Kochan, T., et al. 1991. Proposal for comparative research on industrial relations and human resource policy and practice. Mimeo. Sloan School of Management, Massachusetts Institute of Technology, Cambridge.

Lansbury, R. D. 1985. The accord: A new experiment in Australian industrial relations. *Labour and Society* 10:223–35.

Lansbury, R. D., and E. M. Davis. 1990. Employee involvement and workers' participation in management: The Australian experience. *Advances in Industrial and Labour Relations* 5:33–57.

Lansbury, R. D., and D. Macdonald, eds. 1992. *Workplace Industrial Relations: Australian Case Studies*. Melbourne: Oxford University Press.

Lansbury, R. D., and A. Quince. 1989. Australia. In M. Roomkin, ed., *Managers as Employees: An International Comparison of the Changing Character of Managerial Employment*. Oxford: Oxford University Press, pp. 97–130.

Mcintyre, S., and Mitchell, R., eds. 1989. *Foundations of Arbitration*. Melbourne: Oxford University Press.

Macken, J. 1989. *Award Restructuring*. Sydney: Federation Press.

Marchington, M. 1992. The growth of employee involvement in Australia. *Journal of Industrial Relations* (forthcoming).

Mathews, J. 1989. *Tools of Change: New Technology and the Democratisation of Work*. Sydney: Pluto Press.

Metal Trades Industry Association. 1992. *Building Enterprise Productivity*. Sydney: MTIA.

Milkovich, G. T., and A. K. Wigdor, eds. 1991. *Pay for Performance: Evaluating Performance Appraisal and Merit Pay*. Washington: National Academy Press.

Niland, J. R. 1989. *Transforming Industrial Relations in New South Wales: A Green Paper*, vols. 1, 2. Sydney: NSW Government Printer.

Niland, J. R., W. Brown, and B. Hughes. 1991. *Breaking New Ground: Enterprise Bargaining and Agency Agreements for the Australian Public Service*. Canberra: AGPS.

Niland, J. R., and K. Spooner. 1991. Australia. In J. R. Niland and R. O. Clarke, eds., *Agenda for Change: An International Analysis of Industrial Relations in Transition*. Sydney: Allen and Unwin, pp. 147–63.

Norrington, B. 1993. How the power brokers lost their edge. *Sydney Morning Herald*. August 16, p. 11.

OECD. 1989. *Economic Outlook*. Paris.

Plowman, D. H., and M. Rimmer. 1992. Bargaining structure, award respondency and employer associations. *UNSW Studies in Australian Industrial Relations* No.33. Industrial Relations Research Centre, UNSW, Kensington.

4

Developments in Industrial Relations and Human Resource Practices in Canada: An Update from the 1980s

Noah Meltz
Anil Verma

The Canadian industrial relations system has followed a course of incremental change and adjustment over the past decade that leaves intact the basic institutional framework and relationships among labor, business, and government. Essentially the system has changed in ways that reflect employment relations in other industrial nations but without undergoing any dramatic transformation. While the political forces that influence industrial relations policy and practice predict continuation of this incremental pattern of adjustment, economic pressures to adjust rapidly to a changing market context are likely to test the resilience of this political equilibrium in the 1990s. If the pace and pattern of innovations in industrial relations policy and practice do not accommodate changes in the marketplace, we may expect, at the margin, some decline in investments in Canada contributing to slow growth in employment and income and lagging national competitiveness. Such economic stagnation will, inevitably, put new strains on the political alignment that has made incremental change possible over the last decade.

The broad features of Canada's employment relations system are derived primarily from the (American) Wagner Act model which was grafted on to some significant Canadian innovations that preceded developments in the United States. The system relies on the Wagner Act model of union certification, exclusive bargaining agency, and voluntarism between labor and management through collective bargaining. The most important distinction between the Canadian and the U.S. systems is the interventionist role given to public policy within the law. The Canadian tradition of government supervised conciliation (mediation) embodied in law since 1907, dates back to the disputes of the last century. In keeping with this tradition, there are also some important limitations of the right to strike in contrast to the provisions of the Wagner Act.

In practice, the legal framework has created a decentralized system in which the vast majority of contracts are negotiated at the plant level especially in the private sector. Public sector bargaining tends to be more centralized, particularly in Quebec and in the civil service at both the federal and provincial levels. Working days lost due to strikes and lockouts, for the past two decades, have been above that in the United States, and on occasion in large disputes in the public sector there have been interventions by the government, in the form of back-to-work legislation. As in the United States, the collective agreement is characterized by detailed work rules that are enforced by submitting disputes to a primarily private system of arbitration.

Although this system of industrial relations performed reasonably well in the post–World War II period, the changing economic context in the 1980s, as a result of computer-based technological change and some deregulation, privatization, impact of computer-based technological change, and freer international trade, along with such demographic changes as increased female participation rates and greater ethnic diversity in the workplace, brought intense pressures for change (Chaykowski and Verma 1992). We assay the evidence on changes that took place within collective bargaining agreements in response to external pressures to conclude that these changes have been similar to those in the United States, in that innovation within collective bargaining has been slow and limited. Innovations in human resource practices in non-union firms likewise take on a similar pattern but they are less widely diffused than in the United States. This assessment, however, hides considerable divergence between the two systems in four important and related areas. First, there has been virtually no decline in overall union density in Canada in recent years, whereas union density in the United States has declined quite dramatically. The difference between the two countries' union density is less striking, though still significant, when the private and public sectors are compared separately. Private sector union density has declined in Canada since the 1970s, though to a lesser extent than in the United States, while public sector union density has risen more than in the United States. Second, in the last ten years there have been some notable successes for organized labor's political strategy. This has given labor relatively greater political clout in setting the social policy agenda at the federal and provincial levels. Third, this policy agenda in the post–World War II period has included comprehensive social legislation—such as a national health care system, broad-ranging employment standards, human rights, and health and safety legislation—and gradual improvements in labor relations legislation supportive of trade unions. Fourth, there have been a number of new tripartite initiatives at the sectoral level that break fresh ground in sharing power in decision making.

The pressures on the Canadian system to improve productivity at the workplace level remain intense and similar to those experienced by firms in the United States. Our analysis suggests that the Canadian successes of the last ten years, such as labor's political clout and cooperation at the sectoral level, could be in jeopardy in the 1990s if these achievements cannot be translated into improvements at the workplace. In the short run, many employers could take the option of investing in new technology rather than in industrial relations and human resource (IR/HR) innovations to improve productivity. But technological improvements alone are unlikely to sustain the productivity growth that firms will be required to maintain in the 1990s. We conclude with the observation that unless the Canadian IR system changes sufficiently to facilitate productivity growth, its integrity will be questioned and increasingly challenged throughout the remainder of this decade.

4.1 Broad Parameters of the IR/HR System

In 1867 the British Parliament passed the British North America Act, which created Canada as a confederation of provinces giving the French and English the same central government but control over their own local affairs. The ten provinces have jurisdiction over labor and employment matters covering 90 percent of the Canadian work force. The positive role of government, together with the primacy of the provinces and the unique institutions in the province of Quebec continue to shape the Canadian system of industrial relations (Meltz 1985, 1990a).

The Economy and IR/HR

The Canadian economy is highly developed with a standard of living close to that of the United States. Three-quarters of Canada's trade is with the United States, making Canada its biggest trading partner. An important factor in the development of Canada is the large extent of foreign (primarily American) ownership of its manufacturing sector, estimated at 48 percent in 1984 (Statistics Canada 1992a). These branch plants have tended to have the same unions as in the United States.

The strong links with the United States were increased with the 1965 Auto Pact which introduced sectoral free trade in automobiles and auto parts, combined with minimum guarantees for production of cars and parts in Canada. The auto sector represents nearly one-quarter of Canada's merchandise exports and imports (Kumar and Meltz 1992). The 1989 Free Trade Agreement with the United States increased the interdependence of the two countries, and the North American Free Trade Agreement among these two countries and Mexico will likely further enhance this interdependence. These close economic links have influenced IR in Canada. Initially unions "followed the market" in the sense that when American companies established plants in Canada, unions in the United States organized locals in Canada and thus became international. Unions that had formed in Canada also sought alliances with American unions for strength of numbers (Morton 1990). But with the growth of the public sector in Canada and public sector unionization, the national unions now dominate the Canadian labor movement with 65 percent of the total membership. An additional factor in the relative decline of the international unions has been the shift of some branches of international unions to national union status. The largest change was that by the Canadian branch of the United Auto Workers whose 150,000 members in 1985 became the Canadian Auto Workers.[1]

Political Parties

The existence of political parties linked to the labor movement has also been an important in development in Canada's industrial relations system (Bruce 1989) and its advanced health care system and employment standards legislation. The New Democratic Party (NDP) was formed in 1961 through an alliance of the Socialist party, the Cooperative Commonwealth Federation (CCF), and the Canadian Labor Congress (CLC).[2] When the CCF formed the government of

---

1. One Canadian local with approximately 2,500 members in Wallaceburg, Ontario, remained with the UAW.

2. Dissatisfaction of some Ontario trade unionists with the policies of the Ontario NDP government in 1993 led a large local of the Canadian Auto Workers to vote to withdraw from their affiliation with the Ontario NDP (Papp 1993). At this point there is no indication that the NDP-Labour alliance will dissolve, but it does illustrate the pressures on this alliance.

the province of Saskatchewan, it introduced the right of civil servants to bargain and strike (1944) and, later, a comprehensive health care program (1961). In 1992 the NDP held power in Ontario, the most populous and most industrialized province in Canada, as well as in British Columbia and Saskatchewan. The Liberals were in power in the second largest province, Quebec, whose opposition was the Parti Quebecois (PQ), a party with the backing of some segments of the Quebec labor movement and committed to a form of independence from the rest of Canada. The Progressive Conservatives held power at the federal level, with the Liberals and the NDP forming the opposition.

The party structure in Canada is significant for industrial relations because for the past three decades the dominant thrust has been toward support for trade unions.[3] This thrust has come not only from the NDP but earlier from the PQ. Even when the NDP or the PQ did not hold power, their voice in opposition or in a minority government has been significant enough to draw attention to labor issues. In most cases the Liberals and Conservatives have been supportive, to varying degrees, of trade unions and progressive employment legislation.

Labor Legislation

Labor legislation in Canada has gone through three stages in the past century. The first stage decriminalized unions from being conspiracies in restraint of trade and established a tradition of tripartism. This tradition was developed in large part by William Lyon Mackenzie King from his experience in the United States when he was employed by the Rockefellers to deal with industrial disputes in their mines. King introduced the Industrial Disputes Investigation Act (IDIA) in 1907 when he was Canada's first deputy minister of labor (Morton 1990). He later became prime minister of Canada.

The second legislative stage began with the introduction in 1944 of a Wagner-type Act (PC1003) that provided for compulsory recognition by employers of unions that represented a majority of employees in a designated bargaining unit. In contrast to the United States,

---

3. In the mid-1980s the Social Credit government of British Columbia passed legislation that reversed many of the pro-labor provisions of the labor relations law enacted by the NDP government of 1972–75. In 1992 the newly elected NDP government brought in new pro-labor amendments to "restore the balance."

employees were not allowed to strike during the term of a collective agreement. Compulsory arbitration of grievances was introduced using tripartite boards. The result of PC1003 was enterprise bargaining, a pattern similar to that in the United States. The dominant form of collective bargaining in Canada is between local unions and management in a single establishment (Craig 1990). There has been some pattern bargaining in a few industries, such as automobile assembly, steel, meat packing, and pulp and paper, but recently there has been a weakening of pattern bargaining especially in the meat-packing industry.

The third phase of labor legislation began in 1964 when the government of Quebec gave public employees the right to organize, bargain, and strike. Twenty years earlier in the province of Saskatchewan, North America's first socialist government, headed by the CCF, gave public sector workers the right to organize and strike. The Quebec initiative was followed in 1967 by the federal government's Public Service Staff Relations Act (PSSRA) which fulfilled an election promise to give federal civil servants the same rights (Morton 1990). Other provinces followed the lead of Quebec and the government of Canada to varying degrees (Meltz 1989a). By the 1990s over 60 percent of the public sector of Canada and the provinces was unionized.

Most recently there has been legislation in the federal and three provincial jurisdictions to provide for first contract arbitration when a union and an employer cannot reach a first agreement. The three jurisdictions also ban the use of replacement workers during strikes, Quebec since 1978, and Ontario and British Columbia beginning in 1993. The banning of replacement workers was introduced when political parties strongly supported by labor were in power. This provision was vociferously opposed by employers, although the employer opposition in Quebec is now muted.

Other Legislation Affecting Human Resource Practices

As was indicated earlier, Canadians have always supported government intervention in economic and social affairs. Over the years Canada has developed a comprehensive social security network. This network provides a framework that affects human resource practices. Coverage of the Unemployment Insurance (UI) program has been comprehensive and generous. Of those unemployed two-thirds receive UI benefits compared with one-third in the United States. Those not covered in Canada include new entrants and re-entrants to the work force, although many qualify for training through Canada's large publicly funded training programs (Meltz 1990b). Recently proposed legislation, intended to be more restrictive, seeks to make ineligible for UI benefits persons who are dismissed for misconduct or those who quit work without just cause.

Employment Standards legislation contains minimum wage rates and maximum hours as well as requirements for advance notice in the case of layoffs and dismissals of individuals. In many jurisdictions mass layoffs (50 or more persons) or plant closings require advance notice or compensation in lieu of notice. The federal jurisdiction and Ontario require severance pay for individual or group layoffs.

Employers under the federal jurisdiction must comply with a program of employment equity, termed "affirmative action" in the United States. This program does not set quotas but does require the tabling of plans. A number of provincial governments have similar programs for their public sector employees. The province of Ontario has the most comprehensive form of pay equity, termed "comparable worth" in the United States. Employers in the private sector are required to set aside up to 1 percent of their payroll costs to raise the pay of women in sectors where they are not receiving the pay rates they should based on a comparison of female-dominated and male-dominated jobs using a composite measure of skill, effort, and responsibility. Pay equity programs must be developed through joint labor-management committees if the workplace is unionized. The programs include the establishment of a job classification system (Stone and Meltz 1993).

Health and safety laws in Canadian jurisdictions usually require joint labor-management committees to administer the legislation at the workplace level. Ontario's Health and Safety Act specifies that establishments with twenty or more employees must establish a joint management-worker health and safety committee with at least two members, and with at least four members in a workplace where fifty or more workers are employed. At least half the members must be selected by the workers, or where applicable, by the union. The committees must have two co-chairs, one selected by the worker members and one selected by the management members. At least one management member and one worker member must be certified in accordance with training criteria by the new workplace health and safety agency. At smaller establishments with five to nineteen employees, and places such as construction sites, the workers are to choose their own health and safety representative.

The members of the joint committee are to identify hazardous situations and make recommendations to the employer on issues of health and safety. They are also to investigate cases of critical injury or fatality and report the findings to the Ministry of Labor. Certified members have the power to stop work in certain circumstances and to investigate complaints that "dangerous circumstances" exist (Stone and Meltz 1993, 669–72).

The general trend has been to increase the scope and nature of workplace regulations. Employer groups have been concerned that the comprehensiveness of Canadian workplace and labor relations legislation will impair Canada's international competitiveness. Specifically the question raised is whether Canada can continue to maintain a more comprehensive social welfare system in the face of product market competition from the United States, and in the future from Mexico, with lower standards and overall lower social welfare costs. Although some recent international assessments of competitiveness have ranked Canada high, in the top five, both in overall terms as well as in many areas of human resources, there is clear indication that Canada's position has slipped relative to its major competitors (IMD International 1991). While these issues are beyond the scope of this chapter, we want to emphasize that such external considerations will influence industrial relations policies in the future.

4.2   The Actors in the IR/HR System

The three traditional actors in the IR/HR system in Canada are each very fragmented, with no one single entity speaking for any of the actors.

The Government

We have already discussed the decentralized nature of the government with labor and employment legislation determined separately by each of the ten provinces and the federal government for the federal sector. There is little or no coordination among agencies that administer these laws, although there are regular discussions through the Canadian Association of Administrators of Labor Legislation. Individual provinces are aware of developments taking place within other provinces and comparisons and even some pattern setting does occur.

Management

Central management organizations exist in Canada, but their major role is to lobby the various levels of government and participate in various tripartite or labor-management boards such as the Canadian Labor Market and Productivity Centre. The most important central body is the Business Council on National Issues. Management is also represented, together with trade unions on the Canadian Labor Force Development Board (1993), a labor-management community-run body established by the federal government to administer its training programs. There are also sectoral management associations in most industries. Some of these conduct negotiations with the trade unions in their sector, such as the various regional and local construction associations. Recently a few sectoral associations have joined with trade unions to examine employment and training issues. These sectoral groups include the steel and the electrical and electronics industries, both groups receiving funding from the federal Department of Employment and Immigration.

Within corporations there has been a significant increase in the importance of the human resource function. A 1988 survey by the Conference Board of Canada (Benimadhu 1989) found that 76 percent of HR managers reported directly to the chief executive officer, and 12 percent to the corporate vice president. Eighty-four percent of HR executives are full contributing members in their organization's strategic planning process and participate in senior planning meetings.

The Conference Board survey also showed that HR departments were smaller in unionized than in non-unionized firms. This suggests that unions provide a degree of fairness in the workplace that management in non-union organizations has to provide at its own expense (Barbash 1989). One reason non-union firms may be willing to expend more resources is to ensure flexibility in their operations and reduce the desire by workers to unionize.

Another example of the increased recognition of the HR function is the Ontario government's 1991 legislation establishing the designation Certified Human Resource Professional, administered by the

Human Resources Professionals Association of Ontario. Ontario is the first government in North America to establish a formal HR designation. Despite this designation the existence of various organizations that have interests in the IR/HR field means that there is no unified voice on either labor or employment issues.

Labor

The house of organized labor is also divided. The largest organization is the 2.4 million member Canadian Labor Congress (CLC), containing 59 percent of union members in Canada. A little over a third (37 percent) of the CLC members belong to international unions such as the United Steelworkers of America, and just under two-thirds (63 percent) belong to national unions, such as the 407,000 member Canadian Union of Public Employees (CUPE), the largest union in Canada (Labor Canada 1992).

The second largest union federation is the Quebec-based Confederation of National Trades Unions, a multisector federation with 212,000 members. Only slightly smaller is the Canadian Federation of Labor, made up of international trades unions in the construction industry that broke away from the CLC over the issue of jurisdiction over construction trades in the province of Quebec. Provincial associations within the CLC, such as the Quebec Federation of Labor, lobby provincial legislatures and also rule on provincial jurisdictional issues. In addition there are local labor councils.

Of the three actors labor is the most unified with the CLC as the labor group that is most called upon by governments for representatives, although the CFL and the CNTU in Quebec are also included in many bipartite and tripartite consultations.

The Changing Composition of the Labor Movement

Canada is one of a small number of countries whose union density has declined very little in the 1980s. Figures 4.1 and 4.2 show the long-term trends in union membership and density in Canada and the United States over the past seventy years. In these tables there are two developments of note. First the major turning points in increases in unionization were associated changes in legislation that were supportive of unions, such as the Wagner Act in the United States in 1935,

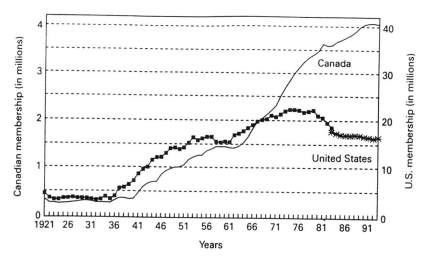

Figure 4.1
Union membership in Canada and the United States, 1929 to 1993. *For Canada:* Annual data from Labour Canada. For 1921 to 1944, from Department of Labour, *Labour Organizations in Canada* (Ottawa: Queen's Printer, 1967, table 1); for 1945 to 1992, from Pradeep Kurmar, *From Uniformity to Divergence: Industrial Relations in Canada and the United States* (Kingston, ON: IRC Press, 1993, 12–13). In 1950 the reference date of Labour Canada's survey was changed from December 31 to January 1; therefore no figure is reported for 1950. The membership figures are as of January 1 of the year shown.

For the United States: Data for 1921 to 1983, from Leo Troy and L. Sheflin, *U.S. Union Sourcebook: Membership, Finances, Structure Directory* (West Orange, NJ: Industrial Relations Data and Information Sources, 1985); for 1984 to 1993, from Bureau of Labor Statistics, *Employment and Earnings* (Washington: GPO, various years).

PC1003 in Canada in 1944, and the Quebec and federal government's granting of public sector rights to organize, bargain, and strike in 1964 and 1967, respectively. Second, the divergence between the U.S. and Canadian patterns began with the passage of legislation but has been sustained at a plateau in Canada of just over 37 percent[4] since the mid-1970s, while the American union density rate has continued to decline to slightly below 16 percent.

---

4. Labour Canada's (1992) *Directory of Labour Organizations in Canada* indicates a union density rate of 37.4 percent in 1992 based on nonagricultural paid employment and 36.2 percent for 1990. CALURA (Sta103tistics Canada 1992), which is the source for table 4.1, shows 34.7 percent for 1990 for all paid employees. If agriculture is excluded, the CALURA density rate for 1990 would be 35.2 percent. There are a number of differences between the CALURA and Labour Canada figures. CALURA excludes international or national unions with less than 100. In addition Labour Canada's figures relate to January of each year, whereas CALURA's data relate to the end of the year.

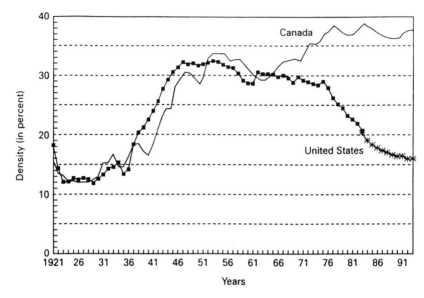

Figure 4.2
Union density in Canada and the United States, 1921 to 1993. *For Canada:* Annual data from Labour Canada. For 1921 to 1944, from Department of Labour, *Labour Organizations in Canada* (Ottawa: Queen's Printer, 1967, table 1); for 1945 to 1992, from Pradeep Kurmar, *From Uniformity to Divergence: Industrial Relations in Canada and the United States* (Kingston, ON: IRC Press, 1993, 12–13). In 1950 the reference date of Labour Canada's survey was changed from December 31 to January 1; therefore no figure is reported for 1950. Union density was calculated using annual averages of nonagricultural paid workers in the previous year.
    For the United States: Data for 1921 to 1983, from Leo Troy and L. Sheflin, *U.S. Union Sourcebook: Membershipp, Finances, Structure Directory* (West Orange, NJ: Industrial Relations Data and Information Sources, 1985); for 1984 to 1993, from Bureau of Labor Statistics, *Employment and Earnings* (Washington: GPO, various years).

Table 4.1 indicates that the general stability (or at most a slight downward trend) masks major shifts in employment distribution and union density by industry. Some of the service sectors that grew in the 1980s, particularly health and social services, have high levels of union density (e.g., 50 percent), while others such as trade and finance have low levels, 11.6 and 3.5 percent, respectively (Statistics Canada 1992b).

In addition the decline in the density within certain private sectors, such as fishing and manufacturing, are readily apparent. By comparison with the United States the decline in private sector union density was much less precipitous. As Meltz (1993) shows, the dif-

Table 4.1
Employment share and union density by industry in Canada: 1980, 1984, and 1990

	Employment (%)[a]			Union density (%)		
	1980	1984	1990	1980[b]	1984	1990
All industries	100.0	100.0	100.0	35.3[c]	34.5	34.7
Goods producing	30.5	27.9	25.2	43.0	38.0	39.3
Agriculture	1.3	1.2	1.3	0.4	1.1	1.8
Forestry	0.7	0.6	0.4	38.6	42.5	58.8
Fishing and trapping	0.1	0.1	0.1	55.3	40.2	33.4
Mines, oil wells	2.0	1.8	1.5	32.5	26.4	28.4
Manufacturing	21.4	19.6	16.8	43.2	39.1	36.7
Construction	5.0	4.5	5.0	57.6	47.5	59.6
Service producing	69.5	72.1	74.8	27.5	33.2	33.2
Transportation, communication, and utilities	8.6	8.2	8.0	53.2	56.4	54.8
Trade	17.5	18.2	18.8	8.9	9.8	11.6
Finance, etc.[d]	6.1	6.1	6.6	2.5	2.7	3.5
Services	29.6	31.9	34.3	24.2	36.9	35.9
Business	3.9	4.0	5.4	N/A	N/A	3.1
Education	6.5	7.4	7.5	N/A	N/A	77.0
Health and social	7.7	9.1	9.9	N/A	N/A	50.8
Accommodation	5.5	5.9	6.3	N/A	N/A	8.8
Other	6.0	5.5	5.2	N/A	N/A	15.2
Public administration	7.7	7.5	7.1	67.8	72.4	80.6
Canada: Private[e]	69.5	66.7	67.5	N/A	20.6[g]	20.7
Public[f]	30.5	32.2	32.5	N/A	63.1[f]	64.3
United States: Private	82.6	82.9	82.9	20.1	15.3	11.9
Public	17.4	17.1	17.1	34.7	35.8	36.9

Sources: For Canadian data, Statistics Canada, *CALURA Labour Unions*, catalogue 71-202, 1980, 1984 and 1990 editions. For U.S. data, 1980 data are taken from Troy and Sheflin (1984, 28–31, 1985, A.1); 1984 and 1990 data are from *Employment and Earnings*, Bureau of Labor Statistics (January issues).

a. Shares of employment within the service industries in 1980 and 1984 were obtained from Statistics Canada (1992).

b. The industry sector union density figures for 1980 exclude the 1983 amendments to the CALURA survey which raised the density figure by 3.5 percentage points. The 1983 amendments required two types of organizations to report for the first time: single establishment unions that are unitary unions with no locals, and professional organizations whose avowed primary purpose is the professional development of their members, such as teachers' federations and nurses' organizations (CALURA 1990, 22).

c. The total union density in 1980 of 31.8 percent was increased by 3.5 percentage points for comparability with the post-1983 figures (see note b).

d. Finance, insurance, and real estate.

e. Private include agriculture, forestry, fishing, mines, manufacturing, construction, trade, finance, business services, accommodation, and other services.

f. Public includes transportation, communication and utilities, education, health, and public administration.

g. The division of the service sector unionization between the public sector and the private sector was based on the calculations in Meltz (1993).

ference in union density in manufacturing went from 6 percentage points in 1966 (43.3 percent vs. 37.4 percent) to 16 percentage points in 1990 (36.7 percent vs. 20.6 percent). In 1975, according to Troy (1990), the private sectors in the two countries were identical at 26 percent, whereas the 1985 figures for the two countries were 21 and 15 percent and the 1990 figures 18 and 12 percent (Troy 1992), the later being a gap of nearly 50 percent.

An alternative estimate, prepared by the authors, indicates that private sector union density did not decline from the mid-1980s but remained at approximately 21 percent in both 1984 and 1990.[5] The source of this stability appears to result from increases in density in forestry, construction, trade, finance, and other commercial services that offset decreases in union density in manufacturing, fishing and mines. Table 4.1 shows that with the exception of forestry, the private sector industries whose union density declined were also the sectors whose share of paid employment declined. Similarly the sectors whose employment share increased also had increases in union density (trade, finance). While the level of union density varies enormously in the private sector, the data indicate that unions were increasing their success rates in the growing sectors.

Other estimates prepared by Riddell (1992) from Statistics Canada's 1984 Survey of Union Membership show private union density at 29 percent and government (public sector) at 74 percent, respectively. Riddell (1992) and Chaison and Rose (1991) observe that in both the public and private sectors the rate of union density in Canada is twice that in the United States.[6] Not only is the public sector more highly organized in Canada than in the United States, but also its share of employment is greater. Statistics Canada (1992c, A-15, A-17) estimates public sector employment in Canada in 1991 at 19.8 percent of employment, excluding self-employed and unpaid family workers, com-

---

5. No precise estimate is available for 1990 on public versus private sector union density in Canada. Troy (1990 and 1992) bases his estimate of the division of sectors between private and public on a study by the Economic Council of Canada (1986) using 1983 data. Our estimates for 1984 and 1990 are determined in a less precise way by allocating whole industrial sectors. This method produces the same figure of private sector union density of 21 percent for 1984 as Troy (1990) found for 1985. However, we find that in 1990 private sector density remained at 21 percent, whereas Troy's (1992) estimate is 18 percent.

6. In a recent study Farber and Krueger (1992) concluded that approximately half of the Canada–U.S. gap in union membership is due to differences in worker demand for union representation and half due to the supply of union jobs.

pared with 17.5 percent in the United States. Using these estimates, the larger Canadian public sector contributes to the difference between the densities of the two countries, but the impact is less than 10 percent of the overall difference. This figure would rise to a maximum of 33 percent if the public sector in Canada is defined as including all employees in those sectors in which there is a high proportion of public employees, that is, transportation, education, health, and government (see table 4.1).

There are two additional developments concerning unions in Canada. As Verma and Meltz (1990) have shown, a great deal of organizing continues to take place in Canada, particularly in the service sector, by what have been traditional private sector unions. For example, the Service Employees International Union has organized a McDonald's restaurant (in Orangeville, Ontario), which is the first time this has happened in North America. Finally, a major restructuring appears to be beginning with a number of mergers, such as the 1992 merger of the Communications and Electrical Workers of Canada (which had previously separated from the Communications Workers of America), the Energy and Chemical Workers, and the Canadian Paperworkers (which in 1974 was formed by a merger of the Canadian branches of the International Pulp and Sulfite Workers and the United Paperworkers). This new union, the Communications, Energy and Paperworkers (CEP) union, will rival in size the Food and Commercial Workers International Union, the Canadian Auto Workers, and the United Steelworkers.

The implication of the major restructuring within the Canadian labor movement is that labor is adapting itself for the changed competitive and changed economic structure that is emerging in Canada. This development could and hopefully will present an opportunity for constructive explorations for new approaches within the various public forums that exist for labor-management consultation.

4.3 Recent Developments Affecting the IR/HR System

A number of recent developments have had significant impacts on the Canadian IR/HR system. Three developments will be discussed below: the changing demographic composition of the labor force, the increase in the unemployment rate during the recessions of 1981–82 and 1990–91, and the economy's lagging productivity growth.

The Demographic Composition of the Labor Force

There were two significant changes in the demographic composition of the Canadian labor force that affected the IR/HR system. The greatest change was the 50 percent increase in the employment of adult women between 1980 and 1990. Although women are less organized than men, their rate of unionization increased in the 1980s, narrowing the gap with men to 8.2 percentage points. The second major change was the progressive aging of the labor force. While the adult labor force grew by 30 percent in the 1980s, the number of youth (aged 15 to 24 years) decreased by almost 16 percent. Since youth are the least represented by trade unions, the aging of the work force, together with more female unionization, implies a greater potential for organizing by the trade unions.

The Recessions of 1981–82 and 1990–92 and Unemployment

In the past decade Canada experienced two severe recessions that have had sizable effects on the IR/HR system. For the first time in the postwar period large numbers of professional and white-collar workers were unemployed. While the level of unemployment was unchanged, at the beginning and end of the 1980s two differences emerged. The first was a regional change with Ontario experiencing a rapid postrecession recovery in the 1980s. Second, in the rest of Canada unemployment rates reached an unprecedented 2 percentage points above the United States. The recession of 1990–91 was more severe in Canada than in the United States, with the difference in unemployment rates widening further to almost 4 percentage points in 1992.
 For the IR/HR system the high unemployment rates have meant a weakening of trade unions' bargaining strength. Strike rates, while remaining above the United States, declined dramatically and wage increases moderated significantly. Unions emphasized employment security and large severance packages. In non-union organizations the high rates of unemployment eased earlier recruiting problems for skilled labor and reduced turnover rates.

Lagging Productivity Rates

Although Canada has a high level of productivity, recent rates of increase have lagged behind those recorded by the other countries (Rao and Lempriere 1992). Part of this lag may be the result of Canada having had the highest rate of labor force increase. The increase was initially in inexperienced youth and later in women with less continuous work experience. The up side of this development was that employment increased as well, with Canada ending the decade of the 1980s with a higher employment to population ratio than the United States.

The down side of this development was that in manufacturing Canada's unit labor costs were rising faster than those of its competitors. This was the result of lower productivity increases and higher wage rate increases, the latter presumably the result of Canada being more than twice as unionized as the United States. Following the beginning of the Free Trade Agreement with the United States in 1989, the 10 percentage point increase in the value of the Canadian dollar, in comparison with the American dollar, placed Canada's manufacturing sector in a less competitive position than many U.S. and other foreign companies (Meltz 1991; Rao and Lempriere 1992).

The result was massive plant closings and the shifting of many U.S. branch plant operations to the United States. Ontario, the manufacturing heartland of Canada, was hit the hardest. Between 1989 and 1992 employment in manufacturing in Ontario declined by 18.4 percent (Statistics Canada 1993). This meant that sectors with high union densities declined. The response of trade unions has been to organize vigorous nontraditional sectors (Verma and Meltz 1990). For example, the United Steelworkers of America have been organizing janitorial and security service workers in the service industries.

The combination of the three major changes has weakened the bargaining position of unions in Canada and encouraged organizations to seek ways to be more cost effective. At the same time the aging of the work force, together with governments' supportive legislation for trade unions, has given unions an opportunity to at least maintain their substantial level of organization. These developments in turn underlie both the gradual changes in IR/HR in Canada and the significant role played by management-labor cooperation on a sectoral basis.

4.4   IR/HR Practices: Dominant Patterns, Changes, Diffusions

Collective agreements in Canada cover approximately 40 percent of the paid work force, that is, the 35 to 37 percent who are union members plus another 4 to 5 percent who do not belong to the unions.

Table 4.2 presents statistics on specific IR/HR practices as contained in major collective agreements. While these data only provide broad indicators of the formal arrangements between the parties and do not indicate the extent of informal arrangements, the fact that they represent approximately 60 percent of persons covered by collective agreements in Canada does indicate the major direction that formal provisions are taking. These data were prepared by the Canada Department of Labour's Bureau of Labour Information from its collective agreements files.

No comprehensive statistics are available on HR developments that are occurring in the non-union sector. To describe HR developments in the non-union sector, as well as informal arrangements in the unionized sector, we have used case studies and the results of selected surveys conducted by such groups as the Conference Board of Canada. The statistics in table 4.2 contain selected measures on trends in labor–management cooperation, employment security, wage incentive arrangements, fairness and equity, and training. Specific IR/HR practices will now be examined.

Governance

Firm-Level Developments
The traditional patterns of workplace and firm–level governance in Canada are very similar to those found in the United States. At the firm level, management rights to make business decisions exclusively are well entrenched in corporate law. However, there are a small number of cases where employee representatives have gained the right to participate in decisions to hire, fire (for just cause), and to be consulted on choice of technology, new investments, or plant closures. At the workplace level, the Wagner Act framework has led to a system of decentralized collective bargaining in which work rules with respect to wages, benefits, hours, job classifications, and the like, are negotiated.

Many scholars have argued that as in the United States, this system of governance with its detailed substantive work rules encoded in long collective agreements formed a stable symbiosis with labor's "job-control" philosophy, on the one hand, and a growing North American market that was relatively free of offshore competition, on the other (Chaykowski and Verma 1992). In the 1980s this system of governance came under intense pressures to change. Competition intensified due to freer trade, deregulation, privatization, and rapid

Table 4.2
Canada: Collective agreement provisions, 1980–92 (% of contracts and employees)

	Agreements			Employees		
	1980	1987	1992	1980	1987	1992
Number	1,028	1,198	1,238	2,114,100	2,392,504	2,437,765
Labor-management cooperation						
Labor-management committees	72	41	48	79	42	55
Joint committee technical change	14	17	17	24	26	26
Joint committee powers in H&S	N/A	25	27	N/A	23	23
Joint job evaluation	N/A	41	46	N/A	46	47
Joint administration pension	8	5	5	8	5	6
Job sharing	N/A	6	7	N/A	4	7
Work sharing	a	3	2	a	3	2
Quality of working life	a	9	12	1	10	12
Employment security						
Contracting out prohibited	44	40	46	50	43	48
Employment guarantees (duration)	N/A	11	12	N/A	24	21
Income guarantees	N/A	17	19	N/A	19	20
Wage incentives						
Piece rate	N/A	6	5	N/A	5	4
Group rate	N/A	1	1	N/A	b	b
Productivity bonus	1	2	1	b	1	1
Profit sharing	b	1	1	b		1
Other	N/A	3	3		2	2
No provision	86	89	91	88	93	93
Fairness and equity						
Affirmative action plans	N/A	3	5	N/A	6	9
Sexual harrassment	N/A	18	25	N/A	40	43
Equal pay for equal work	N/A	3	4	N/A	4	4
Equal pay for work of equal value	N/A	1	9	N/A	1	18
Training						
Training on the job	N/A	40	43	N/A	45	48
Training outside courses	N/A	26	31	N/A	33	35
Apprenticeship	N/A	33	33	N/A	32	30
Educational leave, job related	37	28	15	51	38	19

Sources: For 1980, Wood and Kumar (1981) and Kumar, Arrowsmith, and Coates (1991); for 1987, 1992: Bureau of Labor Information (1992).
Note: Includes all collective agreements in establishments with 500 or more employees under provincial jurisdiction and 200 or more employees under federal jurisdiction.
a. Figures do not add to total.
b. Less than 5.

technological change. This resulted in erosion of profits, forcing firms to look for rapid improvements in productivity. In collective bargaining, employers pushed two agendas: moderate increases in compensation and the introduction of quality improvement programs within the framework of increased employee involvement. The push for lower wages resulted in some high profile strikes in the early 1990s.

Overall, the employer push for quality improvement and employee involvement has resulted in small incremental changes in workplace governance. Both labor and management have contributed to the slow diffusion of innovations in the area of workplace governance. In the eyes of many unionists and other critics, employer initiatives in quality improvement and employee involvement (EI) are employer attempts to reduce the power and influence of labor collectives by coopting workers into a managerial agenda (Wells 1986). Many unions believe that it is politically hazardous for them to support programs that allow workers to be coopted without some degree of union participation in the governance process. In the main, the critics see quality and EI programs as a threat to traditional collective bargaining.

Early opposition to such programs by the broad band in the Canadian labor movement through much of the 1980s has resulted in two developments. First, in the sectors that have high union density (public sector, resource industries, autos, steel, etc.), quality and EI programs have diffused very slowly. A small but significant number of employers have pushed ahead with these programs on their own, isolating or at least attempting to isolate the union. Second, in sectors where unions are weak or absent, employers have essentially implemented such programs unilaterally. Although there are no comprehensive studies of the diffusion and effectiveness of such programs across union and nonunion sectors, much of the case evidence points to research findings in American workplaces (Verma and Weiler 1993). EI programs in the unionized sector are more difficult to start, but once launched, they are easier to sustain if the union is supportive. If the union is cool or opposed to the idea, the probability of sustaining the program in the long-run declines sharply (Cutcher-Gershenfeld, Kochan, and Verma 1991; Verma 1989).

By 1992 an increasing number of unions were coming to terms with the reality of these initiatives. Only a handful of major unions—notable among them, the Communications, Energy and Paperworkers (CEP) Union, and the United Steel Workers (USWA)—have proactively embraced policies supporting employee involvement and flexibility. These unions have articulated a set of conditions under which they would be willing to support innovations. These conditions include a formal role for the union in joint decision making and safeguarding union principles such as seniority rights and job security (CWC 1990; USWA 1991). Other unions are reluctant to become involved in such efforts. The Canadian Auto Workers (CAW) has set its own agenda, which rejects Japanese production methods but supports efforts to involve and empower workers (Kumar and Meltz 1992, 73–74). Many employers see the CAW stance as unfriendly to their efforts to introduce employee involvement and team-oriented work organization.

Most firms that wish to implement quality and EI programs do not see the need for broader changes in workplace governance. Managers would like to retain exclusive control of such initiatives and, at the same time, have unions support them. Under the provisions of the law and of almost all collective agreements, employers have the exclusive right to implement quality and EI programs. It is a traditional right that few employers are willing to give up. In a recent study of ten industrial sectors,[7] Chaykowski and Verma (1992, table 12.1, 459–61) reported that few joint labor-management initiatives addressed governance issues.

Despite the slow pace of change, there are indications that a small number of companies and unions have begun to experiment with alternate governance structures (Verma and Cutcher-Gershenfeld 1993). As table 4.2 shows, quality of work life provisions have increased over the years but remain confined to a small proportion of all collective agreements. Not all of these concern quality and EI programs. Some are traditional areas such as contracting out and joint committees to deal with technological change. Table 4.3 shows a representative sample of cases where the parties have agreed to govern jointly.

Table 4.2 identifies other joint labor-management cooperation including health and safety, joint job evaluation, joint administration of persons and labor-management committees, excluding the 1993–96 social contract in Ontario. Overall, there appears to be an increase in many specialized forms of labor-management cooperation, with the major exceptions being joint administration of pension plans and

---

7. Auto, steel, mining, construction, textile, clothing, public sector, education, airlines, and telephones.

Table 4.3
Firms and unions with joint governance

Site	Union	Number of employees		Products	Area of joint governance	Year started
		Company	Bargaining unit			
Zehrs Markets	United Food and Commercial Workers (UFCW)	5,400	4,000	Retail food, supermarkets	Training	1987
B.C. Telephone	Telecommunications Workers' Union (TWU)	14,997	11,990	Telephone and related services	Contracting out and technological change	1978
Forest Industrial Relations Ltd. (FIR)— bargaining agent for employers in the industry.	International Woodworkers of Americas (IWA)	—	14,000	Logging and lumber	Contracting out	1988
B.C. hydro	International Brotherhood of Electrical Workers (IBEW)	5,498	2,000	Power utility	Employee involvement	1989
Manitoba Telephone System (MTS)	Communications and Electrical Workers of Canada (CWC)	5,308	612	Telephone and related services	Ergonomics and other work-related issues	1988
Shell Canada	Energy and Chemical Workers Union (ECWU)	200	138	Petroleum products	Wide variety of work operations	1978

Source: Verma and Cutcher-Gershenfeld (1993).

general labor-management committees. In the latter case there was a substantial decline from a high of 72 percent of all collective agreements in 1980 to 41 percent in 1987 and then an increase in 1992 to 48 percent. It would appear that there was a shift in the 1980s away from general labor-management committees to joint committees in selected areas such as technological change and job evaluation. The onset of the 1990–91 recession seems to have brought back the general labor-management committee while leaving the other specialized committees in place. In general, most of the general labor-management committees have no decision-making authority, and hence their contribution to general governance is minimal. Such committees are mostly a forum for exchange of information and some consultation.

Although their numbers are small, the experiments in joint governance mentioned above are nevertheless significant because they offer an alternative to traditional management-dominated governance for the workplace. It is possible that the industrial relations system may evolve to a new equilibrium around joint governance because it allows cooperative solutions to form around integrative issues without giving up the right of either party to raise disputes. In this sense, joint governance permits the ideals of pluralism to coexist with the market-driven need to collaborate (Verma 1991).

Sectoral Initiatives

Although industry-level joint committees have a long tradition (Adams 1985), they received increased attention in the 1980s as a way of focusing on the mutual interests of labor and management. The theoretical assumption behind these initiatives, even if not fully stated, is that if the parties can share a common view of the problems facing the industry, they will be able to proceed with needed reforms at the workplace. The Canadian Textile Labor Management Committee was formed in 1967 and has been active in the area of trade policies affecting the industry (Sexton, Leclerc, and Audet 1984). Similarly the Canadian Steel Trade and Employment Congress (CSTEC) was established in 1985 as a joint initiative of the United Steelworkers (USWA) and the major steel companies. Since 1987 it has also received funding from Canada's Industrial Adjustment Service (IAS) to operate adjustment programs for laid-off workers in the steel industry (Worklife Report 1990). In the same spirit the IAS has also signed agreements with the Canadian Automotive Repair and Service Council and the Joint Human Resources Committee of the Canadian

Electrical/Electronics Manufacturing Industry (CEEMI), both formed in 1988. Both of these committees are primarily concerned with developing and implementing a strategy to improve the skills available to the industry (CEEMI 1989).

A different type of sectoral initiative occurred in Ontario in 1993 when the NDP government divided the broader public service (950,000 workers in health, education, and government, over 20 percent of the provincial work force) into eight sectors and required labor and management in these sectors to agree to a reduction of compensation of $2 billion a year for three years without a reduction in employment. Instead of introducing across-the-board wage cuts, as the Parti Quebecois did in Quebec in 1982, the Ontario NDP government wanted unions and management to negotiate a mutually acceptable approach to reducing compensation. In addition the government wanted to change the relationship between labor and management by encouraging greater involvement of public service employees in the planning program structure and training of staff. Other aspects of the government policy included increases in taxation of $2 billion and reduced expenditures of $2 billion as a means to contain the provincial government deficit. The Ontario legislature passed the Social Contract Act of 1993 which permitted public sector employers to unilaterally impose wage freezes or cuts plus up to 12 days of unpaid leave over a three-year period (1993 to 1996) if a social contract was not achieved by August 10, 1993. The legislation also provided for a 20 percent reduction in the amount by which budgets were to be cut if a voluntary agreement were reached. Virtually all of the sectors reached voluntary agreements. In the process some units within the sectors established labor-management committees to administer aspects of the agreement, for example, a committee to ensure that qualified employees, or recently released employees, are offered new openings before external hiring takes place.

While some positive labor-management consultation was induced by the social contract process, the legislation so embittered the Ontario labor movement that support for the federal NDP collapsed during the national election in October 1993. The NDP, which at the time was in power in three provinces (Ontario, British Columbia, and Saskatchewan), saw its strength in the national parliament reduced from 43 to 9 seats, less than the 12 seats necessary for the designation and perquisites of a national party. The political implications of this failed attempt at imposed labor-management cooperation will not be lost on political parties.

While a full assessment of these initiatives is somewhat premature, some observers have already noted that sectoral level cooperation has not necessarily spurred the consideration and adoption of innovations at the firm or plant level (Warrian 1990; Docquier 1989). It is possible that the newer initiatives of the 1990s need more time to percolate down to the firm level. On the other hand, it is also likely that sectoral initiatives facilitate innovations only in a very indirect way.

National Level

It is important to note that the 1980s saw a number of both private and public initiatives at the national level in which labor and management tried to arrive at broad understandings. The Canadian Chamber of Commerce (1988) issued its report, FOCUS 2000, after consulting labor leaders in which it affirmed its resolve to "building an atmosphere of mutual confidence and trust" with the labor movement. In another initiative the Niagara Institute (1987) assembled an impressive array of leaders from both labor and management whose report, *The Search for a Better Way*, spells out a code of conduct for labor-management relations. These initiatives may well have a positive impact on firm–level adoption of innovations. It is simply too early to tell at this time. There is no doubt, though, that such inputs are important in sending a positive signal to the labor and management community at large.

In the area of public policy, in 1988 the federal government initiated the Advisory Council on Adjustment to examine ways in which Canadians could not only withstand the shock of adjustment to the Canada–U.S. Free Trade Agreement (FTA) but also benefit from it. The council, under the chairmanship of A. Jean de Grandpré in its much publicized report *Adjusting to Win*, recommended a series of measures to invest in labor skills among other things. It urged a review of the nation's training and education infrastructure. It also recommended that the government should "shift the emphasis of government assistance towards employment promotion rather than income maintenance" (Advisory Council on Adjustment 1989, xix). As a result of these recommendations the federal government initiated a number of task forces with the help of the Canada Labor market and Productivity Centre (CLMPC) in 1990 to develop a national training policy. The task forces, seven in all, completed their report by late 1990. In early 1991 the government announced its intention to set up a national training board (the Canada Labor Force Development

Board) that will be managed at arm's length from the government by representatives from labor, business, the community, and educational institutions. The government also enacted a bill in 1991 that transfers $800 million from the unemployment insurance fund to the newly created training funds. At the time of this writing, it is hard to tell if this initiative will breathe new air into Canada's private sector training programs that generally lag behind those of other nations (Economic Council of Canada 1991). It is clear, however, that the process of consultation followed by the government and the willingness to move training away from the political winds that blow on Parliament Hill are positive developments.

A major innovation in union initiatives was introduced in Quebec in 1983 by the Quebec Federation of Labor (QFL) with the Quebec Solidarity Fund (Fonds de Solidarite) at the initiative of the then president of the QFL, Louis Laberge. This investment fund has two objectives: to create employment in the province of Quebec and to enhance the nationalistic goals of the province. Seventy percent of the over 100 firms in which investments are made are unionized. The fund has 186,000 shareholders and assets worth $800 million. Approximately 27,000 jobs have been created or maintained since the first investments were made in 1986. Of the 145,168 subscribers in the fund, 68,839 persons belong to QFL affiliates. Many local unions have clauses in their collective agreements that include automatic deduction from workers' paychecks. Up to 80 percent of the contributions are tax deductible. In some cases employers match the worker's contribution. The QFL initiative is not only viewed as a success in Quebec but has also become the model for the Working Opportunity Fund established by the NDP government in British Columbia. (Boivin 1993; Fonds de Solidarite des Traivailleurs du Quebec 1992; Fournier 1993)

Another major innovation in Quebec is the "social contract," a labor-management initiative with provincial government support. This social contract is a document signed by the parties. The provisions include no-strike pledges for periods of up to eight years, together with a commitment by companies to invest in job creation or at least in job preservation. The technical term that is used to refer to these initiatives is "concertation" among labor, management, and government (Fournier 1993).

For example, most of the agreements negotiated with some government input are of longer duration. Longer-term contracts were negotiated at Sammi-Atlas (6 years), Mil-Davie (4 years), Soreltex (4.5

years), Sidbec-Dosco (4.5 years), Tapis Peerless (5 years), Goodyear (9 years), Domtar[8] (6 years), Abitibi-Price (6 years), Société des alcools du Québec (5.5 years), Alcan (6 years), and Expro (6.5 years) (Bourque and Vallée 1994).

The longer duration is accompanied by provisions such as employment guarantees (Sammi-Atlas, Goodyear, Domtar), joint decision-making committees (Sammi-Atlas and Goodyear), new investments (Sammi-Atlas), and productivity gainsharing (Abitibi-Price at Alma) arrangements. The agreement at Goodyear creates a joint labor-management committee for ongoing consultation. It also commits most workplace changes, such as technological change and reclassification of jobs, to joint decision making. The hope is to create a new employment system that will take parties away from adversarialism toward mutual accommodation and a focus on making the operations more productive and competitive through joint decision making.

Work Organization

There have been only a handful of cases in Canada where large-scale innovations have been introduced. The best-known example is the Shell Canada Chemical plant in Sarnia, Ontario, which has successfully used a team–based work organization along with other attendant innovations since 1975 (Halpern 1984).[9] The Shell plant broke new ground in two important ways. First, it reversed the Tayloristic logic of work organization to a high commitment, high involvement form of work organization based on sociotechnical design. Second, it achieved this transformation with the full cooperation and involvement of the union, the Energy and Chemical Workers. The union through its stewards and members on the shopfloor shares decision-making powers with management. In a much larger number of organizations, innovations are diffusing very slowly and tentatively with the parties taking a much more cautious approach. In companies like McDonnell Douglas, Inglis, MacMillan Bloedel, B.C. Hydro, and General Motors of Canada, there are tentative steps by one or both sides.

---

8. An agreement at Domtar Packaging with two unions, the Independent Paperworkers of Canada and the Independent Woodworkers Association produced an eight-year agreement in Ontario, providing for a gainsharing plan and limited employment security to protect workers from "cyclical" layoffs.
9. An overview of such developments until the mid-1980s is provided by Mansell (1986).

In the Canadian auto industry there was an increase in the flexibility of work practices to the benefit of management, but the changes were not quite as great as occurred in the United States when data were compared from 1979 and 1986 (Katz and Meltz 1989). Three types of flexibility were examined: reductions in the number of job classifications, increases in the range of work performed by employees, and other changes in work rules and practices such as the use of small discussion groups to deal with production or quality problems and pay for knowledge. A reduction in the number of job classifications removes barriers to flexibility in the use of labor, while broadening the range of work performed enhances flexibility. The reduction of job classifications was much greater in the United States. There was little difference with respect to the range of work performed, except that Canadians do much less of their own housekeeping. Group consultation and pay for knowledge occurred to a greater extent in the United States.

While these changes indicate more flexibility in the U.S. than Canadian automobile industry, the overall performance measures showed higher productivity levels and better quality of product in Canada than in the United States, although the gap has narrowed. These findings suggest that there were other factors at work in addition to work rules and flexibility. Canadian operations were ahead in measures of industrial relations such as having lower grievance rates and lower discipline rates.

The other factors in differentiating the performances of workers in the two countries could include the quality of management, the quality of the work force, and the history of the relations between the parties. The continuing sizable investment by the Big Three automobile firms (General Motors, Ford, Chrysler) in Canada suggests that the Canadian operations are providing a positive environment for production, even though the Canadian Auto Workers have a reputation for militancy. The union has emphasized fair treatment and has been willing to accommodate changes within the framework of the goals it has set for union-management relations (Kumar and Meltz 1992).

Management is often not sure of how speedily to proceed given the ambivalence or possible opposition of their unions. Unions are similarly unsure of how this may impact their political standing vis-à-vis their constituents or how it may affect collective bargaining (Rankin 1990). In a growing number of organizations, some innovations have been considered and abandoned so completely that their revival on the bargaining agenda appears unlikely in the near future. Among others, innovations involving worker involvement have been tried and abandoned in the Atomic Energy Corporation, Rockwell, and Colgate-Palmolive.

Employment and Income Guarantees

Although it was popular to refer to the need for Canadian industry to adopt Japanese approaches to employees, table 4.2 shows that only 12 percent of collective agreements in 1992 in large (500 or more employee) establishments provided for employment guarantees. Of these, 9 percent were for an indefinite term and covered 19 percent of all employees. A further 2.5 percent of employees were covered for the term of the agreement or for a specified time period. This is a slight increase from the coverage in 1988 (Meltz 1989b). For most Canadian employees seniority provisions and the prohibition of contracting out are the most that employers will provide (Meltz 1989b). Seniority is taken into consideration in a majority of contracts when there are layoffs, recall, job posting, promotion, and bumping.

Although one in every two contracts prohibits contracting out, there is a wide range in the proportion of agreements with such a clause, from 89 percent in automobile assembly to 27 percent in electrical products. A prohibition of contracting out could have a negative effect on competitiveness in that it prevents an organization from taking advantage of possibilities of reducing costs of operation. In practice these provisions vary in their wording, often allowing for more flexibility than seems apparent. Some provisions prohibit contracting out if employees are to be laid off as a consequence. Firms can contract out if they find other work for the employees. This prohibition could have some element of encouraging employee commitment to the organization. On balance, however, it may tend to reduce competitiveness unless it is accompanied by other forms of flexibility and consultation.

Income guarantees are now more prevalent than employment guarantees (though slightly less in terms of number of employees covered). The trend is definitely toward an increase in income guarantees. This trend was very likely influenced by the major gains in the auto industry in 1990 as well as at International Nickel by the United Steelworkers in the same year (Chaykowski and Verma 1992, 459–61).

The bottom line remains, however, that only 20 percent of employees in the larger bargaining units have employment and/or income protection. For employees of non-unionized firms the trend has definitely been away from secure employment with such large and employment security–oriented firms as IBM Canada, Dofasco, as well as highly unionized Ontario Hydro, which eliminated large numbers of jobs and reduced staff through severance incentives in the early 1990s.

Wage Incentives

In the 1980s there was an accepted view that a greater proportion of pay in the form of contingent wages was necessary to enhance competitiveness. This is what the Japanese did, and conventional wisdom held that it was necessary for wage incentives to occur in Canada. The statistics in table 4.2 show that in general, wage incentives and contingent wages for unionized workers actually decreased in Canada in the 1980s.

The overall decline may be explained by the strong and highly visible opposition to profit-sharing schemes advanced by the Canadian section of the United Auto Workers in the 1982 and 1984 negotiations with the auto assembly firms (General Motors, Ford and Chrysler). Although the American branch of the UAW accepted profit sharing, the Canadian branch refused. The differences over profit sharing in the 1984 negotiations led to the split in the union and the formation of the Canadian Auto Workers in 1985. A recent study indicates that the Canadian Auto Workers received more in earnings by not accepting profit sharing than auto workers in the United States (Katz and Meltz 1991).

If Canadian auto workers received more earnings per person by not accepting profit sharing, does that mean that labor costs were higher in Canada and profits lower? In fact profits tended to be higher in Canada, perhaps because of higher productivity along with lower costs of health care and the lower value of the Canadian dollar. Although the link between the rejection of profit sharing and higher productivity remains unclear, the CAW appears to have adopted the policy of stressing fair treatment of employees and to put the onus of enhancing productivity on management. To this point the CAW's social unionism has been successful in balancing their concerns for equity with enabling management to enhance efficiency (Kumar and Meltz 1992).

The data from collective agreements do not support the view that there was an increase in contingent wages in the Canadian work force, However there appears to have been growth in such forms of compensation for management and some white-collar workers. No general statistics are available but a survey of large organizations showed that in 1990, 35 percent had a stock option plan restricted in most cases to executives, 27 percent had a stock purchase plan for most employees, 22 percent had profit-sharing plans open to most employees, and 28 percent had cash bonus plans for all employees while 61 percent had cash bonuses for management and executives (Lendvay-Zwickl 1990, 6)

Wage incentives are therefore mostly focused on management and executives, though some industries such as clothing, and to an increasing extent steel, make substantial use of wage incentives. The most interesting experiment taking place in Canada in this regard is the employee buy–out by the United Steelworkers of America of the third–largest steel company, Algoma Steel. The employees will own 60 percent of the firm. Initially they will take a reduction in pay and a reduction in employment as part of the restructuring process to restore profitability to the ailing firm. Government assistance has been provided, and there will be an extensive program of employee involvement (Galt 1992; Lancaster Labor Law Reports 1992). The labor movement is divided on the wisdom of the Algoma labor-sponsored buy-out and the subsequent reduction in wages. If the employee-controlled Algoma is financially successful, the door may be opened to a broader range of experimentation involving changes in compensation.

Fairness and Equity

Canada has experienced a major growth in affirmative action (termed "employment equity") legislation in Canada and especially an increase in the extent of legislation on pay equity (termed "comparable worth" in the United States). In the long Canadian tradition of government intervention in the labor market, governments have been proactive on this issue. This contrasts somewhat with the United States which introduced these concepts first in the 1960s but in the 1980s began to move away from them. By contrast, although Canada started later, the federal government and a majority of provincial governments have embraced either employment equity or pay equity (Labor Canada 1991). While legislation in these fields has tended to be limited to the public sector, in Ontario the Pay Equity Act applies to the private sector as well (Weiner and Gunderson 1990).

Perhaps because the federal and provincial governments have embraced these equity concepts, few collective agreements contain provisions for either. Affirmative action plans are found in only 5 percent of agreements, while equal pay for equal work or equal pay for work of equal value are in 9 percent of agreements. The latter covers 18 percent of employees. Not surprisingly, the industries in which these provisions are most prominent are industries with larger numbers of women (clothing and telephones). The steel industry, with a small percentage of female employees, less than 10 percent, is noteworthy for its involvement in equal pay for equal work. The electrical products industry, with a female proportion of 38 percent, has some agreements with affirmative action plans, although the telephone and telegraph industry has moved the furthest with these plans and more than doubled the proportion between 1987 and 1992 from 11 to 27 percent of agreements. Provisions against sexual harassment have also increased significantly, although the proportions of contracts with this clause vary from a high of 56 percent in the auto industry to 0 in clothing. Overall, there has definitely been a move toward more fairness and equity in Canadian workplaces.

Training

As noted earlier the federal government has undertaken some recent initiatives to increase the financial support for training in Canada, especially through earmarking $800 million per year of unemployment insurance funds for this purpose. However, this recent infusion of funds is against a backdrop of a decrease in federal government support for training (Meltz 1990b).

Of even greater significance is the fact that private support for training in Canada (0.25 percent of GDP in 1987) is estimated to be less than half of that in the United States (0.66 percent of GDP in 1987) (Economic Council of Canada 1991, 130). The data in table 4.2 confirm the limited involvement of Canadian firms in formal training. For Canada as a whole, less than half of the larger unionized establishments have provisions for training on the job, while only a third support apprenticeship or training in outside courses. On the other hand, the most recent survey of private sector training, conducted in 1991 by the Canadian Labor Market and Productivity Centre, found that 70 percent of organizations provide formal (structured) training to 36 percent of private sector employees.

The differing results between the earlier Economic Council of Canada (1991) study and the most recent survey by CLMPC may lie partly in the type of training identified. CLMPC reported that 61 percent of firms provided orientation training, followed by computer training (57 percent), health and safety training (44 percent), and managerial training (40 percent). Sales employees were the most likely to receive some structural training. The average training per employee was 14 hours or approximately two days of training. The average trainee received 39 hours of structured training. The CLMPC survey may have cast its net more broadly in defining training than the earlier Economic Council Survey.

A recent survey by the Conference Board of Canada that indicated that both unionized and non-unionized Canadian organizations are increasing their expenditures on training at a substantial pace. The largest spenders on training in terms of the percentage of payroll costs were B.C. Hydro (7.2 percent), IBM (5.6 percent), Xerox Canada (5.0 percent), and the Royal Bank (3.9 percent). (Larson and Blue 1991, 11). IBM and the Royal Bank are non-unionized, while B.C. Hydro and Xerox Canada are unionized.

In the past the relatively low level of private firm spending on training has been offset to some extent by a high level of government spending. In fact in the early 1970s Canada was spending more on training than any other country except Sweden (Economic Council of Canada 1971). That training, however, was institutional rather than in industry or in partnership with industry, and much of the expenditure was for income support. The challenge in Canada has traditionally been to try to shift training toward an industry base. To date there has only been a limited success in this regard. It is important for Canada's continued competitiveness that training be increasingly shifted in an industry–related direction. At present an estimated 36 percent of training expenditures are in or with industry (Meltz 1990b). The newly created Canada Labor Force Development Board and the planned Ontario Training and Adjustment Board (a government agency to be managed by representatives of labor, management, and special interest groups) may help to shift training toward a greater partnership with industry and a redirection of spending from income support to enhancing the amount of training.

4.5 Conclusion

While Canadian developments in industrial relations have been influenced by the U.S. experience, particularly in the economic arena the institutional responses have charted an increasingly divergent and uniquely Canadian course. This makes the Canadian case especially useful for comparative theory construction. The evidence suggests that both labor and management have taken an incremental approach to workplace reform.

Although Canadian management has not adopted the same union avoidance tactics as American management (Verma and Thompson 1989), the desire to avoid unions in Canada is very similar. Some corroboration of this observation comes from the declining union density in the manufacturing sector (Troy 1992), but the slower rate of decline than in the United States also highlights the greater union strength in Canada (Meltz 1993). The financial sector has generally neutralized early union gains made in the 1970s, and some large manufacturers like Northern Telecom and other medium-sized ones like Crown Cork and Seal have pioneered the growth of the high commitment non-union industrial relations systems.

Some degree of union avoidance has always characterized Canadian management practices. What gives them a new flavor is the growing ability of employers to stay non–union in greenfield sites. But perhaps the strongest weapon that employers have used with success against unions and workers in the 1980s is the threat of closure. In response to increasing competition as a result of the Free Trade Agreement (FTA) with the United States and lower tariffs in general, a number of employers (especially, but not only, the U.S. manufacturing companies) began to wind up their branch plant operations in Canada. Even as these plants closed, other employers have missed no opportunity to point to these cases to win concessions or to defeat organizing campaigns.

Despite management resistance the Canadian labor movement as a whole is far from weakened in the way that the U.S. labor movement found itself circa 1980. Labor has gradually increased its involvement both in the political process as well as at the sectoral level during the 1980s (Chaison and Rose 1990). With the election of Bob White (of the Canadian Auto Workers) as the president of the Canadian Labor Congress (CLC), this trend is likely to intensify further. The political strategy has paid some handsome dividends for labor in recent years. Within a two-year period (1990–92), three provinces, Ontario, British Columbia, and Saskatchewan, elected NDP governments with substantial support from the labor movement. This has given labor increasing clout in setting the political agenda of the nation.

As described earlier, labor has also assured itself of a role in sectoral joint committees and in the national Canada Labor Force Development Board. Similar boards are now being constituted in several provinces giving labor a formal voice. These developments run almost counter to organized labor's declining influence in some parts of private sector collective bargaining and on the shopfloor.

Canadian developments raise three research and policy issues that need further examination. First, is increasing clout for labor at the political and industry levels compatible with its decline within collective bargaining in some sectors and on the shopfloor in the manufacturing sector in particular? Or, to state it in policy terms, how can labor use its political clout to prevent a decline in its ranks? In the United States this debate was settled once between the Knights of Labor and the American Federation of Labor in favor of a nonpolitical labor movement that was to concentrate on bread-and-butter issues within collective bargaining. The Canadian developments are rekindling the old debate in a new setting. The CLC has no major rival. It fights against decline of all labor unions. It also believes in collective bargaining but wants to combine such particularistic activities with broader social goals. At the same time labor has received its immediate rewards from the political process with pro-labor amendments to labor relations legislation in 1992 in two provinces ruled by NDP governments, Ontario and British Columbia.[10] Management viewed the changes in legislation in both provinces as a major shift of power to unions. However, academic observers believe that these changes will not drastically alter the balance of power but rather will result in incremental changes consistent with the gradual process of labor law reform in the past (Carter 1992).

In a modern democracy this debate between political initiatives and workplace priorities, like most others, will be settled ultimately at the ballot box. It is tempting therefore to hypothesize that the success of labor's political strategy may well depend on the extent to which unions can add wealth generation to the traditional agenda of equity in the workplace and in the society at large. There is no doubt that for labor, the price of achieving greater clout at the political level will be greater responsibility and involvement at the workplace level where it must demonstrate that it can marshal the rank-and-file forces as much in support of wealth generation as it has in the past in

---

10. At the time of going to press, Saskatchewan, the third province with an NDP government, had begun the process of proposing a labor law reform bill.

wealth distribution. If labor succeeds, its reward will be greater following at the ballot box. On the other hand, should labor fail to broaden its traditional role of emphasizing wealth distribution only, voters could see labor increasingly as part of the problem rather than as part of the solution. In that event, labor's increasing political clout in the early 1990s might be best remembered as Canadians' brief affair with the labor movement.

The second issue is one of Canada's competitive position vis-à-vis the United States, its largest trading partner. Can Canada continue to chart a different economic and labor relations policy course than the United States at a time when the two economies are becoming increasingly interdependent? If the lack of unionization and labor market regulation in the United States reduces the cost of labor relative to Canada, there will be some pressure, especially within companies that operate in both countries, to shift resources from high-cost Canadian operations to the lower-cost facilities in the United States. As suggested earlier, this may already have happened to some extent since the Free Trade Agreement went into effect.

Third and last, from a theoretical point of view, the Canadian experience suggests that labor's political power can modify the behavior of the parties and the influence of market forces on workplace practices and outcomes. Industrial relations theories must therefore take into account the role of labor's political initiatives in workplace reform and economic growth. Since the recent successes of labor's political strategy are without precedent in contemporary Canadian history, it is difficult at this time to estimate its effectiveness in the longer run. Meanwhile it is clear that the stronger political role of labor in Canada relative to the United States will continue to influence workplace reform and collective bargaining as much as the economic forces of the labor and product markets.

References

Adams, Roy J. 1985. Industrial relations and the economic crisis: Canada moves towards Europe. In Hervey Juris, Mark Thompson, and Wilbur Daniels, eds., *Industrial Relations in a Decade of Economic Change*. Madison, WI: Industrial Relations Research Association, pp. 115–50.

Advisory Council on Adjustment. 1989. *Adjusting to Win: Report of the Advisory Council on Adjustment*. Ottawa: Minister of Supply and Services.

Barbash, Jack. 1989. Equity as function: Its rise and attribution. In J. Barbash and K. Barbash, eds., *Theories and Concepts in Comparative Industrial Relations*. Columbia: University of South Carolina Press, pp. 113–22.

Benimadhu, P. P. 1989. *Human Resource Management: Charting a New Course.* Ottawa: Conference Board of Canada. May.

Boivin, Jean. 1993. Personal correspondence with the authors, May 14, 1993, and annotated references to the annual report of the Fonds de Solidarité, 1992

Bourque, Reynald, and Guylaine Vallée. 1994. Contrats sociaux: Ententes de partenariat ou ententes de longue durée? Inventaire et analyse juridique. In *Info Ressources humaines.* Quebec: Association des Professionnels du Québec.

Bruce, Peter G. 1989. Political parties and labor legislation in Canada and U.S. *Industrial Relations* 28:115–41.

Bureau of Labor Information, Labor Canada. 1992. *Provisions in Collective Agreements, Special Tabulations.* Hull, Quebec: June 2 and 3, 1992.

Bureau of Labor Statistics. 1984, 1985, 1990. *Employment and Earnings* (January):A.1.

Canadian Labor Force Development Board. 1993. *Occupational Standards in Canada— Issues and Opportunities.* Ottawa.

Canadian Chamber of Commerce. 1988. *Focus 2000: Report on the Task Force on Harnessing Change.* Ottawa. August.

Carter, Don. 1992. *Labor Law Reform: Radical Departure or Natural Evolution.* Kingston, Ontario: Industrial Relations Centre, Queen's University.

CCEEMI (Canadian Electrical and Electronics Manufacturing Industry). 1989. *Connections for the Future. A Human Resources Strategy for the Canadian Electrical and Electronics Manufacturing Industry.* January.

Chaison, Gary N., and Joseph B. Rose. 1991. Continental divide: The direction and fate of North American unions. In Donna Sockell, David Lewin, and David B. Lipsky, eds., *Advances in Industrial and Labor Relations*, vol. 5. Greenwich, CT: JAI Press, pp. 169–205.

Chaykowski, Richard P., and Anil Verma, eds. 1992. *Industrial Relations in Canadian Industry.* Toronto: Holt, Rinehart and Winston.

CLMPC (Canadian Labor Market and Productivity Centre). 1993. *1991 National Training Survey. Edition* Ottawa: CLMPC. February.

Craig, Alton W. J. 1990. *The System of Industrial Relations in Canada.* 3d ed. Scarborough, ON: Prentice Hall Canada.

Cutcher-Gershenfeld, Joel, Thomas A. Kochan, and Anil Verma. 1991. Recent developments in U.S. employee involvement initiatives: Erosion or transformation. In Donna Sockell, David Lewin, and David Lipsky, eds., *Advances in Industrial and Labor Relations*, vol. 5. Greenwich, CT: JAI Press, pp. 1–31.

CWC (Communications and Electrical Workers of Canada). 1990. An agenda for the future: CWC's position on workplace reorganization. Mimeo. 7th Annual Convention, Quebec, May 7–11.

De Mara, Bruce. 1994. McDonald's first union bid goes to a vote. *The Toronto Star.* February 5.

Docquier, Gerard. 1989. Forging new management relations—Competitive necessity? Notes for remarks made to the Human Resources Section of the Canadian Pulp and Paper Association.

Economic Council of Canada. 1971. *Seventh Annual Review. 1971.* Ottawa: Information Canada.

Economic Council of Canada. 1986. *Minding the Public's Business.* EC 22-135. Ottawa: Information Canada.

Economic Council of Canada. 1991. *Employment in the Service Economy.* Ottawa: Supply and Services Canada.

Farber, Henry S., and Alan B. Krueger. 1992. *Union Membership in the United States: The Decline Continues.* Working Paper 4216. Cambridge, MA: National Bureau of Economic Research.

Fonds de Solidarité des Travailleurs du Québec. 1992. *Rapport annuel. 1992*, Montreal.

Fournier, Louis. 1992. The Quebec Solidarity Fund: A profound revolution in the labor movement. *Inroads* __(2):___–___.

Galt, Virginia. 1992. Algoma workers take pay cut to own the mill. *The Globe and Mail.* April 16.

Halpern, Norman. 1984. Socio-technical systems design: The Shell Sarnia experience. In J. B. Cunningham and T. H. White, eds., *Quality of Working Life: Contemporary Cases.* Ottawa: Labor Canada.

IMD International. 1991. *The World Competitiveness Report.* Lausanne: IMD.

Katz, Harry C., and Noah M. Meltz. 1989. Industrial relations issues for the 1990's. In Michel Grant, ed., *Proceedings of the 26th Conference of the Canadian Industrial Relations Association,* Université Laval, Québec, June 4–6, pp. 384–96.

Katz, Harry C., and Noah M. Meltz. 1991. Profit sharing and auto workers' earnings, the United States vs Canada. *Relations Industrielles* 46:515–30.

Kumar, Pradeep, and Noah M. Meltz. 1992. Industrial relations in the Canadian automobile industry. In Richard P. Chaykowski and Anil Verma, eds., *Industrial Relations in Canadian Industry.* Toronto: Holt, Rinehart and Winston, pp. 39–86.

Kumar, Pradeep, David Arrowsmith, and Mary Lou Coates. 1991. *Canadian Labor Relations: An Information Manual.* Kingston, ON: Industrial Relations Centre, Queen's University.

Labor Canada. 1991. *Labor Standards in Canada.* Hull, Quebec: Minister of Supply and Services.

Labor Canada. 1992. *Directory of Labor Organizations in Canada.* Hull, Quebec: Minister of Supply and Services Canada.

Labor Canada. 1993. *Labor Update, Ottawa: Issue 24.* February.

Lancaster Labor Law Reports. 1992. Contract Clauses, "Steelworkers reach historic deal in bid to save Algoma," vol. 16, no. 5 (May).

Lendvay-Zwickl, Judith. 1990. Compensation planning outlook, 1991. *Survey Results*, 9th ed. Ottawa: Conference Board of Canada.

Larson, Peter E., and Matthew W. Blue. 1991. *Training and Development. 1990: Expenditures and Policies.* Report 67–91. Conference Board of Canada, Human Resource Development Centre.

Mansell, Jacquie. 1986. *Workplace Innovation in Canada*. Ottawa: Economic Council of Canada.

Meltz, Noah M. 1985. Labor movements in Canada and the United States. In Thomas A. Kochan, ed., *Challenges and Choices Facing American Labor*, Cambridge: MIT Press, pp. 315–34.

Meltz, Noah M. 1989a. Interstate vs. interprovincial differences in union density. *Industrial Relations* 28:142–58.

Meltz, Noah M. 1989b. Job security in Canada. *Relations Industrielles* 44:149–61.

Meltz, Noah M. 1990a. Unionism in Canada, U.S.: On parallel treadmills? *Forum for Applied Research and Public Policy* 5:46–52.

Meltz, Noah M. 1990b. The evolution of worker training: The Canadian experience. In Lou Ferman Michel Hoyman, J. Cutcher-Gershenfeld, and Ernest Savoie, eds., *New Developments in Worker Training: A Legacy for the. 1990's*. Madison, WI: Industrial Relations Research Association, pp. 283–307.

Meltz, Noah M. 1991. Sectoral realignment in Canada: Shifting patterns of output and employment and the consequences for labor-management relations. In Elaine B. Willis, ed., *Industrial Restructuring and Industrial Relations in Canada and the United States*. Kingston, Ontario: Industrial Relations Centre, Queen's University, pp. 1–17.

Meltz, Noah M. 1993. Manufacturing sector unionism: Canada–U.S. comparisons. In *Proceedings of the 30th Annual Meeting of the Canadian Industrial Relations Association*, Carleton University, Ottawa, Canada, June 4, 1993.

Minister of Labor, The Honourable Bob Mackenzie. 1992. Introduction of Amendments to the Ontario Labor Relations Act.

Morton, Desmond. 1990. *Working People: An Illustrated History of Canadian Labor*, 3d ed. Toronto: Summerhill.

Niagara Institute, The. 1987. *Code of Conduct for Labor-Management Relations*, Niagara-on-the-Lake. October.

Papp, Leslie. 1993. Civil service revolt builds. *Toronto Star*, March 24, p. A17.

Rankin, Tom. 1990. *New Forms of Work Organization: The Challenge for North American Unions*. Toronto: University of Toronto Press.

Rao, P. Someshwar and Tony Lempriere. 1992. *Canada's Productivity Performance*. Ottawa: Supply and Services Canada and Canada Communication Group.

Riddell, W. Craig. 1992. Unionization in Canada and the United States: A tale of two countries. Department of Economics, University of British Columbia, Vancouver.

Sexton, Jean, Claudine Leclerc and Michel Audet. 1984. *The Canadian Textile Labor-Management Committee*. Ottawa: Labor Canada.

Statistics Canada. 1992a. *Canada: A Portrait*. Ottawa: Supply and Services Canada.

Statistics Canada. 1992b. *CALURA Labor Unions. 1990*. Catalogue 71-202. Ottawa: Industry, Science and Technology Canada.

Statistics Canada. 1992c. *Labor Force Annual Averages. 1991*. Catalogue 71-220. Ottawa: Industry, Science and Technology Canada.

Statistics Canada. 1993. *Labor Force Annual Averages. 1992.* Catalogue 71-220. Ottawa: Industry, Science and Technology Canada.

Stone, Thomas H., and Noah M. Meltz. 1983. *Human Resource Management in Canada.* 3d ed. Toronto: Dryden Press.

Troy, Leo. 1990. Is the U.S. unique in the decline of private sector unionism? *Journal of Labor Research* (Spring):111–43.

Troy, Leo. 1992. Convergence in international unionism, etc.: The case of Canada and the U.S.A. *British Journal of Industrial Relations* 30:1–43.

Troy, Leo, and L. Sheflin. 1984. The flow and ebb of U.S. public sector unionism. *Government Union Review* (Spring):28–31.

Troy, Leo, and L. Sheflin. 1985. *U.S. Union Sourcebook: Membership, Finances, Structure Directory.* West Orange, NJ: Industrial Relations Data and Information Sources.

USWA (United Steel Workers of America Canada). 1991. *Empowering Workers in the Global Economy: A Labor Agenda for the. 1990s.* Toronto: USWA.

Verma, Anil. 1989. Joint participation programs: Self-help or suicide for labor? *Industrial Relations* 28:401–10.

Verma, Anil. 1991. Restructuring in industrial relations and the role for labor. In Margaret Hallock and Steve Hecker, eds., *Labor in a Global Economy: A U.S.–Canadian Symposium.* Eugene: University of Oregon Books, pp. 47–61.

Verma, Anil, and Joel Cutcher-Gershenfeld. 1993. Joint governance in the workplace: Beyond union-management cooperation and worker participation. In Bruce E. Kaufman and Morris M. Kleiner, eds., *Employee Representation: Alternatives and Future Directions.* Madison, WI: Industrial Relations Research Association.

Verma, Anil, and Noah M. Meltz. 1990. The underlying sources of union strength: Certification activity in Ontario. 1982–1988. *Proceedings of the Twenty-seventh Annual Meetings of the Canadian Industrial Relations Association,* pp. 465–74.

Verma, Anil, and Mark E. Thompson. 1989. Managerial strategies in industrial relations in the. 1980s: Comparing the US and Canadian experience. *Proceedings of the Forty-first Annual Meetings, Industrial Relations Research Association,* Madison, WI.

Verma, Anil, and Joseph Weiler. 1993. *Change and Restructuring in Industrial Relations and Human Resource Management in the 1980s: A Review of Firm-Level Responses.* A special report of the Queen's Ottawa Economic Projects. Kingston, ON: Queen's University IRC Press.

Warrian, Peter. 1990. Is the wolf coming to the Canadian steel industry in 1990? Draft manuscript. April.

Weiner, Nan, and Morley Gunderson. 1990. *Pay Equity: Issues, Options and Experiences.* Ottawa: Supply and Services Canada.

Wells, Don. 1986. *Soft Sell: Quality of Working Life Programs and the Productivity Race.* Ottawa: Canadian Centre for Policy Alternatives.

Wood, W. D., and Pradeep Kumar. 1981. *The Current Industrial Relations Scene in Canada,* Kingston, ON: Industrial Relations Centre.

Worklife Report, The. 1990. Community and sectoral approaches to labor market policy, vol. 7, no. 3, Kingston, ON, pp. 1–17.

5

Between Voluntarism and Institutionalization: Industrial Relations and Human Resource Practices in Italy

Ida Regalia
Marino Regini

Fifteen years ago the Italian industrial relations system was easier to describe. It was factious, underinstitutionalized, rather centralized, and beset by a plurality of collective actors competing for members (e.g., see Regini 1980). Today the situation is quite different. With the exception of the public service sector, Italian IR/HR practices are characterized by a high degree of cooperation between labor and management at the level of the firm, by more decentralized levels of bargaining, and by cooperation among interest groups. Notwithstanding several shifts in the balance of power between labor and management, this change in IR practices indicates that the Italian system has the flexibility to adjust to changing markets and production systems without a dramatic overhaul.

The gradual development of relatively stable and cooperative IR/HR practices at the company and territorial levels contrasts so sharply with the traditional features of the Italian system of IR that some researchers have been prompted to look for hidden factors such as (1) formal rules that might decree orderly and cooperative relations between management and labor and (2) institutions that might ensure stable relations by removing the temptation to exploit changes in power structures. Our research in the 1980s, as well as that of others (Regini and Sabel 1989; Locke 1995; Golden 1988), has singled out three factors that may explain this "Italian enigma" (Ferner and Hyman 1992).

First was the implicit acceptance that the official strategies elaborated at the center of the IR system conflicted with those enacted at the company or industrial district levels. The relative isolation of labor-management relationships at the workplace from events in the national arena permitted pragmatic adjustments to changing markets and new production methods.

Second were certain historical legacies of the Italian trade union tradition. The Italian trade union movement's interest in production dates back to Antonio Gramsci but was given its clearest expression in the 1970s during the "struggle for an alternative organization of work." At the core of the union's culture is an antagonism that promotes, rather than resists, technological innovation and economic development. This cultural predisposition contributed to the relatively smooth transition that took place in the Italian economy and IR during the 1980s.

Third was the peculiar structure and role of employers in Italy. Italian entrepreneurs are accorded low legitimacy and often industry is extremely fragmented, consisting mostly of small firms. Most employers need to seek alliances with local trade unions or factory councils in order to increase their legitimacy and, perhaps more important, their access to state resources. As a result a stable and harmonious system of decentralized IR was fostered.

These three factors provide us with an explanatory framework through which we can interpret the workplace reforms of the 1980s (Regini 1994). However, a more historical perspective of the entire post–World War II era illustrates a more enduring factor contributing to the stability of labor-management relationships: the duality of the Italian IR system. On the one hand, the Italian IR system may be accurately described as largely informal and underinstitutionalized in its practices, but on the other, it is less so when analyzed in relation to other features of the system.

Indeed there is little doubt that certain IR practices like the relationships between employers and unions, the system of interest representation, and the structure of collective bargaining (especially in the core sectors of the economy) are minimally institutionalized, and that the behavior of the parties is characterized by a high degree of voluntarism (Cella 1989). However, if one takes into account the regulation of the welfare system and of public services, the role of interest groups appears to be far more formalized and firmly embedded in a network of legally sanctioned institutions (Regalia and Regini 1989; Falcucci and Mesirca 1983; Cammelli 1982). Moreover, although, by law, the state and institutions play a minor role in labor-management relations (Napoli 1989), they do intervene if the labor market and social security policies are at risk.

The high informality and voluntarism characteristic of labor-management relations and the highly institutionalized implementation of social policies, together with extensive evidence of indirect public intervention, have been a structural characteristic of the Italian

IR system ever since its creation. Even the passage in 1970 of the Workers' Statute (Statuto dei Diritti dei Lavoratori)—a significant piece of legislation that recognized workers' constitutional rights in the workplace and ensured legal support for the largest unions[1]—did not substantially alter the rationale of the system.

To be sure, the informality of the Italian IR system and its voluntarism have the most far-reaching consequences. Nevertheless, to protect weak parties (those outside the workplace) and weak individuals (those outside collective bargaining), the less conspicuous, formalized and structured side of the system has developed a dense network of institutionalized interaction. In this way the Italian IR system, to some extent, compensates for its informality and voluntarism.

Since, in comparison with the other features of this duality, the institutionalized side is a much older and a much more constant factor in the Italian IR system's evolution, we will use it as the basis for our discussion. However, it is less appropriate for our needs when we move, in section 5.1, from a background description to an analysis of trends in IR/HR practices during the 1980s. Explanation of both the stability and the evolution of these practices will oblige us to analyze all the factors mentioned above. Only by drawing on their combined effect, can we hope to unravel what would otherwise remain an "Italian enigma."

5.1 The Main Features of the Traditional IR System

The informality and underinstitutionalization of Italian industrial relations is due to the lack of a formal, legal framework regulating the establishment and operation of trade unions and employers' associations. Although the Constitution of the Republic contains two articles establishing the right of workers to form unions and to strike, these rights have never been fully implemented.[2] Indeed Italian trade

---

1. The term used was "most representative"; the precise meaning is unclear, as are the criteria by which the degree of "representativeness" is to be measured. In the 1970s, however, the phrase was generally taken as shorthand for the three main union confederations (Cgil, Cisl, Uil). During the 1980s, as the confederations grew in membership, this expression came to include different forms of "autonomous unions" (those not affiliated with top organizations).
2. In the early 1950s the implementation of these articles was opposed—on the ground that they would grant formal recognition to an organized communist and socialist labor movement. Subsequently the informality of the system was welcomed by all the unions because it allowed greater freedom of action. In the late 1980s, however, there was renewed pressure for the implementation of these two articles of the Constitution.

unions and employers' organizations enjoy no formal or special recognition, and in general, access to the arena of interest representation remains relatively open. This environment has led to the development of a pluralist and diversified (indeed fragmented) system of representation, whose representative capacity is open to some doubt. The early split along ideological lines within the initially unified Confederazione Generale Italiana del Lavoro (CGIL) and the creation of the two other major confederations, Confederazione Italiana dei Sindacati Lavoratori (CISL) and Unione Italiana dei Lavoratori (UIL), in the late 1940s; the subsequent growth of "independent" unions in the service sectors during the 1960s and the 1970s; the occasional upsurges of radical grassroots opposition movements to the official trade unions which sometimes bred new organizations (e.g., the CUB of the Hot Autumn period and the Cobas in the late 1980s)—all of this illustrates the openness and fragmentation of labor representation in Italy. In a similar fashion the employers' system of representation has become increasingly diversified and complex, to the extent that it has recently been called the most fragmented in Europe (Ferner and Hyman 1992). Employers are divided along sectoral lines (i.e., agriculture vs. manufacturing vs. services vs. the artisan sector), ownership patterns (private vs. state-owned capital), firm size, and even by political affiliation (Martinelli and Chiesi 1989; Lanzalaco 1990). The 1980s and early 1990s also saw the emergence of new employer organizations (within the service sector). As a result the degree of representation of even Confindustria, one of Italy's most influential interest organizations, is quite limited.

In contrast, the creation, operation, and responsibilities of workplace structure are governed by a strict set of rules. Workplace-based representative institutions—Commissioni Interne—were re-introduced in the postwar years as a result of a national agreement between the major union confederations and the Confindustria. They were not regulated by law and their impact was always rather limited. In the early 1970s, after the wave of mobilization that culminated in the Hot Autumn struggles of 1969, these original structures were replaced by factory councils. In the manufacturing sector, in particular, an informal (and voluntary) system of factory councils was established. Soon afterward, these councils were recognized by the unions as the official workplace structures, and they came under the legal protection of the Workers' Statute. However, given that this piece of legislation did not prescribe rules for their formation and operation. These workplace representation structures became increasingly controversial and open to multiple interpretations (Regalia 1994).

Until the 1990 enactment of a law prohibiting strikes in key public services,[3] there were no legal constraints on strikes and industrial conflict beyond the legislation safeguarding private property. In fact the right to strike constituted an individual right.[4] Nor were there provisions for the compulsory arbitration or public mediation of industrial disputes.[5] Union confederations found it difficult to exert full control over rank and file workers. In the 1980s labor disputes were especially frequent in the public service sector (Cella 1991).

Fourth, there are no legal rules for collective bargaining; the outcome is treated as any ordinary private agreement (Napoli 1989). In general, the parties to a labor dispute are not obligated to negotiate (though, as we will see, the legislation of the 1970s and 1980s provided indirect incentives for collective bargaining). More important, the collective bargaining structure itself has remained largely unregulated. Since the 1970s three basic levels of collective bargaining have emerged: at the national interindustry level, the industry level, and the company or plant level. But there are no formalized specifications of their respective scope, competence, salience, and procedures. In fact, not only do the relationships between these levels and the balance between centralization and decentralization change frequently over time (according to circumstance and changes in power relationships), but frequently the same issues are also dealt with at different levels simultaneously, with no clear-cut differentiation between them.

The more formalized aspect of Italian IR, that at the level of social welfare programs and the regulation of the public sector, can best be understood in terms of two functions. The first relates to the institutional role assigned to the social part. Immediately after the Second World War, while they were still very weak in the labor market, the unions (and to a lesser extent the employers' representatives) became involved in the administration of a wide range of social security programs: pensions, unemployment insurance, the Cassa Integrazione Guadagni (state-financed redundancy/income maintenance fund),

---

3. This law represents a symbolic break with the liberal tradition, although it encourages self-regulation rather than being rigidly prescriptive (Ferner and Hyman 1992, 579).

4. Lockouts, however, are illegal.

5. Comparative studies invariably show that internationally Italian strike figures are the highest (Bordogna and Provasi 1989; Franzosi 1989).

and special unemployment protection for agricultural and construction workers. The major union and employer organizations were offered seats (currently eight or nine)[6] on the tripartite committees responsible for administering these labor market institutions at both the national and local levels. Union participation was required in the several hundred committees set up to oversee labor regulation in the public service sector, where formal collective bargaining was not allowed until the early 1980s (Ascoli 1984; Isap 1987; Regalia and Regini 1989; Reyneri 1989a, 1990). Over time this institutional involvement has become increasingly widespread, and now the trade unions possess a majority of seats on the supervisory board of the INPS (the national institute for social security).

Although a full assessment of the effect on the IR system of this institutional participation by the unions is not available, existing research shows that over time it facilitated negotiation among the social partners, even in periods of turmoil and high levels of conflict, and created channels for indirect pressure, communication, and even consent between labor and management (Treu 1987). As a result of this participation, Italian unions enjoyed greater and more pervasive influence than standard indicators of union performance (membership figures, collective bargaining outcomes, etc.) would suggest.

Likewise, although formally the state is a neutral partner in labor-management relationships, since the early postwar years a number of institutions have been created to protect the labor force, simultaneously enabling firms to operate more freely in competitive markets. Some of the most important institutional innovations were an economywide wage indexation system (*scala mobile*),[7] income support for temporarily laid-off workers (by the introduction of the above-mentioned Cassa Integrazione Guadagni, which has been extended and improved over time), and the enactment of strict universal labor laws.[8] Until the 1980s these measures continually grew, both in number and complexity.

The duality of the Italian IR/HR system stems from the historical weakness of the unions, in both economic and organizational terms.

---

6. Labor decisions continually changed and grew in complexity, and this did not improve the labor market, at least not until its reform in 1991 (for details, see Reyneri 1989a).

7. The scala mobile was introduced by an interindustry collective agreement in 1945 but without the public institutions necessary for its implementation.

8. Among the most important of these protective measures were the law prohibiting night shifts for women and the law regulating worker dismissals.

Unions were traditionally weak in the labor market because of high unemployment and also because of ideological divisions, dependence on political parties, and underdeveloped organizations (Regalia, Regini, and Reyneri 1978). At the same time, the at least symbolic institutional involvement of the social partners and state interventionism, designed to give minimum protection to the industrial labor force and prevent outbursts of organized protest, substituted for a more elaborate, formalized industrial relations system and helped maintain social cohesion. In the long term, the informality of the system meant that it could more easily adjust to changes in the power and interests of the social partners.

To conclude, the informality and the voluntarism of the IR system helped it to adapt to changing circumstances. The widespread institutional involvement of interest organizations in the administration of labor market policy and the social security system favored social cohesion and, indirectly, industrial adjustment and innovation, but it impeded reform of a welfare system whose disordered structure is becoming increasingly inefficient. As a result, in the early 1980s, the IR system appeared overloaded by its dual function of collective bargaining and legal protection.

The developments of the 1980s can largely be viewed as attempts to reorganize the system and to increase its flexibility in a more competitive environment.[9] It is to these developments that we now turn.

5.2 Changes in IR/HR Practices in the 1980s

Work Organization

Mass production organized according to the principles of the Taylorist-Fordist rationalization arrived late in Italy. After the first experiments in the 1950s, however, this development was very rapid and pervasive in industry. By the late 1960s, when the Hot Autumn struggles swept across the country, and industrial sociologists conducted extensive research on production sites for the first time, it was found that most large industrial firms were based on a clear separation of execution and conception, narrow job descriptions, and

---

9. The substantial reform of labor market regulation in 1991, the partial reforms of the scala mobile in 1984 and 1986 and its de facto abolition in 1992, the tripartite national agreement in 1993 which reorganized the collective bargaining structure and the workplace representation system, were the most important achievements.

specialized machinery.[10] In the 1970s, as part of the ideological thrust of this collective mobilization, the trade unions launched an offensive against traditional forms of work organization. Although their demands concerned proposals for job enlargement, later to become widespread, the unions failed to impose any major changes in work organization. Only a few large firms (e.g., Olivetti, Ansaldo, and Alfa Romeo) had experimented with organizational innovation by the end of the decade (Medusa 1983).

The 1980s witnessed a radical transformation of work organization. More flexible forms of work designed to give workers greater autonomy and responsibility, as well as to adjust working time more efficiently to mass production, were introduced. A fairly rich body of empirical evidence has documented this transformation, but without reaching firm conclusions as to the extent of this break with the strict application of mass production principles.

Attempts to enlarge and integrate formerly distinct tasks were widespread, although their results have been ambiguous. To give just a few examples drawn from a larger research project (Regini and Sabel 1989), at Montedison (chemicals) there was a general flattening of managerial hierarchies, individual jobs were grouped into teams, and workers were rotated through various jobs in the same plant so that they could acquire broader skills and responsibilities. At Italtel (telecommunications) workers were trained not only to set up, operate, and maintain several machines but also to check the quality of their output. Wherever possible workers were organized into semi-autonomous work groups with sufficient technical training to play an active part in organizing the production flow in their area. In the industrial districts (Prato, Modena), where the division of labor had traditionally been extremely informal, the reorganization of work translated into a breakdown of tasks in order to deepen and broaden worker expertise in each area.

However, the experiences of a number of large companies like Fiat (autos) and Olivetti (personal computers) require some caution when assessing the extent of these trends. In these companies machine operators were trained to take responsibility for at least some preventive

---

10. Even later extensive systemization was introduced in agriculture and the service sector. In many cases small firms, which are important to the Italian industrial fabric and which in the so-called Third Italy often form networks or districts, switched directly from artisan to post-Fordist modes of production (Marchisio 1988; Ires Toscana 1991).

maintenance, setup work, and quality control. However, in the 1980s they chose to provide workers with the minimum of skills necessary to reduce downtime and scrap rates to acceptable levels rather than to equip them with the skills necessary to improve the organization of production as their experience with it increased (Locke and Negrelli 1989). The emphasis was on giving workers the knowledge and autonomy necessary to operate just-in-time delivery systems, which included teaching workers to detect defects and help identify and eliminate their causes.

Among the several possible explanations for these differences in the willingness of management to pursue radical innovation is the organization of work, two are of interest to us here (see Regini and Sabel 1989 for further reasons). The first is that the lower rate of innovation may conceal a whole network of capital-goods subcontractors capable of rehauling workstations at short notice.[11] The second relates to an effectively different managerial strategy designed to increase product variety without abandoning the distinction between conception and execution. In this case workers are taught to operate the full range of new equipment so that they can move smoothly from one job to the next. But when the product range is already well defined and the machinery programmed accordingly, there is little incentive to teach employees the fundamentals of a new technology. Not withstanding these differences, in the 1980s the concept of small work units—including both teamwork with low autonomy but providing job rotation and enrichment to group-based work systems with a high autonomy in assigning tasks and responsibilities (see Butera 1987; Dina 1991)—was extensive and has been reported in all case studies of this period (Della Rocca and Zoccatelli 1985; Biliotti and Della Rocca 1986; Colasanto 1987; Bianchi 1988; Cittarella and Vitale 1988; Marchisio 1988). Organizational innovation by no means came to a halt with the end of the 1980s. An annual survey of industrial companies in Lombardy has recently shown that in 1989–1990, 56 percent of the sample introduced new job rotations, 41 percent enriched production jobs with either maintenance or quality control, and 11 percent promoted forms of self-organization of work within the group (Regalia and Ronchi 1991). Group-based work systems appear to be widespread in the service sector as well, especially in supermarkets

---

11. It is clearly less risky to build a number of cheap, rather inflexible plants, and to scrap them as demand changes, than it is to build a single, expensive unit able to accommodate market changes over the long haul.

and department stores, finance and professional services (Regalia 1990).

Flexible working time was another major innovation in Italian employment practices in the 1980s. These experiments involved all sectors of the economy in the extensive use of overtime, additional shifts, and work on Saturdays in exchange for extra vacations (Chiesi 1988). Experimentation in working time flexibility was begun in the textile industry, which is characterized by occasional or seasonal fluctuations in production. In the second half of the 1980s, however, these experiments spread to all sectors of the economy and lost their original connection with the cyclical nature of demand. In fact the negotiation of elaborate shift arrangements allowed for the full exploitation of, and hence increased amortization of, new capital goods in a variety of industries. Sectoral agreements, such as those covering textiles (Guidotti 1986) and chemical workers (Perulli 1986), established the frame of reference for other industries—to the extent that, in the late 1980s, working time issues came to displace wages as the most frequent issue on the agenda for both formal (Baglioni and Milani 1990) and informal (Regalia and Ronchi 1988–92) bargaining.

In general, it was the employers at the enterprise level who pushed for the above changes in work practices. But the trade unions also made a significant contribution by not raising major objections to these organizational changes and, indeed, by often advocating them, as was the case for group-based work in the 1970s and early 1980s (Regini and Sabel 1989). The unions also agreed to place work time flexibility, an issue strongly promoted by employers, at the center of both industry-level and plant-level negotiations.

Besides group-based work and flexible working time, the 1980s saw the development of other forms of employee involvement, the most prominent being quality circles which were introduced in Italy in the early 1980s. However, a national survey conducted by the Italian association of quality circles in 1987 found that they involved a rather low percentage of employees, even though they existed in around 300 firms in the industrial and service sectors (ANCQUI 1987). A later survey estimated that in the early 1990s around 400–500 companies had active quality circle programs (Galgano 1990). Despite their early success and their (limited) quantitative growth, quality circles failed to become widely diffused. Although most trade unions, after their initial skepticism, were moderately in favor of the scheme, middle management was often very much opposed (ANCQUI 1987). Therefore after the initial success of quality circles, and despite their acceptance by unions, widespread skepticism over their usefulness appeared, and they failed to develop outside broader companywide programs of quality control (Regalia 1992) such as those recently introduced at Fiat (Bonazzi 1991).

Public institutions and legislation were very marginally involved in the changes described above, and mainly this stemmed from the shifting interests of the policymakers. It was the union demands and proposals for a more human method of production in the late 1970s that heightened awareness of these issues. Union demands, however, were based more on cultural-ideological concerns, and they did not offer convincing arguments. As a result only a few, sporadic experiments followed. With the shifts in the 1980s, employers began to promote new work systems in an attempt to respond to more volatile markets. The shift in employee strategy explains the widespread diffusion of new work systems in the 1980s. Among the strategies, as we have noted earlier, were product differentiation, the reconfiguration of supplier networks, the introduction of just-in-time production, competition in quality or design, and massive technological innovation.

However, the existing IR institutions had a key role to play in accommodating these pressures for change in ways that favored successful adjustment. As we have already pointed out, most important in this respect was a type of unionism and existing shop floor practices which, far from blocking change, placed a premium on innovative business strategies (Regini and Sabel 1989).

Skill Formation and Development

David Marsden has argued convincingly that there existed a body of evidence that showed "greater reliance upon internal labor markets among manual workers in industry in France and Italy than in either Britain or West Germany" and that "it is fair to suppose that the main form of training for skilled labor in France and Italy consists of work experience and training organized by individual employers" (Marsden 1982, 33–34). More recent research largely confirms that this was indeed the principal way in which skills were formed and developed in much of Italian industry. Research also shows that only minor changes in this approach occurred during the 1980s; so much so that, a decade later, Marsden again drew the same distinction among the four countries, although he specified more precisely how the pattern worked. "Internal labor markets, in contrast to occupational markets, develop less extensive and less transferable skills for which training is usually provided in an extended sequence of ad hoc doses on the job, in association with initial recruitment and subsequent upgrading. Partly to compensate for the inadequacies of such skill formation patterns, public policy in . . . Italy has increasingly complemented training in internal labor markets by initial vocational preparation and qualification in the public school system" (Marsden 1992, 14).

The above passage highlights three major components in the traditional regulation of skill formation and development in Italian industry: (1) the predominance of on-the-job training, (2) incremental skill development, which is reflected in upgrading or internal career paths through an elaborate grade structure, (3) reliance on the public school system to teach basic technical knowledge to a fair proportion of the work force. A number of other features of this traditional pattern should, however, be reviewed before moving to a discussion of the changes that took place during the 1980s.

First, Italian trade unions have traditionally focused much of their attention on devising job classification systems that reflect their egalitarian policies, and on negotiating more or less automatic upgrading in the formal grade structure, than on promoting actual skill development. In Fordist-Taylorist systems of production, where semiskilled workers have predominated and formed the basis of union strength, career advancement has become, for a large segment of the work force, a bargaining objective—often "hidden" in wage negotiation and largely independent of actual job content and training. In the national industry agreements of the 1970s new job classification systems were drawn up in most sectors of the economy that lumped blue- and white-collar jobs together (*inquadramento unico*). The negotiation of collective upgrading within this structure was, however, left mostly to enterprise-level bargaining (Cella and Treu 1989). This has led to an extraordinarily rigid hierarchy of jobs that hardly corresponds to the actual distribution of skills.[12]

Second, vocational training in Italy is institutionally separate from the general educational system. General education, which is predom-

---

12. As we pointed out earlier, rather than safeguarding existing jobs, Italian unions were primarily interested in a general upgrading of wages and a reduction in wage differentials. In many companies they demanded job rotation, enlargement, and enrichment so that semiskilled workers could develop a wide range of skills (Regini and Sabel 1989).

inantly public, falls under the control of the Ministry of Education, while the organization of vocational training is the responsibility of regional governments, which can—and very often do—contract it out to private schools. This entails not only wide variations in the effectiveness of vocational training across regions (ISFOL 1990)[13] but also a lack of coordination between the two systems. Among the different categories of postcompulsory secondary schools, all of which belong to the public educational system, some have specifically "vocational" or "technical" curricula, with continually growing rates of enrollment. By contrast, the vocational "institutes" under regional control, which are theoretically intended to provide not general education but specific skill formation before entry into the labor force, have over time become more similar to the former. This is a major reason for the long decline in Italy's vocational training system, which is seen, as far as initial preparation was concerned, as providing second-class education to dropouts or to young people with lower expectations (ISFOL 1989). Another reason was the hostility expressed by the unions during the 1960s and 1970s, on the ground that apprenticeships might be used as a low-cost alternative to regular work contracts. In general, they saw training less as a means of acquiring skills—which the existing work organization would make little use of in any case—than as a worker's right to enhance his economic and political culture (Garonna et al. 1987).

As we have already pointed out, no dramatic changes occurred in this traditional pattern during the 1980s. The incremental effect of a series of minor changes, however, gradually led to a fairly new mode of regulation of skill formation and development. The attention of employers and trade unions gradually shifted from formal grade structures and more or less automatic upgrading, irrespective of any change in actual job content, to the problem of how training should be regulated. One indicator of this process was the sharp decrease in job classification issues in both national industry agreements and enterprise-level bargaining during the 1980s (Baglioni and Milani 1990). Although upgrading remained relatively prominent in the latter, it was mostly concentrated in more traditional industrial sectors like textiles and construction, and in smaller firms (ibid.).

---

13. Usually training has a vocational purpose, but in this case, for both societal and political reasons, many local administrators used training as a disguised form of financial support especially for artisans and the young unemployed.

Moreover regionally based vocational training—which was regulated by a 1978 law drawn up by the tripartite accord—gradually changed its focus from providing second-class education to supporting labor market flexibility, thereby indirectly attracting greater attention from both unions and employers. In fact another accord on youth employment, first enacted in 1978 and then substantially modified in 1984, introduced "work-and-training" contracts for young people that permitted employers to hire under favorable and flexible conditions young workers and gave youth a chance to receive both employment and training while in vocational schools. On the other hand, a problem with layoffs, which was made acute by the radical industrial restructuring of those years (see section 5.3), was mostly managed at the company level, where in dealing with redundancies heavy use was made of the vocational system to retrain redundant workers.

The combined effect of these changes was the social partners' increased awareness of skill development in contemporary production, and the average skill level of workers rose in Italian industry. In particular, the 1980s saw a massive increase in the proportion of white- to blue-collar workers, with a shift toward higher grades in both categories of employees (see table 5.1 on the metalworking industry for effect in steel and engineering). That this was more than just the outcome of negotiation, and corresponded to a real, qualitative transformation in the labor force, is confirmed by the dramatic change that occurred in its composition by educational level during the second half of the 1980s (see table 5.2).

Further indicative of the social partners' awareness of the special importance of skill development were the national agreements signed in 1989 and 1993 by the peak-level trade unions and employers' associations. The 1989 agreement introduced, on an experimental basis and in a few regions, joint committees to promote vocational training, with instruction and financing provided by both partners (Patriarca and Negro 1990). However, the agreement has remained largely on paper, corroborating the traditional practice of Italian unions to pay scant attention to the implementation of accords. Indeed, such national arrangements do not help unions develop a real awareness of the importance of training, since they do not make this the unions' responsibility. Likewise the 1993 agreement consists of proposals and mutual promises that do not require companies to organize and invest in training (Capecchi 1993). Once again the limitations of

Table 5.1
Distribution of employees in the grade structure of the metalworking industry in 1980 and 1989 (in %)

	1980	1989
Total employees		
White collar	26.33	35.37
Blue collar	73.67	64.63
White collar		
Top level (including middle management)	11.67	20.23
High level	29.28	33.73
Medium–high level	10.14	6.24
Medium level	33.45	29.74
Medium–low level	11.79	8.38
Low level	3.67	1.68
Blue collar		
High level	15.14	20.79
Medium–high level	28.16	30.71
Medium–low level	49.03	40.00
Low level	7.67	8.50

Source: Adapted from Federmeccanica's data cited in ASAP (1992).

Table 5.2
Employees by educational level and sex in 1980 and 1991 (in %)

	1980		1990	
Degree	Male	Female	Male	Female
Primary school or lower	51.7	46.9	26.8	21.2
Compulsory secondary school	29.5	29.1	41.7	37.3
Postsecondary schools	14.0	18.7	24.7	33.5
University degrees	4.8	5.3	6.8	8.0

Source: Adapted from ISTAT data by ISFOL.

voluntarism and the relatively low institutionalization of the Italian IR are manifest by this failure to implement major reforms in Italy's vocational training practices.

Different actors interacting at different levels were responsible for changes in skill development and training: the state and regional governments through their enactment of laws in concert with the social partners, trade unions and employers' associations in peak-level and industry-level bargaining, and especially managers and workplace representatives in plant-level negotiation. Overall, however, there were no clear strategies by which the change could proceed, nor even a full understanding of the process by those concerned, so among IR/HR practices skill development and training in Italy remained largely underdeveloped and clearly inadequate for the needs of a dynamic economy.[14] Previous evidence of plant-level bargaining agreements signed during the 1980s further confirms the extremely low concern for training issues (Baglioni and Milani 1990).[15]

We now turn briefly to the factors that explain both the change that occurred in the 1980s and the limits to such change. As we pointed out in our discussion of work organization at the beginning of this chapter, much of the pressure for change came from the product market and new technology. Rigid classification of jobs was deemed obsolete for post-Fordist production, and adequate skill formation became a far more pertinent issue. Nevertheless, although employers and unions alike were ready to express these opinions in public, the Italian industry's actual path to adjustment during the 1980s was not a sustained effort to develop technical skills in new and more efficient ways. Leaving aside international and national factors such as monetary policy, the major reasons for successful company adjustments

14. For instance, annual surveys by employers' associations in Lombardy have noted an inadequate supply of labor for a number of skilled occupations (Federlombarda-Intersind, 1983–90). Also problematic is the supply of the skilled engineers, technicians, and middle managers. The numbers are affected by high dropout rates in Italian universities. To deal with the problem, a law introducing the mini-laurea (a first-level university degree in some subjects) has recently been passed, but it is still too early for an assessment of its effect on the labor market where higher skills are concerned.

15. Training issues were negotiated in only 22.2 percent of the industrial companies involved in plant-level bargaining in 1984–85, in 17.2 percent in 1985–86, and in 19.2 percent in 1986–87. In the agreements on the nine issues, training is eighth or ninth in importance, depending on the year considered. Moreover, among plant-level agreements dealing with training in general, those providing some form of union participation in training declined from 57 percent in 1984–85, to 36.1 percent in 1985–86, to a low 17.5 percent in 1986–87 (Baglioni and Milani 1990).

were a readiness to experiment with organizational and technological innovation, extensive labor flexibility (see section 5.3), and the largely unexpected cooperation by workplace representatives (Regini 1991). As these elements proved sufficient to ensure success, employers were relieved of both the financial costs of sustained investment in human resource development and the political costs of engaging in serious reform of the vocational training system.

The type of trade unions that the employers had to deal with also contributed to the moderate change. On the one hand, Italian trade unions were not committed to the defense of traditional job definitions but instead were culturally predisposed to support changes aimed at developing broader skills. On the other, the unions' still considerable, albeit declining, strength hindered management in considerably segmenting the labor force, in such a way as to offer training and career opportunities to only a core group of workers while relegating other workers to substandard jobs and work contracts.

5.3   Compensation: Levels, Forms, and Structure

The composition of pay in most Italian manufacturing and service industries comprises four principal components: a countrywide cost-of-living allowance (*indennità di contingenza*) linked to the already mentioned *scala mobile*;[16] a minimum wage rate fixed by industrywide national collective agreements (usually negotiated every three years), and which de facto (though not statutorily) applies to all the firms in a particular industry; a firm-specific set of bonuses, premiums, and so forth, established by collective agreements at the company and/or plant level; and a firm-specific individual component (merit pay, etc.), either unilaterally granted by management or individually negotiated.

In the early 1970s the influence of the old *scala mobile* mechanism accounted for less than 20 percent of average wage increases (see table 5.3). In the early 1980s—after a decade in which the egalitarian wage strategy carried forward by the unions combined with the operation of the flat-rate indexation system of the new *scala mobile* in a period of two-figure inflation—the wage structure was characterized by the predominant role of *contingenza* (which alone accounted for about

---

16. This sliding-scale mechanism automatically links wages to the cost-of-living index. In the late 1970s, after the reform of 1975 negotiated by the top trade unions and the employers' associations, the scala mobile amounted on average to approximately 80 percent of the inflation rate (Asap 1989; Dell'Aringa 1991).

Table 5.3
Percentage of wage increases due to *contingenza*, 1970–80

Year	Wage increase
1970	13.5
1971	12.5
1972	18.0
1973	19.9
1974	18.1
1975	24.5
1976	48.1
1977	66.7
1978	74.1
1979	79.7
1980	66.4

Source: Prometeia, cited by Somaini (1989).

40 to 50 percent of average total earnings; see table 5.4), the limited variability of average pay across firms within each industry (differentials were mainly the result of collective bargaining at the plant level), and a dramatic reduction in skill-based differentials (see table 5.5) (Santi 1981; ASAP 1989; Dell'Aringa 1991).

In the late 1980s, however, all these tendencies began to reverse. After the tripartite national agreements of 1983 and 1984, and the temporary reform of 1986, the leveling effect of the *scala mobile* slowly decreased, and its coverage of inflation growth shrank.[17] The skill differentials established by national and, especially, plant-level collective bargaining again began to increase, and even more so the individual wage drift caused by managerial concessions (see Dell'Aringa 1991; ASAP 1989). In other words, the allocative function of a more differentiated wage structure within workplaces was beginning to be, at least partially, restored.

However, the current situation is not simply one of a return to the former pattern of wider differentials across firms and industries, and between blue- and white-collar workers, which typified the 1960s. Both more flexible and ad hoc forms of compensation (largely negotiated) are increasingly becoming widespread.

---

17. In 1990 the coverage was about 45 percent of the inflation rate (Dell'Aringa 1991, 4). As already mentioned, in summer 1992 the *scala mobile* was finally abolished. New mechanisms for wage determination and minimum protection against inflation were negotiated in the tripartite national agreement of 1993.

Table 5.4
The composition of average earnings in the metalworking industry in 1983 and 1988 (in %)

	1983		1988	
	Blue collar	White collar	Blue collar	White collar
Contingenza	48.9	38.1	47.5	37.6
Minimum rates	32.1	27.9	29.0	28.0
Collective bonuses and other plant-level negotiation	15.0	14.2	16.1	14.1
Individual pay	1.3	12.0	2.1	16.3
Seniority	2.7	5.7	5.3	4.0

Source: Assolombarda, cited in Asap (1992).

Table 5.5
Skill-based differentials in 1969 and 1977

Workers	1969	1977
Skilled	155.1	126.9
Semiskilled	129.0	112.4
Unskilled	100.0	100.0
Apprentices	61.8	71.1

Source: Santi (1981).
Note: Average real wages in the manufacturing sector (unskilled workers' wage = 100).

Since the mid-1980s, research on pay policies has revealed a twofold tendency: (1) the reintroduction of incentive schemes and the experimentation of performance-related pay (PRP) schemes through company-level collective agreements, and (2) a return to more individualized wages and merit pay systems (Cella 1989; Biagioli and Cardinaleschi 1990; Della Rocca and Prosperetti 1991; Santi 1989). For instance, according to a recent survey of company-level negotiation, between 1984 and 1989 around 130 agreements introducing different forms of performance-related pay were signed, covering roughly 700,000 employees (Nomisma 1991). The first enterprises to introduce some form of PRP were the major department stores. Subsequently large companies in most of the manufacturing industries (e.g., the automobile, electronics, telecommunications, and engineering firms in the IRI public sector group) followed suit: In the late 1980s about 66 percent of the workers affected by the agreements were in the manufacturing sector (and mainly in firms with over 200 employees),[18] the remaining 34 percent comprised workers in the banking, public services, and commercial sectors. Different performance indicators were adopted, including productivity, quality, waste reduction, gross operating profit, sales, or a mix of these criteria (Nomisma 1991). It should, however, be stressed that the variable proportion of pay provided by these and other forms of collective incentives was rather low and accounted for no more than 3 to 5 percent of gross pay. A systematic survey of plant-level negotiation has revealed the spread of a new range of incentives during the recent round of decentralized collective bargaining (Baglioni and Milani 1990). Among the blue-collar workers these incentives are mostly collective—either group or enterprise based—while among white-collar employees they are much more individualized.

The move toward a more flexible pay system was the product of both a re-regulation process at the workplace (through collective agreements and some involvement of workers' representatives in the day-to-day management of the schemes adopted) and increasing managerial attention to the more skilled employees. The latter action was viewed with great concern by the unions. Evidence shows, however, that in most cases these two processes have not interfered with each other, since they apply either to different groups of employees or different kinds of work.

Two recent consequences of these combined processes have been the slightly increasing proportion of pay, which is not determined automatically or at the national level, and the broadening of pay differentials across companies and skills. There are of course many factors accounting for these changes. As far as employers are concerned, one may simply cite their interest in increasing productivity and product quality, in achieving greater flexibility in the use of work, and in boosting employee motivation (Nomisma 1991). For the unions there are at least two explanations to consider. The first is the unions' perceived need to allow, or even promote, increasing differentiation in pay levels and to reward mechanisms that remunerate higher skills, responsibility, and so forth, given that these improve their ability to represent a work force that is much more fragmented and heterogeneous than in the past.[19] The second reason is the unions'

---

18. Small firms prefer individual merit pay schemes.
19. Though it remains an exception, the national collective agreement for the banking sector is a particularly important example in that it has enabled the unions to negotiate the criteria and the procedures by which higher supervisory positions are individually compensated by management (Reyneri 1989).

concern to be a party to the redistribution of productivity gains, especially in a period when the economic performance of the enterprises appears largely dependent on cooperative and adaptive behavior and on more flexible work practices (Regini and Sabel 1989; Treu 1989). Finally, the partial overlap of employers' interests with those of the unions (which have largely retained their strength and following among workers) accounts for the fact that change is more often the outcome of negotiation than of unilateral decisions by management.

So far we have focused on the structure of compensation mainly in the private sector. We now turn to wage levels, and include the public service sector, to identify another new trend. In fact, while in the manufacturing industries real wages and salaries remained roughly stable during the 1980s,[20] in the public sector pay levels started to rise considerably in mid-decade—a period marked by public employee unrest, widespread conflict, and the rise of new rank-and-file organizations (*cobas*) (Bordogna 1988; Baldissera 1988). In the late 1980s the overall picture appeared much more diversified, even fragmented, as a consequence of these tendencies, and a more coordinated and fairer compensation system has become an important item on the IR agenda for the 1990s.

5.4   Employment Security and Staffing Arrangements

Since the postwar years the labor market in Italy has been continually regulated by rather ad hoc legislation. Labor policy is the area where state intervention in industrial relations and the participation of industrial relations actors (unions and employers' associations) in the public arena are most inextricably intertwined (Regalia 1984; Reyneri 1990). These policies are regulatory and distributive in nature, as is typical of the Italian political culture (Reyneri 1990). In other words, these policies establish rules that constrain the parties' behavior while at the same time providing them with resources and benefits.

For instance, employers are traditionally not permitted to hire and fire at will, nor can they define the terms of labor contracts as they please. They must comply with a complex set of rules frequently enforced by joint committees in which union representatives participate.

---

20. Labor costs nevertheless increased in the 1980s, as a consequence of the increasing "indirect wage," or "social contributions," paid by companies to finance the welfare system.

In principle, this system guarantees that criteria of universalism and fairness will be applied to recruitment practices, dismissals, and lay-offs.[21] In practice, however, these rules have grown increasingly rigid and inefficient over time and are eluded whenever possible. At the same time a number of income security mechanisms have been pro-gressively introduced to cushion the social impact of layoffs and in-dustrial restructuring, while giving incentives or economic support to the firms. The wage guarantee fund (*Cassa Integrazione Guadagni*), which was repeatedly adjusted to changing needs, is the most promi-nent example of this tendency.

Bearing this institutional framework in mind, we now turn to the evolution of the structure of employment during the 1980s (see table 5.6). Chiesi (1989) has observed the following trend in Italy: First, self-employed positions increased at a much faster rate than wage-earner jobs; second, regular wage-earner workers decreased; third, there were more than 2.5 million unconventional jobs in the Italian labor market; fourth, there was an extremely rapid increase in second jobs reaching more than 7 million; and fifth, immigrant nonresident work-ers more than doubled in these years. If we further consider that ap-prenticeship, work-and-training contracts, part-time, and temporary work (which are all categorized as regular jobs in official statistics), it becomes clear that a large number of workers have atypical posi-tions. The terms of employment here differ in certain respects from the traditional, steady, full-time (and fundamentally male and Italian) work that has typified Fordist mass production, especially in large establishments.[22]

A number of statistical surveys (Regalia and Ronchi 1988–90; Gan-dini 1990) suggest that even regular employment became more loosely articulated in the 1980s. One indicator of this trend was the success of temporary work-and-training contracts (legally introduced in 1984, after a pilot scheme in 1978), which made it possible for young workers to bypass legal restrictions on entry into the labor

---

21. For example, the rules on hiring generally stipulate that job applications must be submitted to a public employment agency. Direct selection of candidates is allowed only in special circumstances. For some time, however, with the tacit consent of the unions the loophole of exceptional circumstances (e.g., a need for very rare skills, the facilities granted to small firms) has legitimized illegal activity (Reyneri 1987).

22. The decrease in intermittent jobs, and especially in undeclared jobs (see table 5.6), stemmed from the more flexible labor market legislation of the 1980s which, together with new fiscal measures, enabled broad sectors of the underground economy to re-surface (Chiesi 1989, 3).

Table 5.6
Dynamics of jobs in the 1980s, according to estimates by the National Institute of Statistics (in thousands)

	1980	1988	Percent
Total jobs in Italian economy	27,501	28,701	+4.36
Employees	16,142	16,372	+1.42
Regular	13,054	12,996	−0.04
Irregular	1,630	1,540	−5.52
Not declared	343	300	−12.54
Immigrants/nonresident	274	560	+104.38
Second job	840	976	+16.19
Self-employed	11,359	12,329	+8.54
Regular	4,351	4,753	+9.24
Irregular	1,024	1,046	+0.02
Not declared	485	340	−29.90
Immigrants/nonresident	—	—	—
Second job	5,499	6,190	+12.56

Source: Istat (Chiesi 1989).

market, and another indicator was the slow but steady spread of part-time, temporary, and seasonal work (whose statutory regulation was relaxed during the decade, and especially in the late 1980s). Survey data also show that during the 1980s an increasing number of young workers entered the labor market through substandard, though legal, forms of employment and that mobility across firms and industries grew considerably (Chiesi 1990).[23]

To conclude, in the 1980s employment became less stable, and long-term attachments to firms decreased. These trends reflect increasing reliance on both more skilled *and* less stable human resources, and not on the unskilled and stable labor force of the past, in order to guarantee quality standards in production (Annibaldi 1989). They were also the outcome of the massive restructuring efforts and consequent labor force adjustments undertaken by most large manufacturing enterprises during the decade.

An full list of the consequences of the different labor reductions has yet to be drawn up. On the whole, though, we may say that the social consequences were less dramatic than expected, although there were

23. According to this survey, at least in the affluent region of Lombardy, workers were favorably inclined toward mobility and change. A stable job is not considered as important a priority as in the recent past.

striking differences depending upon the characteristics of the local economies. The Italian welfare system performed relatively well in this respect—at least compared with the systems of other countries—and it was mostly due to the (unwitting) effects of the *cassa integrazione guadagni*, which directly assisted worker mobility across firms or in some cases cushioned retiremens (or early retirements) by transitions to substandard jobs, thus preventing a great surge in unemployment and reducing the impact on household budgets (Scamuzzi 1989). A number of case studies have shown that collective bargaining among the parties was the principal mechanism by which existing income security mechanisms and welfare programs adapted to the particularities of individual firm's needs for efficiency and worker desire for employee security.[24]

Micro-level analyses (using case studies or surveys) of industrial relations at the company level have moreover shown that since the early 1980s continuous formal and informal bargaining, together with information/consultation practices in workplaces, has been responsible for the flexible and unusual forms of employment that have met with the consent of the social partners.[25] We may therefore conclude that the reform of labor market legislation during the 1980s, which led to a general framework for a law in 1991 (law 223/1991), was somehow preceded and prepared for by the mutual accommodation among the social actors at the local level. The 1991 law is much less regulatory in nature than its predecessor in that its provisions largely require the explicit agreement of parties and/or union control for its enforcement.[26] The new law is based on an obvious trade-off: Employers are allowed more flexibility in managing human resources while unions are given (or, better, gain formal recognition of) a greater say in the process of industrial adjustment and continual innovation (Ambroso 1991).

In conclusion, the last decade was a period of legal innovation rather than simply of deregulation. This was a consequence of both the new needs of the post-Fordist economy and the unions' commit-

---

24. Particularly interesting here are cases studies by Regini and Sabel (1989).

25. For instance, a survey of collective bargaining at the company-level in Emilia Romagna has shown that negotiation on special employment circumstances (i.e., training-and-work contracts, temporary, part-time, seasonal work) is second only to the negotiation of working time and is more frequent than negotiation on wages and bonuses (Gandini 1990).

26. For instance, special contracts, temporary and seasonal work, are allowed as long as they are covered by collective agreements.

ment to change made possible by their institutional involvement and, more important, by their continual presence in the workplace.

5.5   Governance

For a long time after World War II, Italian management largely neglected issues relating to personnel policies or IR strategies. The weak organization of the unions, especially at the plant level, combined with high unemployment due to the weak economy, simply was not capable of encouraging managers to invest in developing modern human resource management practices. Spontaneous and ad hoc procedures consequently prevailed. With few exceptions (most notably Olivetti) either authoritarian or paternalistic managerial styles predominated, with the personnel director performing a somewhat marginal role in corporate management.

The backwardness of Italian IR/HR managerial practices became suddenly evident during the collective mobilization of late 1960s and early 1970s. During the 1970s traditional practices changed rapidly: In most manufacturing companies the personnel manager, and in the larger ones also the IR/HR specialist (mainly responsible for the management of conflict and day-to-day dealings in factory councils), became key actors in the board room.

In the early 1980s the picture changed again. In those years new, differentiated, and even divergent trends came to the fore. Initially the decreasing pressure from unions in the workplace and in the strategic management of companies with conglomerate organizational changes[27] showed a "shift from employment systems and internal labor markets based on the governance of collective transactions and union bargaining to employment systems and internal labor markets based on the governance of individual and group-centered transactions" (Camuffo and Costa 1991, 14). Implicit in this view was that traditional personnel management, and a fortiori the IR function, would progressively decline in importance. Nevertheless, although in the early 1980s this tendency could be observed in cases such as the metal and automotive industries, which were marked by declining

---

27. These changes were modeled on (1) deverticalization in large companies and (2) various forms of hierarchical coordination in small ones (Regini and Sabel 1989; Lorenzoni 1990; Camuffo and Costa 1991); both processes entailed some reallocation of human resources and technological process/product innovations requiring larger work force involvement.

union membership and strength, the broader evidence suggests a rather more complex picture.

In the first place, from an organizational viewpoint, empirical studies show that throughout the decade, there was a growth and diffusion of personnel departments, and of IR specialists within them, even in small- and medium-sized companies (Regalia and Ronchi 1988–92). Second, from a functional perspective, there is no doubt that increasing importance was given to the roles and tasks of HR specialists in dealing with issues such as selection procedures and criteria, career development, training and compensation policies, and direct communications. Simultaneously, however, this new tendency frequently coexisted with the ongoing operation of the IR function, which occupied an increasingly crucial role as plant-level negotiation on flexibility grew to massive proportions (Regini and Sabel 1989). In other cases the intensification of IR practices led to the devolving of some IR functions to the line. Third, the early 1980s saw the experimental introduction of innovative forms of cooperative IR, whereby the unions and worker representatives were given a number of formal responsibilities in the management of labor. The most outstanding example here was the *Protocollo*, or framework agreement, which covered the companies belonging to the IRI public sector group (*Protocollo IRI*). Signed by the social parties in 1984, this agreement inspired similar forms of innovative IR in other state-controlled businesses. As Carinci (1986) has pointed out, the general philosophy of the *Protocollo* was closely akin to that of German codetermination. Its aim was to prevent workplace conflict, as far as possible, by providing structures and procedures for interaction and joint decision making on a number of critical issues. The research available (Ronchi 1986), however, shows that the original system proved rather complicated to operate, so it was subsequently revised.

Similar trends can also be discerned in the private manufacturing sector, and likewise in some service industries. According to a large amount of empirical evidence (Negrelli and Treu 1992; Regalia and Ronchi 1988–92; Regini and Sabel 1989), during the decade a highly differentiated range of information, consultation, and joint decision practices developed, and they involved works councils and the unions more or less formally in the day-to-day management of work and in some more strategic decisions (see table 5.7). Finally in the early 1990s, demands for "new IR" of a more cooperative or participative kind have frequently provoked political debate among the

Table 5.7
Works councils' involvement in the day-to-day management of work in Lombardy, according to plant size (in %)

Issues before management councils	50–100 employees	101–500 employees	>500 employees
Yearly calendar, vacations	84.0	94.8	97.3
Overtime	38.2	57.8	70.8
Internal mobility (across departments)	20.8	50.3	70.4
Effects of technological/ organizational change	13.9	50.0	60.0
Training for blue-collar workers	16.5	41.2	63.1
Training for white-collar workers	11.7	14.4	45.0

Source: IRES Lombardia survey on workplace IR, 1989 (Regalia and Ronchi 1990).

unions and employers, although it still appears unlikely that formal framework agreements will be reached in the near future.

5.6 Conclusion

This chapter has sought to analyze recent developments in Italian IR/HR practices. Yet three warnings are in order. First, focusing on a given set of practices does not entail that they are invariably the most important over time and that other issues may not come to acquire similar or even greater significance in a system of industrial relations. For instance, the issue of working time—which, for our present purposes, we have discussed together with work organization—became increasingly important in Italy during the 1980s. By contrast, an issue like social welfare declined in relevance, whereas in the past it had been a good indicator of the state of labor relations. Second, one should not take the practices discussed here to be equally representative of labor relations in all countries. German industrial relations, for example, place more importance on the regulation of skill formation than on the regulation of employment or staffing, while the reverse is the case in Spain. To give another example, during the 1980s the regulation of work organization was an issue more central to industrial relations in Italy than it was in Britain, where pay was regarded as more important.

Finally, concentrating on specific IR/HR practices should not in-
duce one to overlook more general trends in IR policies and styles. To
give just one example, the generalized and powerful process of decentralization of Italian (and European) industrial relations during
the 1980s cannot be fully appreciated if an analysis only addresses
changes in a given set of IR/HR practices. Attention must also focus
on the reorganization of roles in management structure, on the frequency and character of labor-employer meetings at the company
level compared with those at a national level, and on the changing role
of interest associations in the coordination of their members' activities.

Let us now summarize some critical developments in Italian industrial relations of the 1980s. First, the decade witnessed a decline in tripartite concertation, and in political bargaining in general. This was
accompanied by the emergence of companies (or small firm districts)
as the protagonists of successful economic adjustment and as the
most important *loci* for change in industrial relations. The resulting
increase in company-level bargaining and activity, however, led not
to the disappearance of work regulation at the national level but to an
overlap between national and local institutions and systems of interaction without a clearly specified division of roles.[28]

Second, in Italy as in most other western European countries, the
shift of the center of gravity of industrial relations toward the workplace was attended by the growing strategic uncertainty and eclectic
pragmatism of all who were involved (Streeck 1987; Regini 1994). As a
result there are today more heterogeneous national systems of labor
relations than was the case fifteen years ago. It is therefore harder to
contrast, say, centralized and decentralized or adversarial and cooperative systems, since each of these is more accurately described as a
specific mix of such features (Locke 1994).

Third, this increasingly important IR activity at the company and
workplace levels centered principally on labor flexibility. Whereas in
the late 1970s and early 1980s external or numerical flexibility was the
key factor in industrial restructuring, internal or functional as well as
temporal flexibility grew steadily in importance. Most companies
first sought to adjust by laying off workers, which they were enabled
to do by the *cassa integrazione* (wage guarantee fund). They rapidly
discovered, however, that work reorganization, skill development,

---

28. The first major attempt to bring order to these unregulated, overlapping mechanisms was the reform of the collective bargaining system initiated by the 1993 tripartite
agreement.

and adaptability of the working schedule were more important factors in competitiveness. Although workers' representatives helped, to a large extent, achieve the consensus-based management of redundancies in the early 1980s, employers soon realized that cooperation over internal and temporal flexibility could be obtained in exchange for restrictions on external flexibility (if they also gave up their attempt to introduce downward wage flexibility). The Italian experience suggests therefore that although greater flexibility, in all its forms, might theoretically be better for employers, institutional constraints apply more stringently to some forms rather than others. Hence the likelihood of achieving certain forms of flexibility may be conditional on a willingness to relinquish others.

Fourth (and this is closely connected with the previous point), the 1980s saw no major assault on union rights, prerogatives, resources, and recognition—although it would have been possible for both legislators and employers to launch one. Attempts to develop a network of direct employer/employee relations based on direct communication policies and quality circles increased, but in the end they complemented traditional collective relations and did not substitute for them. These processes resulted in a new type of de facto, pragmatic cooperation between managers and workplace representatives. This cooperation developed initially in industries exposed to international competition and became an important factor in their ability to adjust to new market conditions. In sharp contrast, confrontational relations and a sort of militant business unionism came to characterize the public services and other sectors sheltered against competition (Bordogna 1988; Baldissera 1988).

Turning to explanatory factors, developments in Italy in the 1980s suggest that institutional variables were crucial in that they largely determined the range of options available to firms or else guided their choices among alternative strategies. Conversely, technological and market constraints placed pressure on existing institutional arrangements—although these usually showed considerable resilience and underwent change that was often more piecemeal than dramatic. The Italian case also demonstrates that, among institutional factors, special attention should be reserved for not just industry or national arrangements, such as legal rights, but also to the type of trade unions that employers (and governments) have to deal with. This means that the varying strength, organization, strategy, and attitudes toward change within the unions are likely to exert a strong influence on the way that different IR/HR practices develop and are regulated.

References

Ambroso, G. M. 1991. Nuova legge sul mercato del lavoro, nuovi impegni per le relazioni industriali. *Notiziario del Lavoro* 50:3–6.

ANCQUI. 1987. *Lo sviluppo dei circoli della qualità in Italia.* Mimeo.

Annibaldi, P. 1989. *La Confindustria e la legge n.56/1987.* In Società e Lavoro, ed., *Stato, Regioni, Parti Sociali e Mercato del Lavoro.* Naples: Jovene.

ASAP. 1989. *1989. Rapporto sui salari.* Milan: F. Angeli.

ASAP. 1992. *1991. Rapporto sui salari.* Milan: F. Angeli.

Ascoli, U., ed. 1984. *Welfare State all'italiana.* Bari: Laterza.

Baglioni, G., and R. Milani, eds. 1990. *La contrattazione collettiva nelle aziende industriali in Italia.* Milan: F. Angeli.

Baldissera, A. 1988. *La svolta dei quarantamila: Dai quadri Fiat ai Cobas.* Milan: Ed. di Comunità.

Biagioli, M., and S. Cardinaleschi. 1990. Retribuzione legata ai risultati e incentivi tradizionali nella recente contrattazione aziendale. *Prospettiva sindacale* 75/76:199–222.

Bianchi, G. 1988. La ristrutturazione industriale negli anni '80, fra tentazioni liberistiche e la sperimentazione di nuovi modelli partecipativi. *Quaderni ISRIL* 3:43–59.

Biliotti, E., and G. Della Rocca. 1986. *Azione sindacale e mutamenti dei processi produttivi.* In CESOS, ed., *Le relazioni sindacali in Italia, Rapporto 1984–85.* Rome: Ed. Lavoro.

Bonazzi, G. 1991. Qualità e consenso. L'evoluzione del lavoro operaio alla Fiat Mirafiori (1980–1990). *Rassegna italiana di sociologia* 1:3–24.

Bordogna, L. 1988. *"Arcipelago Cobas": Frammentazione della rappresentanza e conflitti di lavoro.* In P. Corbetta and R. Leonardi, eds., *Politica in Italia. Edizione 1988.* Bologna: Il Mulino.

Bordogna, L., and G. C. Provasi. 1989. *La conflittualità.* In G. P. Cella and T. Treu, eds., *Relazioni industriali: Manuale per l'analisi dell'esperienza italiana.* Bologna: Il Mulino.

Butera, F. 1987. *Dalle occupazioni industriali alle nuove professioni.* Milan: F. Angeli.

Cammelli, M. 1982. Sindacato e istituzioni: La presenza del sindacato nei collegi della pubblica amministrazione. *Prospettiva sindacale* 44:83–117.

Camuffo, A., and G. Costa. 1991. Human Resource Management and Strategic Innovation: The Italian Case. University of Venice, Department of Business Economics and Management. Mimeo. April.

Capecchi, V. 1993. Istruzione, formazione professionale e mercato del lavoro. *Il Mulino* 2:319–34.

Carinci, F. 1986. *Il protocollo Iri nella dinamica delle relazioni industriali.* In CESOS, ed., *Le relazioni sindacali in Italia. Rapporto 1984–1985.* Rome: Ed. Lavoro.

Cella, G. P. 1989a. *Regulation in Italian Industrial Relations.* In P. Lange and M. Regini, eds., *State, Market and Social Regulation.* Cambridge: Cambridge University Press.

Cella, G. P., ed. 1989b. *Il ritorno degli incentivi.* Milan: F. Angeli.

Cella, G. P., ed. 1991. *Nuovi attori nelle relazioni industriali*. Milan: F. Angeli.

Cella, G. P., and T. Treu, eds. 1989. *Relazioni industriali: Manuale per l'analisi dell'esperienza italiana*. Bologna: Il Mulino.

Chiesi, A. M. 1988. *Orario flessibile ed effetti di dislocazione delle rigidità temporali*. In M. Regini, ed., *La sfida della flessibilità*. Milan: F. Angeli.

Chiesi, A. M. 1989. *Lo sviluppo dei lavori atipici. Un quadro di riferimento concettuale e un tentativo di spiegazione*. IRES/Papers, Collana Discussioni 14.

Chiesi, A. M. 1990. *I lavoratori dipendenti lombardi. Strategie di mercato e azione collettiva*, IRES/Papers, Collana Ricerche 27.

Citarella, F., and I. Vitale. 1988. L'esperienza dei circoli della qualità nella industria alimentare. *Quaderni ISRIL* 2:3–27.

Colasanto, M., ed. 1987. *Innovazione e regolazione nell'impresa*. Milan: F. Angeli.

Dell'Aringa, C. 1991. *Collective Bargaining and Wage Determination in Italian Manufacturing*. Milan, CRELI Discussion Papers 22.

Della Rocca, G., and M. Zoccatelli. 1985. *Ristrutturazioni tecnologiche e nuove relazioni sindacali nell'editoria*. In CESOS, ed., *Le relazioni sindacali in Italia, Rapporto 1983–84*. Rome: Ed. Lavoro.

Della Rocca, G., and L. Prosperetti, eds. 1991. *Salari e produttività: Esperienze internazionali e italiane*. Milan: F. Angeli.

Dina, A. 1991. Nuove tecnologie: Chi le giudica? *Meta* 1/2:43–45.

Falcucci, G., and A. Mesirca. 1983. *La rappresentanza imprenditoriale negli organi della pubblica amministrazione*. Rome: Asap-Intersind.

Federlombarda-Intersind. 1983–90. *L'occupazione nell'industria lombarda: Situazione, caratteristiche, previsioni*. Rapporti annuali. Milan.

Ferner, A., and R. Hyman. 1992. *Italy: Between Political Exchange and Micro-Corporatism*. In A. Ferner and R. Hyman, eds., *Industrial Relations in the New Europe*. Oxford: Blackwell.

Franzosi, R. 1989. Strike data in search of a theory: The Italian case in the postwar period. *Politics and Society* 42:453–87.

Galgano, A. 1990. Quality circle movement in the Italian manufacturing and service industries: Eight years of experience. Paper presented in the International Convention of QC in Tokyo.

Gandini, A. 1990. Flessibilità, cambiamenti produttivi e contrattazione sindacale negli anni '80. *Sociologia del lavoro*:38/39:153–65.

Garonna, P., et al. 1987. *Il ruolo delle parti sociali nella formazione professionale in Italia*. Berlin: CEDEFOP.

Golden, M. 1988. *Austerity and Its Opposition: Persistent Radicalism in the Italian Labor Movement*. Ithaca: Cornell University Press.

Guidotti, D. 1986. *Strategia generale e azione decentrata*. Milan: F. Angeli.

IRES Toscana. 1991. *La complessità e la partecipazione*. Florence: EMF.

ISAP. 1987. *Le relazioni fra amministrazione e sindacati*, Archivio no. 4, NS, 2 vols. Milan: Giuffrè.

ISFOL. 1989. *Rapporto ISFOL 1989*. Milan: F. Angeli.

ISFOL. 1990. *Caratterizzazioni regionali del sistema di formazione professionale*. Milan: F. Angeli.

Lange, P., and M. Regini, eds. 1989. *State, Market, and Social Regulation: New Perspectives on Italy*. Cambridge: Cambridge University Press.

Lanzalaco, L. 1990. *Dall'impresa all'associazione. Le organizzazioni degli imprenditori: La Confindustria in prospettiva comparata*. Milan: F. Angeli.

Locke, R. 1995. *Remaking the Italian Economy*. Ithaca: Cornell University Press.

Locke, R., and S. Negrelli. 1989. *Il caso Fiat-Auto*. In M. Regini and C. Sabel, eds., *Strategie di riaggiustamento industriale*. Bologna: Il Mulino.

Lorenzoni, G. 1990. *L'architettura di sviluppo delle imprese minori*. Bologna: Il Mulino.

Marchisio, O., ed. 1988. *Frammenti di innovazione*. Milan: F. Angeli.

Marsden, D. 1982. Collective bargaining and industrial adjustment in Britain, France, Italy and W. Germany. Unpublished paper.

Marsden, D. 1992. European Integration and the Integration of European Labor Markets. *Labour* 6:3–35.

Martinelli, A., and A. M. Chiesi. 1989. *Italy*. In T. Bottomore and R. J. Brym, eds., *The Capitalist Class: An International Study*. London: Harvester Wheatsheaf.

Medusa, G. 1983. *L'impresa tra produttività e consenso: Il caso Alfa Romeo*. Milan: Etas Libri.

Napoli, M. 1989. *Il quadro giuridico-istituzionale*. In G. P. Cella and T. Treu, eds., *Relazioni idustriali*. Bologna: Il Mulino.

Negrelli, S., and T. Treu, eds. 1992. *Le scelte dell'impresa fra autorità e consenso*. Milan: F. Angeli.

NOMISMA. 1991. Retribuzioni, produttività e redditività. *Quaderni di industria e sindacato* 29:11–81.

Patriarca, S., and P. Negro. 1991. Contrattazione interconfederale. In CESOS, ed., *Le relazioni sindacali in Italia, Rapporto 1989–90*. Rome: Ed. Lavoro.

Perulli, P. 1986. *Pirelli 1980–1985. Le relazioni industriali*. Milan: F. Angeli.

Regalia, I. 1984. *Le politiche del lavoro*. In U. Ascoli, ed., *Welfare State all'italiana*. Bari: Laterza.

Regalia, I. 1990. *Al posto del conflitto: Le relazioni industriali nel terziario*. Bologna: Il Mulino.

Regalia, I. 1992. New forms of organisation and direct involvement of the workers in Italy. European Foundation for the Improvement of Living and Working Conditions. Dublin. Working Paper 92/11.

Regalia, I. 1994. Italy: The costs and benefits of informality. In J. Rogers and W. Streeck (eds.), *Works Councils: Consultation, Representation and Cooperation*. Chicago: University of Chicago Press.

Regalia, I., and M. Regini. 1989. Sindacati, istituzioni, sistema politico. In G. P. Cella and T. Treu, eds., *Relazioni industriali*. Bologna: Il Mulino.

Regalia, I., M. Regini, and E. Reyneri. 1978. Labour conflicts and industrial relations in Italy. In C. Crouch and A. Pizzorno, eds., *The Resurgence of Class Conflict in Western Europe Since 1968*, vol. 1. London: Macmillan.

Regalia, I., and R. Ronchi. 1988–92. *Le relazioni industriali nelle imprese lombarde. Annual survey*. Milan: IRES/Lombardia.

Regini, M. 1980. Labour unions, industrial action and politics. In P. Lange and S. Tarrow, eds., *Italy in Transition*. London: F. Cass.

Regini, M., ed. 1988. *La sfida della flessibilità*. Milan: F. Angeli.

Regini, M. 1991. Capitale e lavoro: Nuove frontiere della collaborazione. *MicroMega* 4:174–83.

Regini, M. 1995. *Uncertain Boundaries: The Social and Political Construction of European Economies*. Cambridge: Cambridge University Press.

Regini, M., and C. M. Sabel, eds. 1989. *Strategie di riaggiustamento industriale*. Bologna: Il Mulino.

Reyneri, E. 1989a. The Italian labor market: Between state control and social regulation. In P. Lange and M. Regini, eds., *State, Market and Social Regulation*. Cambridge: Cambridge University Press.

Reyneri, E. 1989b. Contrattazione decentrata e politica retributiva aziendale. In Società e Lavoro, ed., *Il Sistema Retributivo Verso gli Anni '90*. Naples: Jovene.

Reyneri, E. 1990. La politica del lavoro in Italia: Attori e processi decisionali. In B. Dente, ed., *Le politiche pubbliche in Italia*. Bologna: Il Mulino.

Ronchi, R. 1986. Protocollo Iri: Una indagine sullo stato di applicazione. Milan, IRES/Papers, Collana Ricerche 11.

Santi, P. 1981. I differenziali retributivi nell'industria italiana e la politica sindacale negli anni '70. *Rivista internazionale di scienze sociali*.

Santi, P. 1989. Economia della partecipazione e relazioni industriali. *Giornale di diritto del lavoro e delle relazioni industriali* 4:634–70.

Scamuzzi, S. 1989. Cassa integrazione e riconversione lavorativa: Rilevanza dei risultati della ricerca per le politiche del lavoro. In Società e Lavoro, ed., *Stato, Regioni, Parti Sociali e Mercato del Lavoro*. Naples: Jovene.

Somaini, E. 1989. Politica salariale e politica economica. In G. P. Cella and T. Treu, eds., *Relazioni industriali*. Bologna: Il Mulino.

Streeck, W. 1987. The uncertainties of management in the management of uncertainty. *Work, Employment and Society* 1:281–308.

Treu, T. 1987. Italian industrial relations in the past ten years. *Bulletin of Comparative Labour Relations* 16:167–81.

Treu, T. 1989. La retribuzione: Il quadro istituzionale. In Società e Lavoro, ed., *Il Sistema Retributivo Verso gli Anni '90*. Napoli: Jovene.

6

Inertial Choices: An Overview of Spanish Human Resources, Practices and Policies

Víctor Pérez-Díaz
Juan Carlos Rodríguez

This chapter discusses Spanish human resource management practices and policies starting with the democratic transition and the establishment of a Western-style system of industrial relations in the mid-1970s. However, the developments in the field during this period can only be understood against the background of previous political, economic, and cultural processes, between the early 1960s and the mid-1970s, to which some attention will also be paid.

The discussion provides an overview of a number of human resources practices and policies: job stability, compensation practices, vocational training, work organization, and labor mobility, industrial relations, and corporate culture. Since empirical data are fairly limited and uneven, this can only be a first, tentative step in the process of mapping out the field, asking questions, and advancing some lines of inquiry. This chapter is a starting point for research in progress, from which we intend to move into several sectors and case studies that will enable us to revise our original assessment.

A variety of researchers on both sides of the Atlantic have been trying to establish a theory about the transition from one system of production, usually labeled Fordist, to another quite different one and to show that this change is driven by innovations in technology and work organization at the workplace (Piore and Sabel 1984; Streeck 1992; Boyer 1986; for a more detached view see Hyman 1988). Although this is a very stimulating intellectual exploration, we suspect that the connection between the different elements of these various productive systems is itself quite loose and is contingent on too many exogenous factors, mostly of a political and cultural character. Therefore we consider that these explorations (as they stand today) provide us with suggestive heuristics (Homans 1967) but not proper theories through which we can understand recent changes in industrial relations and human resource management practices.

This chapter will explore the loose connections among several human resources practices and policies in Spain. The following introductory section outlines the changes and continuities in the political and economic context of Spain from the early 1960s to the early 1990s, and sketches the main institutional features of the Spanish industrial relations system. In our view, however, contextual and institutional constraints are not enough to explain the human resources practices that will be discussed later. Institutions certainly matter. But traditions and the understandings that actors bring to bear on these institutions, and the uses those actors make of them, are of equal or greater importance (Pérez-Díaz 1993).

6.1   Contextual Constraints: Politics, the Economy, and Industrial Relations Institutions

Politics

The Spanish political context changed dramatically in the mid-1970s when Spain became a full-fledged liberal democracy. However, the political climate of the country had begun changing about fifteen to twenty years before the transition to democracy. Those changes had considerable consequences for labor politics and industrial relations. Three key developments took place in the wake of a period of sustained economic growth and full employment and in response to an emerging independent labor movement that the state, de facto, tolerated. First, the main lines of labor policies aimed at providing employment stability, a legacy of the corporatist/fascist period of the 1940s and 1950s, were confirmed. Second, the basic building blocks (institutions, economic resources, and personnel) of a state-sponsored welfare system were put in place. Third, a rather baroque situation was allowed to emerge in industrial relations. Alongside the facade of the existing vertical unions, which were more or less subservient to the political class, a quasi-Western system of industrial relations developed. The period was characterized by the development of collective bargaining, frequent strikes, and the emergence of independent unions, which were subject to continual state harassment but not the repression that had destroyed their predecessors in the aftermath of the civil war (Pérez-Díaz 1993; Martínez Lucio 1992).

The political transition of the mid-1970s was of paramount importance to critical areas of Spanish life. The political institutions were thoroughly transformed, and there was a very significant turnover of political personnel. But we should not lose sight of important continuities both between the predemocratic and democratic politics and, after the transition, between the center governments of 1977 to 1982 and the socialist governments thereafter. The Constitution of 1978 confirmed the fundamental tenets of a market economy and established formal guarantees for the existing practices of free association, collective bargaining, and industrial action, thereby dismantling the remnants of the authoritarian institutions of Francoism. The Workers' Statute of 1980 preserved most of the labor market regulations of the past, only to be partly altered after 1984.

A climate of political consensus at a time of momentous symbolic and institutional political change and, above all, the goal of social consensus and wage moderation at a time of acute economic crisis combined to push political and social actors into a series of corporatist pacts between 1977 and 1986 (Pérez-Díaz 1985). This was followed by a more ambiguous relationship between the state and the unions. Despite visible and genuine quarrels between the socialist government and the main unions (with the socialist union UGT [Unión General de Trabajadores] in the forefront of these conflicts), some basic understandings were nonetheless respected. Following the national strike of December 14, 1988, the government backed off from some of its key proposals for labor market reform (reform that the unions had objected to) and increased public spending (in pensions, and unemployment subsidies).

The Economy

Spain's economy has experienced two very different stages since the 1960s. During the period of sustained economic growth (annual growth rates of 7 percent and an inflation rate of 6 percent) between 1960 and 1973 (IMF 1989, 1991), fundamental changes took place. Most notable was the transformation of a semitraditional economy with a large agricultural sector into a modern one with a significant industrial sector in both basic industries and consumer goods. The Spanish economy became integrated into, and increasingly dependent upon, Western economies. Full employment during the period was maintained only because about one million Spaniards migrated to other West European countries in search of employment. Exports and imports to Western Europe became more important as the external sector (imports plus exports) grew from 17 to 31 percent of GDP between 1960 and 1973 (Viñas et al. 1979). The inflow of foreign capital and foreign tourists were equally significant.

The mid-1970s proved to be a watershed for the Spanish economy. Inflation jumped from 10 to 18 percent between 1973 and 1976. When Franco died in November 1975, the country faced immense political uncertainties. For the next few years the political class focused its attention on urgent political matters, and the economy and economic policies were ignored. In the meanwhile social demands escalated, unemployment rose to 7 percent, and inflation to 26 percent. The stage was set for a series of austerity policies that were pursued by successive governments through protracted corporatist bargaining that lasted until the mid-1980s. By the end of this long period of crisis, inflation had been reduced to about 6 percent, where it remains to this day. However, Spain's high rate of unemployment (about 20 percent in the mid-1980s) exposed the basic weaknesses of both the Spanish economy and the government's corporatist economic policy arrangements.[1]

Spain shared in the mild prosperity of the late 1980s, when she became a full member of the European Community. The economy grew at about 4.5 percent a year between 1986 and 1990. However, this had only a limited effect in reducing unemployment to about 16 percent of the active population by 1990. At the same time the government committed itself to, or allowed itself to drift into, an inconsistent mix of economic policies. It tried to contain inflation through relatively tight monetary policies. Expansionary budgetary policies fueled the public deficit, the financing of which required fairly high interest rates.

The government managed to muddle through the late 1980s and reach the magical year 1992, when the seriousness of the economic crisis over this period finally exploded. In 1992 economic growth was only 1 percent and was forecast to be negative in 1993 (BBV 1993); unemployment had rebounded to about 23 percent by the end of 1993, and the public debt had reached about 60 percent of GDP by 1994. At the same time the Spanish economy had become more diversified

---

1. Part of the increase in the unemployment rate can be attributed to the return of Spanish migrants from Europe in the late 1970s, and the industrial restructuring policies of the early 1980s (Viñals et al. 1990; Segura and González 1992).

over the years, with the growth of services and with manufacturing contributing a smaller share of the country's total GNP. In 1992 industry and services accounted for 27 percent and 60 percent of GDP, respectively, compared to 29 percent and 55 percent in 1975 (BBV 1993).[2] The economy is more interconnected with world markets, but its high trade deficit (7.26 percent of GDP in 1992) reflects its competitive weaknesses in world markets (BBV 1993).

Industrial Relations

The system of industrial relations has been characterized by a combination of change and continuity. Although, on surface, the contrast between the Francoist system and the present one is striking, some of the most important present-day actors, practices, and institutions came into being in the 1960s. At that time collective bargaining, which was made possible by a 1958 law (Amsden 1974), became common practice at the industrial or provincial level, and to a limited degree at the company level. The decriminalization of strikes in 1965 was a companied by growing official toleration of strikes and as many as 1.5 million workdays were lost per year in 1973 to 1975. Semi-spontaneous organizations, most notably the Comisiones Obreras (CCOO), took the lead in bargaining and strike activities, and became semi-institutionalized in the second half of the 1960s (Foweraker 1989).

These Jurados de Empresa were established under a 1948 law that allowed workers to choose their own representatives. They maintained connections with opposition parties, clandestine unions, and churches, and took advantage of existing institutions for labor representation in the factories. In the new sociopolitical climate of the 1960s, these elections were free enough to encourage a new wave of militants, primarily those affiliated with the CCOO, the USO (Unión Sindical Obrera)—later to split and become the socialist UGT—to participate and win most of the positions in the local committees for their own candidates in 1967. A period of ambiguity followed, with uncertain and rather erratic moves on all sides. But by the time of the transition period (from 1975 to 1978), a new system had been in the making for more than a decade, awaiting formal legal recognition.

---

2. On changes in the internal structure of manufacturing and services in the 1970s and 1980s, see Segura and González (1992) and Cuadrado Roura (1992).

The Constitution and the new legal framework allowed for a dual system of labor representation through the existing institutions. At the plant level, works councils (*Comités de Empresa*) or individual delegates in smaller firms coexisted with local sections of national (or regional) unions, mainly the communist CCOO and the socialist UGT. However, in contrast to the German dual system of local representation, there was no clear-cut division of labor between the *Comités de Empresa* and the unions since both of them could and did conduct negotiations or call a strike. This institutional ambiguity was compounded by the fact that most members of the *Comités* won their posts as union candidates (Martínez Lucio 1992; Escobar 1992). Collective bargaining is conducted at various levels, primarily at the industrial/provincial level where the unions, and not the works councils, do the bargaining. Until 1986, negotiations were conducted within the guidelines of a series of nationwide social pacts. In terms of the legal principle of *erga omnes*, the results of collective bargaining apply to all workers and employers in a given bargaining domain and not only to the parties to the agreement.

Labor and business are usually represented in collective bargaining and social pact negotiations by the two main unions, CCOO and UGT, and by the CEOE (Confederación Española de Organizaciones Empresariales), an all-encompassing business association that was set up shortly after the democratic transition (Martínez 1984). The unions are generally considered as major players in public life. Their membership, however, has never been very large and has decreased markedly over the past fifteen years. By 1993 union density was estimated to be around 10 percent. This would be even lower if unemployed and retired people were not included. The state grants CCOO and UGT the status of "most representative" unions nationwide on the basis of the results of the elections to the works councils held every four years.

The political and economic context has provided Spain's social and political actors with major challenges and constraints. The system of industrial relations institutions has been established in the process of responding to these challenges and constraints. The key to understanding the choices made by the main social and political actors lies in the traditions and understandings that they have brought to bear in those institutions, as they developed over time. To summarize the argument, in the Spanish case we think that the (macro) institutions of the social pacts (explicit before 1986, and tacit thereafter) and the

(micro) institutions of industrial/provincial and company-level collective bargaining and local dual representation have allowed for a
diversity of human resources policies and practices. The choices
made reflect a shared set of understandings between labor, business,
and most of the political class after the transition. These understandings were founded upon the following beliefs: that social pacts were
essential to handle the uncertainties of the time, that keeping inflation
under control was the key provision of those pacts, that labor market
regulations inherited from the Francoist years could be tinkered with
but not changed fundamentally, that increasing the public sector and
developing the welfare state was necessary for the redefinition of the
country as part of a democratic and prosperous Europe, and that
large-scale unemployment was a fact of life to which people would
have to adjust (if necessary through reliance on the extended family
and recourse to the underground economy).[3] By contrast, little attention was usually given to the themes of competitiveness in world
markets or productivity. Those understandings, and the predisposi-
tions that came with them, have had important effects on the human
resources practices and policies which we discuss below. Employment security and compensation have been most salient in the public
debate and in the conflicts and agreements between the state, unions,
and businesses.

Employment Security

For more than forty years the Spanish work force has enjoyed a high
degree of employment security. Changes in the political regime have
made little difference in this respect (except for some recent variations
which we will discuss later). The reasons for this state of affairs have
had little to do with any purposeful attempt on the part of government or business to increase workers' commitment to their workplace
or companies, nor have the workers understood legal provisions for
employment security along these lines either. In the Francoist period
these provisions were part of the social contract the authoritarian
state tried to establish with labor. In terms of the corporatist mentality
of the time, free mobility of labor was seen as a source of social dis-
order: one of the many failures of a market economy that a corporate

---

3. In 1990, 70 percent of the unemployed lived in a family where at least one member
received a wage income (calculated from data in *Encuesta sobre la Estructura Social
Española*).

system was required to correct. Employment contracts between individual workers and entrepreneurs were regarded as completely different from civil contracts: as status rather than contractual relationship. This intellectual construction not only fit the traditional doctrines of social catholicism or fascism but also the political requirements of the regime. Franco had won a civil war where organized labor had been on the other side. Anarchists, socialists, and communists who had led the fight against Franco's armies were executed by the thousands in the aftermath of Franco's victory. Victory was followed by the banning of unions, parties, and strikes. Left without leaders, associations, and any organizational or political means of defense, the working class was, however, granted employment security. This was supposed to be the cornerstone of a set of social policies that, in ensuring a modicum of "social justice," would provide Franco's regime with a corresponding modicum of political legitimacy.

The basic provisions of the Francoist labor legislation of the Fuero del Trabajo of 1938, and the Ley del Contrato de Trabajo of 1944 covering employment security remain in place today. Except in the case of "just cause," dismissals are forbidden. However, legal provisions alone can not explain how, by the time of the democratic transition, there was a well-established tradition that dismissal without just cause required long procedures and costly compensation. The legal provisions were reinforced by the experience of sustained economic growth and concomitant full employment in the 1960s and early 1970s. Under these circumstances employment security came to be taken for granted, as a fact of life.

Employment security in Spain during the last ten to fifteen years must be discussed in the light of the country's experience with massive, unprecedented and persistent rates of unemployment. Between 1970 and 1975—the so-called good old days—Spain's unemployment rate went from 1.1 to 3.4 percent. By 1980 it had climbed to 11.3 percent, which was used by the socialists as the electoral ammunition against the economic and social policies of the centrist government of the time. But, by 1985, under the socialist government the rate had jumped to 21.5 percent. Moreover, despite the economic bonanza in the late 1980s, with an annual growth rate of about 4.5 percent, unemployment never fell below 16 percent. By the end of 1993, it was estimated about 23.4 percent. These rates were about double the average rate of unemployment of the European Community. However, official data may not accurately represent actual unemployment. Discounting people working in the underground economy, the actual rate could be taken to be six to eight points below the official rate. This would leave us with a rate of about 15 to 17 percent in 1993.

Other features of this picture make it even more somber, especially when one considers the overall rate of participation and the structure of unemployment. First, this increasing rate of unemployment applies to a declining proportion of the potential labor force (adults above the age of 16), since participation rates have declined from 52.5 percent in 1970 to 48.7 percent in 1993. These participation rates tend to be lower than the European average: in 1992 participation rates were 69 percent in Germany, 66.4 percent in France, and 75.4 percent in the United Kingdom (Banco de España 1993). Second, a disproportionate share of Spanish unemployment is composed of young people, women, and the long-term unemployed. In 1993 the unemployment rate for those aged 16 to 24 was 41.3 percent, the rate for females was 28.4 percent, and for people who had been unemployed for over one year in 1993, it was 48.3 percent.

Let us examine how the main actors reacted to this situation, and how the institutional system of industrial relations may have influenced their reactions. Labor decided to engage in a two-pronged strategy. To begin with, labor defined the situation in order to privilege those workers already employed. As a result it sought to defend workers from unjustified dismissals by retaining the corpus of labor legislation of the Francoist years. Despite strong protests of businesses to the contrary, state policy reinforced labor's position for some time, with only minor legal adjustments (in 1976, 1977, and 1980; Valdés Dal-Re 1985) and with more significant changes in 1984 (see *infra*). The difficulty Spanish firms face in dismissing individual workers is due to the fairly high compensation they must pay in the case of individual dismissals. The average severance cost in 1992 was 10.7 months' salary for cases that went to the Institute for Conciliation and Arbitration (our own calculations, from data in MTSS 1993).

Legal changes in 1984 opened the way for the introduction of temporary contracts of up to three years, with minor compensation for dismissals at the end of the contract, and with substantial reductions in social security payments (up to 75 percent of the entrepreneurs' contribution). The socialist union UGT reluctantly agreed to these changes when unemployment was about 20 percent, and the unions and the government engaged in discussions that led to the signature of a social pact, the Acuerdo Económico y Social (AES), which also provided the unions with additional organizational resources.[4] As a result temporary contracts became almost immediately the *voie royale* for new hires in the late 1980s. By 1992, 96 percent of all registered new hires were temporary and 81.5 percent had fixed period contracts, 10.4 percent had part-time arrangements, and 2.4 percent possessed other, "atypical" contracts (MTSS 1993). Moreover about one-third of the total work force was employed under temporary arrangements—31.8 percent in manufacturing, 55.7 percent in construction, 26.3 percent in banking and insurance (Segura et al. 1991). Heralded by the government as a way out of the impasse created by the existing rigidities in the labor market, as a way of taking advantage of economic growth in the late 1980s, and of reducing the level of unemployment, the new provisions have nonetheless provided some rather dubious consequences. They have created a situation in which there is no connection between skills and job stability: Only seniority provides workers with employment security. Thus the new generation is jumping from one job to another, with the result that it is unable to develop either particular on the job skills or any attachment or commitment to their workplaces.

The second part of labor's strategy consisted in pressing the state to increase unemployment benefits, which are frequently up to 80 percent of the last salary and may well last up to three and a half years. For some segments of the population, a portion of the benefits may be of indefinite duration. At the same time the unions cooperated, tacitly, with the government in diverting attention from activities in the underground economy and the extensive fraud that takes place in the distribution of unemployment benefits. The rationale being that these illicit practices softened the impact of unemployment as well.

In view of the fiscal crisis in the early 1990s, the government has been trying to persuade labor to accept some cuts in unemployment benefits. The matter was at the heart of the social and political debate in fall 1993. It was also under consideration in the Economic and Social Council,[5] though no more than a protracted compromise

---

4. The new arrangements provided "most representative unions" with seats in different state bodies and enhanced their capacity to control the works councils election system (candidates had to run in closed, blocked lists, and most representative unions were given the right to convoke elections in workplaces where they previously had no affiliates).

5. The Social and Economic Council advises the government on social and economic policy issues and is composed of state officials, employers' and unions' representatives, experts, and academics.

came out of the discussion in the council (see *El Mundo*, October 8, 1993).

This is the landscape in which the individual firms operate. After decades of a rigid labor market and relatively protected product markets (despite the gradual, and uneven, liberalization of the Spanish economy after 1959; see Martí 1975; Viñals et al. 1990), most large companies in the automobile, banking, airlines, and steel industries were overstaffed. In steel, textiles, shipbuilding, and some consumer goods industries, firms reacted to the crisis of the 1970s and early 1980s by downsizing, with or without restructuring plans approved by (and paid for) the state (Navarro 1990). Where this has not yet taken place, as in the case of banking, substantial reductions (at least 20 percent) in personnel are expected in the next few years. Since the work force is underutilized, financial services are currently overpriced, and growing competition is expected to make the status quo impossible to maintain for much longer.

Economic Compensation

For Spanish unions job security and economic compensation have been the primary focus of collective bargaining. For most of the period nominal wages have tended to increase between one and two points above inflation. At some critical moments, however, provisions were made to increase wages on the basis of anticipated rather than past inflation, and this helped to curb inflation, particularly in 1977 and 1978 and again between 1982 and 1984. On the whole, however, both real wages and, most important, labor costs (wages plus social benefits) per unit of production have risen steadily, during the long period of full employment until the mid-1970s and thereafter, exhibiting very little responsiveness to the country's extraordinary levels of unemployment. Even allowing for the moderating effects of the Moncloa Pacts of 1977, wage and labor cost increases were particularly marked during the transition to democracy, in a climate of political uncertainty, acute economic crisis, escalating union demands, weak employer organizations, and the loss of direction in economic policy. Labor costs rose about 60 percent in real terms between 1970 and 1983, with most of the increase concentrated between 1973 and 1980 (Malo de Molina 1985). This was not only the result of increased wages but also of expanded welfare benefits and changes to formal occupational categories. In addition the working day was reduced by about 11 percent between 1977 and 1985.

Real wages were contained between 1980 and 1987 but then started to go up again, both during the upswing of the economy in 1987–89 and in the recession years of 1990–92 (average of 1.7 percent per annum; Raymond 1992).[6] In comparison with labor costs per unit of production in the rest of the European Community, Spanish costs have been increasing at nearly double the average European rate during the last ten years (BBV 1993):

	1983–86	1986–89	1990–92
Spain	7.2 percent	5.8 percent	7.1 percent
Europe	4.8 percent	3.2 percent	5.1 percent

Given that Spain's strongest competitive advantage had been lower prices (Viñals et al. 1990), these increases, together with other factors such as an overvalued currency and high energy and capital costs, have contributed significantly to the loss of competitiveness of Spanish exports.

The explanation for this pattern of real wages and labor costs in the face of huge unemployment lies in a combination of institutional, political and cultural factors. Labor markets are structured in such a way that increases in wages in the protected labor markets may be accompanied by a gradual shrinking of the protected labor force (covered by collective agreements) and an increase in the number of people operating in the underground economy, and/or living off unemployment benefits. This is certainly the case in Spain where three quite differentiated labor markets coexist. First, there is a market for permanent jobs, with wages governed by collective agreements. This market includes about two-thirds of the officially employed work force but only a minor proportion of the new hires. Second, there is a market for jobs with no employment guarantees but with wages and social benefits also governed by collective agreements. This is the most important market for new entrants. Third, there is a labor market that operates in the underground economy and possesses no protection of any kind; its size is dependent on the degree of protection, or rigidity, of the other two and inversely dependent on the level of unemploy-

---

6. This happened despite the increasing percentage of the labor force working under conditions of temporary employment. Other circumstances kept constant, temporary workers tend to earn 8.5 to 11 percent less than workers with an indefinite contract. Temporary workers' lower wages were quite probably counterbalanced by raises in the permanent workers' salaries (Bentolila and Dolado 1993).

ment benefits. Estimates of irregular employment in the underground labor market in 1986 ranged from 22 to 30 percent of total employment (Trigo 1988; Muro et al. 1991).

Political and cultural factors have helped this state of affairs and this institutional setting to develop and persist for so many years. Labor has been an important contributing factor but not the decisive force behind these arrangements. The ensemble of the political class (both center-right and socialist parties) bears the main responsibility, aided and abetted by labor, despite the vocal opposition of organized business (but only the mild reluctance of businessmen themselves). Between 1977 and 1986 the parties generally concurred on the desirability of social pacts to control the growth rate of real wages. This provided satisfactory guidelines for collective bargaining for the protected labor force (García de Blas 1985; Espina 1990). At the same time these pacts have confirmed the basic regulations for entry and exit from the labor markets (and allowed for the policy shift that made room for temporary employment in 1984) while adding pressure to increase public social spending. The public has acquiesced, sharing in the general opinion of the desirability of those pacts. Finally, the main thrust of these arrangements and understandings outlived the explicit, formal social pacts of 1977 to 1986 into the early 1990s. In this way Spanish socioeconomic policy and politics presided over the formation of the three differentiated labor markets mentioned above.

Wage differentials in the official, protected labor market tended to decrease in the 1970s and then expanded moderately in the 1980s. For example, the wage differential between an employee with a university diploma and an employee of the lowest occupational rank was 4.19 in 1973, 3.11 in 1977, and 3.73 in 1988 (Revenga 1991). Wage differentials among industrial sectors decreased sharply in the second half of the 1970s, and again during the 1980s (but kept below the level of intersectoral variation of the late 1960s) (García Perea 1991). Reductions in the wage differentials can be attributed to labor's successful moves in the mid-1970s to escalate social demands (including egalitarian demands for equal nominal increases of wages) and increase the rigidity of the labor market. The reverse tendency in the 1980s may be related to the different economic and political climate and the government's moves to introduce some flexibility in the market.

A pointed illustration of this recent trend is management compensation. During the few years of prosperity in the mid-1980s, wage differentials rose considerably so that by the time the economic crisis exploded, the compensation of Spanish general directors had become among the most generous in Western Europe (just after the Swiss; *El País*, February 16, 1992; *El País*, January 3, 1993). At the same time the narrow margin of difference between the wages agreed to in multiple-company agreements (mainly for small- and medium-sized companies) and those agreed to in single-company agreements suggests that differentials between small- and medium-sized companies, on the one hand, and large companies, on the other, are minor. (The average annual difference was +0.3 percentage points in the period of 1983 to 1992; MTSS 1993.) No significant difference can be attributed to public/private and foreign/domestic ownership, nor to the profitability of the company (Ministerio de Hacienda 1984–90).

The increasing rigidity of the wage structure and the general tendency to narrow the wage differentials during the 1970s was reinforced by a complementary tendency to reduce the variable component of wages. During the long period of economic growth in the 1960s and early 1970s, when adjustments of labor to changes in the level of demand were made mainly through adjustments in extra-time payments, the variable components of wages had become extremely important, eventually amounting to about 50 percent of wages (Sánchez Fierro, 1987, 189). As the result of union pressure, overtime payments were drastically curtailed by legislation enacted during the democratic transition (including the Workers' Statute). By 1983 variable compensation accounted for only 17.3 percent of gross salary for firms with more than 200 employees. Attempts to introduce productivity agreements during the second half of the 1980s only had very limited success, increasing those components to 18.5 percent in 1990. However, compensation of upper- and middle-managers (about 4 to 5 percent of the work force of firms with more than 200 employees) who are excluded from collective agreements, increasingly took individual performance into account (*El País*, January 3, 1993).

Finally, from the mid-1970s to the early 1990s a very strong trend emerged to increase the social welfare of Spanish workers as a variety of social transfers including social security benefits (financed up to about two-thirds by the employers' contributions; CEOE and CEPYME 1987, 212) were introduced. This was due, first, to the general uncertainty that the successful transition and consolidation of democracy in Spain required the development of the Spanish welfare state, bringing it into line with the welfare systems of other Western European nations. There was consequently a general disposition to accept substantial increases in the welfare state despite the economic crisis of the time. Second, the unions were fairly successful in persuading their followers and large segments of the public and the political class that the social pacts implied a trade-off between union wage moderation and the state's (and business') contribution to increased social provisions. As the result of these two converging developments, public social spending rose from 9.2 to 16.6 percent of GDP between 1975 and 1992, while total public expenditure increased from 25.6 to 46.7 percent (BBV 1993).

Having redefined the slowdown in wage increases as a "concession" to the state and the business community, the unions were also keen on developing two related arguments. On the one hand, claiming no connection between the high rates of unemployment and the labor market policies the unions defended, unions refused to accept any responsibility for the increase in the social needs. On the other, the unions felt responsible for, and concerned with, the defense not only of the workers' interests but also of the people's interests, particularly the unemployed and pensioners, thus defusing the potential conflict of interest between the core work force with protected jobs and the large periphery of the growing unemployed. In this way the unions succeeded in using their social demands to add legitimacy to their core claims regarding wages and employment security.

Work Organization and Functional Mobility

The analysis of work organization and functional mobility in Spain faces the almost unsurmountable difficulty of the lack of empirical information. Whatever is said about these matters can only be tentative and subject to revision by future research, but some general observations seem in order. The prevailing type of work organization within Spanish firms during the 1950s and 1960s was Taylorist—entailing a bureaucratic and hierarchical authority structure, a clear-cut division of labor between management focused on planning and workers concentrated on production-related issues. Most of the engineering and economic literature of the time took for granted that this structure more or less reflected the reality of big firms (Guillén 1992).

But regardless of how accurate this picture actually was for large Spanish firms, it seems quite unlikely that it ever fit the small- and medium-sized companies that dominate the Spanish industrial landscape. In 1989, 97.4 percent of Spanish firms employed less than 50 employees and accounted for 52.9 percent of the work force (Escobar 1989; see also Viñals et al. 1990; Segura et al. 1993). Throughout the rosey days of economic growth of the 1960s as well as during the economic and political turbulence of the 1970s, the authority structure of those firms was more akin to a patrimonialist bureaucracy than to a modern and rational bureaucracy (González Olivares 1985). Tasks were either diffusely assigned or allocated through well-established routines on the shop floor. Accounting and financial controls were rudimentary and confused. There was little "strategic thinking" vis-à-vis production or marketing, not to speak of personnel policies. Managers were unrepentant short-termists so to speak, taking advantage of the opportunities provided by the favorable environment of the 1960s. The general climate was one of toleration for an inflation rate of about 6 to 7 percent in which labor demands were easily accommodated by translating increased costs into price hikes. Production was geared to domestic markets, still fairly protected from foreign competition despite some moves to the contrary between 1959 and 1964 (Martí 1975), and exports were primarily viewed as a means to compensate for downturns in domestic demand. In the much harsher conditions of the 1970s, these firms had to face escalating energy and labor costs at a time of falling demand. This situation was aggravated by the erratic and particularistic style of management and rigid forms of work organization practices prevalent in most of these firms.

Rigid forms of work organization were partially the result of state policy. Since the 1940s the state has issued quite detailed regulations (*Ordenanzas Laborales*) which have indicated precisely which tasks should be fulfilled by every occupational category in every productive branch. The *Ordenanzas Laborales* were originally part of the grand corporative/authoritarian strategy of the Francoist state. They were understood as providing workers with a defense mechanism in the face of the discretionary powers of management, in much the same spirit as employment security was supposed to compensate for the lack of free unions or the right to strike. In due course, however, independent unions, which began to organize in the 1960s and 1970s, took over the task of defending the *Ordenanzas* and/or made their contents part of their collective agreements with management (Amsden 1974, 124; Durán 1989, 121). The unions continued this strategy into the democratic era. Thus the rigid framework of the *Ordenanzas* was basically confirmed by the Workers' Statute of 1980 and remained in place until the early 1990s.

Pressures from organized business to change the *Ordenanzas*, and to include more flexible work organization arrangements in collective agreements, have had very limited success, not only because of union resistance but also because of splits within the business community. This issue is not especially important for small companies (Fina 1991, 134). The present state of affairs generally favors small companies because they can deal with their personnel individually on an ad hoc basis, and they are unwilling to pay the price (wage increases) that the unions demand in exchange for greater flexibility. Thus multiple-company agreements have introduced little flexibility so far. Big companies are much keener to change the *Ordenanzas*, for they need more functional and geographical mobility, and this is reflected in arrangements that gradually developed in the 1980s. On the whole, there has been a slight increase of agreements with clauses on geographical mobility (present in 8.7 percent of the collective contracts in 1986 and in 14.7 percent in 1988) and the replacement of occupational categories by broader professional groups (present in 14.4 percent of agreements in 1986 and 19.7 percent in 1988; CEOE and CEPYME 1987, 1989; CEOE 1988).

Big companies, however, can find themselves in rather complicated predicaments when they seek to change their work organization. The result may be a mixture of experimental moves and conservative tactics, as the case of the automobile industry illustrates. The automobile sector is central to Spanish manufacturing and the overall economy, accounting for 6.6 percent of industrial employment in 1990 (Miner 1993), 12 percent of total exports, and 5 percent of GDP, in 1991 (*El País*, March 15, 1992). Since the sale of Spanish-owned SEAT to Volkswagen in 1986, the industry has been in the hands of foreign companies: 30 percent of car production in 1992 was controlled by Volkswagen; 39 percent by two American companies—GM and Ford; and 31 percent by two French companies—Renault and Peugeot. In addition Nissan and Suzuki produce trucks in Spain (ANFAC, quoted in Ford-España, 1993). Multinationals such as these automakers have become committed to introducing a variety of changes in work organization which most Spanish observers label as "Toyotism," the equivalent to "lean production" (Womack, Jones, and Roos 1991). However, there is no clear evidence that innovations such as quality circles, just-in-time procedures, and group work have become widespread. FASA-Renault has experimented with variants of quality circles since 1973, and Ford introduced them in 1979, reaching up to 331 circles and involving one-third of its employees by 1985. In contrast, Peugeot/Citroën had established only 12 circles by 1986, and SEAT/Volkswagen, which began with 140 circles in 1987, had no more than 113 by 1989 (Castillo 1990; Castillo et al. 1991; Ford-España, 1993). Just-in-time arrangements have been applied at GM and Nissan, and they seem to have been given particular importance in the design of the Martorell factory of SEAT/Volkswagen. However, only 15 of its 440 suppliers are located near or in the surrounding area, and 215 were located abroad, with more than half of the parts coming from Germany (SEAT 1993). Group work seems to have become predominant in Renault, where it involved as much as 80 percent of the personnel in 1992 (FASA-Renault 1993); it is also quite important in SEAT's Martorell factory but is much less prevalent at GM, Nissan, and Suzuki (CCOO 1992). These moves must be seen in the context of an overall business strategy that responds to a fairly pessimistic view of the immediate and medium-range prospects for the European automobile industry as a whole. This leads to a sustained attempt at numerical flexibility and cost-cutting to meet falling demand and increasing competition. Thus almost 50 percent of Renault's investment in Spain in 1991 went to pay for a 10 percent reduction of its work force (*El País*, March, 15, 1992). In the fall of 1993 Martin Bangemann, the Industry Commissar of the European Community, stated that the European automobile industry work force is expected to be cut by half in the next few years (*El Mundo*, October 21, 1993). This statement was apparently corroborated by the recent closing of SEAT/Volkswagen's Zona Franca factory, with the loss of about 9,000 jobs.

A similar mix of halfhearted moves to change work organization and of expected or actual moves toward greater employment flexibility can be observed in industries as diverse as energy, textiles, and banking. Changes in banking—in financial products, in the need for closer and better attention to clients, in granting more autonomy to the local agencies, and in network technology—imply organizational changes (IESA 1987; Castells et al. 1986; Castaño 1990). But all this has to be done in the context of an oversized sector that anticipates restructuring. Financial services in Spain profit from diverse forms of protection that allow for margins much higher than those in most countries. But this is only for the time being. This situation cushions the effects of an excess of personnel (Villarejo 1990) who enjoy job security and compensation, which will not be maintained when the effects of international competition reach Spain, as is expected, within the next few years. By then the latent issue of numerical flexibility will become prominent once again.

Skill Formation and Training

During the Franco years the state set up two main types of vocational training institutions: the so-called Formación Profesional Reglada (FPR) and occupational training. The FPR provided a training program focused on youth before entering the labor market, which, on paper, ought to have prepared them for an occupational career. In fact, it was merely a variant of the general program of secondary education, with some light touches of vocational knowledge, for adolescents lacking the economic resources and/or the intellectual ability to follow the main track of the baccalaureate. These characteristics were accentuated further by the General Law of Education of 1970.

The most important program for vocational training for the adult population was developed in the early to mid-1960s. It was supported by the Ministry of Labor and was managed through the PPO (Programa de Promoción Profesional Obrera, later to become part of the Instituto Nacional de Empleo, INEM). The PPO was fairly effective in providing basic occupational skills to hundreds of thousands of people to prepare them to move from the agrarian sector to the building industries, tourism-related activities, and manufacturing. It also helped large segments of the agrarian population to learn the fundamentals needed to manage the new agricultural machinery such as tractors and mechanical harvesters (Pérez-Díaz 1972). The PPO set up hundreds of courses of about 100 to 200 hours to be given by mobile teams of skilled trainers in villages, factories, schools, or city halls. Successful as it was, the PPO was mainly an ad hoc response to the immediate needs created by the growth of cities, industries, and the affluence of tourists.

Until the late 1980s to early 1990s, vocational training ranked low in the agenda of both center and socialist governments. This combined with the effects of the economic crisis to create a situation where the old institutions remained in place and were allowed to drift along for a long while. The FPR continued to act as a residual track for general secondary education, not withstanding that it was common knowledge that the kind of training provided by the FPR was disconnected from the demands of the economy and was basically fulfilling the role of a convenient parking lot for about a third of 14- to 19-year-olds. By the late 1980s, however, the administration started to consider this state of affairs unacceptable and began to search throughout Europe for better alternatives. With the backing or the acquiescence of organized business and labor, the Ministry of Education introduced an interesting reform that is now being implemented. The program of vocational training is addressed to youngsters aged 16 to 18, and it requires them to take about 1,000 hours of professional courses and to spend about 300 to 500 hours working in firms. The plan has been conceived as a variant of the German system and includes the Chambers of Commerce, organized business, and unions in the implementation of the plan. The designers call it a system of training *en alternancia* because it alternates between classes in school and hands-on experience in the firm.

6.2   Industrial Relations and Corporate Culture

The final section of our discussion deals with changes in industrial relations and corporate culture. The theme of industrial relations includes and goes beyond that of firm governance insofar as industrial relations concern (1) the institutional mechanisms of voice for both the employees and their representatives in the decision-making processes at the micro level of the firm and (2) the institutional mechanisms of collective bargaining and sociopolitical pressure that take place outside the firm, at the macro level. The theme of corporate culture refers to some of the cultural premises of the industrial relations system.

In Spain the law guarantees the presence of union representatives in firms under two guises: as members of the local sections of the national unions and as members of the works councils, which workers choose in nationwide elections that take place about every four years. This system was put in place after the transition to democracy but built upon prior experience when local militants were simultaneously part of semispontaneous workers' commissions and local representatives of the official unions. This helps to explain the ambiguity of the institutional design of workers' representation at the local level where union sections and factories' committees coexist rather peacefully and tend to reinforce each other. Nonetheless, this mutual reinforcement has *not* resulted in a strong local tradition of worker representation in either small or large firms. This weakness is closely related to the existing traditions in collective bargaining.

Collective bargaining had already become a central feature of industrial life in the 1960s but its full development came with the transition to democracy. Its coverage has extended from 2.8 million employees in 1977 to about 6 million in 1982, and 7.4 million in 1992. At the same time the number of agreements has grown from 1,300 in 1977 to 3,300 in 1982 and 4,800 in 1992 (Ruesga 1991; MTSS 1993). Most of those agreements, however, have been concluded at the provincial-sectoral and national-sectoral levels, with company agreements (primarily involving big companies) affecting only about 1 million employees in 1992. Agreements above the company level require bargaining between organized business and leaders of the territorial branches and/or the trade federations of the most representative unions, with little direct involvement on the part of the local unions and the works councils. These local organizations have weak foundations, and in many cases they barely exist. They are set up at the time of the elections, when the national unions come to the shops and persuade mostly unaffiliated workers to stand as union candidates. Once the elections are over, the unions present "their delegates" to the government. If the union has more than 10 percent of the works council delegates nationally, they gain their credentials and the legal prerogatives attached to their status as "most representative unions." Chief among these prerogatives is the right to engage in collective bargaining, as well as to gain time off for their activists, to call a strike, to call the next elections for the committees, and to participate in an array of state- and parastatal organizations.

Labor leaders engaged in multiple-company negotiations for entire sectoral-provincial aggregates of small- and medium-sized firms will seek relatively high levels of compensation for the entire sector if they fear that otherwise the wage level to be obtained in subsequent negotiations with large companies will be reduced. The problem is that the two types of collective bargaining are not articulated. The sectoral-provincial agreement does not provide a floor for company-level negotiations. Union leaders are also aware that workers and management in small- and medium-sized firms are not particularly interested in issues related to work organization. As we have shown, small-firm practice tends to be characterized by a combination of bureaucratic paternalism and ad hoc arrangements aimed at enhancing flexibility. Hence multiple-company collective bargaining has been traditionally concerned, above all, with wages. The mechanism has worked for many years by setting as a goal a range of wage increases of about

three points above and below past cost-of-living increases, with business and labor generally converging around one point above, which
is expected to become 2 points above inflation once wage drift is
taken into consideration. During most of the 1980s this roughly corresponded to the guidelines proposed by the social pacts or to the government's recommendations, in the absence of pacts after 1986.

In their roundabout way to an agreement, organized business usually takes comfort in the government's discreet encouragement, and
labor flexes its muscle with fairly frequent use of short, massive
strikes (6.2 million workdays lost in 1992; MTSS 1993). But the end
result has not changed much over the last decade or so. From the
viewpoint of the work force of small- and medium-sized companies,
this is a rather mechanistic and ritualistic endeavor that requires neither much commitment nor deep involvement in local unionism.
Company agreements are certainly more important for companies
with over 200 workers. Collective bargaining in this case may be
extended to cover issues other than wages: changes in occupational
categories, forms of payment, productivity, and the like. Still, wages
have been the most important element, and the crisis of the early
1990s has reinforced this characteristic. There is no evidence of a
developing pattern of agreements and understandings between management and local representatives of the work force on so-called qualitative issues, which could both respond to and reinforce local unions
and/or works councils.

From the viewpoint of that segment of management, particularly in
the large companies, more inclined to take a long-term view, the
unions are basically interested in wages and employment security, defensive when the time comes to discuss matters of work organization
and functional mobility, inattentive to vocational training and skill
formation issues, and only marginally interested in the variable component of the compensation and the forms of temporary employment
that management is most keen to implement. These managers think
that the unions' basic cultural premises correspond to a mentality of
confrontation and suspicion regarding the management's goals and
modus operandi, and of deep distrust regarding the basic rules of the
game of a market economy. Therefore they consider long-term understandings (e.g., of a so-called productivist nature) with such unions
quite unlikely.

In response to this situation, some major companies like BBV, Rep-
sol, Iberdrola, and El Corte Inglés have begun a process of redefining
their corporate culture. They are trying to articulate values, criteria,

and objectives to guide a process of internal restructuring, enhanced product quality, relations with the public, and so on. Primarily they are in a search of common ground to develop understanding and motivation of the several layers of management but also for common ground between management and the most stable and qualified part of their operations—their core work force. This is an ongoing process, still in its early stages with uncertainty about the form and direction it will take.

6.3   Concluding Remarks: The Four-Cornered Society

For all their apparent inconsistencies, Spanish human resource management practices and policies and industrial relations exhibit a basic systemic or quasi-systemic character. Its several elements are loosely connected to each other in that changes in one of them may have significant effects on the others. But in order to understand such an underlying system, we have to dispense with the notion of a homogeneous arena where all the rules and institutions apply evenly. The key to understanding the true picture lies in differentiating between several arenas and in following the links between them.

First, the most visible arena seems to be the protected core of the labor market (space 1). In this arena the rigid rules for exit and entry to the labor market have already been applied for about five decades without interruption. Although there have been significant changes in the rhetoric and the political underpinnings of the rules, from the "concessions" of an authoritarian corporatist regime to the "social conquests" acquired by the new democratic regime, the rules of the game remain remarkably similar. The unions are basically geared to represent and defend the interests of the seven to eight million employees in this arena: increasing the costs of their dismissals while raising their wages and their social benefits.

However, the very success of the unions in providing the core labor force with employment stability and real wage increases at a time of deep, continual economic crisis since the mid-1970s has been a determining factor in the creation of three quite different labor markets, each with its own rules: for temporary workers, for workers in the underground economy, and for redundant workers living off public subsidies.

Since business has been quite reluctant to create jobs under conditions of low demand, increasing real wages and social security payments, and expensive and lengthy dismissal procedures, the socialist government has sought to promote some flexibility into the labor market through a variety of public policies. As a result in the mid-1980s a secondary labor market for temporary workers was created, and with such a success that by the early 1990s about three million workers were operating under new rules. Almost every new entrant, and therefore a sizable part of the new generation, is now working in temporary jobs. These young workers usually have contracts for up to three years, at the end of which they are given a fairly modest sum of money (about 12 days of salary for every year worked), and receive unemployment benefits until they secure a new temporary job. Only a small minority (17 percent) succeed in securing permanent contracts (Segura et al. 1991). While they are covered by the collective agreements, their lack of seniority and their limited skills make their wages lower than those of the core work force. Moreover, because of significant reductions in social security payments, business pay is considerably less for these temporary workers.

Permanent and temporary workers are only the visible, official part of the labor market. A third labor market, that of the underground economy, also exists in Spain and is quite important in certain sectors like agriculture, textiles, and the footwear industry. Thus export success and dynamism of Spain's footwear industry, located mainly on the Mediterranean coast, is dependent on the existence of a widespread underground economy, which in different ways is protected by both local authorities and a variety of local leaders (parties, churches, unions, and the media). In 1986, estimates of employment in the underground sector of these consumer industries ranged from 280,000 to 270,000 with a total of 1.5 to 2.5 million for the whole economy (Trigo 1988; Muro et al. 1991). In this labor market, firms and workers operate under different rules: Jobs are dependent on performance, wages are low, and social security payments are nonexistent. However, there are different ways in which people working under these arrangements do get access to complementary provisions. They achieve this by using the rules, institutions, and material resources of the public subsidies and by making the boundaries between the underground economy and public subsidies as porous as possible.

A fourth arena is that of the officially ex-employed or unemployed population. By "ex-employed population" we mean the significant segments of relatively old workers who were persuaded to take early retirement and receive pensions, which were substantially raised in the late 1980s. They also benefited from generous compensation offered by entrepreneurs eager to reduce their work force, and assisted by the state to facilitate restructuring in the early 1980s. The officially unemployed population, which has fluctuated between two and three and a half million over the past ten to fifteen years, receive a sizable part of their last salary for a period of time. The boundaries between the underground economy and this segment of the labor force are fuzzy, thus permitting people to live off subsidies *and* work in the underground economy. It is also possible to alternate between the secondary labor market, composed primarily of young people working in temporary jobs, and this last subsidized segment of the working population by working for about one or two months in the country-side and then receiving a subsidy for the rest of the year (the so-called PER plan: Plan de Empleo Rural).

We have characterized a segmented, four-cornered system, with people operating in each of these four corners by different rules and moving from one corner to another, a sort of massive rehearsal (and "eternal return") of the classical Spanish children's game of the four corners. In that game four children are located in four corners of a room or a garden, under the watch of a fifth one standing in the mid-dle. The four children play around and feel safe so long as they stay close to their spots. But of course they move, and run from one corner to another, switching places. The moment any of them moves and leaves his spot unguarded, the fifth child runs into it and tries to take his place. The aim of the game is to remain in any one of the four safe corners, and to move around swiftly and carefully, while the unlucky child in the middle tries to replace any of the movers. Spanish work-ers play a similar game by moving from one safe corner to another, while unlucky watchers who just missed the safety net sit in the mid-dle because their unemployment benefits have run out, because there is no slot in the underground economy to fill or because they do not have an extended family to take care of them. Foreign immigrants play this game, beginning often as unlucky watchers in the middle.

The stability of such a system lies in the peaceful coexistence between, and the complementarity of, the subsystems, and in their anchoring within the same basic societal unit: the extended, or quasi-extended family of two or more generations living together, or main-taining close ties to each other, and helping each other survive through difficult times. The family is the open secret of the Spanish la-bor market and the explanation for the fact that Spain may have sur-vived about fifteen years of high unemployment without apparent sociopolitical trauma. The family survives on a variety of sources of income and of social provisions, which can be pooled: wages of permanent and temporary workers, salaries earned in underground activities, pensions and unemployment benefits.

The relative rigidity of the rules concerning job stability and wages in the primary labor market are to a significant extent responsible for the scope and the characteristics of the other three arenas: instability and low wages for temporary and underground workers and subsidies and benefits for ex-employees and the unemployed. They may even reinforce each other. For instance, paying lower wages and social security payments to temporary workers provides firms and unions with these margins necessary to pay for wage increases for the core work force (Bentolila and Dolado 1993). But the interdependence and linkages among the different arenas also appears in the realm of human resources practices and policies, and in industrial relations.

People living under temporary arrangements or in the underground economy are usually not given the incentives or the opportunity to develop professional skills. Indeed temporary arrangements and underground work often have low skill requirements, and the workers lack any prospect of obtaining a professional career that will enhance their professional skills. At the same time the core work force's basic motivation to protect their jobs and wages make them reluctant to undertake any systematic, sustained efforts at professional re-training. Hence low priority is usually accorded to vocational training. On the other hand, since professional categories are strongly connected with seniority and wage levels, and weakly connected with skills, workers and unions have considerable incentive to resist changes in the labor ordinances of the past. Thus shop floor negotiations to change work organization and enhance functional mobility become more difficult and erratic.

The stability of traditional patterns of on-the-job training and work organization fits fairly well with a system of industrial relations in which comparatively modest emphasis is put on company or local bargaining. Despite their symbolic salience, and the extraordinary visibility of their sociopolitical initiatives, Spanish unions are rather weak not only because they have few affiliates but above all because their local roots, which perhaps could be extended (as reflected in the numbers of the union-related members of the works councils), are in fact quite superficial. The unions have not developed, nor helped to develop, a strong tradition of local bargaining. Nonetheless, the unions have developed fairly strong sociopolitical personalities, which they have used to increase the stability of the system. Thus they have focused public attention on increasing the welfare state provisions for pensions and unemployment subsidies; they have diverted the public's and the (central and regional) political authorities' attention away from the problems of the underground economy and toward the potential conflict of interest between the people working in the primary and secondary (temporary) labor markets.

So here we have what we might label a segmented, four-cornered society, or socioeconomic system, that stands as a sort of "model" of adjustment (with no normative implications) to the prolonged economic crisis of the last two decades (with the brief interlude of the late 1980s bonanza). It has provided a modicum of socioeconomic, political, and cultural stability. Of course it may be suggested that the long-term prospects for such a system are quite dubious. In a sense it is a system that seems inimical to the actors spending much energy on considerations of the future. Young people are provided with slim prospects of professional careers and socialized into developing low professional expectations. Long-term policy decisions can be put off, and as in the case of vocational training, they may be realized after a delay of many years (and then with only cursory attention to the critical issue of the bottleneck in trainers, which in turn would take a number of years to train). The entire productive system, in the meanwhile, may lose competitiveness vis-à-vis other countries. But all of these may be considered (by some) just "prices to be paid" in exchange for the benefit of social peace and the system's resilience to survive the transition from one critical stage to another without losing its composure.

Now, without further exploration here into that disquieting question about the price to pay for the stability of the system, let us explore what can be said about how and why this system has come into being. About the genesis of the system, the most interesting point is that nobody designed it. As Hayek would say, it was the result of human action and not of human design (Hayek 1978). Nobody has deliberately set up this curious, and so far stable, combination of permanent workers, young temporary workers, underground workers, and structurally unemployed people. The various governments, political parties, unions, business organizations, media, and academes—none of them has designed the system, nor would any of them ever describe the above arrangements as a "system." In fact the four-cornered society has been allowed just to "happen," so to speak, each key actor lending a helping hand. But to impute this outcome to the conscious strategies of either the state or the social actors (unions and business) would be clearly out of the question.

Likewise the state and the main socioeconomic actors cannot be blamed for pushing along an entrenched institutional setting. During the last twenty years or so, building on previous foundations, politicians, civil servants, union officials, and business leaders collaborated in designing new industrial relations and public policy institutions: most notably, that of the dual structure of worker representation, multilevel collective bargaining arrangements, and social concertation. This institutional system, which has contributed to the segmented, four-cornered society just described, could have been put to work with quite different results, providing for more flexible and less segmented arrangements in matters of job stability and wages, work organization, and training.

An explanation for this paradoxical outcome may lie less in strategic choices or the institutions of Spain, and more in "inertial choices" of organizational actors which, faced with unprecedented challenges and uncertain circumstances, stuck to their traditions, and the explicit or implicit understandings that went along with them. The liberal-democratic state of the late 1970s through the 1990s has been in the hands of politicians and civil servants keen on an expansion of the welfare state, and on the maintenance of a relatively high level in job stability and real wage increases for a fairly extended protected core of the labor force. Unions have never acknowledged their strategy could be other than the one of playing on and reinforcing such inclinations, and to soften the impact on the nonprotected labor force by means of social welfare provisions, and de facto toleration with the underground economy. Spanish business has a well established tradition of deference toward the state, and short-termism in its dealings with their work force and the unions. Business and unions have a consistent tradition of avoiding face-to-face company level bargaining where a large or complex array of issues may have had the opportunity to be thought over, debated, and possibly solved. Such absence of a strong local tradition in collective bargaining fits in a tradition of giving low priority to the issues of expanding the variable components of the economic compensations, work organization, and professional training. More generally, these traditions fit easily in with the absence of a tradition of continual compromise, mutual understanding, and in the end, possibly a modicum of mutual trust, which can only be built on such experiences of shared local knowledge and intense interactions.

It may also well be that these traditions and understandings have been, and are, dependent on a soft economic environment: soft in the sense of allowing easy translations of labor cost increases into prices and of protecting inefficient firms from domestic and foreign competition. So it may well be that structural economic preconditions for the persistence of those traditions are being gradually eroded by the much harsher environment of the late 1980s and early 1990s, wherein toleration for inflation and for low competitiveness are being drastically reduced. Economic sectors more exposed to external competition may be those more congenial to the emergence of new local traditions of the collective bargain encompassing the issues of work organization, training, and creating a climate of mutual, realistic understanding between business and workers. To what extent these new traditions depend on local/regional political and cultural arrangements, and to what extent emergent traditions may be compatible with the persistence of the four-cornered, segmented system will be the matter for another discussion.

References

Amsden, Jon. 1974. *Convenios colectivos y lucha de clases en España*. Paris: Ruedo Ibérico.

Banco de España. 1993. *Cuentas financieras de la economía española*. Madrid: Banco de España.

BBV (Banco Bilbao Vizcaya). 1993. *Informe económico 1992*. Bilbao: BBV.

Bentolila, Samuel, and Juan José Dolado. 1993. La contratación temporal y sus efectos sobre la competitividad. *Papeles de Economía Española* 56:112–30.

Bentolila, Samuel, and Luis Toharia, comp. 1991. *Estudios de economía del trabajo en España III: El problema del paro*. Madrid: Ministerio de Trabajo y Seguridad Social.

Boyer, Robert. 1986. *La théorie de la régulation, une analyse critique*. Paris: La Découverte.

Bushell, Rober, and Julia Salaverría. 1992. Proceso de formación de precios y salarios y limitaciones del mercado laboral. *Papeles de Economía Española* 52/53:108–25.

Castaño, Cecilia. 1990. *Tecnología y empleo en el sector financiero español: Informes del Instituto de Prospectiva*. Madrid: Ministerio de Economía y Hacienda.

Castells, Manuel, et al. 1986. *Nuevas Tecnologías y Sociedad en España*. Madrid: Alianza.

Castillo, Juan José. 1990. Diseño organizativo, formación y participación en una fábrica de motores. *Revista de Economía* 7:58–62.

Castillo, Juan José, et al. 1991. Nuevas formas de organización del trabajo y de implicación directa en España. *Revista Española de Investigaciones Sociológicas* 56 (October–December):115–41.

CCOO. 1992. *Toyotismo y sindicalismo en el automóvil: el caso español*. Mimeo.

CEDEFOP. 1988. *El papel de los interlocutores sociales en la formación profesional en España.* Mimeo.

CEOE. 1987. *Mesa Redonda: Estructura Salarial. Octubre, 1986.* Madrid: CEOE.

CEOE. 1988. *Mesa Redonda: Normas estatales y negociación colectiva en materia laboral. Febrero, 1988.* Madrid: CEOE.

CEOE and CEPYME. 1989. *Mesa redonda: La negociación colectiva en España y en Europa.* Madrid: CEOE/CEPYME.

CIFP (Comisión Interministerial para la Formación Profesional). 1981. *Formación Profesional en España: Situación y perspectivas.* Madrid: Ministerio de Economía y Comercio.

Cuadrado Roura, Juan R. 1992. El sector servicios. *Papeles de Economía Española* 50: 258–94.

Durán López, Federico. 1989. La Negociación colectiva y la vigencia de Reglamentaciones de Trabajo y Ordenanzas Laborales. In *Mesa redonda: La negociación colectiva en España y en Europa.* Madrid: CEOE/CEPYME.

Escobar, Modesto. 1992. Works or union councils? The representative system in medium and large sized Spanish firms. CEACS. Estudios/Working Papers. Madrid: Instituto Juan March.

Espina, Alvaro. 1990. *Empleo, democracia y relaciones industriales en España: De la industrialización al mercado único.* Madrid: Ministerio de Trabajo y Seguridad Social.

Eusebio Rivas, Pedro de. 1987. La Formación Profesional en España: Fondo Social Europeo y Plan Nacional de Formación Profesional. In *II Jornadas: Formación profesional y Fondo Social Europeo.* Madrid: CEOE.

FASA-Renault. 1993. *Informe Anual 1992.*

Fina, Lluis. 1991. *El problema del paro y la flexibilidad del empleo: Informes sobre un debate.* Madrid: Ministerio de Trabajo y Seguridad Social.

Ford-España. 1993. *Informe Anual 1992.*

Foweraker, Joe. 1989. *Making Democracy in Spain: Grass-roots Struggle in the South, 1955–1975.* Cambridge: Cambridge University Press.

García de Blas, Andrés. 1985. La negociación colectiva en España: Situación y perspectivas. *Papeles de Economía Española* 22:329–42.

García Perea, Pilar. 1991. Evolución de la estructura salarial española desde 1963. In Samuel Bentolila and Luis Toharia, comp., *Estudios de economía del trabajo en España III: El problema del paro.* Madrid: Ministerio de Trabajo y Seguridad Social.

González Olivares, Luis. 1985. Crisis en la pequeña y mediana empresa industrial. *Papeles de Economía Española* 22:38–61.

Guillén, Mauro. 1992. *Dirección, Ideología y Organización de Empresas.* Mimeo.

Hayek, Friedrich von. 1978. *New Studies in Philosophy, Politics, Economics, and the History of Ideas.* London: Routledge and Kegan Paul.

Homans, George. 1967. *The Nature of Social Science.* New York: Harcourt.

Hyman, Richard. 1988. Flexible Specialization: Miracle or Myth? In R. Hyman and W. Streeck eds., *New Technology and Industrial Relations.* Oxford: Basil Blackwell.

IESA. 1987. *Cambios de cualificación en las empresas españolas. Banca.* Madrid: Fundación IESA.

IMF. 1989, 1991. *International Financial Statistics Yearbook.*

Malo de Molina, José Luis. 1985. Coherencia del sistema de relaciones industriales y eficiencia del mercado de trabajo. *Papeles de Economía Española* 22:244–64.

Martí, Luis. 1975. Estabilización y desarrollo. *Información Comercial Española* 500 (April):42–55.

Martín, Carmela, and Francisco J. Velázquez. 1993. El capital extranjero y el comercio exterior de las empresas manufactureras. *Papeles de Economía Española* 56:221–34.

Martínez, Robert. 1984. Business elites in democratic Spain. Ph. D. dissertation, Yale University.

Martínez Lucio, Miguel. 1992. Spain: Constructing institutions and actors in a context of change. In Anthony Ferner and Richard Hyman, *Industrial Relations in the New Europe.* Oxford: Blackwell.

Martínez Serrano, José Antonio, and Rafael Myro. 1992. La penetración del capital extranjero en la industria española. *Moneda y Crédito* 194:149–98.

Miguélez, Faustino, and Carlos Prieto, dir. 1991. *Las relaciones laborales en España.* Madrid: Siglo XXI.

MINER (Ministerio de Industria y Energía). 1993. *Encuesta Industrial (1987–1990).* Madrid: Ministerio de Industria y Energía.

Ministerio de Economía y Hacienda. 1984–1991. *La negociación colectiva en las grandes empresas.* Madrid: Ministerio de Economía y Hacienda.

MTSS (Ministerio de Trabajo y Seguridad Social). 1992. *Anuario de Estadísticas Laborales.* Madrid: MTSS.

MTSS (Ministerio de Trabajo y Seguridad Social). 1993. *Boletín de Estadísticas Laborales,* no. 103 (June).

Muro, Juan, et al. 1991. Estimación del empleo irregular en la economía española. In Samuel Bentolila and Luis Toharia, comp. 1991. *Estudios de economía del trabajo en España III: El problema del paro.* Madrid: Ministerio de Trabajo y Seguridad Social.

Navarro, Miquel. 1990. *Política de reconversión: balance crítico.* Madrid: Eudema.

Pérez-Díaz, Víctor M. 1972. *Cambio tecnológico y procesos educativos en España.* Madrid: Seminarios y Ediciones.

Pérez-Díaz, Víctor M. 1985. Economic policies and social pacts in Spain during the transition: The two faces of neo-corporatism. *European Sociological Review* 1, 3 (December).

Pérez-Díaz, Víctor M. 1993. *The Return of Civil Society: The Emergence of Democratic Spain.* Cambridge: Harvard University Press.

Piore, Michael, and Charles Sabel. 1984. *The Second Industrial Divide.* New York: Basic Books.

Raymond, José Luis. 1992. Salarios reales y empleo. *Papeles de Economía Española* 52/53:126–28.

Revenga, Ana. 1991. La liberalización económica y la distribución de la renta: La experiencia española. *Moneda y Crédito* 193:179–223.

Ruesga, Benito, and M. Santos. 1991. La negociación colectiva. In Faustino Miguélez and Carlos Prieto, dir., *Las relaciones laborales en España*. Madrid: Siglo XXI.

SEAT. 1993. *SEAT-Martorell. Nueva Fábrica*.

Segura, Julio, and Arturo González Romero. 1992. La industria española: Evolución y perspectivas. *Papeles de Economía Española* 50:140–72.

Segura, Julio, et al. 1991. *Análisis de la contratación temporal en España*. Madrid: Ministerio de Trabajo y Seguridad Social.

Segura, Julio, et al. 1993. *Un panorama de la industria española*. Madrid: MICYT.

Streeck, Wolfgang. 1992. *Social Institutions and Economic Performance. Studies of Industrial Relations in Advanced Capitalist Economies*. London: SAGE.

Trigo Portela, Joaquín. 1988. *Barreras a la creación de empresas y economía regular*. Madrid: Instituto de Estudios Económicos.

Valdés Dal-Re, Fernando. 1985. Flexibilidad en el mercado de trabajo y ordenamiento laboral. *Papeles de Economía Española* 22:302–15.

Villarejo, Esteban. 1990. La renovación en la aplicación de los recursos humanos en la Banca española. *Sociología del Trabajo* 9 (Spring):55–70.

Viñals, José, et al. 1990. Spain and the "EC cum 1992" shock. In C. Bliss and J. Braga eds., *Unity with diversity in the European Economy*. Cambridge: Cambridge University Press.

Viñas, Angel, et al. 1979. *Política comercial exterior en España (1931–1975)*. Madrid: Banco Exterior de España.

Weber, Max. 1978. *Economy and Society*. Berkeley: University of California Press.

Womack, J. P., D. T. Jones, and D. Roos. 1991. *The Machine That Changed the World*. New York: Harper.

7   Industrial Relations and Human Resources in France

Jean Saglio

The industrial relations (IR) system in France is currently undergoing a process of fundamental change. It is being transformed by a long-standing economic and political crisis, whose symptoms include shifts in unemployment and in work forms and patterns. The most critical change, however, is not in terms of employment practices but in the development of new managerial concepts. In section 7.1, I review the employment trends and discuss my analytical approach. In the three subsequent sections of this chapter, I describe the features of the French IR system, analyze the evidence of rupture and continuity, and discuss the implications for theory.

7.1   Global Perspectives

A Long-Term Perspective on Crisis and Change

When analyzing work and employment in France, there is one point on which virtually all observers agree: The current situation makes a profound and significant break with the past. Left behind is one system of employment, and we are now witnessing the development of new forms. What historical reference can we use to evaluate these changes? For most commentators, the first oil crisis in the mid-1970s marked the break with the past and ushered in the current period, but the new situation has not stabilized nor become homogeneous.

For some, this is the end of thirty "glorious" years of rising prosperity and the impetus for economic growth provided by reconstruction.

This chapter is a product of work carried out collectively by researchers in GDR 41/CNRS. In writing it, the author was greatly assisted by the observations, discussions and criticisms offered by many colleagues, notably Jean Bunel, Alain Chouraqui, François Michon, Marie Laure Morin, Edward Lorenz, Emmanuèle Reynaud, and Jean Daniel Reynaud.

For others, it signals the collapse of the Fordist mode of production, characterized by mass production technologies, mass consumption, and by a political balance based on the sharing of productivity gains. Still others see the crisis as the end of a political-economic equilibrium that began in the early years of the century and that was characterized by state intervention in the economy and a particular relationship between economic actors and employment institutions.

The debate remains unresolved, but there seems to be one point of agreement: To understand such phenomena, it is necessary to conduct an investigation with a long-term perspective. At the very least we would need to consider the whole postwar period, and perhaps even the interwar period and the early years of the century.

"The Crisis": The Rise of Unemployment and
Precarious Employment

The most pernicious aspect of the crisis is the level of unemployment, which has been rising inexorably for the past fifteen years. But unemployment trends are themselves the result of other shifts in labor force participation and in employment levels. First, the working population, which had remained stable for a long period before 1960, has grown steadily since that date. Second, until the mid-1970s total employment was growing in such a way that unemployment remained at a low rate. After this date the growth in jobs was insufficient to absorb the increasing labor force. Even with the cessation of immigration, total unemployment increased to a current level of about three million people. These changes in total employment are the product of various trends: the decline of agricultural employment, the growth of employment in services, the decline in industrial work after the mid-1970s, and the stabilization in public administration during the 1980s.

In France, as in most developed countries, unemployment has mainly affected women and less-skilled workers. However, in other ways the unemployment trends are unique. The extent of youth unemployment[1] and the high level of long-term unemployment suggest that France's record in dealing with unemployment is particularly poor.

---

1. Youth unemployment rates are lower in France than in the United Kingdom or the United States. There is, however, a low rate of labor force participation among French young people and this depresses the unemployment measure. See Elbaum and Marchand (1993).

Successive governments have enacted a series of measures to combat this increase in unemployment. Policies particularly designed to stimulate employment (in both the public and private sectors) were introduced in the periods 1977 to 1981 and 1984 to 1987 (see table 7.1).

Measures have also been taken to improve the circumstances for individuals seeking employment (training schemes, early retirement, etc.). The number of individuals benefiting from these policies has increased steadily from 1973 to 1984 and has since leveled out (IRES 1991; see table 7.2).

Throughout the 1980s the increase in unemployment was accompanied by an increase in poorly protected jobs, to the point where

Table 7.1
Subsidized employment (in thousands)

	Total employment[a]	Subsidized employment in profit sectors	Subsidized employment in nonprofit sectors	Nonsubsidized employment
1973	21,411			21,411
1974	21,597			21,597
1975	21,401	1		21,400
1976	21,565	8		21,557
1977	21,730	92		21,638
1978	21,818	322		21,496
1979	21,835	315		21,520
1980	21,847	344		21,503
1981	21,716	451		21,265
1982	21,752	403	8	21,341
1983	21,668	272	8	21,338
1984	21,467	258	8	21,201
1985	21,401	261	123	21,017
1986	21,423	444	195	20,783
1987	21,485	767	202	20,516
1988	21,644	542	204	20,898
1989	21,879	536	167	21,176
1990	22,140	613	149	21,378
1991[b]	22,375	652	245	21,478
1992[b]	22,318	769	339	21,210
1993[b]	22,068	769	373	20,926

Sources: Until 1990 Gautié et al. (1994, 171); for 1990, 1991, 1992, and 1993, *Premières Synthèses* 30, 48, 71 (as of December 31).
a. Data from Comptes Nationaux until 1990 and MTEFP thereafter.
b. Estimates as of December 31.

Table 7.2
Unemployment and employment policies (in thousands)

	Unemployed without job search obligations	Early retirement	Professional training stages	Total measured jobs	Unemployed
1973		44	47	91	394
1974		59	48	107	498
1975		75	62	138	840
1976		93	83	184	933
1977		102	79	273	1,072
1978		137	95	554	1,163
1979		158	89	562	1,350
1980		188	87	619	1,451
1981		280	83	814	1,773
1982		413	101	925	2,008
1983		650	112	1,042	2,068
1984	1	684	119	1,070	2,340
1985	27	637	135	1,183	2,456
1986	99	561	145	1,445	2,517
1987	141	470	151	1,731	2,622
1988	209	394	202	1,551	2,563
1989	220	344	206	1,473	2,532
1990	230	288	242	1,522	2,505
1991[a]	232	175	134	1,438	
1992[a]	233	176	213	1,730	
1993[a]	252	192	129	1,715	3,400

Sources: Until 1990 Gautié et al. (1994, 171); for 1990, 1991, 1992, and 1993, *Premières Synthèses* 30, 48, 71 (as of December 31).
a. Estimates as of December 31.

skilled, full-time, permanent jobs became more the exception than the rule. However, some remarks must be made about the development of new hiring practices, such as by temporary or fixed-term contracts. First, this development has not been continuous; rather, it seems to have come to a temporary halt at the end of the 1980s (IRES 1991). Second, it is clear that over the long term, although precarious forms of employment have evolved, the overall number of jobs threatened by this phenomenon has not changed significantly (Fourcade 1991). Third, in some ways, in France, the increase in part-time working arrangements in response to the rise in unemployment has not been comparable to that found in some other countries, so the development of new work forms has been relatively limited.[2] Fourth, the changing employment situation affects individuals differently. Some people, at least in certain stages of their careers, manage to maintain satisfactory career paths even in precarious jobs, whereas others fall into a succession of precarious jobs because they come upon serious difficulties in entering the labor market and integrating into society (Drancourt 1991).

A Shift in Production Systems

Throughout most of the 1900s,[3] employment in industry grew, driven by considerable productivity gains (Dewerpe 1989).[4] After World War I this growth in productivity and employment was due to the increasingly dominant Fordist production model. The Fordist system was based on large industrial establishments where relatively unskilled workers carried out repetitive tasks under the strict control of a large body of supervisory staff. Productivity gains were achieved essentially through the use of more efficient machinery.

In the 1970s, as increases in productivity slowed down considerably,[5] a new model of industrial employment gradually emerged. It offered promise, as some argued, of regenerating postwar levels of productivity and growth: Plants became smaller and workers' emphasis was placed on investment in training. This new trend was reflected in the ratio between skilled and unskilled workers in industry, which kept rising for fifteen years. The increasing demand for skill has now reached the point where a definite shortage of skilled workers can be observed, while unemployment among unskilled workers is widespread.

In part, this new mode of production was a move away from the concentration of firms. Until the 1950s and 1960s France was a country where the concentration of firms was low and where small and medium-sized firms predominated (Carre et al. 1972). Then, starting in the 1950s, large financial groups began to form, and the physical

---

2. Only 12 percent of male and 24 percent of female workers are employed part time (Eurostat 1990).
3. The slump of the 1930s is an exception to this growth trend. Between 1931 and 1936, employment in the secondary sector fell from 7.2 to 5.9 million.
4. From 1949 to 1973, hourly productivity rose by 5.1 percent each year.
5. It should be noted that the rate of increase (3.1 percent) is still higher than that recorded in past periods.

size of the average firm increased. It was in the larger establishments that new jobs tended to be created. From the mid-1970s onward, however, the trend toward growing employment in establishments with more than 500 employees was reversed, and with the exception of 1989 and 1990, employment in large establishments has declined. Thus concentration, as measured by the average size of firms, has fallen (*Liaisons sociales* 1991).

Though it is clear that French employers' practices have changed, the extent of this shift is less apparent. Certainly there is no uniformity in the adoption of the new production model, and it is not as prevalent as many of its proponents claim. Even in large firms that claim to be implementing such a policy, wage-employment relationships have not changed rapidly.

Modes of Managerial Thought: Paternalism, Taylorism and Beyond

The changes in work levels and practices have been accompanied by a remarkable change in the attitude of employers toward their employees. For a long time employers' attitudes could be characterized by a sort of authoritarian paternalism: Even before being a capitalist or a businessman, the head of a French company was above all a "patron," the natural, unchallenged leader of a working community (Bunel and Saglio 1979). This conception was modernized when French managers embraced "scientific management"—a theory of work design and compensation particularly consistent with Fordist mass production that was created by F. W. Taylor. In the Taylorist system, employees are perceived as interchangeable, and productivity gains are mainly expected to accrue through tightly engineered jobs, incentive pay, and technical innovation. Since the 1970s it has been the fashion, even among company managers, to criticize Taylorism for introducing depersonalized working relationships. Productivity gains, it is argued, should be sought through investment in training and the involvement of workers in decision-making processes, as in the new employment model outlined above.

In analyzing the trend toward Taylorism and the subsequent shift to a new approach, researchers often focus on the influence and significance of market and technological change. But, we are dealing above all with a conceptual change—that is, with an evolution in modes of thought that managers wish to explore when putting forward their programs. Managers are conceptualizing work and their relationships with workers in distinctly new ways.

7.2 The French Industrial Relations System

Industrial relations systems are complex historical constructs (Reynaud et al. 1990). It is therefore futile to look for a single structuring principle running through all of them at all times. Accordingly I will not attempt to characterize the French IR system in any simple, static way but will explore the historical development of several of its features. I will examine six characteristics of the French system. The first three are concerned with the definition of the leading collective actors, namely the trade unions, the employers and the state; the fourth with the formal rules governing the system; the fifth with commonly shared conceptions of conflict and negotiation;[6] and the sixth with the role of the industrial relations system in training and welfare policies.

Trade Union Pluralism and Representativeness

At the end of World War II the French government conferred to trade unions the power to engage in negotiation. The legitimacy of the role of unions in negotiations rests primarily upon this state anchor, rather than upon elections or consultation of the membership. Thus trade union institutions presently empowered to negotiate employment conditions for all French employees, even inside a plant, were so designated by their political stance almost half a century ago.

When French trade union confederations agree to engage in collective bargaining, they do so because they claim to represent all employees and not simply their own members. Trade unions do not derive their legitimacy in negotiation from membership mandates but rather from their existence as institutions.[7] This conception of legitimacy influences the way in which the articulation of interests is

---

6. The description presented here is a framework for an analysis of the dynamics on which I am currently at work. Thus the reader should not be surprised by my singling out as leading characteristics elements that are perhaps not so obvious in current industrial relations practice.

7. "Thus the representativeness of the trade union does not have to be proved or measured by an electoral procedure: it is substantive in nature since it is based on a communality of interests and a natural community of sentiment. To this extent, it is possible to speak of virtual representation and essentialist representativeness" (Rosanvallon 1988, 209).

conceived: At the highest level, trade unions claim to represent the collective interests of employees, which is differentiated from the general interests of society at large (Rials 1987). Elections in such a system offer both a means of selecting employees' legitimate representatives for contract negotiations and a measure of the power of the opposing forces.[8] As a result French trade unions can be said to function as general political institutions representing the collective interests of employees rather than as pressure groups representing specific interests.

Because of the political capacity of trade unions, the practice of restricting advantages to union members is rare in France. It is forbidden by law to limit the gains of collective bargaining to union members only, just as it is illegal to make membership compulsory.[9] Nevertheless, the situation is not so straightforward, insofar as trade unions are active both in the defense of employees' individual claims and in the negotiation of collective benefits.

The frequently "political" implications of trade union decisions can also be linked to their nature as political institutions, as can the fact that union pluralism is seen as a democratic requirement, a consequence of the freedom of expression and association. This conception of unions has encouraged activists to focus on general political projects put forward by the confederations rather than participating in the collective construction of the representation of interests. As a consequence trade union sensibilities as a whole must be represented everywhere, and the securing of a majority in industrywide elections does not provide one trade union with an opportunity to exclude the others.

To conclude this brief survey of trade unionism, it should be pointed out that the particular character of union pluralism and representation in France has historically seemed to meet the interests of unions as well as those of employers and the state. On the one hand, employers and the state have been able to thwart the development of revolutionary trade unionism by dealing with more reformist unions, even if they remained in a minority. On the other hand, French trade unions have been able to continue to develop notions of trade unionism as a mass movement and revolutionary vanguard not engaged in the day-to-day representation of employees' interests. Without being

---

8. Presently there are signs of both a decline of union membership (Bevort) and of union strength being preserved in elections (Labbe).
9. Indeed this prohibition of closed shops is to a large extent the purpose of the 1956 law on trade unions (Lyon Caen 1984).

quite as radical, unions have also been able to participate actively in the negotiation of gains for employees without having to endorse compromises, since agreements come into force as soon as one of the representative unions signs them. In this way unions have been able to adopt a critical stance, taking the credit for any gains acquired without having to enter into compromises in order to make them permanent. However, the chronic lack of members from which French trade unions suffer may be viewed, in part, as a consequence of this institutional form.[10]

The Role of the State

Extensive government intervention is a well-known characteristic of the French industrial relations system. For this reason I will limit my discussion to a brief survey of some of its main implications.

First, government involvement in IR has been fostered by pressure from unions and employers in order to ensure the stability of their agreements by enlisting state support. It is only in exceptional cases that pragmatism wins the day and understanding between the actors is sufficient to guarantee the legitimacy of an agreement. State intervention is desirable in agreements between parties because the agreements can be translated into law through the legal mechanism of extension. As a result agreements are typically couched in terms that bring them close to the law.[11] Agreements, like the law, tend to be applicable *erga omnes* for an indeterminate period. Thus when bargaining takes place, discussions focus more on general principles than on precise conditions under which the agreement will apply.

Second, the state can intervene as a third party in the processes leading to agreement between the other actors. In some circumstances the state may arbitrate disputes; in other circumstances it may encourage and coordinate negotiations, at the workshop or company

10. "The general weakness of the French trade union movement is primarily due to the law, . . . the whole structure of economic and social law is based on this notion of [trade union] plurality . . . it has become inaccurate to say that some trade unions are representative. They 'exist.' And because they exist, they have a duty to speak on behalf of all employees" (Lyon Caen 1984, 7–9).

11. The debate on the nature of the collective agreement is shared by analysts of industrial relations in France. It has been part of their intellectual baggage from the early days of the debate at the beginning of this century (Pirou 1909; see Dezes 1993) up to the most recent times (Morin 1991); it reached its classic high points in the 1930s (Durand 1939).

level (through a factory investigator) and at industry or interindustry levels (through the organization of collective bargaining).

The state can advance its policy aims by limiting the permissible content of collective agreements. For example, the state may police contracts between unions and employers when wage controls are in force. It can also introduce legislative and regulatory measures (from health and safety regulations to legislation on vocational training or the monthly payment of salaries).

One of the most striking characteristics of the French government is that it does not limit its intervention to the sphere of industrial relations. There is a long-established tradition in France of political leaders[12] having so little faith in the virtues of the market that they enact an "industrial policy" to strengthen French industry in the face of competition. These industrial policies have not always been consistent with government policies on industrial relations, however.

Finally, no discussion of industrial relations can ignore the fact the government is the biggest employer in France. In its role as employer in the public sector, it assumes the right systematically to depart from the rules that it imposes on other employers. The government is also the owner of hybrid companies that are both public and private in character. As a result the government has at its disposal, even if only by setting an example, a considerable capacity for action in granting new privileges to employees or in determining wage policy.

United Employers and Autonomous Firms

For a long time it was possible to characterize French employers' strategies toward industrial relations in terms of one concern: the elimination of collective bargaining from the company level (Sellier 1961). As a result the main task of the employers' organizations was to take responsibility outside the firm for maintaining necessary relations with unions and government authorities. The employers' primary hope was that this would limit disputes. They were convinced that disputes were fomented by organizations outside their companies and that it was therefore necessary to keep unions at a distance. This opposition was responsible in part for the very belated recognition accorded to unions within firms.[13]

---

12. Often included among these are high-level civil servants.
13. Recognition came by a law in December 1968.

However, by eschewing involvement in negotiations, employers also hoped to preserve their independence. The French concept of authority considers it more important for the person in charge to be independent, and thus not consult with others, than it is for him or her to make strategic decisions. In the eyes of many traditional French bosses, it is better to be small and independent than to be large and involved in mutually dependent relationships.[14] This behavioral model has prevailed for a long time for French company directors.

Employers' organizations have traditionally had to contend with a double role: a *social* one of maintaining relations with employees' organizations and an *economic* one of engaging in dialogue with various government agencies responsible for the implementation of industrial, financial, and customs policies. To accomplish the latter, particularly in the interest of maintaining social order, employer organizations have become closely allied. Thus pluralism on the trade union side has had to contend with unity on the employers' side, not only at the company level but also at higher, industry and interindustry, levels. However, notwithstanding the unity of the employers' organizations and the fact that they represent the vast majority of businesses, they are limited in their ability to negotiate and to maneuver.

For a long time, with the aim of avoiding potentially constraining cross-firm cooperation, whether industrywide or involving only a few organizations, employers wielded control over their immediate environment. The traditional large French company could maintain its autonomy by taking on a number of social functions unconnected with the production process, such as housing, town planning, education and vocational training (Bunel and Saglio 1979). French employers preferred regulated markets to free markets, whether it was a question of the supply of labor, housing, or raw materials or indeed of the consumer market itself.

In recent years, however, although employers have undoubtedly achieved more stature, they have abandoned many of the social functions they previously assumed. "We owe it to ourselves to ensure the full employment to which the French people are rightly committed" declared the head of social committee at the French employers' confederation in 1973. This objective has manifestly been abandoned

---

14. In the early 1970s a majority of directors of firms or plants with more than fifty employees chose independence when presented with the question: "If you had to choose between expansion and independence for your company, what would you do?" (Bunel and Saglio 1979).

by his successors. Neither the temptations of protectionism nor the control of employees' lives outside work now figure on the employers' agenda. French employers claim to have been converted to the virtues of the free market.

Linking the Various Levels and Firms' Independence

From a legal point of view, the French IR system is often described as a series of interrelated levels, the whole constituting "law and order in the social domain" (*l'ordre public social*). General law articulated at the highest level is adapted and clarified through agreements at lower levels, as it passes from national interindustry, to national industry, to regional industry, and down to the firm. However, the social partners can depart from higher law in their agreements only in ways favorable to employees.

This system is designed to have rigor, elegance, and simplicity. But, in practice it is not quite so simple or elegant. First, certain elements cannot be modified, even in a way that would be considered favorable to employees. For example, procedural rules, such as the definition of electoral jurisdictions within firms, cannot be changed by agreement at a lower level. To some extent then, the hierarchy of levels corresponds to a division of roles, with more general and fixed rules decided at higher levels. However, the number of derogations and exceptions permitted under other regulations is so great that the relevance may well be questioned.

More fundamentally, despite the hierarchical arrangement of levels, the authority vested the various levels is neither straightforward nor stable. One of the first issues in any negotiation is to determine the level at which the problem is to be resolved. The actors' strategy must be to designate within the changeable structure of authority the level allocated for a decision of comparable significance. However, disputes about the designation of levels can be also disputes about the description of rules. The determination of the appropriate level for negotiations is as much a question of strategy as of logic, or even of just a power struggle (Sellier 1961). The same applies to the definition of levels: The composition and definition of the relevant body for negotiation is itself often a matter for negotiation, and this is particularly true when it comes to defining industries.[15]

15. "What defines an industry or an occupation for the purposes of negotiation is very far from being explicit or even clear. The division into industries is clearly a product of

In recent times two different tendencies have combined to displace the negotiating process. On the one hand, the voluntarist policies adopted by successive governments have led to an increase in the number of people covered by collective agreements at industry level (Jobert et al. 1993). On the other hand, company-level agreements have increased significantly, particularly in the 1980s in the wake of the Auroux laws.[16] Questions can be asked about the concomitance of this increase in the number of agreements and the weakening of the trade union movement: Is it an indication that employers have developed the habit of negotiating agreements, or is it merely a new means of declaring employers' decisions in the sphere of labor force management (annual reports by the CSNC;[17] Ferec and Loos 1988)?

The Negotiated Agreement: Armistice Rather than Contract

The conception that French social partners have of the agreements they reach with each other and of the formal rules within which they operate differs from that prevailing in most English-speaking countries. The standard French agreement is not seen as an instrument for prescribing the partners' actual behavior, but rather as a declaration of a minimum standard to which an employer has to conform.[18] Thus wage agreements do not list the wages that are paid or the increases that will be granted, but the minimum levels that employers agree to take as a baseline in the determination of actual wage rates. However, the precise fixing of such rates remains the prerogative of employers.[19]

---

unmitigated empiricism. It seems difficult not to conclude that everything depends on circumstance" (Reynaud and Verdier 1990, 59).

16. In 1993 there were 6,122 collective agreements signed at the level of the firm (or plant). Covered by such agreements (11 percent by agreements on wages) were 2,564,000 (18 percent) employees. The rates were 29 percent in secondary sector, 6 percent in construction, 9 percent in trade, and 17 percent in services (Mabile 1994)

17. The CSNC (or Commission Supérieure de la Négociation Collective) is a national commission that evaluates collective agreements and public policy in industrial relations.

18. Gérard Lyon Caen, on the matter of the negotiating collective agreements, says: "collective agreements have hitherto been nothing more than a *concerted statement of the minimum level of protection* to which employees in a given industry may lay claim" (Lyon Caen 1984, 13).

19. The real rules and customs are more complex. Agreements on wages at the level of the branch or at the level of interindustry bargaining are only for fixing minimums (sometimes the minimum increase, so-called bargaining on "actual" wages). Since the Auroux laws of 1982, there must be annual bargaining (but no obligation of agreement) in the plant about overall wage increases. In the public sector the procedure represents fixed actual and real wages.

Thus legal or negotiated regulation is not predictive because the law permits employers to depart from it. However, it should also be realized that employers very often do not feel bound even by these minimum levels. For example, for more than forty years it has been a legal requirement that a works council should be elected in all firms with more than fifty employees, but the minister of labor has published statistics that reveal the slow pace at which this statutory institution was being established. Some industry-level agreements remain similarly unenforced, and there are examples of collective agreements that have remained virtually unimplemented because employers consider their wage provisions excessive. Furthermore, in theory, minimum wage guarantees are compulsory, but exceptions are now often permitted as a means of reducing unemployment.

If agreements are not always respected, one of the reasons is that the actors show little interest in monitoring their implementation. There are very few grievance procedures that function effectively, and rather than trying to improve the functioning and implementation of an agreement, negotiators seem to prefer to embark on new, dramatized negotiations of a technical nature. In such a situation the view of these negotiation shared by the actors may be likened to a temporary truce between two armies determined to renew hostilities at a later date, rather than a compromise or the signing of a contract as a stable method to resolve their disputes even if only for a limited period.

Even if collective agreements cannot be predicted and are not always implemented, they still play a considerable role in France's industrial relations system. They provide the standards for actors to refer to in assessing each other's behavior.[20] Thus sectoral wage agreements are by no means useless, even if they result in wage agreements that are lower than the minimum wage rates imposed by the government.

Training and Redistribution

Are French modes of training and redistribution products of its industrial relations system? Clearly all three institutional actors are con-

---

20. A Ministry of Labor circular of 1915 gives a good definition of this regulatory effect on wage statements: "wage statements . . . make known a wage rate . . . based on practice and general agreement and which everyone, employers and workers alike, knows to represent . . . the standard rate for the region. Employers and workers naturally take it as a basis for their contracts, and are influenced by its regulatory effect even when they depart from it" (Oualid and Picquenard 1928, 164n).

cerned with training and redistribution. However, although the rules governing these systems are sometimes negotiated by the social partners, the state has been for a long time, since 1967, the major actor in this arena.

The policy concerning training and redistribution is highly centralized. It is often carried out by institutional mechanisms in which the state plays a dominant role. This has long been true of initial education and training, of which the state education system is the principal provider. Most educational facilities, including higher education institutions, belong to this centralized system. Curricula, requirements, qualifications for degrees, and even the faculty are all managed centrally. Private or jointly managed institutions play a more important role in technical training, especially for shorter courses of lower social status (table 7.3).

The state exerts even greater control over the redistribution and welfare systems. Health, pensions, family income supplements, and unemployment insurance are all managed by mixed systems in which interindustry negotiation at the national level plays a role, even though the state is the dominant partner. The greater part of the financial flows linked to training, health, pensions, assistance to families, and unemployment benefits are thus under state control (tables 7.4 and 7.5). However, unlike education spending, most of this expenditure is not financed out of taxation but rather by a direct levy on companies, which have to contribute a proportion of their wage bill. Agreements between the social partners, whether at the industry or company level, merely supplement or modify this basic system.

Table 7.3
Financial support of firms to vocational training (in millions 1990 FF)

1972	11,417
1974	15,551
1976	16,619
1978	19,821
1981	20,723
1983	23,123
1985	25,102
1987	28,323
1989	33,572
1991	37,868
1992	40,206

Source: *DSTE* 104 (December 1993).

Table 7.4
Professional training funding (in millions 1992 FF)

	First employment	Unemployed	Employed	Miscel- laneous	Total	Percent
State	11,385	12,093	28,344	2,447	542,698	44.5
Local col- lectivities	2,032	2,447	1,332	315	6,126	5.0
Other public agencies	96	302	2,539	128	3,065	2.5
UNEDIC[a]	0	7,425	0	183	7,608	6.2
Firms	8,758	91	37,315	3,352	49,516	40.6
Households	63	0	1,164	241	1,468	1.2
Total	22,334	22,358	70,694	6,666	122,052	100
Percent	18.3	18.3	57.9	5.5	100	

Source: Osbert et al. (1994).
a. Joint national institution for funding unemployment.

Table 7.5
Welfare accounts (in billions 1992 FF)

	Social security	National social effort	Social insurance
General	1,500		
Social aid		450	
Voluntary or private agreement			130

Source: Join Lambert et al. (1994, 324).

The burden of this system of redistribution has increased steadily overall, even though successive governments have tried for fifteen years to put a brake on its expansion. On the other hand, the relative share of these various methods of redistribution has gradually changed: The insurance components (health, unemployment) and pensions now play a more important role than those directly connected to redistribution (family allowances and housing benefits; Join Lambert et al. 1994).

7.3   Rupture and Continuity in the 1980s

An Era of Changes

The changes that have taken place in industrial relations since the mid-1970s are significant but contradictory. The Auroux laws brought an end to the trade union monopoly in expressing workers' views. The ability of the traditional actors, both trade unions and employers, to mobilize support declined sharply, and new actors, often short-lived, emerged during labor disputes. At the same time bargaining increased: New collective agreements were signed in industries that had not hitherto been the subject of such accords, and old agreements were systematically revised. Similarly the obligation to hold annual wage negotiations at the company level was a significant change, and the number of agreements signed increased considerably.

Was this simply an effect of the growth in unemployment? Labor disputes have even decreased in number and changed in nature, with disputes limited to certain categories of employees taking the place of one-day general strikes.[21] At the same time, however, the major conflicts that pose a threat to the social fabric no longer seem to be closely linked to labor disputes. For more than a century, social explosion, whether hoped for or feared, was expected to arise out of changes in wage-employment relationships. The social movements likely to bring about radical changes seemed to be associated with the labor movement. For at least ten years this system of dispute management linked to the world of work has seemed incapable of papering over the considerable cracks in the social fabric. Even though they are certainly not unconnected with problems of employment and unemployment, the greatest tensions in French society seem rather to have their roots in the problems besetting urban areas than in those experienced by firms.

Productive Flexibility: Fashion or Reality?

Traditionally the modes of work organization in French industry, both in firms and in the commercial and industrial relationships between firms, were neither homogeneous nor identical. Taylorism gradually became established in industries based on mass production, particularly the automobile, domestic goods, and clothing industries. Yet it was in the more bureaucratic sectors that this philosophy took greatest hold. It may seem paradoxical, but it was in the large public-sector service organizations, such as the post office and the railways, and in

---

21. From 1970 to 1975, in the private sectors four million days, on average, were lost to strikes; the number decreased to three million in the late 1970s and even more in the 1980s. In 1991 to 1993 it was less than half a million. In the public sector (state-owned firms and agencies), about 2 million days were lost in the early 1980s and less than one million in 1991 to 1993 (Furjot 1994).

banking, that Taylorism became most firmly entrenched in the 1970s. In these sectors Taylorism led to the development of standardized working conditions, job descriptions, and methods of payment but only rarely to strict performance-related payment systems. In such organizations, while work organization closely followed the dictates of Taylorism, other elements of personnel management were driven instead by an absolute priority given to internal labor markets. In other large firms in which production runs were shorter and the average skills of operatives higher, the system of work organization made room for technicians and engineers, but efforts to standardize behavior made less headway. Here again, in line with the tradition of paternalism, personnel management was governed to a large extent by the priority given to the internal labor market.

Interfirm relations were also ambiguous. Employers desired independence, but they wanted it to be guaranteed through constraints on their employees rather than through strength in the open market. This value system had its source in the tradition of the cartels and accords of the interwar period, and it did not disappear during the postwar period of economic expansion, although it did take a new form (Bunel and Saglio 1979). Thus French firms favored long-term relationships, custom, and tradition and remained reluctant to expose themselves to competition.[22] It required all the power and intervention of the state to persuade firms to accept, reluctantly, the workings of the free market.[23]

After Taylorism company directors had to change direction. Whereas before it was necessary to be well organized and have control over everything, faith now was placed in employees' resources and skills; whereas before it was necessary at all costs to stabilize production by seeking to extend production runs, it now became fashionable to operate with tightly controlled flows, reducing turnaround times and batch size; whereas before it used to be thought necessary to integrate activities within the organization in order to stand a better chance of remaining independent, it was now considered appropriate to place faith in the market and to forge links with other firms. The French economy became subject to the same management practices as other developed economies.

---

22. J. R. Pitts, an ingenious and mischievous observer of the French bourgeoisie, attributes this reluctance to face competition to the fact that causing the collapse of a rival firm brought social disgrace to a middle-class family, a serious crime for which no member of the bourgeoisie wanted to take responsibility (Pitts 1963).
23. Such intervention fostered the free trade treaty negotiated during the Second Empire and the construction of the European Common Market between 1958 and 1975

Such prescriptions did accord with certain long-established informal practices, but they came up against resistance from certain quarters. Strictly controlled work flows require cooperation between firms and their suppliers. Such cooperation is easier to establish in France, where competition is considered an anomaly by company managers, than in other countries where interfirm relations have always been governed by the laws of the market. However, the particular methods that French firms had long used to retain labor (which led to fairly high versatility among workers) proved to be obstacles to the standardization of production and increases in production runs. Likewise social distinctions and hierarchical boundaries within firms blocked the development of real cooperation. The barriers between production workers and technicians and between these two categories and middle managers are still considerable, and are reinforced by separate types of training, career paths, and ways of life. Change in these spheres remains stubbornly slow.

The Auroux laws of 1982, in their attempt to change the behavior of organizing groups within firms, provided for the direct expression of employees' views. After an initial period of extensive experimentation, the number of organizing groups declined. In part, this decline could be said to have been due to an opposition of a political/ideological nature. Company directors, opposed to the intervention of the state, preferred to establish quality circles rather than direct expression groups. This response could be said to be only temporary, and there are obvious cultural issues contributing to this decline. In establishing more participatory practices on a permanent basis, it is important to involve all actors in the firm, middle managers and executives as well as workers, supervisory staff, and trade union organizations. This vast undertaking cannot be completed by simply introducing a law.

Training

The state education system has traditionally enjoyed a position of unrivaled supremacy in the field of vocational training. It has often been pointed out, quite rightly, that within that system the various routes toward vocational qualification are perceived as subject to a hierarchy in which the greatest prestige is attached to academic or theoretical training and the least value to preparation for specific jobs in industry. Alongside the state education system, industry and commerce has established a number of vocational training institutions that maintain close links with firms. However, the training offered in these establishments is generally perceived to be second rate, suitable only for youths who have failed in the state system.

The presence of this alternative second system, for the most part controlled and sometimes directly financed by firms, is a clear indication of the value that firms attached to training. For paternalistic French employers who have sought to combat the influences of craft organizations and to escape the pressures and constraints of open labor markets, direct organization by firms of the training they require is an effective and lasting means of ensuring a stable supply of labor.[24] Since the early 1970s this long-established tradition has been progressively incorporated into a system managed by interindustry agreements and laws on vocational training and education.

This regulatory framework, based on agreements and legislation, reflects the expectations of industrial firms. In order to cope with new technologies or to implement organizational changes, firms have frequently utilized continuing training, and there are many firms that have far exceeded the compulsory levels of expenditure on continuing training.[25] The development of the continuing training market has had the unexpected effect of furthering change in the state education system itself, and the various institutions within that system are increasingly adapting to the needs of these lucrative markets. Whether they are offering training for unskilled workers, technicians or even managers, the technical schools, the *grandes écoles*, and the universities are devoting increasing resources to training, developing links with firms and changing the training they offer in order to meet demand.

However, firms are not the only players in the management of continuing training. Training centers are administered by representatives of some associations of firms and trade unions. In consequence the

---

24. Training was possible at the level of the firm or at the level of a regional industry, and many private vocational schools for workers and technicians were founded by associations of local employers.

25. Since the early 1970s, following a national interindustry agreement on July 9, 1970, between the trade union confederations and the employers' confederation and the subsequent introduction of legislation on July 16, 1971, firms having more than ten employees have been obliged to devote a certain percentage of their wage bill to continuing training. Since then, this regulatory structure has been supplemented and clarified by various laws and agreements. The minimum level of contribution was initially 0.8 percent and is now 1.5 percent. Many firms exceed these minimum levels: The level of contribution, which was 0.51 percent of the gross domestic product in 1972, was 1.77 percent in 1992 (Osbert et al. 1994).

Table 7.6
Vocational training by firm size

Size	10–19	20–49	50–499	500–1,999	>2,000	Total
Financial participation rate[a]	1.50	1.63	2.32	3.45	5.24	3.32
Employee participation rate[b]	7.13	11.57	26.00	42.51	55.15	34.32

Source: *DSTE* No. 104 (December 1993).
a. Vocational training expenses as percent of total wages.
b. Percent of employees participating in a training course during the year.

continuing training system supports cross-firm links at the industry level. And this long-established practice has not been challenged in recent decades.

Whatever obligations firms have in the sphere of continuing education, and whatever benefits they draw from it, there remain a considerable number of firms that are not very concerned with the training of their work forces. These are largely, but not exclusively, smaller enterprises (table 7.6). These firms, which make systematic use of the external market for their labor supply and scarcely concern themselves with continuing training, fall into two categories. On the one hand, they are fairly small firms, in traditional sectors with low levels of technology, and on the other, they are more modern firms for which systematic recourse to the external market is considered by managers to be a criterion of good management, a means of avoiding training costs.

In addition to the efforts made by firms, the state has made sustained attempts to adapt the initial training system to the needs of firms. The school leaving age has been raised, and in 1993, 54.7 percent of the age group attained the *baccalauréat* (high school graduation). At the same time new courses and special procedures have been put in place to give youths who leave the school system without training another chance to acquire qualifications.

Of course diplomas are not sufficient to ensure that the training they certify has real content. The state, including the state education system, offers internships and work-study positions in these programs to secure a young, well-educated work force at low cost without altering the structure or the content of a job.[26] As a result, and

---

26. In 1993, 13.2 percent of people employed with a CES contract (restricted to short-term, half-time, and minimum wage employees in nonprofit organizations) had baccalaureate or higher degrees (Monchois 1994).

Table 7.7
Wage increases and type of agreement

Rate of firms giving:	10–49	50–199	200–999	1,000–4,999	5,000+	Total
No increase	24	29	1	0	3	24
Increase	76	71	99	100	97	76
Only general	62	69	51	21	10	62
Only individual	23	11	14	18	9	21
Mixed	15	20	35	61	81	17

Source: Mabile (1994).

despite all the public statements about valuing training and education, there is a certain skepticism among young people about the measures being taken in this sphere. This dissatisfaction with "dead-end courses" or "fraudulent training programs" has been articulated by the trade unions, but they have not really put forward any positive alternative proposals for the organization of training.

Wages and Income from Work

It has always been difficult to ascertain with any accuracy the state of wages in France. Collective agreements at the industry level only lay down minimum wage levels that employers can alter. Even firm-level agreements seldom contain complete and accurate pay scales. With the introduction of the Auroux law of 1982, firms of a certain size became obliged to hold annual wage negotiations. However, an obligation to negotiate does not necessarily translate into actual agreements on average wages. Except for government employees, whose wages and earnings are determined by national rules, the determination of individual pay rates is still for the most part the prerogative of company directors. In fact the trend toward the development of individualized forms of payment has strengthened this traditional characteristic of the French system (table 7.7).

Average wages are often considerably higher than those stipulated in collective agreements.[27] So the various forms of wage bargaining are not totally devoid of meaning. Negotiations on job classifications,

---

27. In February 1990 the average monthly basic wage for manual workers in 1989 was 21 percent higher than the average guaranteed monthly minimum wage for skilled workers on the first rung of their job classification scale. Comparable discrepancies are found at all levels of the pay scale (*Liaisons Sociales* 1991).

which take place at the industry level, produce lists of job categories and pay differentials to which the various actors constantly refer, even if only to distance themselves from them (Eyraud et al. 1989). If firms do not stick to the provisions of agreements in determining their pay levels, they certainly seem to adhere faithfully to the rates of increase recommended by the employers' organizations. In these respects perhaps more than in others, the role of negotiations is only to establish common reference points by which the various actors give direction to their strategies.

Bargaining is all the more difficult in the French situation, since determination of the various elements that make up income lies partly outside the control of decision makers at the firm or industry level. Thus the breakdown between direct and indirect wages is only marginally influenced by decisions made at firm level. For a long time the French system could be characterized by the size of and the continual increase in the share of indirect wages in pay.[28] For the past fifteen years the state and employers' organization have been seeking to reverse that trend. But the financing of unemployment benefits, like that of pension schemes and social security, falls within the scope of these indirect wage mechanisms rather than the tax system or voluntary sector.

If efforts to reduce the proportion of indirect wages in overall pay have not been overwhelmingly successful, there have been other changes. For a long time the trend toward a rise in the level of earned income relative to income from capital seemed ineluctable. For the past fifteen years, despite the increase in the number of wage earners, this trend has clearly been reversed, and income from capital has increased at a much faster rate than earned income.

For earned income there was a tendency for a slow contraction of the wage spread. The statutory minimum wage was systematically increased by amounts slightly in excess of the cost of living, and since this tended to rise more rapidly than other earned income, it helped to compress the wage spread. In 1984 the trend was reversed (Sandretto 1994). As part of the fight against unemployment, those in charge of government economic policy seem finally to have accepted the argument that the main factor in the growth of employment, in sectors where investment is low and the labor force unskilled, is

---

28. In the household total income, the rate of "welfare" income was 20.3 in 1960, 29.1 in 1975, 37.1 in 1985, and 38.3 in 1992 (Sandretto 1994, 70).

reduced labor costs. Thus special dispensations from the obligation to pay social security contributions have been granted (tables 7.1 and 7.2). This has led to the creation of several types of exceptional pay categories in which, under the pretext that they are undergoing training or preparing for entry into the labor market, workers, especially youths, are legally paid below the statutory minimum wage even though they are engaged in normal production work. As a result, and without taking any account of moonlighting, the wage spread has been extended downward.

The other causes of common wage hierarchies in the French industrial relations system do not seem to have changed as much. There is still a positive correlation between wage levels and size of firm. The hierarchies between industries have remained stable, and regional wage differences continue to favor the Paris region and, to lesser extent, a few other vital regions.

The weakening of the long-established system of employee representation is slowly beginning to make its effects felt. Employees were traditionally represented in wage negotiations by trade unions that took it upon themselves to bargain with employers on behalf of all employees in the firm or sector. One of the effects of the French system of trade union representation was to give the unions a not inconsiderable role in a harmonious management of wage claims. The weakening of trade unions has prevented them from acting as moderators and coordinators. The past few years have seen the emergence of genuinely corporatist wage disputes, a situation where neither the system of representation nor the system of negotiation is suited to the task of dealing with these problems.

Social Welfare: Differentiations and Challenges

The traditional French system of social welfare is commonly described as a "cascade" model. Bargaining or decision making enhances employees' social benefits. Thus all employees are said to be entitled to the social benefits accorded them by law as well as those stipulated by national interindustry agreements. At the other extreme, negotiations or decisions taken at the shop floor level can only improve upon decisions taken at the company level, which must themselves comply with the provisions of industrywide agreements. However, such a model requires that two conditions be fulfilled: that the definition of what constitutes an improvement for employees be obvious and commonly accepted, and that there be very few departures from the relevant law or agreement.

There is more chance of the first condition being met if only a small number of legitimate partners are involved in the determination of the hierarchy of benefits. When the French trade union confederations were considered to represent all employees, and one of them took the lead, the determination of that hierarchy was a fairly simple process. However, when trade union authority is blunted, agreement becomes more difficult. Thus for a long time it seemed that the exclusion of women from night work and the restriction on authorizations for weekend work represented improvements in employees' conditions. And the trade union confederations, led by the CGT, taught their activists to defend these hard-won gains and to extend them. For the past few years, the situation has been more complex: Even activists have openly questioned whether the principle of sexual equality at work should not lead to the ending of restrictions on women doing night work, and whether greater freedom in the management of working hours and free time is not a justification for weekend work. There have been similar developments in the area of dispensations. These were in fact common practices. In principle, labor law was supposed to be identical for all people, but it was determined far from the actual conditions on the shop floor. As a result grassroots activists found it difficult to know exactly what the law entailed, and a significant number of company agreements, though negotiated and signed in due form, contained provisions that should have been accompanied by requests for dispensation. Such practices are now more widely accepted, and are even enshrined in law which, in certain spheres, lays down the general rule and the procedures by which dispensations can be obtained. If the agreement of all the parties involved is all that is required for dispensations to be granted, the normative function of the higher level becomes nothing more than the ability to determine points of reference.

In identifying recent developments in social benefits, it may be useful to make a distinction between the various modes of industrial relations management adopted by firms and their employment practices.

In firms that place great emphasis on the internal labor market, the social benefits accorded employees—in addition to those laid down in law, statute, or collective agreements—have usually been quite large and have not generally been challenged. However, using the need for more flexibility in production as a justification, employers have tended to restrict entitlement to senior skilled workers within the company. Further, in subcontracting where there has been considerable expansion, it is difficult for suppliers generally to give their employees the level of social protection prevailing in the principal company. Such differences may also exist within firms as a result of the development of temporary and fixed-term employment contracts. To a certain extent good indicators of this phenomenon are the increasing share of SMEs in total employment and the growth in the number of employees with precarious employment contracts.

Among government employees similar differences exist. Here, the long-established tradition was for the statutory benefits to be guaranteed to civil servants, but other employees, whose presence would depend on an increase in employment numbers, would not even be guaranteed the benefits laid down by the labor code. The policy introduced at the end of the 1970s, and taken up and extended by the socialist governments of the 1980s, was an attempt to correct this phenomenon. However, the public sector cannot be compared with a company, and it is not sufficient for the government simply to issue directives on employment strategy for decisions taken on employment conditions to comply with government policy in that area. The end of growth in government employment has enabled social protection to be extended to state employees, and since 1983 this phenomenon has been reduced as it has been made more difficult to employ people without the protection afforded by labor law or contract.[29]

Finally, in companies that depend on the external labor market, with all its constraints, employees seldom had any significant social benefits over and above what was determined or negotiated outside the firm. This situation has probably not changed in traditional firms of this type, which are often manufacturing firms employing unskilled or semiskilled workers.

The differences in social protection among the employed are heightened by problems that affect the entire system. Notable among these systemic problems is the growth in the number of retired people. Also the persistence of very high unemployment has increased the burden on the social security system (table 7.8). As far as health care is concerned, the French experience is very similar to that of

---

29. By the end of 1993, in nonprofit sectors there were 372,800 part-time employed with short-term contracts and minimum wages; 63.2 percent of these workers were female and 30.3 percent were under 25 years old (Abrossimov et al. 1994).

Table 7.8
Public expenses for employment policies (in billions of current FF)

	1973	1980	1990	1991	1992	1993
Unemployment compensation	1.89	26.15	87.41	101.80	115.14	122.95
Retirement incentives	1.58	11.18	37.12	32.66	28.92	27.64
Employment preservation	0.14	2.51	3.47	3.48	4.06	6.28
Employment promotion	0.50	2.67	14.58	18.36	22.83	34.36
Job creation	0.08	1.39	4.50	4.43	4.44	5.14
Vocational training	5.72	19.82	67.37	74.06	81.59	87.43
Employment market	0.26	1.06	3.78	4.23	4.74	5.00
Total	10.17	64.77	218.22	239.02	261.72	288.80

Source: Roguet (1994).

other developed countries: expenditure on health care has been significantly exceeding economic growth. This phenomenon is reflected in increased pressure on the whole system of social protection.

Reform of the social security system and the continued viability of the national pension system are of continuing concern to politicians and those involved in collective bargaining. Some changes, such as the establishment of the national social security fund in order to finance the social security system by taxation, have greatly improved the system. Nevertheless, this system of social protection, once put in place to ease major social tensions at the workplace, is now experiencing great difficulty in coping with threats to the integrity of a social fabric that is no longer linked to the world of work.

Management and Supervision Methods

The character of old style management in French firms has been scrutinized in sufficient detail elsewhere (Sellier 1961; Hoffmann 1963; Crozier 1963; Bunel and Saglio 1979; Maurice et al. 1982), so it is not necessary to devote more than a few lines to it here. In the past the actors in the firms tried to avoid not only face-to-face confrontations but also competition that might disrupt congenial work relations. The industrial relations system was organized in such a way as to maintain managerial autonomy and independence, just as the system of economic management sheltered firms from the risks of unbridled competition. Any radical activity, even by trade unions representing employees, that occurred was external to the management process and the commitments extracted did not, by definition, have to be kept. In fact the slightest protest or demand put forward by employees was very often interpreted as a evidence of anticapitalist leaning.

The climate of work relations at the end of the 1980s bore very little relation to this model. Activity against the firm and the development of state control have given way to support for the open market: The social achievements of company managers and entrepreneurs had become symbols of success. Concurrently there had been a steady decline in the number of disputes, as indicated by the number of industrial conflicts in companies and on the shop floor. By the end of the 1980s labor disputes had fallen to their lowest level in many decades, and a large proportion of the disputes that did occur involved state employees.

There are many factors that might account for this change. The rise in unemployment is frequently mentioned. Fear of unemployment has made workers more cautious about making demands or entering into disputes that might well endanger their jobs. Workers also now could observe that it would be easier than in the past for an employer to make employees redundant. Yet another factor was the enhanced social status of those who provide employment: As "bosses" become "managers," they find themselves enjoying higher public esteem.

However, the rise in status of managers and entrepreneurs is not simply a consequence of the growth in unemployment. The mode of supervision and management in firms has also evolved: Productivity gains used to be sought through an intensive utilization of the labor force and through the standardization of products, machinery, jobs, and processes. Company directors in France were more than mere representatives of shareholders, but not all were the best salespersons or the most subtle politicians in managing internal disputes in the best possible way. The legitimacy of hired managers was their academic abilities, and particularly their scientific competence. In both the private and public sectors they were recruited from among engineers. Thus, with the greatest value placed on technical solutions to problems, their competencies could not challenged by their peers.

The new concept of management that has emerged stresses the need to mobilize the skills of the work force. It is in this mobilization of employees' resources that the greatest source of productivity gains now lies. At the level of the firm, particularly the larger ones, there has been created a craze for management and industrial relations that emphasizes employee participation and consultation. Progressive managers have been receptive to such methods and to such thinking for some time, and there has been a veritable proliferation of training seminars and popular works. Human resource management was traditionally considered to be a secondary function in French industry. In firms, it was entrusted to managers promoted from the shop floor or to retired army officers. These practices have been largely abandoned, and human resource management in firms has been added to the list of management functions.[30] Such changes in management methods have no doubt affected the shop floor work environment. The new trends have further been encouraged by the government: One of the Auroux laws, enacted in the early days of the socialist government, sought to promote direct consultation of employees about their working conditions and to introduce employee representation into small establishments and at sites with more than one employer.

To some extent the inspiration for these developments in management style can be traced to trade union ideologies, practices, and orientations. Although in most cases employers might have taken little notice of these views, it has long been one of the unions' most cherished ambitions to take an active, critical part in the debates of works councils. To achieve this goal, activists acquired training in the economics of the firm, accounting and management. Similarly, in advocating joint worker-management control, the CFDT made significant progress in strengthening managerial initiative among employees. In some disputes activists even embarked upon experiments in direct worker management by establishing workers' cooperatives in order to safeguard jobs threatened by redundancies. In this way the workers became aware of management problems and of market constraints, and they shared this awareness with other activists.

In light of this new passion for economic management and decision making, there has not been any strengthening of the institutions through which employees participate in decision making at company level. The vogue for "direct expression groups" seems to have died out, even though quality circles might be thought of as a continuation of that trend. Opposition to Taylorism and authoritarianism is a leitmotif that sometimes conceals thinking that is virtually indistinguishable from the targets being attacked. The efficacy of institutions through which employees are represented within firms has further been affected by the decline in trade union membership. With the

---

30. Evidence for this can be found in the increase in the number of vacancies for personnel managers appearing in publications specializing in executive recruitment and in the presence of this category in studies of managers' pay during the 1980s.

decline in the number of activists, it has become increasingly more difficult for many trade unions to appoint representatives to the many bodies in which they are invited to participate. Thus those management teams that would like to establish active participation policies through the trade unions sometimes find it necessary to take measures to support trade unionism.

7.4 Questions for Researchers

This chapter has not sought to summarize the evolution of industrial relations in France over the past ten years. Rather, it has highlighted certain factors that lead us to question the relevance of currently accepted theories in the fields of human resource management and industrial relations. In view of the French case we might make two general observations of a theoretical nature. The first relates to the history and varying rates of change of various elements of the IR system, and the second to the need to take into account changes affecting the character of work in our societies.

History, Industrial Relations Systems and Change

The analysis presented here has been conducted within an institutionalist framework, in the widest sense of the term. It has looked at relationships between individuals and between social groups, including market relationships, and has considered how these relationships operate and are regulated as they exist within and are structured by the social framework. However, in any given society there are different levels and forms of regulation, and these levels and forms do not necessarily form a coherent system. In particular, that coherence is not determined by the functional links that can be identified between the various subsets in the system. When the industrial relations system works, it is a social construct that is constantly modified, reshaped, and restructured by the participating actors (Reynaud 1989).

This notion is supported and clarified by this chapter on the French IR case. To reach an understanding of the entire IR system, it is necessary to take account of several different contributing factors and levels: industrial relations in the firm, interfirm relations, relationships between political actors, the evolution of international trade, demographic changes, and the like. None of these ingredients can be said to be entirely external to the system of employment.

For these various ingredients to be incorporated into the analysis, they cannot be reduced to any single explanatory system nor follow the same lines of development. This chapter's analysis is based on the fact that since the mid-1970s the French system of employment relations has had to cope with new circumstances and several related crises: at the very least, that of the international economic system, on the one hand, and that of the French political system, on the other, while coping with dramatic demographic changes.

To a certain extent these are circumstances external to the employment system and can thus be regarded as exogenous variables. However, such a position is not wholly tenable. The evolving political legitimacy of the various social actors and changes in the firms' place in society are mediated by, and in turn influence, the industrial relations system. Likewise there are other areas of change that can be seen as induced by rather than imposed on the IR system, including demographics which concerns the political management of immigration with regard to economic and industrial policy.

There are undeniable historical reasons for the different paces of change associated with heterogeneous social subgroups. To understand the ways in which the French IR system evolved, this chapter breaks with a tradition of analysis that makes economic situations the main elements in the explanation of actors' strategies. In certain circumstances we have to accept the fact that politics can be more important than economics in determining and structuring the strategies of actors (Bunel 1991).

The Social Functions of Labor Disputes

The history of industrial relations in France leads me to question the relevance of a certain number of widely accepted assumptions about the behavior of the various actors. As has been noted above, any understanding of the French system of employment requires an understanding of the actors' concept of the accord that links them to each other and the temporary agreements that they construct.

It is probably not enough to view the workplace as a market exchange in which the protagonists seek to maximize their financial interests, be they short, medium, or long term. Workplace relationships are also a means of socialization, an instrument through which individuals and social groups construct their identities. Conversely, we have to consider the fact that these relationships form part of and are structured by political agreements and by social concepts. Any attempt to understand the significance of current developments must take this into account. Traditionally, and in ways that differed from country to country, work, whether paid or not, served as a reference point around which one's social idenity was constructed. In controlling labor disputes, the workplace managed the integration of individuals and groups into society, and as a consequence those failing to be controlled were perceived by all others to be potential insurrectionists.

Work is certainly no longer central to the management of social conflict. This change took place in France around the beginning of the 1970s, and the events of 1968 can be considered both as the last great social movement of the age of industrialization and as the moment at which a new type of society began to emerge. The paradox of French society in the 1970s, and perhaps of other societies as well, is that the dissatisfaction that created major social tensions was clearly associated with the employment situation and yet could no longer be controlled within the old system through which employment and industrial relations were managed.

Despite this social evolution most of our current theories are based on the assumption that the social structure is immutable, particularly as far as the articulation of the economic and political spheres is concerned. We have to understand that the classical models were, in this respect, of relevance to the study of industrial societies and of the centrality of work and economics in managing conflicts in that type of society. The situation that faces us today is perhaps not yet radically different, but it is forcing us to ask whether the connection that we commonly make between the management of industrial relations and the strength of the social bond is merely one of many possible social configurations, and one which our societies are already in the process of leaving behind.

References

Abrossimov, C., D. Gelot, and B. Roguet. 1993. Bilan de la politique de l'emploi en 1992. *Premières Synthèses* 30 (September).

Abrossimov, C., and D. Gelot. 1994. En 1993, une politique de l'emploi très active. *Premières Synthèses* 71 (September).

Abrossimov, C., D. Gelot, S. Amira, B. Belloc, O. Marchand, and B. Roguet. 1994. Premier bilan de l'emploi et du chômage en 1993. *Premières Synthèses* 48 (April).

Adam, M., J. D. Reynaud, and J. M. Verdier. 1972. *La Négociation collective en France.* Paris: Ed. Economie et Humanisme.

Bunel, J. 1991. *Pactes et agressions.* Lyon: Ed. CNRS.

Bunel, J. , and J. Saglio. 1979. *L'Action patronale.* Paris: PUF.

Carre, J. J., P. Dubois, and E. Malinvaud. 1972. *La Croissance française: Un Essai d'analyse causale de l'après guerre.* Paris: Ed Seuil.

Crozier, M. 1963. *Le Phénomène bureaucratique.* Paris: Ed. Seuil.

Dewerpe, A. 1989. *Le Monde du travail en France, 1800–1950.* Paris: Ed. A. Colin.

Dezes, M. G. 1993. La préhistoire des conventions collectives françaises. In A. Jobert, J. D. Reynaud, J. Saglio, and M. Tallard, eds., *Les Conventions collectives de branche: Déclin ou renouveau.* Paris: CEREQ.

Durand, P. 1939. Le dualisme de la convention collective. *Revue Trimestrielle de Droit Civil:* 353–92.

Elbaum, M., and O. Marchand. 1993. Emploi et chômage des jeunes dans les pays industrialisés: La spécificité française. *Premières Synthèses* 34 (October).

Eyraud, F., A. Jobert, P. Rozenblatt, and M. Tallard. 1989. *Les Classifications dans l'entreprise.* Paris: La Documentation Française.

Ferec., G., and J. Loos, eds. 1988. *Négociation colective quels enjeux?* Paris: La Documentation Française.

Fourcade, B. 1991. L'Évolution des situations d'emploi particulières de 1945 à 1990. Paris: Document CEJEE.

Friedberg, E. 1975. L'État et l'industrie en France. Report CSO CORDES.

Furjot, D. 1994. Les conflits du travail en 1993: La défense de l'emploi au coeur des préoccupations. *Premières Synthèses* 67 (August).

Gautie, J., B. Gazier, R., Silvera, D., Anxod, P. Auer, and F. Lefresne. 1994. Les suventions à l'emploi : Analyses et expériences européennes. Paris: La Documentation Française, Série Document Travail et Emploi.

Hofmann, S., ed. 1963. *A la Recherche de la France.* Paris: Ed. Seuil.

IRES. 1991. Trois années de croissance forte de l'emploi en France. Working paper 91-05, IRES. November.

Jobert, A., and M. Tallard. 1993. Le rôle du diplôme dans la construction des grilles de classification professionnelle. In a. Jobert, J. D. Reynaud, J. Saglio, and M. Tallard, eds., *Les Conventions collectives de branche: Déclin ou renouveau.* Paris: CEREQ.

Jobert, A., J. D. Reynaud, J. Saglio, and M. Tallard, eds. 1993. *Les Conventions collectives de branche: Déclin ou renouveau.* Paris: CEREQ.

Join Lambert, M. T., A. Bolot Gitler, C. Daniel, D. Lenoir, and D. Meda. 1994. *Politiques sociales.* Paris: Presses de la FNSP et Dalloz.

Liaisons Sociales. 1991. Les effectifs salariés du secteur privé et concurrentiel à la fin 1990. *Liaisons Sociales* 2 (September).

Lorenz, E. H. 1987. L'offre de travail et les stratégies d'emploi dans la construction navale en France et en Grande Bretagne (1880–1970). *Le Mouvement Social* 138:21–44.

Lyon Caen, G., 1984. Droit syndical et mouvement syndical. *Droit Social* 1:5–14.

Mabile, S. 1994. La négociation d'entreprise en 1993; moins d'accords salariaux plus d'accords sur le temps de travail et l'emploi. *Premières Synthèses* 61 (August).

Marchand, O., and C. Thelot. 1991a. *Deux siécles de travail en France.* Paris: Ed. INSEE.

Marchand, O., and C. Thelot. 1991b. La montée du chômage. In M. Levy Leboyer and J. C. Casanova, eds., *Entre l'État et le marché. L'économie française des années 1880 à nos jours.* Paris: NRF, Gallimard.

Maurice, M. F. Sellier, and J. J. Silvestre. 1982. *Politique d'éducation et organisation industrielle en France et en Allemagne.* Paris: PUF.

Monchois, X. 1994. Les contrats emploi solidarité en 1993. *Premières Synthèses* 52 (May).

Morin, M. L. 1991. Le dualisme de la convention collective de Branche, aperçu historique. Paper presented at Conventions Collectives du GDR 41, Paris.

Najman, V., and B. Reynaud. 1995. *Les règles salariales au concret: Enquête auprés de grandes entreprises en France.* Paris: La Documentation Française, forthcoming.

Nicole Drancourt, C. 1991. *Le Labyrinthe de l'insertion.* Paris: La Documentationb Française.

Osbert, G., Sanchez, R., and A. Ait Kaci. 1994. Le compte économique de la formation professionnelle pour 1992. *Premières Synthèses* 68 (August).

Osbert, G., ed. 1993. Bilan statistique de la formation professionnelle en 1992. *Dossiers Statistiques du Travail et de l'Emploi* 104 (December).

Oualid, W., and P. Picquenard. 1928. *Salaires et tarifs.* Paris: PUF.

Pirou, G. 1909. *Les Conceptions juridiques successives du contrat collectif de travail en France.* Rennes: Thèse.

Pitts, J. R. 1963. Continuité et changement au sein de la France bourgeoise. In S. Hofmann, ed., *A la Recherche de la France.* Paris: Ed. Seuil.

Reynaud, J. D. 1979. Conflit et régulation sociale: Esquisse d'une théorie de la régulation conjointe. *Revue Française de Sociologie.*

Reynaud, J. D. 1989. *Les Règles du jeu.* Paris: Ed A. Colin.

Reynaud, J. D., et al. 1990. *Les Systèmes de relations professionnelles: Examen critique d'une théorie.* Lyon: Ed. CNRS.

Rials, S. 1987. Les représentations de la représentation. *Droits* 6.

Roguet, B. 1994. Les comptes de l'emploi et de la formation professionnelle. *Premières Synthèses* 76.

Rosanvallon, P. 1988. *La Question syndicale.* Paris: Calmann Lévy, Fondation Saint Simon.

Sandretto, R. 1994. *Rémunérations et répartition des revenus.* Paris: Hachette.

Sellier, F. 1961. *Stratégie de la lutte sociale.* Paris: Ed. Economie et Humanisme.

Sellier, F. 1984. *La Confrontation sociale en France, 1936–1981.* Paris: PUF.

8 Continuity and Change in the "German Model" of Industrial Relations

Martin Baethge
Harald Wolf

German industrial relations (IR) since World War II have been characterized by stability, efficiency, and a high degree of institutionalization. Relations between capital and labor have, for the most part, been marked by the cooperative regulation of interests and a partnership between the actors in order to minimize conflict. The institutional structure of the IR system and the behavior of the major participants have played an important role in Germany's postwar export-driven economic upswing. Clearly this unprecedented phase of prosperity has been the most important stabilizing factor of the industrial relations system as a whole.

During the 1980s a gradual transition took place as the bargaining process shifted from the industry to the firm level. Attempts to deregulate and increase the flexibility of employment, shifts in wage policies, a new framework for performance evaluation in factories, changes in enterprise-level decision making, and new rationalization strategies all contributed to this steady development. Increasingly works councils, rather than the unions, are assuming the primary role in interest representation and are being subjected to the pressures of new problems and intensified negotiations. Despite these challenges the institutional continuity of the German system is striking, especially in comparison with other highly developed capitalistic economies.

This essay is divided into three sections. In the first we outline the distinctive features of the German IR system. In the second we discuss both the continuities and the changes that characterized the 1980s. In the final section we address the challenges of the 1990s: Germany unification and European integration.

8.1   Distinctive Features of German Industrial Relations

The institutional balance of power between capital and labor, which appears to have promoted both economic growth and adaptation in Germany, rests predominantly on a dual system of interest representation. Autonomous collective bargaining at the industry level and codetermination at the firm level are separated legally and institutionally. The autonomy of collective bargaining is legally guaranteed and remains free of direct state intervention. This primary arena of unionized representation is precisely structured by a closely meshed fabric of legislation and regulation that determines how negotiations, arbitration, and industrial conflicts are conducted.

The system of codetermination or co-decision making rests on two institutional channels of employee representation at the firm level: (1) works councils at the enterprise and plant levels, and (2) employee representation on the firm's supervisory board. Legislation that provides for works councils at both plant and the company levels in firms with more than five employees has had a far greater impact on German IR than the three versions of supervisory board participation which we outline below.

Supervisory Boards

German company law provides for a two-tier board system: the supervisory board to which the top executives are accountable, and the management board which comprises these executives. The powers of the supervisory board include the appointment and dismissal of top management, the determination of their remuneration, and advice on general company policy.

The three models of supervisory board codetermination are summarized in figure 8.1. The strongest version was introduced in 1951 in the coal and steel industries—the Montan sector. This is the only version with full parity representation. Workers and shareholders elect equal numbers of representatives to the supervisory board, and the chair cannot be elected against union opposition. This form of codetermination also ensures that worker representatives have a direct influence on the management board, since the labor director cannot be appointed in the face of opposition from the worker representatives.

The 1976 Codetermination Act covers all firms with over 2,000 employees and provides for a weaker form of parity representation on

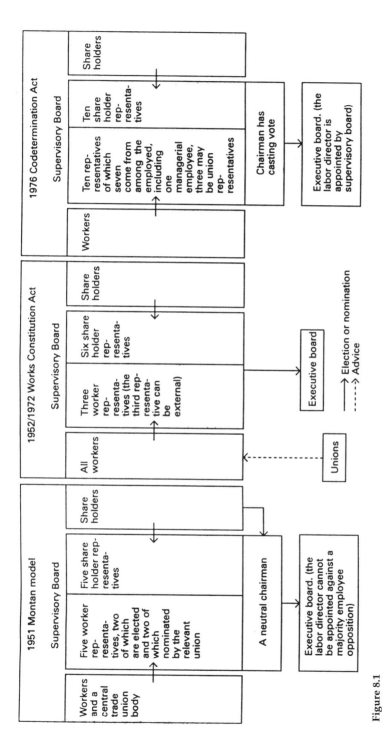

Figure 8.1
Three models of company codetermination in Germany. The size of the supervisory board varies in accordance with company size, but the number of representatives from the two sides remains the same.

the supervisory board in the sense that one of the employee representatives must be of managerial status and the chairman (normally a
shareholder representative) has a casting vote. The third and weakest
version of supervisory board participation covers firms with between
500 and 2,000 employees. It stipulates that one-third of the supervisory board consist of worker representatives. Consequently they tend
to play only an advisory role.

Works Councils

Works councils are the second institutional channel for firm-level
codetermination. The origin of the works councils can be traced back
to the 1891 enactment of the Law for the Protection of Labor which
provided for factory committees in almost all plants employing
twenty or more workers. The 1920 Works Council Act strengthened
the hand of the councils with a range of decision-making powers but
prevented them from encroaching on the responsibilities of trade
unions in traditional bargaining areas. Although prevalent in larger
workplaces, the councils were not universally instituted, partly because of employer opposition but also because some workers did not
enthusiastically embrace them. Although these councils subsequently
collapsed, they provided the context for the debate about industrial
organization and worker participation after the Second World War.

The Industrial Relations Regulation Act (*Betriebsverfassungsgesetz*)
was passed by the conservative government in 1952. This law established works councils (*Betriebsräte*) as separate, non-union organs for
employee representation. Members of the works councils are selected
by the entire work force, not just union members. The Act was partly
an attempt to isolate the unions from the shop floor and to limit their
influence to industrywide bargaining processes. Nonetheless, the majority (75 to 80 percent) of those elected to the works councils are
union members, and the works councils work closely with the unions.

The councils are obligated to maintain labor peace within the plant
(*Friedenspflicht*) and have been granted a series of carefully defined
rights, which were expanded through amendments passed by the
SPD-FDP government in 1972. Works council rights include consultation and information rights on economic matters, codetermination
rights on social concerns and personnel issues such as selection criteria and in-house training, and veto rights over personnel issues, including recruitment, redeployment and dismissal. Fuller details are
provided in table 8.1.

Table 8.1
The most important participation rights of the works council (Works Constitution Act 1972)

Degree of influence	Social concerns	Personnel issues	Business issues
Codetermination rights (can be enforced)	Beginning and end of daily working time; planning of holidays; design of payment system; piecework and premium rates; humane organization of work in accordance with established scientific knowledge	Staff file; selection criteria; in-firm training	Social plan (regarding layoffs)
Veto rights		Recruitment; redeployment; assignment to wage group; dismissal	
Consultation and information rights	Labor protection; accident prevention	Personnel planning	Information about major business plans or changes in the firm; consultation about building or extending plant, about changing/ introducing equipment, and about changes in work processes or places

Source: Translated from Müller-Jentsch (1986, 223).

Because the focus of their activities is primarily enterprise related, works councils tend to be oriented toward the particular interests of their plant or firm and workers' professional interests rather than toward broader labor or industrywide issues. By negotiating at the firm level, works councils generally relieve the unions from having to represent special interest groups and from having to deal with problems related to developments in production technology and work organization (so-called qualitative issues).

Unions negotiate industrywide agreements at the state level with employer associations, which represent the vast majority of employers. These wage agreements are negotiated within the context of the industry's overall economic performance, with the export oriented sectors tending to set the pattern for settlements in other sectors. These agreements are supplemented by agreements negotiated between works councils and company management at the firm level. These firm-level agreements allow for more flexible implementation of the standards established by law or collective bargaining in accordance with the specific competitive situation and balance of power at each plant.

This institutional structure has provided the German industrial relations system with a relatively high degree of flexibility, permitting it to adapt to changing situations and problems. The combination of extensive legal regulation, centralized conflict resolution, and worker representation divided between works councils and unions is quite effective in mediating and minimizing the ever-present tensions between enterprise, industry, and macroeconomic interests and goals. The ability to mediate these tensions accounts for a large portion of the positive contribution that the IR system has made to Germany's economic growth and prosperity.

At the industry level the unions and employer associations pursue their respective interests within the prescribed institutional framework through highly centralized, bureaucratic organizations. Since World War II the politically divided unions of the Weimar Republic (*Richtungsgewerkschaften*) have been replaced by industrial unions which organize both blue- and white-collar workers in a particular sector. The sixteen autonomous industrial unions are united under the umbrella organization of the German Federation of Unions (DGB), which is the largest labor union confederation in Germany. The DGB's functions are limited to representation in the political arena and the formulation of basic principles for social and economic policy. Two smaller union federations, the German White-Collar Union (DAG) and the German Civil Servants Federation (DBB) also exist and organize a smaller share of workers. With union density at about 40 percent, there are about 14 million organized workers in the Federal Republic. The DGB unions, which represent the vast majority of those organized, take the lead in collective bargaining and policy debates. In particular, the largest union in the DGB, IG Metall (*Industriegewerkschaft Metall*) which organizes 3.6 million metalworkers, plays the most prominent role.

Most enterprises in industry and in the important service sectors are members of one of 47 employer federations that negotiate with the unions over wages and provide mutual support for affiliated firms during strikes. The employers' federation of the mechanical engineering industry (*Gesamtmetall*) is the largest and most important member of the United Federation of German Employers (BDA). Although employers' associations affiliated with the BDA negotiate directly with their respective industry unions, the Federation of the German Industry (BDI) focuses primarily on the economic policy interests and political lobbying.

As mentioned above, collective bargaining is formally independent of state intervention. The state cannot impose its will on the parties but exercises influence indirectly through public pronouncements on wage demands or by exerting political pressure. The state retains an important direct influence on the relationship between capital and labor through traditional legal regulatory functions under the Industrial Relations Regulation Act.

Through the national social insurance program the state also plays an important role in assuring the material security of employees against such risks as illness, industrial accidents, unemployment, and retirement. The offices for social insurance, and especially the Federal Agency for Employment (BA) which administers job search assignments, unemployment insurance, and various aspects of German active labor market policy (job creation, further education, etc.), have become important participants in the field of industrial relations. They relieve the participants in collective bargaining and works councils from having to deal with these issues and thereby encourage them to concentrate on wage and working hours issues. Due to the tripartite composition of their central decision making and administrative bodies, with equal state, employer, and union representation, these institutions are constantly involved in the process of interest mediation between capital and labor.

The political and social foundations of the German IR system originated in the early postwar period, and these influences are still felt today. Three sets of circumstances have helped to ensure the longevity and stability of the German model.

First, in addition to their legally secured rights to influence enterprise decisions, the unions earned social acceptance and a lasting position of political strength by pursuing moderate wage policies during the postwar phase of economic reconstruction. Subsequently this acceptance and political strength were enhanced by their involvement in a "productivity pact" throughout the long phase of postwar prosperity. In this period the unions advocated "technical progress" and did not oppose rationalization as long as the employees received a fair share of the growth in productivity in the form of wage increases.

In exchange for this exceptionally constructive posture—which contributed to the formation and expansion of West Germany's industrial capacity and its success in world markets—the unions gained considerable political and organizational power in many industrial sectors. This was especially true in the mining, steel, and vehicle construction industries, where almost 100 percent of the blue-collar work force is unionized. This strength also allows the unions a considerable influence in some enterprises in the service sector such as banking, insurance, and retailing, even though union density is not nearly as high as in the main industrial sectors.

The second condition that helped structure the German IR system involved the dominant Taylorist-Fordist mode of production and socioeconomic regulation which underlay the country's postwar economic development. Some structural characteristics of the German model of relations between capital and labor proved to be especially appropriate for Fordist forms of mass production and mass consumption and for Keynesian regulation of consumption. It appears as if the type of union organization and politics found in Germany was especially well matched to inflexible Fordist mass production. Standardized, centralized, and legally prescribed forms of negotiation and regulation ensured the stability of both the economic actors and the rigidly connected production and distribution processes essential for this form of production. A collective bargaining strategy that focused almost exclusively on wages and work hours complemented the need to standardize working conditions in the mass production model (Mückenberger 1985).

Third, although the degree of complementarity between Fordism and the German model cannot be discussed in detail here, undoubtedly this production and rationalization model contributed decisively to transforming the core mass production industries into important centers of union organization and mobilization. The unions' organizational and mobilizational abilities were also supported in the important industrial centers by the stable, traditional culture of a reformist labor movement, soundly anchored in the well-established milieu of an urbanized, hierarchically organized and disciplined working class. This culture of the manual industrial worker defined the self perception and the political style of the West German industrial unions (see Hoffmann 1992, 139).

Although these political, social, and cultural pillars played key roles in the development of the German IR system over the last forty years, they have been undermined during the last two decades by changes in the social structure, in sociocultural patterns, and by new social problems. Following a description of developments in the 1980s which will trace the ways in which the IR system absorbed and digested these changes, we will discuss future scenarios for the German model.

8.2   Continuity and Change in the 1980s

Excessive economic displacement, a renewed rationalization thrust, and a more general shift toward conservative politics have all helped to destabilize the established relationship between capital and labor in almost all developed capitalistic economies since the beginning of the 1980s. German unions have been confronted with employer and state initiatives which represent the greatest challenge they have experienced since World War II. Yet, when compared to the labor movements of other advanced industrialized nations, the German model appears to be relatively stable and capable of adapting to changes in global markets.

Unemployment and the Struggle for Shorter Hours

In Germany the economic and political circumstances surrounding industrial relations have also changed significantly. As a result of economic crisis, the level of unemployment increased sharply to over 9 percent at the beginning of the decade (1983) and remained at high levels until 1989–90, when it declined to about 7.2 percent (Statistisches Bundesamt 1991, 130). The replacement of the pro-labor SPD-FDP government by a more conservative CDU-FDP administration in 1982 reduced the influence of the unions in the political arena. As a result organized labor has been increasingly vulnerable to business cycles and consequent developments in the labor market.

The CDU government of Helmut Kohl refused to enact deficit finance programs to stimulate economic growth and create new jobs. Instead, it implemented a comparatively moderate monetarist macroeconomic policy combined with supply-side measures focused on research and industrial policy that aimed at rapidly diffusing new technology. This was accompanied by limited deregulation of the

labor market, allowing for temporary work contracts and the simpli-
fication of regulation concerning temporary and part-time jobs. The
employer federations simultaneously pursued an ambitious policy of
more flexible work hours.

In the early 1980s the looming possibility of long-term, high unemployment and the increasing level of labor market segmentation
threatened to weaken, and in the long run thoroughly undermine, the
strategy and strength of the unions. In this politically and economically precarious situation, shorter working hours became the cornerstone of the unions' collective bargaining policy. The primary goal
was to fight unemployment at the bargaining table by decreasing the
supply of labor. The leading proponent, the Metalworkers Union (IG
Metall), placed the demand for an introduction of the thirty-five-hour
week at full pay on the collective bargaining agenda. At the same time
the unions exercised noticeable restraint in wage demands. This restraint not only helped enterprises improve their weak profits but
also allowed the unions to concentrate their energy and financial resources on the work hours issue.

The breakdown in negotiations over work hours led to the harshest
labor dispute in the history of the Federal Republic. A nine-week
strike in 1984 resulted from the IG Metall's demands. Of the 455,000
workers affected by the strike, 58,000 were officially on strike, 147,000
were locked out, and about 250,000 were out of work due to missing
parts deliveries. Although strike benefits cost the IG Metall DM500
million, or about one-third of its total financial reserves, the conflict
cost the employer federation around DM800 million in mutual support payouts (see Streeck 1988, 9).

This strike had contradictory consequences/benefits for both labor
and employers. Average work hours were reduced to 38.5 per week,
and employers were granted increased flexibility vis-à-vis working
hours. One positive result was that the most important union in Germany proved to be a powerful force despite unfavorable political and
economic conditions, and it established a precedent for other unions
to pursue throughout the decade. Subsequent agreements called for
the gradual shortening of the work week to 35 hours by 1995, which
undoubtedly has had a positive although limited effect on employment patterns in the West German metal industry. From IG Metall's
perspective the increased working time flexibility granted to employers has created problems such as longer production runs and longer
weekend hours for part of the work force. Although the union's origi-

nal goal was to standardize regulations through centralized collective bargaining agreements, the result has been increased differentiation brought about by permitting works councils to reach firm-level agreements with employers (for a discussion of the course of the strike and its results, see Weber 1986; Hinrichs and Wiesenthal 1986).

The strike provoked an unintended change in the social insurance system, which has affected the future bargaining power of the unions. To minimize the drain on its financial resources, IG Metall used its usual strike tactic of targeting selected plants in certain regions, with the aim of achieving broader national results. However, a new tactical variation was added. Strikes were organized at the most important automobile suppliers so that the auto manufacturers were forced to cut production due to parts shortages. The union was not required to provide strike support to the affected workers, since they were entitled to receive unemployment insurance benefits. As a result of the subsequent debate about the use and interpretation of paragraph 116 of the Labor Market Act (*Arbeitsförderungsgesetz*), the state and the employer federation were able to weaken the negotiating power of the unions by passing a new version of the law[1] that removed this entitlement.

From Fordism to "New Concepts of Production" and "Systemic Rationalization"

Shifts in world markets have had an especially strong effect on the Federal Republic's export-oriented economy, given that sectors such as the chemical, machine tool, and automobile industries export more than half of their production. During the 1980s this led to a new orientation in enterprise strategies and production concepts. In the context of changing patterns of trade, marked by increasingly unstable and at times even shrinking markets, many enterprises have rationalized by introducing new technologies and reorganizing their strategies and structures. These restructuring efforts gained momentum throughout

---

1. The political controversy over the large housing construction organization (*Neue Heimat*) owned by the German Federation of Unions should also be mentioned here. At this time the organization was nearly bankrupt and some of its top managers were even suspected of corruption. The CDU-FDP government exploited the affair in the media, and an indignant debate about mismanagement and fraud in the union-owned enterprises quickly overshadowed the conflict over paragraph 116 which till then had gone well for the unions. The scandal led to a lower public opinion of the unions and a loss of trust among its members.

the 1980s. Innovations included the flexible automation of production and administrative processes, increased use of computer technologies, and new forms of labor organization. These last changes entailed a departure from the Taylorist and Fordist principles of the previous era and increased the importance of highly skilled blue- and white-collar work. This new phase in the history of capitalist rationalization has been described by German industrial sociologists as "new concepts of production" (Kern and Schumann 1984) or "systemic rationalization" (Altmann et al. 1986; Baethge and Oberbeck 1986).

Research conducted by the Sociological Research Institute of Göttingen (SOFI) in the automobile, machine tool, and chemical industries (Schumann et al. 1990) has shown that the new forms of rationalization and labor practices are now relatively widespread in the core industrial sectors. In these sectors a new category of worker, the so-called system regulator, has emerged and is gradually increasing in importance as the changeover to the new production concepts occurs. By the end of the 1980s this new type of worker made up 5 percent of the production work force in the auto industry, 9 percent in the machine tool sector, and 33 percent in the chemical industry.

The growing number of highly qualified workers is especially conspicuous in the automotive industry, which until recently was considered a stronghold of Taylorist work organization. Following the recent reorganization of this industry the work allocation and production monitoring roles of foremen and planning technicians have been increasingly assumed by system regulators who function with greater autonomy and self-direction. To enhance the optimal operation of the automated system, management is no longer seeking to limit the sphere of worker activity in the high-tech areas. In the low-tech areas management strategy has been to preserve mass production principles while trying to reduce complexity and control variety in final assembly. Here work reorganization includes the following:

1. Lengthening the cycle time of individual jobs.

2. Expanding job content by incorporating QC, maintenance, logistic organization, and process control functions.

3. Creating internally regulated work groups that rotate through a variety of operations.

Together these changes have had little impact on the character of assembly work and can be characterized as "modernized Taylorism." These different rationalization strategies in high- and low-tech areas have provoked cleavages between highly skilled and semiskilled workers, who have been the core groups represented by the works councils.

In the electronics industry producers introduced sophisticated automation projects in parts production and assembly, shifting from a predominantly unskilled female work force to a more skilled and integrated one. The traditional division of labor was deemed inappropriate given that high skills were necessary to optimize the continuous flow of production systems and were moved closer to the line. Diverse production tasks have been integrated to create much broader job classifications (Voskamp and Wittke 1992).

To address these needs, older workers have been retrained and younger, highly skilled workers hired. Training has also changed. Rather than traditional learning by doing and the application of accumulated experience, workers are now trained to develop highly analytical and abstract problem-solving skills. These new "problem-solvers" adopt a systematic and strategic approach and actively seek out production problems. As a result the initiative to transform work is coming from below as problem-solvers exploit the grey areas in the formal organization of work to expand their sphere of influence. Although these workers have enhanced production quality and maintenance processes, firms have experienced problems in socially integrating these highly energetic, aggressive, younger skilled workers into established work groups consisting primarily of older skilled workers.

New forms of rationalization have also provoked a variety of new problems for the works councilors, and the consequences cannot simply be passed on to the peripheral work force. Negotiation procedures and the range of bargaining topics that had been clearly delimited between unions and works councils (e.g., worker remuneration) are losing their validity or becoming more difficult to administer. Conflict between labor and capital is now taking place on a less well-defined negotiating terrain (e.g., work design and further training) with fewer formalized opportunities for labor participation in codetermination (see Düll and Bechtle 1988).

Another consequence of the current rationalization process has been that in some forms of new work organization, like quality circles or group work, management has begun to allow employees to influence and directly participate in decision making, a privilege previously restricted to works council members. In the past, works councilors often attempted to block the introduction of these forms of work organization in the hope of retaining their representational monopoly. More recently, however, the works councils and unions have tended to accept the implementation of participative work concepts as supplementary representational opportunities rather than as threatening competition and thus have sought to integrate them into the traditional system of representation (see Dörre and Wolf 1992).

Transition in Work Performance Policies: New Approaches to Collective Bargaining

A fundamental change in work performance policies has accompanied recent shifts in work organization. This change is illustrated by the persistent difficulties experienced by the traditional performance-related pay system and the promotion of so-called work-rate pay (*Pensumlohnformen*). This is essentially the same as hourly pay rates except that systematically implemented performance expectations and controls are included, and the performance portion of the wage is determined using less specific criteria, such as rising productivity. Work-rate pay has not been interpreted as a replacement for traditional performance pay but rather as an expansion of employer performance demands using new performance instruments better adapted to the new production and work structures (Schudlich 1990)

However, due to the related neglect of traditional, supposedly scientific, performance pay methods, especially in those areas where the introduction of group work includes new performance regulations, a shift in emphasis toward negotiating plant-level performance measures has emerged. In setting performance standards, what is really involved is a political process that accommodates the performance demands of employers and the compensation claims of employees.

As a result of these changes in compensation arrangements, unions now need to keep an eye on company performance when bargaining for new wages. The relation between wages and performance remains the most important field of battle in industrial relations. Under the "collective bargaining reform 2000" (*Tarifreform 2000*) initiative, the IG Metall has begun to develop a wage policy that addresses this problem, primarily by achieving agreement on the obligatory objects of negotiation and regulation at the company level. The unions plan to integrate the concept into future master agreements covering conditions of employment.

In a departure from previous practice, IG Metall is also attempting to achieve uniform wage and collective bargaining agreements to cover both white- and blue-collar workers. The goal is to equalize wage payments for comparable skill levels and also to equalize promotion opportunities for all employee groups. The Industrial Union for Chemicals, Paper, and Ceramics Workers (*Industriegewerkschaft Chemie, Papier, Keramik*) ratified a similar agreement in 1987. In practice, however, the contract is more likely to "make small corrections at the boundary between white and blue collar workers . . . rather than remove or weaken the border itself" (Kädtler 1991, 2).

The IG Metall is calling for the replacement of conventional methods of work evaluation and wage setting based on differential work requirements and job levels with a more skill-based system. Due to strong employer opposition this concept has only been applied in a few exceptional cases, such as at the mid-sized mechanical engineering firm Voegele, which is not a member of the employer association. The wage differentiation contract (LODI) negotiated at Volkswagen in 1980 also represented a step in this direction, since the agreement replaced individualized job evaluation with a more collective principle based on "work systems" that include diverse jobs (see Brumlop 1986).

Changes in Company and Employment Structures and the Threat to Union Solidarity

The organizational restructuring of firms and plants has added another dimension to the extremely complex process of redefining responsibilities and opportunities for participation in decision making. Large enterprises and conglomerates have begun to simultaneously-centralize and decentralize decision-making structures. Strategic decisions, like the location of production facilities, product line decisions and important investments are being centralized, while decisions dealing with particular arrangements at individual plants have been decentralized to include more employees at lower management levels in the decision-making process.

These changes have consequences for plant-level bargaining processes. Plant-level managers are no longer authorized to handle the "big questions." Regional or national union representatives, who had previously served as a sort of counterbalance to management, no longer have an effective means of influencing the decisions that have been transferred to central headquarters. Decentralization to the local level requires that plant-level management must also be internally restructured. As a result the key subjects of negotiation and the principal negotiating partners are simultaneously disappearing from the bargaining system: on the one hand, heading up and, on the other hand, going down. An effective union strategy to counteract these developments has yet to be developed.

This combination of centralization and decentralization could be observed during the second half of the 1980s in the automobile industry, especially by the German affiliates of GM and Ford, Opel AG, and Ford AG. GM established a small but influential European headquarters in Switzerland and transferred responsibility for important strategic decisions such as purchasing and supplier relationships from its various European production facilities to headquarters. At the same time GM reduced the extent of vertical integration at Opel and converted some departments into independent firms. In the 1980s similar patterns could also be observed in the German steel industry, especially at Mannesmann and Hoesch.

Human Resources Development: A Continuing Strength of the Unions

Decentralization and contracting out have changed corporate culture, especially where research and development or data processing functions have been separated from production sites. This has often led to the formation of exclusively white-collar facilities with highly qualified personnel. These employees have always been difficult for the unions to organize and the lack of work council representatives makes the task even more difficult. The proportion of white-collar workers represented by unions in these new installations is often much lower than in traditional factories where union density among white-collar workers has never been especially high. The unions have yet to find a solution to this problem.

The union's role in vocational training has not come under threat in the 1980s and remains an important and characteristic part of the relationship between capital and labor in Germany. The vocational training system has always been an especially important element of the German model. The system provides a steady supply of highly skilled workers (*Facharbeiter*), which Germany's export-oriented, specialized, quality production depends on. Organized labor and business have both realized the importance of the human resources provided by the system of vocational training. Decision making about the development and operation of the system continue to be achieved through mutual agreement among the employer associations, unions, and the state. In the 1980s these actors jointly attempted to adapt the vocational training system and qualification structure to the new technological developments. This meant instituting new training measures in response to the growing need for skilled labor required as a result of the application of post-Taylorist rationalization strategies. For example, in 1987 the vocational training regulations for metalworkers and electricians were reformed by replacing 42 apprenticeships (*Berufsbilder*) with 6 new apprenticeship tracks for metalworkers, and 4 for electricians.

The modernization of the vocational training system implies some problems for the future supply of skilled labor as a result of three trends that will affect the supply of skilled labor in the 1990s. Employers and unions fear the emergence of a skilled labor shortage at the end of this century because of (1) the demographics of the age groups now reaching employment age, (2) the extension of high school education and increasing university attendance, and (3) the growing emphasis on the theoretical part of vocational training. Together these trends will reduce the absolute and proportional influx of young people into the vocational training system and will lower the likelihood of skilled workers remaining in their jobs.

The first effect results from the growing attractiveness of university studies in comparison with vocational training. The latter is due to the growing interest of young skilled workers in further education as a result of increasing emphasis on the theoretical part of vocational training. After finishing vocational training many pursue further education at technical colleges and universities. Five years after finishing their vocational training only 40 percent of highly skilled metalworkers and one-third of highly skilled electricians remained at the jobs in which they underwent training. Thirty percent of the metalworkers and 45 percent of the electricians were attending schools for further training or universities (1989 figures). More so than in the past, vocational training is becoming just one step in the overall educational career of young people, and it no longer serves predominantly as preparation for a particular job.

In the late 1980s vocational training programs, and in particular, company programs for further training, became important collective bargaining issues for the unions. Due to the rapid transition in production technology and work organization, company programs have become increasingly important. Unions such as IG Metall and the Chemicalworkers have attempted to achieve more precise and uniform regulations for company training programs in order to protect the skills and material interests of employees.

In 1988 a new collective bargaining master agreement for metalworkers (a new version of the *Lohnrahmentarifvertrag II*) in North Württemberg and North Baden was negotiated that addressed some of the issues involved in regulating further training. The agreement stipulated that management had to advise the works council of its skill requirements and the implementation of training measures. This had led to some expansion in works council responsibility, although it falls far short of codetermination.

Increasing Emphasis on Enterprise-Level Representation

In general, one might say that during the 1980s a gradual shift took place in the focus of the dual system of representation. The bargaining process shifted perceptibly to the firm level. Attempts to deregulate and increase the flexibility of employment, developments in wage policies, a new framework for performance evaluation in factories, changes in enterprise decision-making processes, and the new rationalization strategies have all, in one way or another, increased the importance of worker representation at the plant or the firm level (described in the German discussion as *Verbetrieblichung*). For the most part it was works councils, rather than the unions, that were forced into the key role of interest representation and were subjected to the pressures of new problems and intensified negotiations.

These developments have already had a long prelude. They are related to a change in the themes and pattern of rules of union collective bargaining. As early as the second half of the 1970s the collective bargaining politics of the unions in the specific industrial branches increasingly began to lose their substantive and programmatic character of redistributive bargaining for the benefit of workers. The wage level kept pace with the inflation rate, but on the whole the unions were clearly on the defensive. On the other hand, the so-called qualitative areas of regulation—rationalization, protection of working conditions, flexible work hours—became relatively more important in collective bargaining agreements. However, the actual contract provisions for the implementation of the agreed-upon standards do not appear as uniform or generalized regulations but rather as minimal provisions that can be adapted to suit the conditions at each factory. Accordingly more and more areas arose—owing to so-called opening clauses—in which the stipulation of the actual working conditions were set through supplementary negotiations and agreements between the works council and management within the individual enterprises (see Müller-Jentsch 1986, 239–40)

Consequently plant-level codetermination structures have developed into a genuine and obligatory second negotiation system. This added responsibility at the company level has proved to be exceedingly difficult for the unions. First of all, the negotiations only provide a marginally greater role for works council participation to alter the imbalance of power, given the external pressures of persistent long-term unemployment. Numerous works councils in small- and medium-sized firms have trouble meeting the challenge of effective participation in decisions about systemic rationalization because they are overburdened, and active participation is often replaced by mere playing along or passive acceptance.

The union's role at the plant level could become questionable unless the unions develop beyond their role as centers of organizational support and coordination for works council activities. Whether this transition will lead to an organizational form similar to the enterprise union model is one of the central open questions about future developments in German IR.

Interim Summary and Tentative Conclusions in the Current Period

Many of the questions we have raised in this essay remain open. The risks of erosion and upheaval which we have expressed certainly played a role in the 1980s. While their effects challenged the foundations of the IR system in one place or another, they were not powerful enough to destroy the system's basic edifice. The supporting columns, which we outlined in our first section, are still sound. In comparison with other highly developed capitalist economies, the institutional continuity of the German system is striking, particularly in light of the pressures and challenges it has faced. This continuity has induced many observers to use formulations like stability and flexibility (Jacobi 1989, 184) to capture the essence of the past decade.

Union membership figures and the results of collective bargaining also indicate the lasting strength of DGB unions. The breakthrough in the reduction of working hours was unparalleled in the international

labor movement. As a rule German unions retained sufficient negotiating power to ensure that real wages could be maintained, although
the distribution of national income shifted considerably at the expense of workers during this period. Remarkably the organizational
strength of the unions was hardly affected by the economic crisis. This
contrasts sharply with the drastic membership loss experienced by
unions in some other countries. This organizational and political
stability is a consequence of the less dramatic course of the economic
crisis in Germany, of the ability of unions to secure their members' interests in traditional industrial sectors, and of the relatively good recruiting conditions for the unions in those firms that are locked into
the dual system of representation. A quasi obligation to retain union
membership will remain as long as the alliance between work councilors and the unions remains in place, especially in the large enterprises (Streeck 1988, 20–21).

Just because the formal structures of the German model have not
yet collapsed, we should not obscure the important changes that have
taken place in recent years. These social developments raise questions
about the assumptions of how the society ought to function and confront the unions with the specter of the intensification of various
problems. In some cases these trends and their corresponding problems have already begun to influence the political arena of industrial
relations and human resource practices. In the long run, when one
briefly reviews the following five factors, it becomes clear that these
trends will effect the traditional forms of interest representation and
mediation:

1. The socioeconomic patterns of development have been marked by
a flat growth rate and an increasing rate of unemployment. Against
this background the gradual erosion of the Fordist regime of accumulation is taking place. In particular, long-term unemployment and the
increasing segmentation of the labor market have created and stabilized divisions within the employed population. At the same time,
due to the diffusion of post-Taylorist rationalization strategies, the interests of the traditional core membership of the industrial unions
have become more differentiated. The modern highly skilled worker
not only gains relative importance but also develops new priorities as
he follows his interests, which are more likely to concern his professional perspectives and opportunities rather than performance and
work conditions. The claims and demands of these so-called winners

of the rationalization process are no longer easy to combine with the interests of less skilled workers.

2. Besides this tendency toward fragmentation there has also been a rearrangement of the entire industrial structure with crises in sectors such as shipbuilding and steel that were traditional strongholds of the unions. At the same time sectors such as computers and electronics—sectors that the unions had only partially cultivated or ignored outright—have increased in importance. Consequently there is a growing likelihood that core sectors of the new post-Fordist accumulation model will remain free of union influence and that new forms of industrial relations without union participation—perhaps at the enterprise level—may be permanently established.

3. The tendency to reduce vertical integration and increase contracting out has led to new cooperative relations between enterprises that cut across the conventional borders separating industries. This reorganization of industrial and enterprise structures is challenging the traditional organizational principle of the unions. In this situation the application of the industrial union principle leads to difficult constellations: Activities that previously took place within a specific enterprise and therefore within the sphere of influence of a specific union may suddenly be carried out in an independent firm that falls under the jurisdiction of a different union with a different organizing tradition.

4. Although the general shifts in the employment structure of the entire society can only partially be explained by these trends, they seem to point in a similar direction. The continuing shift from industrial to service employment is reducing the organizing potential of the unions. The model of union organization based on the industrial worker employed in large Fordist factories appears more precarious because of employment shifts toward the service sectors. The problem is magnified in that even in most industrialized firms, the employment structure shows a distinct trend toward a relative increase in technical and commercial white-collar employees. Consequently employee groups that have been very difficult for the German unions to organize now constitute the majority of the work force.

5. Just as the socioeconomic and social structure has been transformed, so too have cultural patterns. The dispositions and orientation of the employed now represent an additional challenge to the uniform collective representation of the traditional IR system. Over

the past few decades, higher average incomes, more free time, longer training, and greater social security have expanded the creative possibilities and personal autonomy of many blue- and white-collar workers. This has fostered the individualization of their life styles and has made the development of personal interests possible. The unions have to recognize this development, especially among young employees who tend to be somewhat older when they begin employment. Due to longer periods of schooling and training, these newer workers are generally more critical and self-confident and hence more difficult to organize. This becomes more evident as the old worker milieu of large factories and urban industrialized regions, which for generations were fertile grounds for union recruitment and mobilization, slowly lose ground and relevance in the wake of recent shifts in the industrial structure. Consequently the organizing potential of the unions is under pressure on various fronts. In the long term this will have negative effects on the negotiating power of the unions if no antidote is found. The situation in many areas and factories is already disquieting, particularly if one considers the weak relationship between highly qualified white-collar workers and both works councils and unions (see Baethge et al. 1992).

During the 1980s the unions became increasingly conscious of these pressing problems. The dangers of social segmentation and loss of social solidarity, resulting from differing perceptions and effects of labor market and rationalization risks and the process of interest pluralization, have been recognized and discussed. At times unions have attempted to deal with these problems through their collective bargaining policy. Qualitative themes such as flexible work hours, further training, and the design of technology and work are being integrated into the collective bargaining agenda to better accommodate the new interests and claims of the increasingly important problem groups within unions.

New politically controversial themes have gradually been introduced into the collective bargaining agenda, including environmental protection, risks of high-tech development, and women's liberation issues. Unions such as IG Metall began to move in the direction of issues that seemed to interest segments of the new individualized employees and that were articulated by emergent social movements. As some unions began to arrange congresses to discuss these issues, many observers predicted that these postmaterial issues would define union policy and the industrial relations system of the 1990s (see Hoffmann et al. 1990).

The above analysis was formulated before the reunification of Germany. This unexpected political event with its far-reaching historical ramifications has caused considerable confusion for the unions' agenda in the 1990s. It also necessitates a revision of many established assumptions about the development of German society.

8.3   Uncertainties in the 1990s: German Unification, European Integration, and Increasing Globalization

In the 1990s a new phase began in the history of the Federal Republic of Germany. Unification and the integration of the European community have fundamentally changed the points of reference and the fields of action of the entire political landscape. Above all, the unification of the two Germanies, executed in the context of the disintegration of the communist bloc, has nullified once valid coordinates for political orientation without creating new, equally stable replacements. Never before have the future political and economic prospects and the circumstances surrounding the German IR model appeared so uncertain and presented so many unsolved problems as at the beginning of this decade.

The collapse of the centrally planned systems in eastern Europe and German unification occurred at a time of intensified competition in world markets. One effect of this tendency on German industry was increased price competition, even in traditionally strong industries like automobiles, machine tools, and chemicals. This development led many German manufacturers to actively seek more efficient global sourcing. All West European economies, especially the German economy, have turned toward eastern Europe in an effort to locate production in lower wage areas and thus to lower production costs. The repurcussions of this process for the national labor markets and human resources policies are extensive although not yet entirely foreseeable. In view of the current German situation, characterized by problems inherent in unification, increased globalization, and greater decentralization, we would like to sketch some new problems and issues facing German industrial relations.

The abrupt collapse of the GDR's political and economic system was followed by the equally abrupt importation of West German institutions. This has created the opportunity to witness a truly outlandish spectacle. Although events in the east confronted political actors with a variety of economic, political, and social problems, which had no clear solutions, the key players, led by the West German government, attempted to implement unification as quickly as possible. As conditions were largely dictated by West German interest groups, the accelerated pace of unification thwarted any genuine public debate over options for the development of the future economic and social structure in the new reunified Germany or the forms of integration of the former GDR into the economic texture of a united Germany. The results quickly discouraged the majority of East Germans who had looked forward to the benefits of national unity.

This reckless unification process has produced deep economic and social divisions in Germany. In eastern Germany the collapse of east European markets, combined with the sudden pressures of international economic competition, have led to the bankruptcy of almost half of the ex-GDR's industrial enterprises.

In 1991 the GNP of the former East Germany declined by almost 35 percent and stabilized at this level before rising moderately in 1994. Huge financial transfers (between 150 and 180 billion DM yearly) could not impede the 40 percent reduction of employment (from 10 million to about 6 million people) in the new German states that took place between 1990 and 1994. The sectors most profoundly affected were agriculture (which experienced an 80 percent decline in employment), mining and energy (a 52 percent reduction in jobs), and manufacturing (a 67 percent decline, or a reduction from 3.4 million to about 1 million employed workers). The actual loss in employment in eastern Germany is even higher, since throughout the last few years over 500,000 people have been involved in publicly financed work programs or further training schemes (see Wissenschaftszentrum Berlin 1994).

With this rapidly darkening economic and political horizon, the industrial relations systems have also moved quickly toward uniformity. West German institutions have spread to the east. The Federation of Free German Unions (*Freier Deutscher Gewerkschaftsbund*) with an official membership of 8.6 million, the largest organization of the former German Democratic Republic, disbanded in fall 1990. As a result the organizing territory of the West German industrial unions spread to the east. Regional organizational structures analogous to those in the west have been established in the new regions.[2]

---

2. The former GDR now consists of five *Neue Länder* (new regional governments).

For the West German unions, unification seemed to promise a rich legacy. Union membership, which had stagnated and at times even declined during the 1980s, took an unexpected jump. By recruiting members in the east, DGB unions increased their membership by almost 4 million (from about 8 million to almost 12 million) between 1990 and 1991. However, this success was short-lived. The rapid decline of employment and the disillusionment this provoked led, as early as 1992, to a 20 percent reduction in union membership in East Germany, and this trend has continued in subsequent years (Kittner 1994). The impressive collective bargaining accomplishments of the unions could not hinder this process. It appears now, four years after unification, that the unions in the new German states will have membership figures and organizational levels comparable to those found in the Federal Republic (see Höhrlein 1994). However, this situation should not blind us to the fact that notwithstanding the transfer of the institutional framework from the west, new developments have emerged in union policies from which German unions can learn for the future.

The collective bargaining parties of the Federal Republic quickly decided to apply the West German collective bargaining system to the new federal states. Initially the master agreements covering regulations on wage and salary structures were adopted and applied in the plants but, given their lower productivity, at only 60 percent of the West German level. Soon afterward negotiations were held over the gradual increase of East German wages and salaries so that they could reach parity with West German levels. In some cases agreements already concluded will lead to equalized pay levels in the coming years. This process of institutional transfer and the application of the West German collective bargaining regulations to the new states was difficult, since East German membership in employer associations still varies widely and the degree of organization is at times very low. This has led to blank areas on the collective bargaining map of the new states (Bispinck 1992; Behrens 1995).

The relatively low degree of organization of employer associations in the east has recently been accompanied in the west by notable cases of firms leaving employer associations. For example, IBM Germany has left the mechanical engineering employers organization (*Gesamtmetall*), apparently in order to avoid the working conditions that had been agreed upon with IG Metall. The CDU/FDP government in Bonn and some employers have proposed that collective bargaining, particularly in East Germany, be conducted at the individual plant or company level. It is argued that firms should be able to negotiate locally and pay employees below industry levels.

The *Mittelstand*, the medium- and small-sized employers, have also begun a push for the decentralization of bargaining and greater sensitivity to their interests in employer federations dominated by the largest firms. They object that industry agreements on shorter working hours favor larger firms that are able to schedule multiple shifts. They argue that recent agreements increasingly restrict their flexibility and fail to take adequate account of sectoral and regional differences as variations are progressively eliminated. Reforms have been proposed to establish broad framework agreements at the industry level, leaving the implementation of the details to the local level in order to facilitate flexibility.

In 1993 the dispute over the preservation of the phased wage contract—through which, by 1996, wage levels in the east were to achieve parity with those in the west—and the introduction of the hardship clause, whereby economically weak firms were given the possibility of deviating from national industry contracts, made it clear that the principle of industrywide collective bargaining contracts (*Flächenverträge*) was being undermined and that union representatives at the firms were gaining importance. The hardship clause compromise in the east was the result of a situation that might serve as a model for the future: a deep economic crisis affecting enterprises to varying degrees and a strongly heterogeneous set of interests on the part of the predominantly midsized firms, which made it difficult for the employers to agree on a uniform policy (see Behrens 1995). The institution of industrywide collective bargaining contracts owes its existence and acceptance at least in part to the era of the large mass-production firm. As large firms become less numerous as a result of decentralization strategies, and midsized and smaller firms increasingly define the industrial structure, problems will become more heterogeneous and the enterprise will gain importance and serve as the principal arena for collective bargaining.

The importance of decentralized political activities can also be seen in labor market and industrial policies. Due to the radical economic collapse and the sharp decrease in employment, centralized labor market and industrial policies have proved ineffectual. They could do nothing more than provide financial resources. The realization of promising training measures and job creation projects required the capacities and cooperation of local and regional actors and political networks, including all regional institutions—state governments, employment offices, the *Treuhandanstalt*, chambers of commerce, enterprises, unions, and work council members (see Andretta 1995; Behrens 1995). As economic crises of the future lose the character of widespread recessions, the field of regional labor market and industrial policies will become more important for the trade unions. Although in both cases described above—collective bargaining and industrial policies—the role of the actors at the enterprise and regional level became more meaningful, it is also true that in the areas of legal expertise and the monitoring of political developments at the national level important centralized functions still exist. New forms of decision making between centralized and decentralized organizational units will become the key to survival for the German unions. From the experiences in the new states, we can also learn that under the circumstances of extreme crisis, one should never overestimate the influence of the works councils and union representatives at the firm level. Normally, under such circumstances, the works councilors have been genuinely included in management strategy discussions about product and production concepts, and this is where one finds forms of comanagement with worker representatives (see Jürgens et al. 1991). Even in these few exceptional cases there is a risk that participation may lead to identification with management goals and to firm-level egoism, at the expense of broader union goals. This situation could lead to serious problems. The danger exists that cleavages will develop between works councils and unions, which may undermine the dual system of industrial relations throughout Germany. The emergence of a separate works councils movement in the new *Länder,* which has been subject to sharp criticism from the unions, is a signal of this potential for division.

One thing seems sure: For the long term the questions of company survival, job creation, and equalization of wages between East and West Germany will receive priority. These bread and butter issues will probably dominate the collective bargaining agenda throughout the Federal Republic over the next few years. The post-Fordist issues of the west now have to compete with the old social questions of the east. This collision has generated a heterogeneous social maelstrom in which the fragmentation of interests among the employed will increase in intensity. The increasingly visible costs of unification, aggravated by a deepening recession, threatened to revive traditional social conflicts over distributional issues. These are expected to play a more important role in IR than in the recent past (see Bäcker 1992; Mahnkopf 1991).

Present conditions represent a break with the past. Previously the system functioned so well because it distributed the fruits of increased labor productivity and economic growth. In the future, redistribution will demand that workers of western Germany sacrifice a significant portion of their wealth in order to finance the rebuilding of the economy of eastern Germany. Workers in the west have to accept that the pie may not be getting any larger and that their share will probably shrink. In the long term negotiations will become a struggle to defend present wage levels or prevent significant losses. In any case there will be losers. Recent breakdowns in wage negotiations reinforce this interpretation. The Retail, Wholesale, Banks and Insurance Union (Handel, Banken und Versicherungen), a union with little labor conflict experience, went on strike, and the second largest union, the Public Service, Transport and Traffic Union (Öfentliche Dienste, Transport und Verkehr), was forced to wage a difficult, politically loaded public sector strike.

The question of class solidarity among increasingly differentiated interests takes on an added complexity. Unions are now concentrating their energies on securing present wage levels and employment, and they are pressed to reduce their staff due to decreasing membership and financial resources. The danger therefore exists that only traditional collective bargaining issues will survive as the single common denominator binding together organized interests. The qualitative themes that were emphasized in the 1980s, and involved a wider spectrum of employee interest in issues such as further training or work design, may lose their importance. Union discussions about the future and the debate within unions about an expanded concept of interests may end before any conclusions can be reached. The long overdue development of union policy on these issues could be blocked, and traditionalist forces may regain the upper hand.

Such a return to traditional union policy would be fatal. The problems that endanger the underlying assumptions of the German model will continue to exist, though they may currently be overshadowed by the unification process. If the first timid attempts to confront these problems are lost in the wake of unification and the current economic crisis, there is a danger of an even faster erosion of the organizational abilities and bargaining power of the unions.

The current German transformation is further complicated by the exchange of impulses between the German situation and the process of European integration. It is clear that in a European community involved in the process of installing supranational legal, economic, and production structures, the development of the relationship between capital and labor will be noticeably affected by the balance of power and institutional arrangements in the IR system of its most economically powerful member, Germany. Simultaneously, as the European process of social standardization and adjustment continues, the unions will face challenges to their solidarity that are similar to those posed by German unification. And these processes will correspondingly affect the development of the German economy and IR.

Until recently the German model appeared exemplary: It was considered a positive point of reference by many within the European labor movement. In the 1980s the system proved—in contrast to other European models such as the French or British—able to function and remain stable even in difficult times. As a result it became attractive for unions in other countries that found themselves in a deep crisis, and European-wide diffusion of the German codetermination institutions at the company level was viewed as a possible way out of their own organization crisis. The chances for such a diffusion seemed, at first, relatively good as the German business association moved in the same direction as the unions and endeavored to establish a European "social charter." Furthermore the association seemed interested in a European-wide institutional alignment at the German level. This consensus has eroded as a result of the sharper conflicts between the German social partners and an intensification of the distribution struggles arising from German unification. If the German model loses its operating basis within Germany, its exemplary function will weaken, as will the chances of its diffusion. Additionally, by expanding their fields of operation across national borders, European enterprises can avoid national regulations, for example, codetermination and collective bargaining agreements (see Dörre 1995). As a result perspectives and reference points in the European IR have become increasingly uncertain in recent years.

Simultaneously one must expect repercussions from the economic integration process to affect the balance of power and the negotiation topics of the German IR in the near future. The problems of adjustment in East Germany illustrate how difficult it will be to reduce the large discrepancies in levels of economic development and to bring divergent social interests closer together. Our outline of the problems show that, at present, the formulation of definite prognoses for the development perspectives in IR and human resource practices is more of a risk than ever before.

Besides the threat of a return to traditional union politics, two additional dangers might fundamentally weaken the German IR system: Wage agreements may become less binding due to the so-called opening clauses, and political solidarity within the unions might weaken due to the contrasts between east and west. Squeezed by high unemployment, lack of investment, and lack of competitiveness, many East German firms are calling for lower wages in the hope of saving jobs. Some firms are not joining the employer organizations in order to avoid being bound by their wage agreements. These developments are viewed as very dangerous by many West German firms because they might completely unhinge the wage agreement system and lead to unpredictable and unstable wages.

The greatest threat in Germany, and probably worldwide, is a new path of development that breaks radically with current patterns. In the past, labor's struggle for wealth dealt with the distribution of increases in GNP. Since the *Wende* (German unification) and the collapse of many east European economies, the distribution struggles may only deal with redistribution. These struggles may be limited to collective bargaining issues but may also include tax and budget policies, and thus affect the system of social security and public goods. Struggles over redistribution require more solidarity than struggles for portions of a growing pie. In Germany no one—not the unions, not the political parties, nor the man on the street—is prepared for this new type of distributional struggle.

References

Altmann, M., M. Deiss, V. Döhl, and D. Sauer. 1986. Ein "Neuer Rationalisierungstyp": Neue Anforderungen an die Industriesoziologie. In *Soziale Welt* 37(2/3):191–206.

Altmann, N., and D. Sauer, eds. 1989. *Systemische Rationalisierung und Zulieferindustrie.* Frankfurt.

Andretta, G. 1995. Das Mobilitätsdilemma: Arbeitsmarktpolitische Lehren aus dem Transformationsprozeß. In Soziologisches Forschungsinstitut Göttingen (SOFI), eds., *Gesellschaft im Umbruch—Beiträge zu einer anderen Standortdebatte.* Opladen.

Bäcker, G. 1992. Gespaltene Gewerkschaften in einem gespaltenen Land. In *Blätter für deutsche und internationale Politik* (5):616–30.

Baethge, M., J. Denkinger, and U. Kadritzke. 1992. Zum Wandel von BerufsperspektiVen und sozialen Interessenlagen von hochqualifizierten Angestellten. Research report, SOFI-Göttingen.

Baethge, M., and H. Oberbeck. 1986. *Zukunft der Angestellten: Neue Technologien und berufliche Perspektiven in Büro und Verwaltung.* Frankfurt.

Behrens, M. 1995. *Die Gewerkschaften in den neuen Bundesländern am Beispiel der IG Metall: Tarif- und Industriepolitik.* Dusseldorf: DGB.

Bergmann, J. 1986. Technik und Arbeit. In B. Lutz, ed., *Technik und sozialer Wandel.* Verhandlungen des 23. Deutschen Soziologentages in Hamburg 1986. Frankfurt, pp. 114–34.

Bispinck, R. 1992. Tarifpolitik in der Transformationskrise. In *WSI-Mitteilungen,* WSI-Tarifarchiv (3):121–35.

Brumlop, E. 1986. *Arbeitsbewertung bei flexiblem Personaleinsatz: Das Beispiel Volkswagen AG.* Frankfurt.

Dörre, K. 1995. Auf der Suche nach einem neuen Kompromiß. In Soziologisches Forschungsinstitut Göttingen (SOFI), eds., *Gesellschaft im Umbruch—Beiträge zu einer anderen Standortdebatte.* Opladen.

Dörre, K., and H. Wolf. 1992. Partizipative Wende im Management? Unpublished paper, SOFI- Göttingen.

Düll, K., and G. Bechtle. 1988. Die Krise des normierten Verhandlungssystem: Rationalisierungsstrategien und industrielle Beziehungen im Betrieb. In K. M. Bolte, ed., *Mensch, Arbeit und Betrieb.* Weinheim, pp. 215–44.

Hinrichs, K., and H. Wiesenthal. 1986. Bestandsrationalität versus Kollektivinteresse. In *Soziale Welt* 37 (2/3):280–96.

Hoffmann, J. 1992. Neuer Produktivitätstyp:Alte Vertretungsstrukturen. In *PROKLA,* pt. 1, 22 (86):137–54.

Hoffmann, J., et al., eds. 1990. *Jenseits der Beschlußlage: Gewerkschaften als Zukunftswerkstatt.* Köln.

IG Metall, Board of Directors, eds. 1988. *Wofür wir streiten: Solidarität und Freiheit.* Internationaler Zukunftskongreß 1988 in Frankfurt. Köln.

IG Metall, Board of Directors, eds. 1991. *Tarifreform 2000: Ein Gestaltungsrahmen für die Industriearbeit der Zukunft.* Frankfurt.

Jacobi, O. 1989. Industrielle Beziehungen im Wandel. In H. Martens and G. Peter, eds., *Mitbestimmung und Demokratisierung.* Wiesbaden, pp. 173–87.

Jürgens, U., L. Klinzing, and L. Turner. 1991. Scrapping the East German industrial relations system. Unpublished paper.

Kädtler, J. 1991. Der Bundesentgelttarifvertrag für die chemische Industrie:Leitbild einer neuer Tarifpolitik? Berliner Arbeitshefte und Berichte zur sozialwissenschaftlichen Forschung, Nr. 43. Freie Universität Berlin.

Kern, H., and M. Schumann. 1984. *Das Ende der Arbeitsteilung? Rationalisierung in der industriellen Produktion: Bestandsaufnahme, Trendbestimmung.* München.

Kittner, M. 1994. *Gewerkschaften heute: Jahrbuch für Arbeitnehmerfragen 1994.* Köln.

Kotthoff, H. 1994. *Betriebsräte und burgerstatus: Wandel und Kontinuität betrieblicher Mitbestimmung.* München.

Mahnkopf, B. 1991. Vorwärts in die Vergangenheit? In A. Westphal, et al., eds., *Wirtschaftspolitische Konsequenzen der deutschen Vereinigung*. Frankfurt.

Mückenberger, U. 1985. Die Krise des Normalarbeitsverhältnisses. In *Zeitschrift für Sozialreform* Nos. 7–8, pp. 415 ff.

Müller-Jentsch, W. 1986. *Soziologie der industriellen Beziehungen: Eine Einführung*. Frankfurt.

Pehl, G. 1992. Deutsche Wirtschaft 1991/92. In *Gewerkschaftliche Monatshefte* (3):169–80.

Schudlich, E. 1990. Die "Autonomisierung" der industriellen Leistungspolitik und neue gewerkschaftliche Konzepte leistungskontrollierender Entlohnungsmethoden. In H. Dabrowski et al., eds., *Jenseits des Taylorismus*. Düsseldorf.

Schumann, M., V. Baethge-Kinsky, U. Neumann, and R. Springer. 1990. Breite Diffusion der Neuen Produktionskonzepte: Zögerlicher Wandel der Arbeitsstrukturen. In *Soziale Welt* 41(1).

Schumann, M., V. Baethge-Kinsky, M. Kuhlmann, C. Kurz, and U. Neumann. 1994. *Trendreport Rationalisierung—Automobilindustrie, Werkzeugmaschinenbau, Chemische Industrie*. Berlin.

Statistisches Bundesamt, eds. 1991. *Statistisches Jahrbuch 1991 für das vereinte Deutschland*. Wiesbaden.

Streeck, W. 1988. Industrial Relations in West Germany, 1980–1987. *Labor: Review of Labor Economics and Industrial Relations* 2 (3):3–44.

Weber, H. 1986. Konflikt im Interorganisationssystem. *Soziale Welt* 37 (2/3):263–79.

Wissenschaftszentrum Berlin, eds. 1994. *Beschäftigungsobservatorium Ostdeutschland* 13 (December).

9   The Swedish Model: Demise or Reconfiguration?

Andrew Martin

The constellation of institutions, practices, and policies convention-
ally described as the "Swedish model" is being transformed. Evolving since its inception in the 1930s, the model attained its "classical"
form in the 1950s and 1960s. Starting in the 1970s and accelerating
over the past decade or so, its key features have undergone substantial changes. So far the transformation has been uneven, and there are
conflicting visions of what its outcome should be. While the Swedish
model may be "dead," as some have declared, what will replace it,
and how much and in which ways it will differ from what existed in
the past remains unclear. Following a brief overview of the Swedish
model, I analyze the changes that have taken place in recent years.

9.1   The Swedish Model and Its Evolution

Broadly conceived, the Swedish model comprised not only a structure of union-management relations but also a pattern of economic
and social policy. It evolved in the context of almost continuous
control of the government by the Social Democratic Party (SAP),
alone or in coalition, from 1932 to the present, except 1976–82 and
1991–94. Crucial to the party's extraordinary political dominance
has been the support provided by the blue-collar unions affiliated to
the largest confederation (LO). However, the SAP's control of government always required the support of cross-party parliamentary or
cross-class electoral coalitions. This configuration of political power
underpinned a consensus, or "historical compromise," over the allocation of functions in governing Sweden's mixed economy (Korpi
1983). It gave the state responsibility for maintaining full employment by managing demand, providing collective services by channel-
ing resources to them, and assuring economic security and equity by

redistributing income through taxes and transfers. At the same time it largely excluded the state from the domain of production for the market, over which private capital retained control, and from regulation of the labor market, which was left up to the private organizations of employers and workers. When this consensus began to break down in the 1970s, the Swedish model started to unravel, but the continued dominance of the SAP has so far limited the extent to which it has been eroded.

Agreement between the two principal peak organizations of unions and employers, the LO and the SAF, defined the Swedish model of labor-management relations. Most private sector employer associations belong to SAF, while almost all blue-collar workers belong to LO unions. Over time, nearly as high a proportion of white-collar workers were covered by unions affiliated to two other confederations, TCO and SACO-SR, which negotiated similar agreements with SAF. Rules and procedures for settling disputes and conducting strikes and lockouts were embodied in a Basic Agreement between LO and SAF in 1938. Beginning in 1956, these two organizations also negotiated agreements setting the overall rate and pattern of wage increases for all their affiliates on a continual basis until 1983. A high degree of centralization within each organization enabled it to deliver on its commitments to the other. Thus LO and SAF operated what has been aptly characterized as a system of "centralized self-regulation" (Kjellberg 1992, 94). However, joint regulation did not extend to hiring and firing or work organization, which remained exclusive managerial prerogatives, eventually becoming an issue that contributed to the erosion of the Swedish model.

Public law still had a narrow but important role. A 1928 law barred strikes or lockouts during the life of collective agreements and established a tripartite labor court to adjudicate disputes over their interpretation. The unions' rights to organize and bargain collectively in the private sector were guaranteed by a 1936 law (to overcome employer resistance to white-collar unionization), and extended to the public sector in 1965. Minimal regulation of child labor, health and safety, hours, vacations, and safety stewards was also introduced at different times. Otherwise, unions and employer organizations were left essentially alone to govern their relations with each other as well as with their members.

The evolution and operation of labor-management relations was fundamentally conditioned by the pattern of economic and social policy pursued by successive SAP governments. The SAP pioneered

Keynesian demand management in the Great Depression, although it contributed little to Sweden's modest recovery. In the postwar context of rapid growth in trade and output, unemployment was more easily minimized than inflation. For the SAP, the problem was not just to curb inflation without sacrificing full employment but to do so consistently with the organizational cohesion of the LO unions comprising its core constituency.

An innovative strategy for doing so, the well-known Rehn-Meidner (RM) model, was devised by LO economists in the later 1940s. Its premise was that demand high enough to maintain full employment inevitably generated inflationary wage pressures, and that any attempts by unions to restrain such pressures were bound not only to fail but also to undermine member support. It accordingly prescribed instead the combination of a more restrictive macroeconomic policy and labor market policy (training, placement, income support) with a standard rate, or "solidaristic," union wage policy (equal pay for equal work, regardless of firms' profitability) implemented through the coordination of wage bargaining by LO. The interaction of these policies was expected to achieve noninflationary full employment in two ways. One was by cost-reducing structural change. Squeezed between standard rates and restrictive policy, firms unable to pay the standard rates had to become more efficient or go out of business, while more efficient firms would retain profits with which to expand. The complementary role of labor market policy was to counteract the unemployment of workers losing jobs in contracting firms by facilitating their transfer to expanding firms, while simultaneously averting inflationary imbalances between the resulting demand for labor and its skills and location. The other was by curbing the inflationary pressures generated by interunion wage rivalry through LO's coordination of its affiliates' wage bargaining.

Policy largely conformed to the RM model in the following years. The inauguration of centralized wage negotiations in 1956 bolstered LO's capacity to coordinate wage bargaining. The reorganization and vast expansion of labor market policy beginning in 1957 met another of the RM model's requirements. Demand management met them less consistently, achieving unemployment rates among the lowest in the OECD but often at the cost of tight labor markets that undermined solidaristic wage policy and fueled inflation.

Interacting with this macroeconomic strategy was a comprehensive array of transfers and services. Transfers replaced lost work income at high rates, especially since universal earnings-related pensions were enacted in 1958, while work income was supplemented by flat-rate child allowances and income-related housing benefits. The social wage was further enlarged by free education, from day-care through university, health care with token copayment, and subsidized housing on a massive scale. The latter, together with the expanding public service sector, also meant that social policy was itself an important source of employment, a by-product of which was the rapid growth, but also segregation, of female participation in the labor force. Because most of the entitlements were available to all on the same terms rather than on the basis of occupation, employer, or some test of need, Sweden had a "universal" as opposed to "occupational" or "residual" welfare state (Esping-Andersen 1990). Yet that welfare state also established strong links between welfare and work by tying the level of most transfers to earnings, and relying on high labor force participation and low unemployment to finance generous universal benefits (Pierson 1993). Characteristically the response to unemployment emphasized labor market policy measures aimed at preserving attachment to the labor market and facilitating reentry into employment rather than straight unemployment benefits. Finally, by severing the link between benefits and specific jobs, universalistic social policy supported the labor mobility required for the structural change on which full employment in Sweden's open economy was believed to depend. Thus, while the welfare state depended on full employment, it in turn decisively conditioned the operation of the labor market.

This conception of the Swedish model as a set of mutually reinforcing institutions, policies, and practices was most closely approximated during a relatively brief period from the late 1950s through the late 1960s. In the subsequent decades the coherence of the Swedish model was undermined by changes both within the country and in its international environment. I now turn to the impact of these changes on employment relations.

9.2   Work Organization

Taylorism and the Swedish Model

While it is taken for granted that Taylorist work organization pervaded Swedish industry (Broström 1991), comprehensive evidence seems lacking. In any case Taylorism was quite compatible with key features of the Swedish model. The restriction of collective bargaining to wages and the related terms of employment left managers free to organize work in whatever way they deemed most efficient, Taylorist or otherwise. At the same time the standard rates and reduction of differentials resulting from centralized wage bargaining, together with mobility among different jobs at similar wages, were consistent with the fragmentation of work into simple, narrowly defined, closely controlled tasks, readily performed by highly interchangeable workers with low and nearly homogeneous skills. There were contradictions, however, between Taylorism and other key features of the Swedish model, particularly full employment and the universalistic welfare state. Although unions could not challenge Taylorism through collective bargaining, tight labor markets gave workers other ways to do so. One was to voice their own protests through wildcat strikes, most notably the 1969–70 wave of strikes begun at LKAB, the state-owned iron mine. More generally, however, workers took the exit option that tight labor markets gave them, for most workers who quit had good prospects of finding comparable alternative jobs. High turnover rates in such quintessentially Taylorist contexts as the auto industry illustrate this phenomenon. Short of quitting, workers could stay away from their jobs without significant economic penalties since lost wages were largely offset by sickness and other benefits.

The effects of the choices available to Swedish workers are strikingly suggested by the contrasting experience of Electrolux refrigerator manufacturing plants in Sweden and England in the late 1980s summarized in table 9.1.

The contrasting effects of differences in the broad policy context were also reflected in the diverse approaches to job design taken by

Table 9.1
Absenteeism, turnover, and labor markets in Electrolux: Sweden and Britain (in %)

	Sweden	Britain
Absenteeism, due to:		
Short-term sickness	15.0	5.0
Other reasons	13.0	0.0
Turnover	25.0	2.5
Unemployment in plant locations	0.9	10.0
Number of days waiting for sickness pay	0	9

Source: Adapted from Berggren (1990, 88).

the production managers of the British and Swedish Electrolux plants. While managers at the British plant pursued a classical Taylorist effort "to simplify jobs and divide them into short cycles as much as possible so as to minimize sources of defects . . . and simultaneously increase production," management and labor in Sweden were engaged in the "construction of an experimental workshop in which to try out different organizations of work" with the aim of "eliminating the most meaningless jobs and replacing them with robots, all in order to develop more stimulating work" (Berggren 1990, 88). Comparisons of auto assembly plants in Sweden and other countries, including plants owned by the same company, reflect similar divergences.

Management Initiatives and Union Responses

Manning problems—recruitment, absenteeism, turnover—were undoubtedly a major factor triggering a search for alternatives to Taylorism by Swedish employers. Another was that, in the context of tight labor markets, local bargaining over piece-rates, strongly associated with Taylorist practice in Sweden, drove up wage costs. Yet another factor driving these changes was a recognition of previously overlooked efficiency losses in assembly line production (Berggren 1990, 131–33). In turn, management efforts to develop alternative forms of work organization posed challenges to unions that were difficult for them to meet within the confines of the Swedish model. The unions responded by turning to legislation to overcome employer resistance to collective bargaining over work organization issues, especially at the workplace level. In both process and substance this marked a major departure from the centralized self-regulation that had characterized the Swedish model in its classical form.

The employers' search for alternatives reaches back to the Fagersta steel company, where a group-based work organization and wage system, traditional in its process units, was extended throughout the company in the late 1950s. Several of the innovating Fagersta industrial engineers later staffed SAF's Technical Department, set up in 1966 to promote work organization experiments and publicize their results. Its efforts culminated in its New Factories project, completed in 1979. Drawing on the Tavistock sociotechnical approach as well as the experience of many Swedish manufacturing companies, SAF formulated a "new theory of production."

Early efforts by SAF to engage its union counterparts in the sponsorship of job design projects broke down in the face of their diverging views of the unions' role in shaping those projects. Initially the LO and TCO did not contest SAF's view of the matter as essentially one of efficiency rather than industrial democracy, and they were content to leave it up to management. During the 1960s, however, they altered their positions and pressed for employee participation under union auspices. In part, the unions needed to enlarge their capacity to act on workplace issues in order to restore their authority, undermined by processes that were leaving local level unions without much to engage their members' interest and commitment. Although centralized wage agreements did not eliminate local wage bargaining, it limited its scope and took away the strike weapon. At the same time nonwage workplace issues were assuming increased salience. Dissatisfaction with Taylorist work organization was increasing, especially among younger workers. Moreover rationalization increased stress for workers who retained their jobs, while structural change imposed on workers who lost their jobs costs not always compensated by labor market policy. Yet unions were unable to address such workplace issues through collective bargaining at any level as long as SAF insisted that they were exclusively managerial prerogatives. Unions could only participate in projects initiated and controlled by management within the limits of joint consultation, and committees for that purpose were set up in many companies under the terms of successive frame agreements between SAF and the unions. Formally, however, this meant that unions shared responsibility for the projects without much scope for influencing them.

In short, the unions were left in an increasingly vulnerable position. The 1969–70 wave of wildcat strikes convinced them they had to find a way out, and both LO and TCO concluded that it lay in extending collective bargaining to nonwage workplace issues. To make this break with the Swedish model, they found it necessary to seek another: a major expansion in the role of law in the regulation of industrial relations. Since SAF refused any renegotiation of the terms of centralized self-regulation entailing a retreat from the principle of managerial prerogatives, the only alternative was legislation. That route was available because the SAP was still in office and welcomed the opportunity to claim TCO as well as LO union members as its constituency, and because the liberal party, which was also staking a claim for the support of union members, provided the additional parliamentary support needed. Reinforced by a leftward shift in the general political climate, this resulted in an unprecedented stream of labor legislation, summarized in table 9.2.

This stream of legislation meant that employers could no longer refuse outright to negotiate over workplace issues. Moreover on certain issues, such as termination at will, it entirely deprived them of rights previously claimed, while on others, such as deviation from reverse seniority in layoffs, certain options were open only upon agreement with unions. In general, much of the legislation adhered to the self-regulation tradition insofar as it took the typical form of "framework laws," setting various parameters but leaving it to the parties to negotiate agreements spelling out the details of implementation within their bargaining jurisdictions.

The impact of all this legislation seems, however, to have been limited. Local union participation tended to continue where it had been established in the past, as in the cases of Volvo and SKF, but did not increase markedly where it had not been present. This was particularly true of smaller companies, though there are notable exceptions such as Almex (Hart and Hörte 1985; Levinson 1991; Svensson 1984). Thus the extent of work reorganization and the union role in it has continued to vary, depending on management initiatives and labor-management relations at the company level.

The Leading Edge

The innovations in work organization are illustrated most clearly by some of the pioneering firms. Of those, Volvo is best known, best documented, and has made the most radical changes. The varied pace of change in Volvo clearly reflected fluctuations in the world vehicle market. Three developments within Volvo's various plants mark the major stages in the evolution of work organization in the company (Berggren 1993).

The first took place at the Kalmar passenger car assembly plant, which was launched in 1974. Its major innovation was replacing the assembly line by separate carriers bringing vehicles into 4 or 5 parallel docks for assembly by teams in separated work spaces. Some leeway for pacing was created by buffers but limited by computerized central control that moved carriers from one work station to another after just 3 to 4 minutes. However, assemblers following vehicles through two team work spaces could have cycle times of up to 25

Table 9.2
Swedish labor legislation in the 1970s

1973	Worker Protection Law Amendments	Broadened health and safety to include ergonomic, social, and psychological dimensions; prescribed safety stewards in almost all workplaces and committees in all with 50 or more workers; required employers to consult on planned changes; gave safety stewards rights to stop dangerous work and to status quo pending adjudication of disputed changes in their jobs
1974	Status of Shop Stewards Act	Extended protection given to safety stewards to all local officials and established rights to paid time for union work and training
1974	Employment Security Act (LAS)	Required "objective" grounds for termination, advance notice that increases with age, and layoffs in order of reverse seniority unless otherwise provided in collective agreements
1974	Employment Promotion Act	Required advance notice of layoffs to union and local labor market board, and measures to minimize impact on older or otherwise disadvantaged workers
1976	Employee Representation on Boards Act	Entitled unions to select two members of company boards
1976	Codetermination Act (MBL)	Required employers to supply company information to unions and notify and negotiate with them before implementing any work organization changes, and permitted unions to negotiate agreements extending joint determination to any workplace matters including hiring and firing, work assignments, and discipline
1977	Work Environment Act	Extended union participation in design of work organization and changes in physical plant, and provided funding for joint union-management projects

Source: Compiled from Bruun et al. (1990) and Dittmar and Losman (1975).

minutes. In response to the auto market's severe setback in 1977, most of the innovations were eliminated or attenuated, control tightened, and work pace intensified. Though high productivity was achieved, the enduring changes were limited. The teams were merely "geographical without organizational content," and tightly controlled sequencing made the production system operate like an assembly line despite its different physical configuration.

The second development occurred in 1982 at the LB heavy truck plant in Tuve. There the assembly line was "broken" or segmented rather than entirely replaced. Assembly, of much more complex, customized products, took place in two sequential flows with 4 to 5 groups in each, and in off-line subassemblies, organized on a more genuinely group basis. Each group had rotating leaders and could take on a range of responsibilities, including the planning, organization, and even pacing of production, as well as budgets, rotation, timekeeping, and training. As a result of these changes in work organization, the number of supervisors was considerably reduced. Coupled with these changes was a new pay system, comprising a knowledge-based individual component and a group component based on the extent of the group's responsibilities.

With the start of the Uddevalla passenger car plant in 1988, the third and most radical phase of work redesign was reached. At Uddevalla sequential line assembly was completely replaced by small-scale parallel assembly. Final assembly (chassis and trim operations on painted bodies shipped from the main plant) of a whole car was carried out entirely by one of 48 teams of 8 to 10 members. The amount of training provided was extensive: 16 months to qualify as an assembler, that is, an employee capable of building a quarter of a car by him- or herself, and further on-the-job training in order to qualify as team leader and ultimately master-builder capable of building an entire car in 20 hours. A much flatter managerial structure accompanied this team structure. When the new auto market crisis brought Volvo the biggest financial losses in its history, it decided to close Uddevalla in 1993 and Kalmar in 1994. There is considerable debate over these decisions. Although some (Adler and Cole 1993) allege that these plants were shut down because of poor economic performance, others (Berggren 1993; Hancké 1993) argue that other factors were at work, including pressure from Renault, then a major shareholder, to cut excess capacity and the power of workers at the main plant in order to concentrate the cuts at the smaller plants. Regardless of the precise reasons, what is clear is that with the closing of these two plants, Volvo has relinquished its role as pioneer in new work systems.

This position has more recently been taken up by Asea Brown-Boveri (ABB). ABB developed a "multidomestic" structure, combining a central global strategy with a high degree of autonomy, and competition, among its subsidiaries. It makes producers' rather than consumer goods—principally a wide range of equipment for generating, transmitting, and using electricity, and associated control systems and service. Hence much of its business involves close contact with customers, and a central part of its global strategy has been to improve its responses to them, in terms of both quality and speed, requiring all its companies to implement total quality management and time-based management. Within ASEA the latter was translated into the so-called T-50 program, aimed at reducing total cycle time, from order to delivery, by 50 percent over four years.

To that end the program relies heavily on changes in work organization, particularly those permitting the cycle time to be cut by reducing the stages from order to delivery. Central to this is the integration of office tasks involving contacts with customers at either end of the cycle, such as receiving orders and ascertaining satisfaction, into production. ASEA, which could never be as thoroughly Taylorist as mass production companies like Volvo, was a pioneer in developing group production, much of it by teams organized around product projects. Under the impetus of T-50, the functions of production teams are being extended, upward as well as backward and forward in the cycle. Emphasis is accordingly placed on tapping and enlarging the competence of production workers, increasing communication between office and production workers, the flattening of organizational hierarchies, and ultimately eliminating entirely the separate categories of white-collar and blue-collar workers through single local agreements covering members of all unions and providing for uniform pay systems and fringe benefits. While Volvo and ASEA have, successively, been at the leading edge of change, many other companies have been implementing similar changes to one degree or another. Small as well as large companies in other manufacturing, with both short and long series as in ASEA, as well as service sector companies such as banks, insurance, and airlines, have adopted variants of group organization and the whole configuration of associated changes (Bengtsson et al. 1991; SOU 1991:82). A parallel process of change has been spreading in the public sector (von Otter 1992; Wise 1993).

Although there are no comprehensive data on the extent of change in work organization, it is evidently quite limited. The strongest evidence concerns the core engineering sector. A study of firms using NC machines in 1989–90 found that three-fifths had a "high division of labor, . . . few 'self-sufficient' machine operators, and a small portion of programming and planning on the shopfloor" (Bengtsson 1991, 87). An analysis of the knowledge content and work environment of its members' jobs in the engineering industry led the Swedish metalworkers' union (Metall) to conclude that the proportion with "bad" jobs (dull, repetitive, low skilled, and unhealthy) was large and increasing. Between 1977 and 1987 employment grew in the subsectors with a relatively high percentage of low-quality jobs, while it fell in the subsectors with a relatively high percentage of high-quality jobs. The subsectors with the worst jobs and those that grew fastest were also those in which the percentage of women was greatest (Svenska Metalindustriarbetareförbundet 1989). Pointing in the same direction, growth in the knowledge content of white-collar jobs exceeded the growth in educational (especially technical) qualifications among white-collar workers, while that was not the case as far as blue-collar jobs were concerned (Landell 1991). This implies that the jobs of blue-collar workers in Swedish industry are not generally being changed sufficiently to tap and expand workers' knowledge to perform a wider range of tasks with greater autonomy, as was being done in the pioneering companies. This tendency toward a polarization of work has led to a new phase in the LO unions' strategy, referred to as "solidaristic work policy." As the terms imply, however, its scope is much broader than work organization. It is a response as well to the disintegration of centralized wage negotiations and solidaristic wage policy, to which we turn next.

9.3 Wage Bargaining and Compensation Practices

The most fundamental change in the Swedish wage bargaining system has been the end of central negotiations. The initiative for their termination, as for their introduction, came from private sector employers. The continuous sequence of central negotiations since 1956 was broken in 1983 when the engineering employers federation, VF, pulled out and induced Metall to conclude a separate agreement. In the next round, there were no LO-SAF negotiations at all. After alternations between recentralization and renewed decentralization in the following years, SAF ruled out any return to central negotiations. Indeed the aim is now to limit if not eliminate even industry-level bargaining and push decentralization on down to the company level.

The Evolution of Union Structures and Wage Policies

Central negotiations were generally expected to limit wage growth by curbing interunion wage rivalry. In the context of divisions in union structure along occupational and sectoral lines, secular changes in the composition of employment made this increasingly difficult. In the early years of LO-SAF negotiations, the agreements between them could shape wage growth because they covered roughly a third of the labor force. By the late 1980s union density had increased to 85 percent, but the white-collar unions affiliated with TCO or SACO-SR (the small confederation of professional employee unions) had grown much faster than the LO unions, whose share of total membership fell below three-fifths. Moreover public sector bargaining covered more workers than all private sector bargaining, white as well as blue collar. The coverage of LO-SAF agreements consequently fell to just over 16 percent (Calmfors and Forslund 1990; Martin 1992).

Increasing fragmentation and complexity accompanied the declining LO-SAF share. Private sector white-collar unions negotiated on their own or in shifting coalitions, including a bargaining organization, PTK, set up in 1973. Similar bargaining "cartels" of white-collar unions at different levels of the public sector were set up, entering into coalitions with their LO counterparts against the rest of LO on some occasions, most notably when the so-called "gang of four" triggered the massive strike and lockout of 1980. Thus wage rivalry among LO private sector unions became less important than rivalry between them and other unions, in both the private and public sectors. This in turn further diminished the effectiveness of LO-SAF negotiations in curbing the inflationary effects of interunion wage rivalry.

The impact of these developments was amplified by the evolution of solidaristic wage policy. Wage rivalry among LO unions was muted on the basis of agreement on the bargaining demands they authorized LO to make. While the norm of equal pay for equal work invoked to legitimate those demands was consistent with unequal pay for unequal work, the demands were increasingly designed to compress wage differentials. However, their intended distributive effects tended to be offset by wage drift—increases exceeding those set in the central agreements gained in industry- or company-level bargaining. While drift served as a safety valve, enabling its beneficiaries to support the policy without forgoing larger increases, the support contingent on the agreed compression was jeopardized insofar as it was counteracted by drift. To avert that, LO secured earnings guarantees, entitling workers whose earnings rose less than average drift to ex-post increases making up a large portion, though not all, of the difference (Elvander 1988).

The strategy apparently had a considerable distributive impact: The dispersion of LO union members' earnings declined by about 56 percent from 1970 to 1982 and, measured differently, by over 70 percent from the mid-1960s (Hibbs and Locking 1993; Hibbs 1990). Further evidence is provided by the clear reversal of these trends since the break in central negotiations in 1983, with dispersion returning to their early 1970s levels by the end of the 1980s, as well as by more comparative data showing that wage dispersion among blue-collar workers and across manufacturing subsectors was substantially lower in Sweden than in other countries. With respect to gender wage differences, there seems no doubt that they were significantly reduced by solidaristic wage policy, partially offsetting discrimination and a high degree of occupational and sectoral gender segregation (Persson-Tanimura 1988). Average monthly industrial earnings of women relative to men rose from 70 percent in 1960 to around 90 percent in the 1980s (Elvander 1991, 236).

There is more uncertainty about the effects of increasingly egalitarian wage policy on efficiency and stability. While compression is credited with forcing inefficient producers out of business, it is argued that further gains must come to a greater extent from improvements in the skills, allocation, and utilization of labor. But the increasing compression and complex provisions in central agreements designed to enforce it at the company level are cited as obstacles to the wage differentiation and flexibility needed to encourage such improvements. Thus they are described as depriving management of the ability to design pay systems that reward growth in the specific skills, responsibility, and performance corresponding to companies' specific needs, particularly as they vary with changes in work organization (Jonsson and Siven 1986; Tersmeden and Wiberg 1986; Östman 1987). In addition they are blamed for insufficient investment in human capital (Henrekson 1992) and for greater regional and youth unemployment than there would otherwise be (Skedinger 1993; Jungdalen 1993).

At least with respect to pay systems, however, the extent to which centralized negotiations obstructed change is not clear. Reliance on individual piece-rates was particularly heavy in the Swedish variant of Taylorism, but their use declined markedly as the search for alternative ways of organizing work accelerated. Piece-rates of all kinds in the engineering sector accounted for around 70 percent of hours worked at their peak around 1960, dropping to a little over 40 percent by the early 1980s. A rise of several percentage points since then reflects a shift toward new, primarily group-based forms of pay for performance (Holmlund 1991, 35). Similarly, in all of industry, individual straight piece-rates for blue-collar workers declined from a third to 12 percent of hours from 1970 to 1985. Growing criticism of stress associated with piece-rates initially led to their replacement primarily by time wages, including fixed monthly wages. However, alternative forms of performance-based pay increased from a little under a third to nearly half over the same period. The latter trend accelerated after 1983, when the engineering sector broke away from centralized negotiations. Still, the proportion of all hours of performance-based pay accounted for by various forms of pay tied to the performance of groups rather than individuals, ranging from teams to whole establishments, already increased from 47 to 67 percent from 1970 to 1983 (Elvander 1991, 50–51). This suggests that significant change in pay systems was possible even while central negotiations were still in effect. A variety of compensation forms not subject to collective bargaining also proliferated, including profit-sharing schemes and convertible bonds, redeemable in the form of shares at prices permitting large capital gains, popular during the 1980s stock market boom but no longer (Elvander 1991, 52–53). While change and variation in pay systems have undoubtedly been essential then, central negotiations were not necessarily an insuperable obstacle.

Negative inflationary effects have also been attributed to the LO's evidently successful efforts to achieve compression (Hibbs and Locking 1993). In negotiating with SAF, LO sought aggregate contractual increases high enough to give all private sector LO union members some increases while enforcing some compression despite expected drift. As other unions won similar earnings guarantees aimed at preserving their members' positions relative to those benefiting from drift, the inflationary impact of drift was diffused across the labor market. Thus the capacity of central negotiations to perform the macroeconomic function expected of it seems to have been impaired by both the proliferation of multiple bargaining organizations and the LO's increasingly egalitarian version of solidaristic wage policy. While there have been episodes of excessive wage growth, however, they may have been due more to excessively expansionary macroeconomic policy, especially in the mid-1970s and mid-1980s, than to any autonomous effects of centralized negotiations. Thus, precisely as predicted by the RM model, macroeconomic policy errors made it impossible for centralized negotiations to limit wage growth (Martin 1985; Notermans 1993).

The Employers' Strategic Reorientation

The breakdown of the SAP's macroeconomic strategy assured success to the employers' drive to end central negotiations. The events of the 1980s reinforced the view within SAF that the trade-off between what central negotiations delivered and what they cost had worsened: less wage restraint and more wage rigidity. It worsened not only because of changes in the operation of central negotiations but also in the priorities against which they were evaluated (Pontusson 1992). As the need to adapt pay systems to changing work organization increased, and as financial as well as technical responsibility for production was decentralized, higher priority was put on wage flexibility. Moreover firms increasingly claimed that they needed to be able to pay wages as high as necessary in order to attract and retain skilled labor.

While all these considerations fed the decentralization drive, it followed an unsteady course. In response to a 1975–76 wage explosion, a new, more militant SAF leadership sought to remedy the economic flaws of centralized negotiations by using them more aggressively, including industrial action to back its demands for both lower wage growth and its more decentralized distribution. Put to the test in 1980, this strategy failed. SAF responded to selective strikes by locking out all its affiliates' employees belonging to LO unions, closing down the whole economy. But instead of providing the expected backing, the government pressured SAF to back down.

This experience renewed VF's determination to end central negotiations, on its own if necessary. This it did in 1983, inducing Metall to make a separate settlement by conceding several of Metall's long-resisted demands, including the addition of a higher wage class enabling its highly qualified members to get higher pay without having to switch to SIF, the white-collar union. VF also split the white-collar unions off from the central negotiations. There were no such negotiations at all the following year. To the SAP government then back in power, the ensuing proliferation of successively higher separate settlements of widely varied duration posed a dire threat to its whole "Third Road" economic strategy for an export-led recovery. So it summoned all parties to discussions from which it extracted a commitment to limit wage growth to 5 percent, which LO and SAF translated into an agreement confined to this overall level. Industry-level agreements that largely conformed to the limit and terminated at the same time laid the groundwork for a more nearly complete restoration of central negotiations in 1986. Despite the employers' initial resistance a combination of circumstances (e.g., the dramatic assassination of the prime minister) enabled LO and the government to get SAF, including VF, back to the table.

Yet the 1986–87 agreement was the last of its kind. Given a boom that had completely escaped the government's control, there was no way the reduction in wage growth could be continued. Moreover complicated provisions for controlling the distribution of increases retained in the agreement were condemned as a "straitjacket" by VF, which vowed to never again give SAF a mandate to negotiate. In 1988 it persuaded the rest of SAF's affiliates to negotiate only at the industry level, as in 1984, and it settled separately with its union counterparts after defeating a strike by SIF, aimed at securing greater control of wages at the company level. To those in SAF opposed to VF's position (primarily small and medium employers), however, the leap-frogging and wage drift substantially greater than contractual increases confirmed their fears, leading them to return to central negotiations in 1989, though without VF, as in 1983. Unlike 1983, however, Metall refused to settle with VF until the rest of SAF and LO reached a two-year agreement, forcing VF to accept similar terms.

VF concluded that negotiating on its own was not enough and that SAF had to be precluded from ever negotiating for any employers again. It accomplished this by taking a key role in changing SAF's leadership, policy, and organization. In 1989 a new leadership committed to VF's position was installed. In February 1990 the SAF board formally declared that wage negotiations should henceforth take place only at industry and company levels, a decision described by its new chair as "historic," marking the death of the so-called Swedish model, to which "there is no turning back" (*SAF Tidningen*, February 16, 1990). SAF subsequently replaced its negotiating department with a support function for its affiliates and established several bargaining cartels of employer associations, of mostly small- and medium-sized firms, that felt unable to go it alone. In addition SAF brought down the "corporatist" structure of tripartite boards responsible for administering a wide range of government agencies, including the labor market policy agency, AMS, by unilaterally withdrawing its representatives. Finally, it elaborated a program for extending this "system shift" across the whole spectrum of institutions comprising the Social Democratic welfare state, including labor law, social policy, and taxation (Martin 1992). Thus the strategic reorientation of Sweden's organized employers was completed.

The Wage-Bargaining System in Transition

The envisioned system shift obviously presupposed an end to Social Democratic rule, which came with the 1991 election. Before that, however, the government took one more wage bargaining initiative. It appointed a national mediation commission whose assignment was not the usual one of averting open conflict but of securing industry-level agreements that would lower the rate of growth across the whole economy. Wage growth did fall sharply from just over 10 percent in 1990 to 3.5 percent in 1992, but this resulted less from the commission's efforts than from an even greater rise in unemployment to the highest levels since the Great Depression. Precipitated by the international recession, this crisis in the Swedish economy was aggravated by domestic factors, including the collapse of a late 1980s speculative bubble and restrictive policies begun by the SAP government and sharply intensified by the conservative coalition that followed.

In the new political context, SAF set out to go further on the road to decentralization. The next step was to sharply curtail the effect of industry agreements, reserving as much as possible to the company level. As before, VI (the former VF after merger with the industry association), now headed by ASEA's CEO, took the lead. Further decentralization was expected to encourage the kind of single local agreements covering members of all unions sought by ASEA, but so far reached at only a few of its units (Mahon 1993). At ASEA, as in other leading engineering firms like Ericsson and Volvo, separate agreements with blue- and white-collar unions, embodying contrasting pay and job assignment rules, were viewed as obstacles to the re-organization of work into teams responsible for a wide range of tasks, among which all team members rotate, cutting across the unions' jurisdictions (including separate ones for different categories of white-collar workers). The prospects for overcoming these organizational divisions piecemeal at the company level were believed better than at the confederal and national union level where they are so strongly institutionalized. While overcoming these divisions, single local agreements could also bring the best of both worlds—blue-collar job flexibility and white-collar pay flexibility. Thus the practice of individual wage setting prevailing for white-collar workers, which SIF unsuccessfully sought to overcome in its 1988 strike, could be extended to blue-collar workers, whose collective agreements now control the "price" though not the "work obligation" of labor, on the German model. At the same time a manager's freedom to assign blue-collar workers to any jobs covered by a given collective agreement could be extended to white-collar workers, whose collective agreements now control their assignment to jobs within an elaborate classification system, more akin to the Anglo-Saxon job-control model (SIF 1991; Bröms 1992). Accordingly the employers entered the most recent wage round with the declared common goal of confining industry agreements to minimum wage rates—with no general increase or special low-wage provisions—and general conditions such as sickness insurance and vacations, leaving pay systems and rules entirely to local negotiations and actual earnings to discussions between managers and individual employees.

To the national unions this threatened their role in wage setting not only at the industry but also company level, raising the specter of enterprise unionism. In response they managed to establish an unprecedented degree of strategic cooperation across blue- and white-collar lines in two major sectors, engineering (where all negotiations for employee agreements were broken off) and retail trade. In both sectors broadly similar agreements, brokered by the same mediators after talks deadlocked, were reached with both blue- and white-collar unions, setting the pattern for the rest of the private sector (*SAF Tidningen*, April 16, May 14, October 22, 1993; *LO Tidningen*, June 11, 1993). They mark some advances by the employers toward their declared goals, providing for both a further decentralization of wage bargaining to the company level and some convergence of blue- and white-collar pay systems. Both should facilitate the negotiation of employee agreements. At the same time they reflect some success by the national unions in developing a strategy for meeting the challenges posed by the employers. They managed to preserve at least some role for national agreements in regulating earnings rather than just minimum wages, though more so in the retail than the engineering agreement. Thus the unions have so far headed off the danger of being shut out entirely from the wage determination process. Moreover they built mechanisms for joint action across the blue–white-collar line. While this may facilitate the spread of employee agreements, it makes it more likely that the national unions can influence the process, providing support for their workplace units, establishing common standards to protect union rights, and preventing employee agreements from turning local representation into enterprise unions, isolated from organization that links workers across different companies and sectors.

Thus, as long as Sweden continues to be so highly unionized, there seem to be limits to how far decentralization can be pushed without sacrificing industrial peace. Moreover, although the 1991–94 government took some measures that weaken unions, the prospects for sustained political support for deunionization have dimmed as Depression levels of unemployment restored support for the SAP to the highest level it has ever had. Without attaching undue significance to such fluctuations, no fundamental political realignment capable of sustaining a far-reaching system shift has so far occurred. Still the wage bargaining system has clearly undergone significant and probably irreversible change. The center of gravity has shifted downward; the peak organizations no longer negotiate. Local bargaining controls much more of total earnings, more of which is calibrated to performance, with an increasing residual that is individualized.

9.4   Skill Formation and Development

Schooling for Work

The widely held belief that "a well-educated labor force is one of [Sweden's] competitive advantages" has been dismissed as a "myth" (SOU 1991:2, 180). Sweden did lead Europe in establishing universal elementary public education, already creating a literate labor force prior to industrialization and long before the Social Democratic era, during which reforms were aimed at lengthening education and reducing its stratifying effect. During the 1960s compulsory education was reorganized into a comprehensive or common basic school (*grundskolan*) extending through the equivalent of early secondary education. Subsequently the proportion of each age group attending either two- or three-year advanced secondary education (*gymnasium*) rose from 60 to over 90 percent from 1965 to 1990, and the proportion of the labor force with at least three years of *gymnasium* rose from 6 to 31 percent between 1960 in 1986. The share of each age cohort going on to higher education rose from 13 to 31 percent between 1965 and 1990. Notwithstanding these postwar reforms, the proportion of the labor force with no more than 10 years of schooling was still 44 percent in Sweden in 1987, less than in Britain or Finland, but considerably more than in the United States, Germany, and Japan. Reflecting high attrition in higher education, only a little over 11 percent of the labor force had university degrees in 1987, higher than in Germany but lower than in the United States, Britain, and Japan (SOU 1991:2, 178–80). By other measures as well, Sweden does not have an exceptionally well-educated labor force. Although a larger share of its GDP was devoted to education than of any other OECD country during the 1980s, less time was spent in school. Moreover in certain crucial subjects like mathematics Sweden ranked low in comparison with other nations (Fägerlind 1991, 226–45).

Postcompulsory secondary education is claimed to be more closely linked to subsequent work life in Sweden than elsewhere, though on the basis only of the numbers in what is defined as occupationally oriented education rather than evidence of its effectiveness (Osterman 1988, 195). In 1984, 51 percent of Swedish 17-year-olds were in two-year occupationally oriented *gymnasium* programs, compared with 27 percent in such programs in Japan, 18 percent in West Germany, and 12 percent in Britain. Of the Swedish 17-year-olds not in *gymnasium*, only 2 percent were in apprenticeship programs, compared with 18 percent in Germany and 12 percent in Britain, reflecting the relatively small role apprenticeship has until recently had in Sweden (Landell and Victorson 1991). However, the school-work linkage is where the main change is occurring. Three-year *gymnasium* has just become standard, with a large part of the third year in occupationally oriented programs that include work experience. Young people not continuing in *gymnasium* (some 13 percent) are also entitled to work experience in the form of six months of full-time paid employment subsidized by local governments. The increasing provision of apprentice- or intern-like work experience is seen as making the transition from school to work in Sweden more like that in Germany (Fägerlind 1991, 245).

Sweden ranks among the lowest OECD countries in the share of both GDP and education expenditures allocated to higher education. An inadequate supply of university-trained labor has been blamed on a return on investment in higher education described as lower than in most other comparable countries (Henrekson 1993), yet the demand for higher education places is apparently higher than the supply—2.6 applicants per place in 1989 (Fägerlind 1991, 249). The supply of engineers, of which shortages have been greatest, is notoriously prone to boom and bust cycles which Sweden has not escaped. During its rapid expansion in the mid-1980s, industry experienced shortages of technically qualified white-collar workers, particularly engineers, but this reflected industry's declining demand in the 1970s, resulting in decreasing entry into and completion of engineering studies and reduction in available places (SOU 1991:82, 182). Moreover industry experienced even greater shortages of skilled blue-collar workers during the 1980s boom (NIER 1991, 70). Thus inadequate investment by industry in skilled labor at all levels over the longer run, for whatever reasons, may have retarded growth in the supply of such labor, not only by pre-employment schooling but also through training and retraining after entry into employment.

Competence Development in the Labor Force

Sweden has a particularly abundant array of programs for training and education subsequent to entry into the labor force. By the late 1980s over half of Swedish adults annually participated in some form of adult education (Fägerlind 1991, 246–47). The most distinctive form is the labor market training provided as part of labor market policy. Recall that in the RM model, such training was assigned a key role in the continuing process of structural change on which the macroeconomic strategy was predicated, enabling displaced workers to qualify for new jobs while avoiding skill shortages in the expanding firms and sectors.

Between 1970 and 1990, roughly 0.70 to 1.25 percent of the labor force has been in courses at any one time, typically a minority of participants in all programs, which ranged between 1.5 to 3.5 percent of the labor force over the same period. Training as well as the total tended to vary with unemployment, though not consistently. Although data on the flow of trainees over the course of a year over the same period is not available, it is substantially larger. During FY

1988–89, when average participation was about 1 percent, the total number of participants was the equivalent of 2.9 percent of the labor force, though the actual proportion was less since some take more than one course. Measured in terms of how many participants are employed a half year after completion, training effectiveness declined somewhat and then recovered, reaching 74 percent in 1989–90 (AMS 1990).

Dissatisfaction with AMU's ability to meet skill demands, in terms of speed and content, led to a major reorganization in 1986, resulting in a more decentralized structure and self-financing fee structure. The present conservative coalition government has converted the AMU group into a joint-stock company as a step toward its eventual privatization and the creation of markets for training as well as placement services (Arbetsmarknadsdepartementet 1992).

AMU's reorganization was partly aimed at increasing its role in firms' employee training. Whereas AMU had been designed to facilitate mobility on the external labor market, where the RM model assumed most of it to be, external labor market mobility appears to have decreased relative to that on the internal labor market. There appears to be a growing tendency of employers to fill positions from among their existing employees, relying increasingly on investment in firm-specific knowledge, with a corresponding interest in protecting that investment (Le Grand 1991). This is in turn attributed to the more diversified and technically advanced competence, and its continuous development needed for the new, more flexible, group-based forms of work organization (Eckstedt 1991; Rollén 1991). To adapt AMU to the growing importance of internal labor markets, then, means integrating it with employee training more than in the past (SOU 1991:82, 193–94).

Yet the amount and distribution of training provided by employers has been viewed as far short of needs. Most training is typically very short. Of the 24 percent of the labor force who had any employee training in 1986, 70 percent had only one to five days. Moreover the distribution of training is highly skewed. One study found that relative to share of labor force, those with the most prior education, two years of *gymnasium* or more, were most overrepresented among those with the longest employee training, more than four weeks, while those with the least, nine years or less, were most overrepresented in the category with no such training (Fägerlind 1991, 246). Included among those who did get some training was 13 percent of those with less than nine years (i.e., older workers) and 41 percent of those with more than two years beyond *gymnasium* (LO 1988, 36–37). A parallel finding is that the skills required by white-collar technical workers' jobs went beyond their training to a greater extent than the skills of blue-collar workers, which was interpreted as reflecting relatively greater investment in training of white-collar workers (Landell and Victorsson 1991).

Fragmentary evidence indicates extreme variation in company practice. Volvo Udevalla, described earlier, is at one extreme, but Volvo as a whole also invests heavily in training, allocating 18 percent of its wage bill and 14 percent of work time to training (Fägerlind 1991, 247). While this is fairly characteristic of large companies, it is much less so of medium-sized companies and rare among small companies. Of four medium-sized companies in one study, one was a training organization that made continuing education an integral part of its business strategy, production organization, and pay system, while the other three provided minimal, ad hoc, ill-designed training that was marginal to management's concerns (Bäcklund et al. 1987). How representative this distribution is of Swedish industry cannot be assessed from the information at hand, but since the breadth and depth of competence firms need depends on how they organize work, great variation in the provision of training is to be expected from the great variation in the reorganization of work (SOU 1991:56, 92).

9.5   Employment Security

Employment security was a fundamental promise of the Swedish model, but it was not a promise of security in the particular job a worker had at any time. There was essentially no protection, legal or collectively bargained, against dismissals; firing as well as hiring and deployment were solely up to employers. Instead, employment security meant assurance of alternative jobs—through demand management—and of information about those jobs, training needed to do them, and income maintenance during the transition to them—through labor market policy. In short, employment security was to be provided through mobility in the external labor market. Much in this pattern has changed. Job tenure was given legal protection, which was somewhat relaxed by the 1991–94 government; there has been a shift from external to internal labor market mobility; and most recently, and most drastically, unemployment has risen sharply.

For decades, open unemployment in Sweden remained below the OECD average. This gap grew during the 1970s, in which unemployment averaged 2.1 and 4.3 percent in Sweden and the OECD, respectively, and became even greater during the 1980s, when the corresponding averages were 2.5 and 7.3 percent. But in the 1990s the gap closed rapidly as unemployment in Sweden reached the OECD average of 8.2 percent in 1993, reflecting the breakdown and abandonment of the full-employment policy regime (Standing 1988; OECD 1990; LO 1993).

Job Security Regulation

Managerial discretion over staffing has been restricted in many ways by legislation, particularly the 1970s surge of labor legislation that marked a major break with the classic Swedish model. Employers have pressed for some relaxation of these restrictions on the ground that they hamper flexibility, with adverse effects on efficiency and employment. Adverse incentive as well as cost effects have also been attributed to many aspects of both legislated and negotiated forms of replacement for work income lost because of termination or temporary absence.

From the employers' standpoint, as articulated by SAF, limitations on varying work force size in the 1974 law on employment security (LAS) are among the most burdensome. A decline in business satisfies the law's requirement of reasonable grounds for layoffs, but they have to be in order of seniority and those laid off have preference in new hires.

Also cited are the obstacles to temporary work force increases in LAS and other laws. One is the prohibition of for-profit employment agencies, which extends to the business of providing temporary workers. Contractors can be used for special tasks or services but subject to union veto. Especially restrictive is the six-month limit on the duration of fixed-term contracts, shorter than in any of the EC countries except Italy. Yet in Sweden such contracts account for as much as 10 percent of employment. Some of this consists of workers hired for special tasks or to meet temporary peak period shortages. Another portion is accounted for by internships or probationary periods for new hires, many of whom will be converted to regular status. Still another consists of replacements for workers on leave to which they are legally entitled, such as parental or study leave, and from which they are entitled to return to their old or fully equivalent jobs. Time lost for such leave was recently estimated as equivalent to about a fifth of all hours worked, but much of that is short term leave for personal or family illness for which there would not be temporary replacements. Given the volume of fixed-term contracts and their short duration, it is not surprising that they should account for about half of all new hires during the 1980s (OECD 1993, 19; Holmlund 1993, 440–41).

The growth of insecure "atypical" forms of employment has probably been strongly inhibited by these restrictions, including the fact that they along with social charges are generally applicable to part-time as well as fixed-term workers, minimizing incentives to expand atypical employment. There is certainly some evasion, but it tends to be concentrated in services individuals can provide. The underground economy has been estimated as equivalent to only 5 to 7 percent of total tax potential (Standing 1988, 84). There is dispute over whether the wide ranging employment security for most has been bought at the expense of unemployment for some, especially young entrants into the labor market. Whatever the answer to this question, current controversy over the restrictions clearly reflect conflicts between management and unions over their relative roles in defining employment relations.

Policy Responses

A variety of changes in labor law and social policy have been made or proposed in response to the issues raised by employers and some economists, including the so-called Lindbeck Commission (SOU 1993, 16). The last SAP government took an initial step to reduce absenteeism by lowering the replacement rate. The 1991–94 conservative government took much bigger steps, first by shifting responsibility for sick pay to employers for the first 14 days and lowering the replacement rates further. These changes undoubtedly contributed to a fall in absenteeism by about half between 1989 and 1993.

The 1991–94 government also shifted the aim of a review of labor law initiated by its predecessor to address the employers' concerns but proposed changes that meet their demands only part way. The changes include: extending the limit on fixed-term contracts to one year; authorizing employers to exclude two employees from layoffs in order of seniority in the absence of satisfactory negotiated agreement on deviations from the rule (benefiting small firms but not the large ones that sought a 20 percent exclusion); and eliminating the unions' right to veto use of contractors and other nonemployees. A separate decision was reached to lift the ban on for-profit employment agencies, eliminating a central element of the Swedish model.

The sick pay reform was joined by modifications of other income replacements. Major changes were made in unemployment benefits, which had not been part of the universal social insurance system. The benefits have been administered by separate funds, controlled by unions, to which most but not all employees belong. Members make small contributions, often together with union dues, while employers pay in a much larger amount. But the bulk of the benefits are financed by the government, which also sets the levels and eligibility rules. The system has now been made universal and compulsory: All must contribute either to one of the union funds or an alternative set up by the government.

Some proposals go beyond such reforms to challenge the universality of the social insurance system. Predicated on full employment, it was bound to be strained by high unemployment, rendering the system vulnerable to far reaching changes. Those debated include a reversion from the prevailing income-replacement principle to a Beveridge-style flat rate basic guarantee, leaving protection against sharp income reductions up to supplementary private insurance, through collective agreements or individual purchase (SOU 1993, 16; Eklund 1993). Whether such a drastic departure from the Swedish model is necessary to deal with the problems that have been identified and widely acknowledged even by defenders of universality is by no means clear. The alternative responses to these problems reflect divergent visions of the future of employment relations in Sweden, to which we turn in our conclusion.

9.6   Conclusion

The vision of the future articulated by SAF is one in which managers' autonomy to shape employment relations would be greatly expanded. The constraints imposed by both unions and the state would be significantly diminished. Preferably the end of central negotiations would be followed by eliminating sectoral negotiations. Short of that, the latter would be restricted to nonwage and nonworkplace issues such as rules governing dispute resolution, working conditions such as vacations, and industrywide fringe benefits such as sick pay and

pensions (which would replace the earnings-related components of
public social insurance). Wage bargaining would take place exclusively at the enterprise level, where single agreements would be negotiated with representatives of the entire work force, all of whom
would be coworkers, no longer differentiated as blue- and white-
collar workers represented by separate unions. Even such single,
enterprise-level agreements would be confined to pay systems, aggregate changes in pay, and procedures for redressing pay grievances.
All actual earnings would be determined on the basis of managers'
evaluations of individuals' performance, reviewed with each, as is
already done with most white-collar employees. Pay determination would accordingly be decentralized to the individual level,
where it would be one of the tools of human resource management
at the employer's disposal, effectively removing wages from collective bargaining. Legal as well as bargained constraints would also
be removed on the use of other tools, such as selecting employees to
be retained in case of work force reductions or for various kinds of
training, setting the duration of probationary periods, employing
temporary workers, and replacing in-house work by contractors. Par-
alleling decentralization of responsibility for production and financial
results down to product units, whether parts of large corporations
or separate small- and medium-size firms, decentralization of human resource management would give unit managers the flexibility
to respond creatively and quickly to diverse and rapidly changing
markets. Work reorganization would certainly be an important kind
of response, but it would take a great variety of forms, developed by
managers in collaboration with their coworkers, unconstrained by
collective bargaining. In this vision, what replaces the Swedish model
is the "market and multiplicity" (SAF 1991).

Having seized the initiative, Swedish employers have made some
headway in the direction of this vision, especially in decentralizing
wage determination. This confronts Swedish unions with a fundamental challenge. Although LO still urges the restoration of central
negotiations, SAF's position precludes it. Now even the national unions are threatened with the loss of their wage bargaining role. Their
response has been to concentrate on preserving it. Their emerging
strategy for doing so is to accommodate some of the employers' main
declared objectives while retaining a voice in how they are met. Thus
unions have been accepting increased differentials, individualized
pay, and elimination of the distinctions between blue- and white-

collar employees, while insisting that the determination of individual pay be governed by norms negotiated at the sectoral level and applied in collective bargaining at the local level—in short, they accept change in the pattern of compensation while rejecting managerial autonomy in determining the content of that change. The strategy is aimed not only at preserving the role of collective bargaining in determining pay but also at extending collective bargaining more directly than the 1970s legislation did to changes in work organization and training by tying them systematically to changes in pay. The implementation of this strategy is envisioned as transforming rather than replacing the Swedish model, reorganizing employment relations in such a way as to reconcile productivity and justice through "solidaristic work" (Metall 1989; LO 1991).

As the terms imply, this vision rests its legitimacy on the traditional norm of equal pay for equal work underpinning solidaristic wage policy. While the latter came to mean increasing compression of pay for different work, however, the conception of "solidaristic work" reflects renewed acceptance of unequal pay for unequal work. The egalitarian thrust of the norm is retained but shifted from equalization of pay to equalization of work, which would then provide the economic basis for the equalization of pay. This would be accomplished by redesigning the organization of work so as to create for all workers opportunities to develop their skills and productivity, and hence their earning capacity, by advancing through a successsion of increasingly demanding jobs, for which all would be guaranteed the required training, on or off the job. As each climbed to the next rung on such a job ladder, he or she would be entitled to the higher level of pay established for the job by a local collective agreement. Pay would be individualized in that it depended on the pace at which individuals were able and willing to climb the job ladders. But while managers might have a say in whether a worker has demonstrated the required skills for a job, they would have no discretion, via any kind of individual evaluation that opened the way to favoritism and unequal pay for equal work, concerning the level of pay to which the worker is entitled. Nor would they have any discretion concerning who was entitled to the training needed to advance to higher paid jobs—continuous upskilling would be every worker's right. Continuous upskilling would in turn create the possibility and incentive for continuous job redesign, so as to capitalize on the investment in training. The model for job redesign is essentially that provided by the leading edge firms:

the organization of work into autonomous groups in which a wide range of indirect functions have been integrated with direct production of goods or services, whose members learn the widest possible range of tasks, among which they can rotate. What distinguishes the vision of solidaristic work is the use of collective bargaining to diffuse that model, not only within firms and agencies but also throughout the economy, in order to equalize opportunity for work in which workers' skills, and hence pay, can be developed, across the entire work force.

This vision clearly contrasts with the employers' vision, which the unions condemn as a formula for inequality that would only intensify the polarization between a minority with good jobs and relatively rising pay and a majority with bad jobs and relatively declining pay. Which of these visions is likely to be realized? Probably neither. There are formidable obstacles to pursuing either very far. Both are utopias, projecting those values and interests on which employers and unions diverge the most. There are other values and interests on which they converge. It is at least as possible that a new "historical compromise" will be hammered out, shaping a "new Swedish model" (Brulin and Nilsson 1991) embodying diluted elements of both visions. Collective bargaining would remain a fundamental feature of it, but it would certainly be more decentralized. National sectoral negotiations would retain a role in wage determination, though much more of it would occur locally. At both sectoral and local levels the lines between blue- and white-collar jobs, pay, conditions, and ultimately union structures would blur, facilitated by the further diminution of the separate confederations' roles. Job redesign would concomitantly become the subject of negotiations but would largely occur through informal collaboration.

There are many signs of something like this occurring, but not of major shifts in the patterns of change in employment relations already observed. The diffusion of new forms of work organization continues to be slow and uneven. There is little to reverse the observed tendency toward polarization in the distribution of training and of work that is rewarding in terms of both pay and satisfaction, nor of the larger tendency toward inequality to which the polarization contributes. Sweden continues to become a more unequal society but, as the Social Democrats' return to office in 1994 suggests, there is no political basis for dismantling the universalistic welfare state and producing the deeper social exclusion that would turn Sweden into a "two-thirds" society. Market forces may be more effective in eroding it over the longer run, but collective bargaining and law will continue to regulate their impact on the labor market, even if they are modified in detail. Sweden's prospective entry into the European union could accelerate the erosion of any new Swedish model, but it would not appreciably change the pressures on Sweden's already highly integrated economy, and it might indeeed diminish the pressures because it assures access to continental markets and because it alters the political configuration of policymaking in European institutions. In short, employment relations at the workplace may be changing less than the large and dramatic changes in their political and economic environment might lead us to expect.

References

Adler, Paul S., and Robert E. Cole. 1993. Designed to learn: A tale of two auto plants. *Sloan Management Review* 34:85–94.

AMS. 1990. *Annual Report 1989–90*. Stockholm: Labor Market Administration.

Bäcklund, A.-K., et al. 1987. *Kompetenskravens förändring och behovet av personalutveckling*. Malmö: Lärarhögskolan i Malmö, Lunds Universitet.

Bengtsson, Lars, et al. *90talets industriarbete i Sverige*. Stockholm: Carlsson Bokförlag.

Berggren, Cristian. 1990. *Det nya bilarbetet: Konkurrensen mellan olika produktionskoncepti svensk bilindustri 1970–1990*. Lund: Arkiv Förlag.

Berggren, Cristian. 1993. Volvo Uddevalla: A dead horse or a car dealer's dream? An evaluation of the economic performance of Volvo's unique assembly plant 1989–1992. Stockholm: Royal Institute of Technology. Department of Work Science.

Björkman, Torsten. 1992. *ABB Project Report. 1992 03 15*. Stockholm: Royal Institute of Technology.

Broström, Anders. 1991. Arbetsorganisation och produktvitet. In Anders Broström, ed., *Arbetsorganisation och produktvitet*. Expertrapport Nr. 5 till Produktivetsdelegationen. Stockholm: Allmänna Förlaget

Brulin, Göran, and Tommy Nilsson. 1991. *Mot en ny svensk modell: Arbete och förhandlingsystem i förändring*. Stockholm: Rabén & Sjögren.

Bruun, Niklas, et al. 1990. *Den nordiska modellen: Fackföreningarna och arbetsrätten i Norden—nu och i framtiden*. Malmö: Liber.

Calmfors, Lars, and Anders Forslund. 1990. Wage formation in Sweden. In Lars Calmfors, ed., *Wage Formation and Macroeconomic Policy in the Nordic Countries*. Stockholm: SNS Förlag.

Dittmar, Kai, and Sten Losman. 1975. *Den nya arbetsrätten*. Stockholm: Wahlström & Widstrand.

Eckstedt, Eskil. 1991. Arbetsorganisation: Förändringar och kompetensutveckling. In *Efter Taylor: En debattskrift från produktivitetsdelagationen och arbetslivsfonden*. Stockholm: Produktivetsdelagationen och arbetslivsfonden.

Eklund, Klas, ed. 1993. *En "skattereform" för socialfösäkringar?* Stockholm: Publica.

Elvander, Nils. 1988. *Den svenska modellen. Löneförhandlingar och inkomstpolitik 1982– 1986*. Stockholm: Almänna Förlaget.

Elvander, Nils. 1992. *Lokal lönemarknad: Lönebildning i Sverige och Storbritannien*. Stockholm: SNS Förlag.

Esping-Andersen, Gøsta. 1990. *The Three Worlds of Welfare Capitalism*. Princeton: Princveton University Press.

Fägerlind, Ingemar. 1991. Utbildningsstandarden i Sverige 1970–1990 och produktivitetsutvecklingen. In Eskil Wadensjö, ed., *Arbetskraft, arbetsmarknad och produktivitet*. Expertrapport Nr. 4 till Produktivitetsdelegationen. Stockholm: Allmänna Förlaget.

Hart, Horst, and Sven Åke Hörte. 1989. *Medbestämmandets stagnation: Medbestämmandets utveckling 1978–1985*. Göteborg: Arbetsvetenskapliga Kollegiet.

Hancké, Bob. 1993. Technological change and its institutional constraints: The politics of production at Volvo Uddevalla. Cambridge: Center for Science and International Affairs. Harvard University.

Henrekson, Magnus. 1992. *Sveriges tillväxtproblem*. Stockholm: SNS Förlag.

Hibbs, Douglas A., Jr. 1990. *Wage Compression under Solidarity Bargaining in Sweden*. Stockholm: Trade Union Institute for Economic Research.

Hibbs, Douglas A., Jr., and Håkan Locking. 1993. *Wage Compression, Wage Drift and Wage Inflation in Sweden*. Stockholm: Trade Union Institute for Economic Research.

Kjellberg, Anders. 1992. Sweden: Can the model survive? In Anthony Ferner and Richard Hyman, eds., *Industrial Relations in the New Europe*. Oxford: Blackwell.

Jonsson, Lennart, and Cleas-Henrik Siven. 1986. *Why Wage Differentials?* Stockholm: Swedish Employers Association.

Landell, Elin, and Jonas Victorsson. 1991. *Långt kvar till kunskapsshället*. Sttockholm: Statens Industriverk.

Le Grand, Carl. 1991. Rörlighet och stabilitet på den svenska arbetsmarknaden. In Eskil Wadensjö, ed., *Arbetskraft, arbetsmarknad och produktivitet*. Expertrapport Nr. 4 till Produktivetsdelegationen. Stockholm: Allmänna Förlaget.

Levinson, Klas. 1991. *Medbestämmande i strategiska beslutsprocesser. Facklig medverkan och inflytande i koncerner*. Uppsala: Department of Business Studies.

LO. 1988. *Personal utbildning*. Stockholm: LO.

LO. 1991. *Det utvecklande arbetet. En rapport till LO-kongressen 1991*. Stockholm: LO.

LO. 1993. *LO Tidningen* (June 11).

LO. 1994. *Ekonomiska Utsikter* (Spring).

Mahon, Rianne. 1991. From solidaristic wages to solidaristic work: A post-Fordist historical compromise for Sweden? *Economic and Industrial Democracy* 12:295–325.

Malm, Lars, and Marianne Pihlgren. 1991. *Medarbetare i Service: Ett förändringsprojekt inom ABB i Sverige.* Stockholm: Pihlgrens Förlag.

Martin, Andrew. 1985. Wages, profits, and investment in Sweden. In Leon N. Lindberg and Charles S. Maier, eds., *The Politics of Inflation and Economic Stagnation.* Washington: Brookings Institution.

Martin, Andrew. 1992. *Wage Bargaining and Swedish Politics: The Political Implications of the End of Central Negotiations.* Stockholm: Trade Union Institute for Economic Research.

Matthiessen, Lars. 1971. Finanspolitiken som stabiliseringspolitik instrument. In Erik Lundberg, ed., *Svensk finanspolitik i teori och praktik.* Stockholm: Aldus-Bonniers.

Metall. 1989. *Solidarisk arbetspolitick för det goda arbetet.* Stockholm: Svenska Metallindustriarbetareförbundet.

NIER. 1991. *The Swedish Economy.* Stockholm: National Institute of Economic Research. Autumn.

Nilsson, Leif Åke. 1992. Human Resources Manager, ABB Sweden. Interview. November 20.

Notermans, Ton. 1993. The abdication from national policy autonomy: Why the macroeconomic policy regime has become so unfavorable to labor. *Politics and Society* 21:133–67.

OECD. 1991. *OECD Economic Outlook 49* (July).

Osterman, Paul. 1988. *Employment Futures: Reorganizaion, Dislocation, and Public Policy.* New York: Oxford University Press.

Östman, Lena. 1987. *Lönepolitik: Företagets och chefens styrinstrument.* Stockholm: Svenska Arbetsgivare föreningen.

Persson-Tanimura, Inga. 1988. Economc equality for Swedish women: Current situation and trends. Lund: Department of Economics, University of Lund.

Rollén, Berit. 1991. Nu behovs ett samlat program för kompetensutveckling. *Efter Taylor. En debattskrift från produktivetsdelagationen och arbetslivsfonden.* Stockholm: Produktivetsdelagationen och arbetslivsfonden.

SAF. 1991. *Den nya svenska modellen: Föredrag och kommentarer från SAFs konferens om svensk ekonomi.* Stockholm: Svenska Arbetsgivare Föreningen.

SAF. 1993. *SAF Tidnignen* (April 16, May 14, October 22).

Schager, Nils Henrik. 1988. Den svenska löneökningstakten. *Ekonomisk debatt* 16:615–23.

SOU 1991, 82. *Drivkrafter för produktivitet och välstånd.* Stockholm: Statens Offentiliga Utredningar.

SOU 1993, 16. *Nya villkor för ekonomi och politik.* Stockolm: Statens Offentiliga Utredningar.

Standing, Guy. 1988. *Unemployment and Labour Market Flexibility: Sweden.* Geneva: International Labor Office.

Svensson, Lennart. 1984. *Arbetarkollektivet och facket: En lokal kamp för företagsdemokrati.* Lund: Department of Sociology.

Swenson, Peter. 1989. *Fair Shares: Unions, Pay, and Politics in Sweden and West Germany.* Ithaca: Cornell University Press.

Tersmeden, Patrick, and Claes Wiberg. 1986. *Lönepolitik för konkurrenskraft.* Stockholm: Sveriges Verkstadsförening.

von Otter, Casten. 1992. Personnel management in the public service: Sweden. Stockholm: Swedish Center for Working Life

Wise, Lois R. 1993. Whither solidarity: Transitions in Swedish public-sector pay policy. *British Journal of Industrial Relations* 31:75–95.

10 A Social-Democratic Order under Pressure: Norwegian Employment Relations in the Eighties

Karl Henrik Sivesind
Ragnvald Kalleberg
Svein Hovde
Arvid Fennefoss

Changing political goals and closer connections to the world economy caused less dramatic changes in Norway than we have seen in several other countries during the 1980s and the early 1990s. The main sources of transformation in Norwegian employment relations during the 1980s were structural shifts between production sectors and an increased number of employees in the skilled and semiskilled professions. This climate has empowered new employee organizations with the potential to change old corporatist bargaining systems. Nonetheless, throughout the 1980s, income policies and relatively small wage differentials were sustained in Norway. The number of work reforms was smaller than in the preceding decade, and activities in this field concentrated on putting old laws and agreements into practice.

This chapter discusses the changes, continuities, and tensions in Norwegian employment relations in the 1980s and identifies some factors that can explain these phenomena. In sections 10.1 and 10.2 we take a brief look at Norwegian political policies, modes of economic regulation, and the relationship between the labor market parties before 1980 and describe changes that took place during the decade. In section 10.3 we consider the changes in five characteristics of employment relations pratices during this period: work organization, skill formation, compensation, employment security, and governance.

10.1 The Social Democratic Order in Norwegian Work Conditions

Norwegian employment relations are embedded in a social democratic order. According to the historian Berge Furre (1991), the rise of the Norwegian social democratic order began in 1950 after the postwar reconstruction period. Sometime around the beginning of the 1980s, it began to decline. Although it is difficult to give a precise year for the end of this order and the beginning of another one, it is reasonable to claim that the social democratic order, which had previously met little opposition, came under increasing pressure during the 1980s. A conservative government was elected in 1981 and a number of new policies were introduced, including the liberalization of the capital and housing markets. The Labor governments that returned to power after 1986 also had different political goals and used different means of economic regulation than had Labor governments in previous decades. It appears that in the 1980s many politicians, including social democrats, had more confidence in the market as a mode of regulation. The social democratic order traditionally included the following:

1. A large, ambitious plan for influencing the direction of social change.

2. Extensive redistributive policy aimed at promoting social equalization. (Furre 1991, 316–18, uses the term "welfare-municipalities" to describe the extent to which these tasks were decentralized.)

3. State regulation of agriculture, fishing, and transportation.

4. A consensus-based negotiation system with the major interest organizations, the state, and the parliament as participants.

"Viewed from a comparative international perspective, after the 1950s, for three decades the established social democratic order made considerable progress in all societal spheres, economic, political, social welfare, and cultural. Although at the turn of the century Norway had been among the poorer countries in Europe, by 1970 before the extraction of Norway's oil reserves, Norway was ranked ninth by *The Economist* in terms of GNP per capita in the world. In 1982 it was ranked third (Hodne 1983, 251). In the second half of the 1980s GNP per capita in Norway was somewhat higher than in Japan and the EC and somewhat below the average U.S. standard (Kvinge et al. 1992, 72). This growth was achieved as large segments of the economy were subjected to international competition: "exports averaged 44 per cent of GNP in the 1946–80 period. With imports of corresponding magnitude, Norway thus has a trade–income ratio surpassed only by the Netherlands" (Hodne 1983, 10).

Two important preconditions for the success of the social democratic policy in Norway were the national consensus developed during World War II combined with a well-established, general culture of equality, partially based on the lack of a feudal tradition. The Labor party's prime minister, Einar Gerhardsen, expressed what many felt in the first decade of the postwar period: "It is no use in fighting over sharing of too small a cake. It is better to put effort into making a cake that will be large enough to be the material basis for a decent standard of living for all citizens" (Gerhardsen 1971, 140). Individual wants and needs were put aside in the joint effort to rebuild the country after the war and to create social democratic welfare institutions.

But political success can be self-defeating. As the living strandard rose and institution building was completed by the end of the 1970s, this spirit of solidarity wore off. There were limits to how much money the taxpayers were willing to put into redistributive arrangements, especially when the large majority seemed to be well off and reasonably secure. Institutions that were designed to secure a fair distribution of goods and services, such as restrictions on housing, became viewed as unnecessary by many people as the economy flourished. In many ways traditions also eroded. Consumers and clients from the new middle class protested against short opening hours and rigid arrangements in both the private and the public sectors. All this contributed to the rise in conservative votes at the end of the 1970s and gave three nonsocialist parties a majority in the 1981 parliamentary election,[1] called the "blue-wave" (Bjørklund and Hagtvedt 1981). Although the Labor party was able to regain political power in 1986, it too began to move away from some of its traditional policies. Against these shifting background conditions we now turn to an indepth analysis of recent changes in Norwegian employment relations.

10.2 The Relations between the "Labor Market Parties" in Norway

Traditional Pattern

Traditionally the two main actors in wage bargaining in Norway have been the Norwegian Confederation of Trade Unions (LO), established in 1899, and the Confederation of Norwegian Business and Trade (NHO) which, until 1989, was called the Norwegian Employers' Confederation (NAF), formed in 1900. LO has close ties to the Labor party. The main features of the relations between the labor market parties

---

1. A minority Conservative party government (Høyre) was installed with support from two other nonsocialist parties. In June 1983 a coalition government of these three parties was formed. After the 1985 election the coalition government continued but with a nonsocialist majority in parliament; in April 1986 it resigned.

date back to the Basic Agreement of 1935 and the reconstruction period after World War II.

The 1935 agreement's institutional presuppositions rested on traditions, laws, and institutions that had existed since the beginning of the century: the first agreement, the Metal Agreement of 1907,[2] and the Labor Disputes Act of 1916, which established the Labor Court and the state as key mediators. In the reconstruction period the unions accepted compulsory arbitration, which had previously been rejected, in the government's accepting "ultimate responsibility for preventing labor conflicts from causing serious damage to society" (KAD, info-series 3, p. 13).

The traditional system was based on the hegemony of the LO, which was dominated by unions organizing the manufacturing sector. Until 1976 the LO was the only federation in Norway. In 1956 it organized 48 percent of all employees, while 10 percent were organized in unions outside the LO (Fennefoss 1988). In the 1950s and 1960s LO, and its different unions, constituted the essence of the labor movement.

The traditional collective bargaining system was based on a solidaristic wage policy, with different levels of bargaining. At the same time there was local wage bargaining in the industrial sector. The government was often a part of the bargaining process and, even when not a direct participant, its influence through the Labor party was substantial. Table 10.1 shows the different forms of bargaining and the occurrence of state involvement in the different bargaining years.

In the article "Norway: Numerical democracy and corporate pluralism," Stein Rokkan first presented his classical analysis of the interdependent relationship between the Labor party, the LO, and the state as it developed in the 1950s and 1960s. Because of its role as broker among the major interest organizations representing employees, farmers, and employers, the Labor government not only took into account various electoral constituencies when shaping policy but also included them, through consultations and negotiations, in the policymaking process (Rokkan 1966, 105–10). For example, on incomes policy, the LO advocated a reduction of wage differentials within the blue-collar sector as well as between blue and white-collar workers (Gustavsen and Hunnius 1981, 23). Since its formation LO strongly pushed for equality. The balance between wages in trading

---

2. The Metal Agreement was the first large, formal mutual recognition of employer prerogatives and basic trade unions rights.

sectors and sheltered sectors has also been an important income policy goal.[3]

Because of this emphasis on equality, job-control unionism has been
less important in Norway than in the United States. Norwegian wage
agreements usually specify different wages according to the complexity of the tasks and the workers' level of education, but in most industries wage gaps tend to be small. In some firms the local union and the
management agree to have less differentiated wages than provided in
the wage agreement. Equity also distinguishes the wage distribution
between management and workers as the ratio between top management and average workers is only about 3:1 (Johnsen and Joynt 1986).

Labor conflict in the postwar period has been low, and the labor
movement considers rationalization of industry to be essential for the
economy and the maintenance of a democratic welfare society (Gustavsen and Hunnius 1981, 24). Since the LO congress in 1923 there
have been conflicts about the organizational structure of the confederation. In 1923 it was decided that LO should have industrial unions
organized across occupational boundaries, but this reform was never
really implemented. In a way some difficulties arising from a mix of
organizing principles have haunted LO ever since; first in relation to
occupational unions and later in relation to white-collar workers, the
skilled and semiskilled professions. However, these problems remained latent and did not surface until the YS (Confederation of Vocational Unions) and the AF (Federation of Norwegian Professional
Association) were founded in 1976–77. One reason for the establishment of these new labor organizations was dissatisfaction with LO's
policy of equality in wage questions. YS unions, regarded as "yellow
unions" by the LO, were established as a nonpolitical alternative to
the LO, and they recruit members in the same sectors and occupations
as LO.

AF, however, primarily organizes more educated employees in the
skilled or semiskilled professions. However, the LO has not given up
on competing for these members. In particular, the growth in the professional work force in the public sector has caused the professional
unions, most of which are not affiliated with LO, to struggle over
the demarcation of territories. This has occurred recently with hospitals. The LO has many members in unions cutting across occupational

---

3. This is the so-called Aukrust model for avoiding inflation (Aukrust 1970). Rødseth
and Holden find empirical support for the assumption that wages in the nontraded
goods sectors in large are kept proportional to wages in the traded goods sectors from
in the period 1962 to 1986 (Rødseth and Holden 1990, 248–52).

Table 10.1
Collective bargaining in Norway, 1974 to 1989: Some important features within the LO/NHO area

Year	Type of settlement	Level of bargaining	Centrally agreed wage increase	Locally bargained wage drift	State intervention	Government
1974	Main settlement	Industry by industry	16.9	7.9	No intervention	Labor party
1975	Intermediary	Tripartite	8.9	4.3	No intervention	Labor party
1976	Main settlement	Tripartite	9.4	5.8	No intervention	Labor party
1977	Intermediary	Tripartite	2.9	7.1	No intervention	Labor party
1978	Main settlement	Centrally coordinated	2.1	3.9	Compulsory arbitration	Labor party
1979	No regular bargaining	Wage stop	0.3	2.4	Wage and price freeze	Labor party
1980	Main settlement	Industry by industry	5.0	8.2	No intervention	Labor party
1981	Intermediary	Centrally coordinated	1.7	6.8	Compulsory arbitration	Labor party
1982	Main settlement	Industry by industry	5.4	6.0	Compulsory arbitration	Conservative minority government
1983	Intermediary	Centrally coordinated	0.9	5.7	No intervention	Nonsocialist coalition from May
1984	Main settlement	Industry by industry	2.9	6.5	Compulsory arbitration	Nonsocialist coalition
1985	Intermediary	Centrally coordinated	0.5	7.2	No intervention	Nonsocialist coalition
1986	Main settlement	Industry by industry	11.5	7.2	No intervention	Labor party from May
1987	"Exception year"	Centrally coordinated	0.2	8.5	No intervention	Labor party
1988	No regular bargaining	Irrelevant	1.6	0.6	Wage law	Labor party
1989	No regular bargaining	Irrelevant	4.1	–0.2	Wage law	Conservative minority government

Table 10.1 (continued)

Year	Type of settlement	Level of bargaining	Centrally agreed wage increase	Locally bargained wage drift	State intervention	Government
1990	Main settlement	Centrally coordinated	3.3	3.0	No intervention	Labor party
1991	Intermediary	Centrally coordinated	1.6	2.5	No intervention	Labor party
1992	Main settlement	Centrally coordinated	0.5	2.4	No intervention	Labor party
1993	Intermediary	Centrally coordinated	—	—	Contribution to early retirement scheme	Labor party
1994	Main settlement	Industry by industry	—	—	—	—

Sources: Høgsnes (1994, 102–103) and NOU (1991, 23; 1992, 27; 1993, 26).
Note: Figures for wage growth refer to percentage increase from one year to another.

borders and has pursued an unprofessional policy in many respects. It may be argued that the conflicts are generated at the central level and are really conflicts between organizations, rather than between different groups of professionals. The competition among the LO, AF, and YS has created a pattern, or a climate, quite different from that of Sweden and Denmark, where the equivalent federations have reached agreements about recruitment areas.

Changes and Tensions Emerging in the 1980s

Although the economic situation and the politics of the Labor party changed during the 1980s, the main institutions of the labor market remained the same. The high-level organizations play a big role in bargaining, and the state takes part, either directly through wage laws or through more informal channels. In the section on compensation we argue that wage bargaining is still handled as a type of social democratic regulation. Our argument is that there have been significant changes at another level, changes that have produced a new "social climate." In the 1990s this may cause further changes in institutions and social structures.

Union density was 57 percent in 1980, and it remained static throughout the decade. However, as shown in table 10.2, LO's share

Table 10.2
Share of the working population in the different unions (in %)

	1980	1989
LO (Norwegian Federation of Trade Unions)	38.2	31.9
YS (Confederation of Vocational Unions)	5.6	9.5
AF (Federation of Norwegian Professional Association)	5.2	9.9
Members in unions without affiliation to any federation	7.8	5.9
Unorganized	43.4	42.8

Sources: Fennefoss and Stokke (1991, 129) and Fennefoss (1994).

Table 10.3
Model for segmented wage formation

	Precondition	Pay determination by	Normative basis	Principle of justification	Typical employees
1	Competition about labor	Market power	Effective allocation of resources	Formal equality = freedom of contract	Unionized part of the oil sector
2	Different qualifications	Functional status	Societal importance	Relative equality = status/ performance	Upper-level public sector
3	Political legitimacy	Political governance	Just distribution	Outcome equality = needs	Service sector workers

Source: Høgsnes and Hanisch (1988, 73).

has declined to 56 percent of the unionized workers and from 38 to 32 percent of all employees. LO consists of 29 unions which had 573,000 members in 1992. Unions affiliated to AF and YS had 178,000 and 171,000 members, respectively, whereas 106,000 workers were organized in unions outside any federations. Although the total union density has been more or less constant since the 1950s, it is significantly lower than in Sweden and Denmark.

During the 1980s new patterns emerged. Most of the labor market in the retail, hotel, and building sectors, as well as in small businesses, has been deregulated. The number of people working in retail, for example, has increased, but only around 10 percent are organized in unions. In this sector several flexible work arrangements, not based on traditional full-time employment, have appeared.

At the same time the new labor federations have become powerful in the public sector. AF is organizing skilled and semiskilled professionals, and YS is recruiting some semiskilled professionals among white-collar workers. During the 1980s these organizations have grown stronger, putting pressure on the earlier institutions favoring LO. Competition between the LO-affiliated unions and the federations has had consequences for both wage policy and union-Labor party ties. The Labor party now has more voters among the employees outside the LO than in the LO, and in the long run it has had to redefine its policy from worker orientation to employee orientation.

At the firm level, fragmentation and competition within the organization has become a severe problem for bargaining and labor-management cooperation. One consequence of the competition is that it is more difficult for the LO as a confederation to coordinate the unions' policies. Unions outside the LO are members of looser federations, and they often try to outbid the LO unions along several different dimensions. The basis of their identities and strategies is the profession or occupation, whereas LO unions are founded on the division between salaried employees and workersw (*Arbeider/funksjonær*) and between the branch and sector identities. AF and YS unions and the independent unions are acting more like interest groups, and not as parts of a social movement as LO has traditionally done. At the same time LO has experienced internal tensions stemming from the growing importance of the sectoral dividing lines. LO changed the structure of the confederation in 1994 which has resulted in a formalization of four cartels: the private industry sector, the private services sector, the municipal sector, and the state sector. The unions have retained their relative autonomy, but the cartels handle wage bargaining and economic policy issues. The coordinating power of LO as a confederation has been reduced, since the reorganization has resulted in four smaller LOs struggling with each other across the sector lines.

In November 1993 an agreement was made between the LO and AF. It states that the parties have the intention to ". . . develop forms of cooperation founded on mutual respect for the independence of each organization and for its different membership basis and different principal political attitudes." The most important facts are that an agreement exists and that AF has changed its international affiliation from CESI (*Confederation Eropeenne Syndicat Independent*) to ICFTU, ETUC (European Trade Union Confederation), and the Council of Nordic Trade Unions. It is also clear that LO and AF do not intend to cooperate on other levels than the executive board level. Whether the agreement implies that LO and AF have divided the markets for potential members between them, as the confederations in the other Scandinavian countries have, is yet to be seen. The competition with YS will continue as before, however.

One possible interpretation of the agreement is that LO accepts that AF is the only credible confederation for the academics, and that LO wants to form a pressure group together with AF on issues that concern all types of employees. The fact that AF and YS became members of the government's Contact Committee in 1988 is an indicator that LO's hegemony as the Labor government's partner in policymaking is gone. As a consequence LO will probably in the future become less committed to the government's policy and more responsive toward its members.

Our conclusion is that even if the main features of the relations between the labor market parties were the same in the 1980s as earlier, there have been significant changes at the actor level. Cooperation with the Labor party has been redefined, the LO has lost its hegemony, and tensions within LO have increased. The relationship between LO and the other federations has been characterized by tension and conflict, and competition for new recruits has led the employee organizations to look for selective incentives to attract new members. A possible result of these changes is that the labor market may gradually be de-politicized, and union politics removed from the traditional labor movement.

Despite the turbulent economic situation, a change of political sentiment, and increased fragmentation and competition of labor, to date the institutional structure defining the relations between the labor market parties in Norway has remained more or less unchanged. The single most important cause of change has been the increase of personnel in the various skilled and semiskilled professions in both the private and the public sectors. This is an important source of power for YS and AF. However, it is difficult to predict how the strains caused by high unemployment and reduced economic growth might work out in the long run.

10.3   Employment Relations Practices: Traditional Practices, Change and Diffusion

Work Organization

In 1990, 15 percent of the work force was employed in the industrial sector, as compared with 20 percent in 1980. Similar developments occurred in other countries as well. For example, during these same years the proportion of the work force employed in industry declined from 22 to 18 percent in the United States, from 28 to 20 percent in the United Kingdom, from 20 to 16 percent in Canada, and from 25 to 21 percent in France (Kvinge et al. 1992, 79). Nonetheless, in comparative terms the importance and size of the manufacturing sector had become disturbingly low in Norway. To a large extent this was a consequence of the increasing importance of the oil and gas sector. During the 1980s the oil sector generated approximately the same proportion of GNP as the industrial sector but employed less than 1 percent of the work force (Kvinge et al., 76).

Norway had a total labor force participation rate of 80 percent in 1990 which is the same level as in 1985.[4] The female participation rate of 72.2 percent is also comparatively high (OECD 1990b). On the one hand, the Norwegian economy has been able to absorb a larger share of the labor supply than most other OECD countries, with the exception of Sweden and Denmark. On the other hand, by the end of the 1980s Norway was not able to create enough new jobs to avoid growing rates of unemployment (3.1 percent in 1988, 5.8 percent in 1992). The incidence of long-term unemployment (more than 12 months) as a percentage of the total number of unemployed increased from 6.3 to 20.2 percent during the same period (OECD 1992).

Although investment levels have been high, the manufacturing sector has experienced low and decreasing returns on capital throughout the 1980s (1980–86: 9 percent; 1987–90: 8 percent annual average). This development contrasts with that of other West European countries as well as to the United States and Japan. Under these conditions and in a more integrated world economy, it may be difficult to attract investments to Norway.

Some have claimed that this problem is attributable to Norway's high wage levels. As measured by relative wage costs per unit output, Norway's competitiveness decreased by 25 percent from 1970 to 1990, although moderate wage growth since 1989 has led to some improvement. However, Skonhoft's comparison of Norway and nine other OECD countries shows that the low productivity of capital rather than of labor explains more of the low operating surplus of Norwegian industry. To some extent the high cost of labor can be defended

---

4. Although the number of persons employed has increased, the number of man-hours is at the 1970 level, and it has been relatively stable (NOU 1992). The average number of hours worked in a year per person in employment was reduced from 1766 in 1970 to 1417 in 1990 (OECD 1992).

on the basis of its productivity, but investments do not earn a sufficient return (Skonhoft 1992). This may have to do with bad investment decisions and management, a tax system that has motivated unproductive investments, and an oil sector that has attracted too much attention.

Norwegian industry is to a large extent based on primary processing of raw materials, namely the production of aluminum, steel alloys, artificial fertilizers, cement, oil and gas, wood products, chemicals, pulp and paper, and various fish products. In many of these industries, employment was cut over the course of the 1980s. Unfortunately, Norway has not been able to compensate for this by expanding its industries based on semifinished products. The highly profitable offshore oil industry has attracted much investment, and partly as a result of this, the restructuring of land-based industry has lagged behind. The establishment of an offshore oil-drilling industry in Norway remains very important for the country's trade balance, but it has had little direct impact on employment. Although production of oil increased strongly (close to 15 percent a year since 1986), the employment growth in oil-related industries has been moderate.

Because of the labor movement's positive attitude toward productivity increases, trade unions usually represent no serious obstacle to more flexible production systems. To the extent that insufficient productivity of Norwegian industry can be explained by its overly rigid production system, this is the result of a lack of managerial interests and initiative.

Although output levels in manufacturing have remained about the same, the number of employees has declined by almost 25 percent since 1974. The decrease has been particularly strong in the manufacture of clothing, textiles, and footwear, where employment levels declined by 70 percent between 1971 and 1989 (from 33,400 to 10,000). Employment in metal products, machinery, and equipment declined by 25 percent between 1975 and 1989 (from 136,100 to 101,200). For the most part this has meant a reduction of traditionally organized work. This has in turn translated into a reduction of the proportion of blue-collar workers in the work force, partly as a result of the introduction of new technologies. The need for more skilled workers in manufacturing has blurred the dividing line between white- and blue-collar workers. These structural changes have led to a reduction of employment in some of the most Taylorist types of work.

During the 1980s the service sector grew. Banks and insurance companies introduced new products and services based on computer technology. This meant a growth in the number of white-collar employees in skilled and semiskilled professional occupations. During the economic slowdown at the end of the 1980s, however, the new technology's potential for rationalization was gradually exploited, and employment in the sector declined. Although service sector employment increased by 2.4 percent annually from 1983 to 1988, it declined by 1.7 percent in 1989 (OECD's quarterly labor force statistics).

The move from manual operations toward advising customers on the choice of products and services has led to experimentation with new organization structures in banks and insurance companies. Instead of having separate departments for different types of services, groups of personnel with a broad spectrum of skills were introduced (Carlson 1984). Ideally the customer should get all information and services needed from one advisor. Since only a few case studies describe this development, it is difficult to say what impact it has had.

The so-called HFB program constitutes the most important initiative in Norwegian industry in recent years. In 1982 the LO and the NHO reached an agreement to jointly support development projects in firms promoting productivity, broad participation, and codetermination. This is a continuation of the Scandinavian tradition of bi- or tripartite development programs, triggered by the sociotechnically inspired industrial democracy program in the sixties (Gustavsen and Hunnius 1981, 37–84; Kalleberg 1987, 87–92). By 1992 about 500 firms, or 7.5 percent of the 6,685 Norwegian enterprises with more than five employees, had carried out at least one HFB project. Participation varied by sector. For instance, in the mechanical industry 15 percent ($N = 604$) of the firms organized in the employers' union Teknologi-bedriftenes Landsforening (TBL) have taken part in such projects (Hovde 1992).

The aim of the HFB projects is to establish a democratic dialogue between management and employees. The intended outcome of these dialogues is to discover challenges crucial for the firms' well-being and survival and to mobilize all employees in the resolution of these problems. Three or four enterprises in the same sector or region may take part in parallel conferences, promoting the development of networks and a sustainable project development (Gustavsen 1992).

The experience from these projects so far indicates that they reinforce development processes already in action. They seem to be less important for the initiation of organizational renewal. In general, the projects have facilitated work with productivity improvement rather than democratization (Hovde 1992).

Skill Formation and Development

Skill Formation as a Combination of Formal Education and Work Experience
In the Norwegian school system children start school at the age of seven, and the first nine years are compulsory and uniform. The secondary level (*videregående skole*, similar to high school) is voluntary. Students normally start high school at the age of sixteen, and most courses last for three years. Since the Upper Secondary Education Act of 1976, virtually all forms of secondary education have been integrated into a single school system. In 1980, 32 percent of the people aged sixteen years and over had completed a secondary level education. In 1989 the proportion was 41 percent. When it comes to postsecondary school education, 18 percent of the Norwegian population above nineteen years has received higher education. In the European context this figure is surpassed only by Sweden (NOU 1992, 245). In order to reduce the high level of youth unemployment,[5] the educational system has been expanded even further.

Normally secondary education in the trades and in various industrial subjects, as well as in subjects related to the service occupations, consists of a basic course of one year followed by two or three years of apprenticeship. The basic course can also be extended by one or two more extensive courses followed by a shorter apprenticeship. On paper this resembles the German dual system of vocational training. In Norway, however, there are no alternatives building on a combination of practice and basic occupational education corresponding to the German *Meister* or *graduierter Ingenieur*.

The number of people receiving apprenticeship certificates has not been sufficient to satisfy the demand for skilled workers in the 1980s. Therefore some trades and industrial enterprises train their own workers. Such training does not result in certificates that are accepted by other employers. Experienced workers, however, may complete the practical and theoretical tests for an apprenticeship certificate without the basic courses at the secondary school (referred to as the Section 20 Arrangement). Short theoretical courses are offered to prepare workers for these tests. The apprenticeships are administered by the National Apprenticeship Council (*Fagopplæringsrådet*) and regional committees (*Fagopplæringsnevndene*), which include members from the trade unions (LO), the Employers' federations (NHO, *Kom-*

---

5. Youth unemployment rate for16- to 24-year-olds was 5.3 percent in 1988 and 12.8 percent in 1991 (OECD 1992).

munenes sentralforbund), a student-organization (YLI), and educational authorities (KUF).

Despite agreement by the trade unions (LO), the Employers' Confederation (NHO), and the educational authorities that the demand for skilled workers with an apprenticeship certificate has exceeded supply, it was impossible for them to fill the gap in the 1980s. The bottleneck seems to be the inability of students to obtain an apprenticeship contract after finishing a basic course. The goal formulated by the National Apprenticeship Council was that one-third of the persons born in any given year should go through an apprenticeship (Rådet for fagopplæring, Årmsmelding 1990). However, during the 1980s only about 10 percent succeeded in obtaining an apprenticeship.

The number of students in secondary school increased strongly at the end of the 1980s because the Department of Research and Science (KUF) instructed schools to absorb as many students as possible. This was partly a measure aimed at decreasing youth unemployment. However, because of the economic decline employers have been reluctant to train and hire. A large number of students have finished one or more basic courses without being able to obtain an apprenticeship contract.

In 1992 the LO and the NHO reached an preliminary agreement on apprenticeships that may solve these problems. Apprentices are expected to take part in productive work 50 percent of their time during a two-year apprenticeship. The educational content of the other 50 percent will become more specific. Apprentices will only be compensated for time spent doing productive work. In the mechanical engineering industry the wage costs for apprentices will be reduced by 40 percent, according to NHO calculations. This is due partly to reduced wages and partly to an increased state contribution. An apprentice's wage will increase gradually from 30 to 80 percent of a skilled worker's pay during a two-year apprenticeship (*Næringslivets Ukeavis*, August 19, 1994, p. 2). Pressure from the Department of Research and Science enabled the parties to reach this agreement. The educational authorities are also reforming occupational training in secondary schools. For instance, they intend to reduce the number of basic courses from more than a hundred to 13. In addition 58 different advanced courses will be offered. The content will be more standardized in order to increase the efficiency of this school-based system.

Skill Formation at the Workplace

The public authorities have no articulated policy on skill formation and development arranged by enterprises. The extent and shape of this training is determined at the level of the individual work-place. There are, for instance, no laws protecting expenditure on train-ing from taxation, making them vulnerable in periods of economic decline.

Estimates show that the share of the working population that took part in some sort of training arranged or financed by their employers at least once during the last year increased from about one-sixth at the beginning of the 1980s to one-fourth at the end of the decade (Nord-haug 1990, 327). Based on a large national survey conducted in 1989, Hege Torp found that 31 percent of the employees reported to have received some training during the last year (Arbeids- og bedriftsun-dersøkelsen 1989, ABU.[6] Torp 1990, 15 and 18).

Torp (1990, 15–17) reports that the higher employees' level of edu-cation is, the more training they get, and the more further training they need. Jobs that require formal education also require on-the-job training and further courses to keep employees up to date. The high percentage reporting a need for more training (on average 52 percent) may indicate that the quality or quantity of the training they get is in-sufficient, but it may also be that training is wanted for reasons other than its usefulness on the job.

To what extent is this kind of training transferable? Torp finds that 55 percent of the employees in the ABU survey expect that a large part of their training and experience at the present workplace will be use-ful. This percentage increases not only with higher formal education but also with the amount of on-the-job training and courses at the workplace (Torp 1990, 17–18).

Skill Formation by the Trade Unions and the Professional Organizations
Traditionally some professional organizations like the Norwegian Medical Association and the Engineer's Association have provided courses for their members. Since certificates from courses that are accepted by employers may lead to promotion and pay raises, the professional organizations' supply of training can be viewed as part

---

6. The Norwegian Survey of Organizations and Employees in 1989 (ABU in the Nor-wegian abbreviation) gives information about individuals and organizations. The sur-vey was generated by sophisticated sampling. Based on the registers in the Central Bureau of statistics, a representative sample of Norwegian work organizations (from both private and public sectors) was made. The sample consisted of 300 organizations with two to nine employees and 750 with ten or more employees. The representative sample of Norwegian employees (approximately 6,000 persons) was drawn from these firms.

of an indirect wage struggle. This struggle may have increased during the 1980s, as a result of an increase in the number of persons with higher education. The duration of different types of education has been an issue of increasing importance in wage bargaining. Although there is a low acceptance for wage differentials in Norway, it is commonly accepted that better education should result in better pay. The indirect wage struggle may be an attempt to escape from the norms of equality.

Compensation: Levels, Forms, and Structures

The differentials in wages between managers and workers in Norway were often discussed in the public debate during the 1980s. By the end of the 1980s surveys on attitudes toward wage differentials show that larger wage gaps were regarded as more acceptable than at the beginning of the decade (Hovde, Høgsnes, and Skollerud 1991). Analysis of the actual wage distribution, however, shows that there were no important changes. Lorenz curves from 1979 and 1989 show essentially the same cumulative distribution of wages. Some groups have changed places; that is, public sector wages have increased less than private sector wages. But overall the comparatively narrow Norwegian wage differentiation remains the same.

Although Norwegian blue-collar workers are among the best paid in Europe, first-line supervisors' salaries are at the middle, and top and middle management receive less pay than their counterparts in most European countries.[7] The wage differentials between the branches of industry in Norway are close to the European average, but small compared to Japan and the United States (ILO 1991, table 19). The wage level of Norwegian workers in manufacturing increased more rapidly than in other European OECD countries from 1980 to 1988. A wage index for hourly earnings in manufacturing (1985 = 100) shows that the Norwegian wages increased from 65 in 1980 to 135 in 1988, whereas the European OECD countries had an increase from 65 to 118 (OECD 1990a). Subsequently the wage growth has slowed down more than the average of the other countries.

The most common type of payment in Norway is a fixed monthly salary or hourly wage without any productivity, performance or

7. Wages compared without correcting for price level, taxation, or other sources of income than wages. Based on HayGroup's classification of jobs. See NOU (1992, 365), Dagens Næringsliv (1992a), and Dagens Næringsliv (1992b).

production bonuses. The following figures are based on the ABU survey from 1989. On average, about 70 percent of the working population is paid monthly, whereas about 15 percent is paid by the hour. Women receive fixed payment more often than men. Fixed monthly or hourly payment is also dominant for white-collar employees at the lower levels of the organizational hierarchy and among middle and upper management (more than 90 percent). Among workers the share is 85 percent, and for craftsmen it is 80 percent. Just 2 percent of workers and 5 percent of craftsmen are remunerated by piecework. The remaining workers receive a combination of fixed hourly or monthly payment and some kind of bonus. It is difficult to find comparable figures from earlier periods.

During the 1980s the average working hours per week decreased from 41 to 39 hours, while women increased their average working week from 29 to 30 hours. The difference can be explained by the fact that less than 10 percent of the men and 50 percent of the women had part-time work. Despite the fact that unemployment increased at the end of the 1980s, part-time workers as a share of total labor force actually decreased slightly between 1983 and 1990 (OECD 1991). Part-time work may be important in some sectors, but it was not used more extensively as a flexibility measure during the 1980s.

There is a long tradition of state intervention in collective bargaining in Norway, particularly by social democratic governments in the postwar period. Through legislation the government regulates the use of conflict resolution mechanisms and establishes mediation institutions. In addition in the 1980s the state played a rather unpredictable role in the wage bargaining.

There are two forms of wage bargaining in Norway: workplace bargaining and centralized bargaining. In an increasing number of companies, central negotiations are followed by local negotiations. The central bargaining may take place industry by industry or through centralized and coordinated negotiations. The choice is made by the labor market parties. Centralized negotiations facilitate the equalization of wages and the balancing of wages in sheltered and competing sectors, which was one of the goals in the traditional Norwegian model. Top-level interest organizations also coordinate industry by industry negotiations behind the scene. In manufacturing, where local bargaining is common, the central negotiations determine minimum wages, and increases differing between the firms result from local bargaining. At the end of the 1980s NHO's preference was to facilitate wage flexibility as much as possible in the private sector through local bargaining, while in the public sector central negotiations are promoted.

In certain years (1975–77, 1980, and 1993–94) the government participated in the central negotiations. Its goal was to help the labor market parties reach an agreement that would be tolerable in the particular national economic situation. When negotiations break down and mediation is unsuccessful, the government may intervene with compulsory arbitration to avoid damaging conflicts as was the case in 1978 and 1981. On three occasions, negotiations have been interrupted by price and wage freezes or wage laws (NOU 1988, 187–91). In the 1970s and 1980s this has only been done by social democratic governments and with the consent of the LO. How much freedom the market is allowed, varies from government to government, but ad hoc decisions have been sufficient to justify interference in the negotiations.

In the 1988 wage-bargaining round, the LO and the NHO were allowed to reach an agreement, and then a wage law was issued. All other organizations and federations had to bargain within the borders of the LO/NHO agreement. In 1989 all bargaining was suspended (table 10.1 shows the shifting negotiation types and the occurrence of state involvement in the bargaining). The LO supported the Labor party government's suspension of bargaining in 1988 and 1989 to cool down the economy after the neoliberal economic deregulation of the conservative and nonsocialist governments from 1981 to 1986. It was assumed that by reducing inflation, the employment level could be secured. Centralized wage negotiations seem to be important for wage equalization, the balancing of wages between sheltered and trading industries, and for wage moderation to reduce unemployment. Increasing competition between union federations may make it difficult to reach such results in the future.

In the 1980s the oscillation between centralized and industry negotiations, between free negotiations and wage laws, and the use of compulsory arbitration, underlines that wage bargaining was still treated as a part of the social democratic mode of regulation. Because of the high export/import intensity the economy is susceptible to external turbulence. State involvement is therefore regarded as necessary. The market is given free play only as long as it serves intended purposes.

When pay is determined by a wage policy, and not entirely by the market, the principle of justification gains importance. Three segments in the labor market with different types of wage formation can be identified: (1) wage formation based on market power, (2) wage formation based on accepted functional importance in the society (i.e., the traditional professions), (3) wage formation based on political policies (i.e., service-sector workers with low pay).

In the 1970s wage equalization was a valued political goal. For instance, in 1978 the LO and the NAF agreed to a low-wage fund, redistributing pay from high-wage sectors to sectors with wages below a certain level. As a result the groups used to being paid high wages, such as upper-level public-sector employees and highly educated personnel, lagged behind. Employees that traditionally were poorly organized were attracted by the new employee organizations YS and AF. Groups such as workers in the oil sector with potentially high wages (if market power alone were to determine wages) left the LO and started illegal strikes or organized themselves in independent unions. As a result of these changes the acceptability of wage equalization began to diminish.

Because education is an accepted criterion for wage determination in Norway and because public sector wages lost ground in relation to the private sector during the 1980s, it is possible that the latter sector could be the winners of the 1990s. By the end of the 1980s, there were low wage differentials. We still had a wage policy in Norway, but ideologically the market seemed to become more accepted as the determinant of wages. The emergence of new unions and federations has also caused new strains in the old system.

Employment Security and Staffing Arrangements

The Work Environment Act is the most important law concerning the maintenance of employment security. The main contents of section 60 of this law specify that the employer must have "just cause" for dismissing an employee. This means that the employer must argue reasonably and refer to facts that have to do with the economic situation or work organization. "Just cause" could include the need for the firm to restructure or to scale back its operations. When all other factors are equal, the seniority principle is used to select which people are to be dismissed.

Chapter 9 of the Basic Agreement between the LO and the NHO contains procedural requirements in such cases. This agreement specifies that the employer is obliged to confer with the union and to document technical and economic factors requiring dismissals. This combination of laws that are viewed as legitimate by both parties, a complex net of agreements, and sociocultural traditions contribute to a relatively high level of job security for Norwegian employees.

Although Norwegian employees have a comparatively high degree of employment security, based on the above-mentioned laws and agreements, three modifications to this general picture should be mentioned. First, there is a segment in the private service sector with low pay, low union membership, and a limited system of rights. Second, part-time employment has been used extensively in parts of the public sector, namely schools, hospitals, and public administration. Third, a notable share of the working population leaves the labor market and takes early retirement or a reduced pension.[8]

Although the laws and agreements of the social democratic order still are of importance, by the end of the 1980s, increased numbers of people perceived their jobs to be insecure. There may be several reasons for this: First, an increasing number of jobs are not covered by these laws and agreements; second, in the economic slowdown with layoffs and increasing unemployment, the fear of losing the job affected many more than those that received a dismissal notice; and third, Norwegians tend to place more value on having a secure job than people in several other countries. In 1983, when unemployment had remained at a low level for decades, 46 percent of the population feared that they or their closest family members would become unemployed (Valen and Hanisch 1984).

10.4   The Social Democratic Model of Corporate Governance

To what extent, and how, are employee interests articulated in the strategy formulation and governance procedures of the enterprise? When focusing on Norway, it is most important to examine two recent pieces of legislation: the revised Company Act of 1973 and the new Work Environment Act of 1977.

The Company Act

With the revision of the Company Act of 1973, employees gained the right to elect their own representatives as members of company

---

8. In 1950 there were 170,000 retired persons in Norway by reason of age or impairment. In 1980 the corresponding figure was 740,000, and in 1990 it was 847,000 or 20 percent of the population (Kuhnle and Solheim 1991).

boards. Employees elect one-third of the members of the board. The revised Company Act was unanimously accepted by Parliament. From the beginning the clauses in the Act concerning employee representation on boards were valid only for limited liability companies with 200 or more employees. During the two decades of the Act's existence it has been generalized to include smaller firms and has stimulated similar arrangements in other forms of ownership and types of work organizations (e.g., student representatives in the government of universities). This means that during the 1980s the number of firms having employee representation on the board has increased. The most recent changes took place in 1989. In firms with more than 50 employees, the employees have one-third of the board members. In firms with between 30 and 50 employees, the employees may, if they choose, have one full member and one observer.

How should this change be evaluated? From the perspectives of democratic theory and legal theory, this was an important reform. Before the reform, employees were not *de jure* treated as members of the company but rather as factors of production. With the revision of the Company Act, employees are now explicitly recognized as stakeholders complete with governing rights.

When the Company Act was reformed, many owners and top managers initially were afraid of negative consequences for productivity and profitability. The reform did not, however, produce these consequences. Quite the contrary, employees have generally acquired more insight into the economic issues discussed by company boards. Because of the reform many managers now claim that the employees have more confidence in the firms' financial accounts and plans. There has been a small increase in the number and importance of issues taken up in Norwegian boards concerning work environment and welfare issues (Kalleberg 1984, 389–92). This was a remarkable institutional reform, but we lack thorough studies of the long-term consequences that it has had for the distribution of power among employees, management, owners, and trade unions.

The Work Environment Act

The Work Environment Act covers most Norwegian workplaces, in the public as well as the private sector. The Act's general aim is to contribute to improvements in the work environment, which means the physical environment and the psychosocial aspects of work. Because of the decentralized development strategy underlying this Act, it is also of great interest from a governance perspective. An important aspect of the new strategy was the introduction of institutions enabling employees to participate in—and influence—this kind of organizational development. Consequently the Act may well be characterized not only as a strategy aiming at better health and safety in the workplace but also as a participatory, democratic reform (Kalleberg 1994).

When a reform encourages democratization processes in a firm, it involves changes in the distribution of power in the organization. The most striking feature of the Act is the influence given to the Work Environment Committee (WEC) and to the safety delegates. Employees elect half of the members of the committee which is located high in the company's hierarchy. The safety delegates are employees who have gone through a short training period, at least a course lasting forty hours. Each industrial plant has one committee and several safety delegates together responsible for the control and improvement of the various subdivisions of the work environment. The employer retains the primary responsibility for providing a good working environment.

The committee and the delegates have been authorized to make decisions in specified areas. For instance, they may stop dangerous work or conduct an inquiry on working environment problems. The employer cannot reverse such decisions.[9] If the parties run into conflicts and are unable to work out an agreement, a state labor inspector will make the final decision. The substantial authority given to WECs and safety stewards has also been used in practice. For instance, according to three surveys that focused on regions and industries, the right to stop production had been used at least once in half of the firms surveyed during the first five years after the Act was put into practice.

The Norwegian Work Environment Act has the very ambitious aim of shaping a "fully satisfactory work environment." According to a number of surveys and case studies it is clear that this Act has made some headway in improving Norwegian working conditions (Kalleberg 1993). The experience of being a representative of the Work Environment Committee become relatively widespread. The ABU survey shows that 13 to 14 percent of the work force have been representatives in such committees. In 70 percent of the firms that are competing

---

9. This is the case in most other areas, where the employer is in authority; in the last instance, this authority, as in other OECD countries, is based on state-protected property rights.

in international markets, it is said that the WEC has been in some way important.

In recent decades the efforts to improve working conditions in Norway have had wider scope and met with more progress than those in many comparable countries. Nonetheless, compared to the ideal case, there needs to be further progress.

The Importance of Unions and Agreements

There is no doubt that in Norwegian work organizations above a certain size, unions are very important and are regarded as integral to the administrative structure of such firms. Authority, obligations, and rights are specified in various agreements between employer and employee confederations. Numerous forms of power are institutionalized under these arrangements. Typical are the employer's information obligation and the employees' right to be heard and have discussions and negotiations.

During the 1980s new issues were put on the agendas of the Norwegian unions. One of these issues concerned board meetings with the senior officers of the firm. Although the boards meet relatively infrequently during the year and address relatively general issues, they are very important to firms. Some unions have asked to join the regular meetings among senior management that typically take place every week. However, except in a few cases, unions are not represented in such meetings.

Another issue is the participation of union representatives in project groups, at the early strategy formulation stages as well as at the implementation phases. But it has become more of an issue for the future. Unions do not generally participate in the development of projects, although union representatives have begun to participate in relevant pilot projects more often than before. According to some surveys they participate in 30 to 40 percent of such pilot projects. Even if there were few new reforms in the management of firms in the 1980s, there were no setbacks. It is therefore reasonable to say that the social democratic order prevails in this area.

10.5 Conclusion

Norwegian employment relations were less affected by economic turbulence, closer connections to the world economy, shifts between types of employment and between the branches of industry, and political change in traditional social democratic policies than one might expect. At the beginning of the 1990s, as in the 1980s, a majority of the working population belonged to an employee organization (57 percent in 1980 and in 1992), but LO's share was reduced (from 38 to 32 percent) and its political position was weakened.

Since the late 1980s, to counter rising unemployment, the state and top-level organizations have become increasingly more involved in wage bargaining, first by setting up wage laws and later by narrowly defining the framework for local bargaining through centralized bargaining rounds. This effort contrasts with the general political sentiment of the Social Democratic Labor party and the nonsocialist parties, which has turned in favor of a nonintervention policy. This means that the Norwegian bargaining system still fluctuates between centralization and decentralization as it has traditionally done (Dølvik and Stokland 1992). However, with the increased competition between the LO and the unions and confederations outside the LO, the legitimacy of such arrangements could be declining as the industrial relations gradually become de-politicized. New tensions have appeared between such actors as the Labor party and the LO, between the LO and the new central employee organizations, and between confederations and member unions. This tension threatens the prospect of cooperative effort at the local and central levels.

The labor market parties were instrumental in the establishment and reform of Norwegian employment relations institutions. Among their important accomplishments are the bipartite development programs such as HFB, regulation of wage negotiations, employment security, and labor's participation in management decisions. Policymakers also are involved in regulation and the laws and institutions that shape the economy and working conditions both formally, such as by the Work Environment Act, and informally, such as by ad hoc decisions during the mediation and arbitration in wage bargaining. In the latter case certain bargaining rounds have further led to wage laws and government policy. In general, between the beginning of the 1980s and the beginning of the 1990s, the basic Norwegian institutions concerned with working conditions remained more or less the same. The changes that took place were for the most part marginal adjustments of existing arrangements. This institutional continuity would not have been possible without the income from the North Sea oil reserves, which buffered the Norwegian economy from a severe economic slowdown. But it also reflected a tradition among workers' confederations and the government of joint commitment and cooperation on primary working conditions issues that was established in the postwar period. Clearly the strategies of these actors are the important intermediate variables between economic and technological change, on the one hand, and employment relations, on the other hand.

References

Aukrust, Odd. 1970. PRIM 1, A model of the price and income distribution mechanism of an open economy. Arikler 35. Central Bureau of Statistics

Bjørklund, Tor, and Berndt Hagtvedt, eds. 1981. *Høyrebølgen*. Oslo

Dagens Næringsliv. 1992a. Norske ledere billigst i Europa. *Dagens Næringsliv*, 23/4–92. Oslo

Dagens Næringsliv. 1992b. Norske ledere på billigsalg. *Dagens Næringsliv*, 17/12–92. Oslo, p. 17.

Dølvik, Jon Erik, and Dag Stokland. 1992. Norway: The "Norwegian model" in transition. In Anthony Ferner and Richard Hyman, eds., *Industrial Relations in the New Europe*. Oxford: Blackwell.

Fennefoss, Arvid. 1988. Lønnstaker-organisering. FAFO-rapport nr. 081. Fagforeningens senter for forskning utredning og dokumnetasjon. Oslo.

Fennefoss, Arvid, and Torgeir Aarvaag Stokke. 1991. Norske lønnstakeres organisering. *Søkelys på Arbeidsmarkedet*, no. 2.

Fennefoss, Arvid.1994. Hvor står YS etter avatalen mellom LO og AF? *Innlegg for sentralstyret i YS* 5 (January).

Furre, Berge. 1991. *Vårt hundreår: Norsk historie 1905–1990*. Oslo: Det Norske Samlaget.

Gerhardsen, Einar. 1971. *Samarbeid og strid: Erindringer 1945–55*. Oslo: Tiden Norsk Forlag.

Gustavsen, Bjørn. 1992. *Dialogue and Development: Theory of Communication, Action Research and the Restructuring of Working Life*. Assen/Maastricht: Van Gorcum.

Gustavsen, Bjørn, and Gerry Hunnius. 1981. *New Patterns of Work Reform: The Case of Norway*. Oslo: Universitetsforlaget, pp. 11–183.

Hodne, Fritz. 1983. *The Norwegian Economy 1920–1980*. New York: St. Martin´s Press.

Hovde, Svein. 1992. Samarbeid om bedriftsutvikling. ISO-rapportserie nr. 27. Department of Sociology, University of Oslo.

Hovde, Svein, Geir Høgsnes, and Kåre Skollerud. 1991. Holdninger til lønnsforskjeller i privat og offentlig sektor—endringer fra 1982 til 1989? *Søkelys på arbeidsmarkedet* (8):205–14.

Høgsnes, Geir. 1994. Collective wage bargaining and the impact of norms of fairness: An analysis of the Norwegian experience. Report 94:8. Institute for Social Research, Oslo.

Høgsnes, Geir, and Ted Hanisch. 1988. Problemer og motsetninger i norsk inntektspolitikk 1973 til 1985. Rapport 88:9. Institutt for samfunnsforskning, Oslo.

ILO. 1991. *Yearbook of Labor Statistic*, no. 51. Geneva: International Labor Office.

JoJohnsen, P, and P. Joynt. 1986. Industrial relations in Norway: Past, present and future. *Journal of General Management* 11 (4):55–75.

Kalleberg, Ragnvald. 1984. Demokratisering av foretak. In W. Lafferty and B. Hagtvet, eds., *Demokrati og demokratisering*. Oslo: Ascehhoug, pp. 367–404.

Kalleberg, Ragnvald. 1987. Some Scandinavian contributions to the field of technology and organization of work. Verhandlungen des 23. Deutschen Soziologentages in Hamburg 1986, In Burkart Lutz, ed., *Technik und sozialer Wandel*. Frankfurt: Campus, pp. 85–105.

Kalleberg, Ragnvald. 1993. Implementing Work Environment reform in Norway: The interplay between leadership labor and law. In *International Handbook of Political Participation in Organizations*, Oxford: Oxford University Press.

Kvinge, Torunn, Ove Langeland, and Dag Stokland. 1992. Kampen om kapitalen. Report 138. FAFO, Oslo.

Nordhaug, Odd. 1990. Personalopplæring i Norge. In Odd Nordhaug et al., eds., *Læring i organisasjoner. Utvikling av menneskelige ressurser*. Oslo: TANO, pp. 325–37

NOU. 1988. *Intektsdannelsen i Norge*. NOU 1988: 44, Oslo.

NOU. 1992. *En nasjonal strategi for økt sysselsetting i 1990-årene*. NOU 1988: 26, Oslo.

OECD. 1990a. *Main Economic Indicators, 1969–1988*. Paris: OECD.

OECD. 1990b. *Labor Force Statistics, 1969–1989*. Paris: OECD.

OECD. 1991. *Employment Outlook*. Paris: OECD. July.

OECD. 1992. *Employment Outlook*. Paris: OECD. July.

Rokkan, Stein. 1966. Norway: Numerical democracy and corporate pluralism. In Robert A. Dahl, ed., *Political Oppositions in Western Democracies*. New Haven: Yale University Press, pp. 1–401.

Rødseth, Asbjørn, and Steinar Holden. 1990. Wage formation in Norway. In Lars Calmfors, ed., *Wage Formation and Macroeconomic Policy in the Nordic Countries*. Oxford: Oxford University Press, pp. 237–85.

Rådet for fagopplæring i arbeidslivet. 1990. *Årsmelding 1990*. Rådet for fagopplæring i arbeidslivet, Oslo.

SSB. 1991. Statistics ordered from Statistisk sentralbyrå by the authors.

Torp, Hege. 1990. Opplæring i arbeidslivet: Hvem får mest? *Søkelys på arbeidsmarkedet* (2):13–18.

11

Developments in Industrial Relations and Human Resource Practices in Japan

Keisuke Nakamura
Michio Nitta

Despite successive external "shocks" and rising internal tensions over the last twenty years, the Japanese system of industrial relations and human resource management has not experienced fundamental change or transformation. This does not mean there have been no changes in IR/HR policies and practices. Quite the contrary. A number of serious events and significant changes have indeed taken place since the first oil shock in 1973. This chapter examines both the changes and continuities in Japanese employment relations. Tackling this vast issue in a short paper is perhaps an impossible task. As a result we give special attention to the following four points:

First, it is essential to address the issue of what constitutes the "traditional" Japanese IR/HR system before discussing whether or not it has changed. On the one hand, there exists a popular "model" that views lifetime employment, the seniority-based wage system, and (cooperative) enterprise unionism as the "three pillars" of the Japanese IR/HR system (OECD 1973). On the other hand, a number of new arguments have been advanced that contradict this stereotype.

For example, employment contracts guaranteeing employment up to the age of retirement do not exist in Japan, and a high percentage of workers actually change jobs, particularly while they are young. Even in the largest firms (over 1,000 employees), where "lifetime employment" is the most common, separation rates exceed 20 percent when workers are in their early twenties. Separation rates are even higher in smaller firms (Koike 1988). When industries face severe market downturn, companies often promote "voluntary severance," which sometimes is seen as another name for layoff with severance pay, in order to drastically reduce the number of workers.

Likewise seniority-based wage systems, in which wages rise automatically as a worker becomes more senior, are virtually nonexistent in Japan, at least for private sector employees. Each year both blue- and white-collar workers are assessed on their capabilities and performance, and the results of these assessments are normally reflected in the amount of each worker's annual pay increase and bonuses. Thus the wage system captures the amount and quality of work provided by employees (at least indirectly) and encourages competition among them.

Finally, although it is true that the majority of unions are structured as enterprise-based unions, this does not automatically mean that they are cooperative with management. Large-scale labor disputes have been a frequent occurrence during the postwar period, including in the late 1970s, when numerous wage disputes and antirationalization strikes took place.

Interesting new interpretations of the Japanese IR/HR have recently been advanced which argue that the "white-collarization of personnel policy and the formation of intellectual skill" (Koike 1983; Koike and Inoki 1987), "single status and disciplined production management" (White and Trevor 1983), "lean production system and team-based work organization" (Womack et al. 1990), and "arbitrative management that mediates the interests of capital and labor" (Aoki 1988) are in fact the essential features of the Japanese employment system.

Nonetheless, the three-pillar model remains quite popular, particularly among practitioners, and these more recent alternative interpretations have not succeeded in replacing the established views. As a result, to better understand recent developments in Japan, in this essay we follow a methodological suggestion advanced by Ujihara (1989a) that when discussing IR systems and practices, we need to disaggregate them along four different dimensions and analyze how these dimensions are interrelated and understood as a whole. The first dimension focuses on the mutual expectations or normative assumptions held by management and workers. The second one illuminates how objective rules are formed and implemented. The third dimension formulates IR/HR theories or ideologies that consistently and systematically interpret the body of rules and practices. And the fourth one seeks out the economic (and social) basis of the normative assumptions, objective rules and practices, and IR/HR ideologies and evaluates their impact on economy and society.

We would argue that lifetime employment and seniority-based wages are normative assumptions mutually shared by management and workers rather than a set of objective rules and practices. Lifetime employment and seniority-based wages as assumptions survived the turbulent 1970s and 1980s because they were flexible or vague enough to be adjusted to the changing environment. Based on these normative assumptions, for example, firms were able to dispatch and transfer employees to related or even nonrelated firms in order to avoid outright discharge.

The second methodological argument which this chapter poses is that various tiers of the organizational/sociopolitical system and not simply firm-level practices like lifetime employment and seniority-based wages are both important and necessary to fully understand how, why, and which IR/HR policies and practices have changed. We argue that at the very micro level, foremen-led work groups have played a critical role in making work organization more flexible and in enhancing the skill levels of their members while also functioning as a voice mechanism. At the other end of spectrum, neocorporatist schemes championed by the newly unified national union federation (JTUC) are becoming influential in formulating welfare-industrial-economic policies as well as employment policy. Arrangements such as joint consultation on strategic decisions at the firm level and industry and multi-industry coordination of wage determination are also very important.

Third, this chapter primarily discusses practices and policies in private, large- to medium-sized firms. This is a serious limitation, especially given that rationalization measures in the public sector such as the privatization of public corporations was one of the most important events in industrial relations in 1970s and 1980s and also that the "core-periphery" model of Japanese IR/HR systems and practices is currently a hotly debated issue (Osterman 1988).

Notwithstanding these shortcomings, we believe that careful analysis of the internal tensions that exist in large- and medium-sized private firms will illuminate the broader nature of the changes that are taking place in "typical" Japanese IR/HR systems and practices. And these are not resolved only by utilizing the "periphery" as a buffer. It is true that there are mutually reinforcing moments in the systems. For instance, seniority-based pay supports lifetime employment by increasing incentives for employees to stay in a company, and lifetime employment makes seniority-based pay acceptable for employees because everybody can climb up the wage ladder in the end. However, it should also be noted that management has strong incentives to replace highly paid senior workers with younger, less expensive ones. This is the reason that senior workers become the target of "patting on the shoulder" when a company resorts to "voluntary severance" measures. In this sense these two pillars are contradictory. We would argue that the most important way to understand the dynamics of change or of continuity in Japanese IR/HR is to examine how these tensions and contradictions are heightened in certain environments and how IR/HR actors cope with them.

Fourth, as a substantive argument we stress in this chapter that labor unions in Japan have played a very important and active role in the change/no-change process. Unions have been proactive partners in the re-configuration of the Japanese labor movement rather than passive and faceless followers. A popular, rather dominant view of the Japanese labor movement after the mid-1970s has argued that it was seriously weakened as a result of changes in the economic environment and the decisive shift of the leadership from left to right. Widely cited evidence for this argument included declining organization rates and largely reduced wage hikes during the *shunto* ("spring offensive"). On the contrary, we believe that the Japanese labor movement was invigorated by the need to cope with the impact of economic change. In our assessment, double-digit wage hikes in the 1960s and early 1970s were mostly a product of extremely favorable economic conditions such as a tight labor market and superb productivity gains. After the mid-1970s the need for the real organizational strength of the labor movement was acutely felt. The union movement pushed for neocorporatist policies immediately after the first oil crisis.

The remainder of this chapter is divided into sections. In the first section we briefly examine how IR/HR practices evolved and were established as a system after World War II. Then in the sections 11.2 through 11.5, we analyze how and why these practices have or have not changed since the mid-1970s. Our discussion focuses on work organization and skill formation, employment and payment systems, corporate governance, and participation in both strategic decision making and policymaking. To support our argument, we rely on a body of case studies and surveys by Japanese IR/HR scholars that have not been fully exploited in English-language publications.

11.1 Evolution of IR/HR Systems and Practices in Japan

Employment practices that were conceptualized as lifetime employment and seniority-based wages in the late 1950s to early 1960s had been gradually developed since the early industrialization period in pre–World War II Japan. A practice called "regular wage raise" (*teiki shokyu*) began to develop in the early twentieth century. In order to keep scarce skilled workers in-house, management initiated a practice to give periodic wage increases to those who stayed longer and showed good work habits. Then it was interpreted as a basis for the "company as a family" ideology which became the banner used by employers to fend off organized labor and government intervention (Hyodo 1971; Gordon 1985). However, in the 1950s this practice became translated into a set of clearly formulated rules that gave every employee a regular raise once a year, although the amount of the raise for an individual worker varied according to his/her merit rating (Showa Dojinkai 1960). Similarly "severance/retirement allowance," another employment practice central to the lifetime employment concept, was first developed as a measure to encourage longer tenure. The scheme received a boost from the anti–mass-dismissal strikes of the 1920s and 1930s, which in most cases were settled by paying a severance allowance to dismissed workers. Government regulation mandating severance allowances in 1936 helped to diffuse this practice. It is safe to say the practice was also transformed into a system in the 1950s through labor management negotiation (Yamazaki 1989).

Critical to Japan's post–World War II development was the rapid rise of its labor movement. As can be seen in table 11.1, by 1949 union

Table 11.1
Number of unions, their membership and union density

Year	Labor unions	Union membership	Estimate union density (%)
1940	49	9,455	0.1
1945	509	380,677	3.2
1949	34,688	6,655,483	55.8
1950	29,144	5,773,908	46.2
1955	32,012	6,285,878	35.6
1960	41,561	7,661,568	32.2
1965	52,879	10,146,872	34.8
1970	60,954	11,604,770	35.4
1975	69,333	12,590,400	34.4
1980	72,693	12,369,262	30.8
1985	74,499	12,417,527	28.9
1990	72,202	12,264,509	25.2
1991	71,685	12,369,592	24.5

Source: Kuwahara (1993).

membership had grown to 6.6 million and postwar density peaked at 56 percent. From the mid-1950s to mid-1970s union density stabilized, although membership continued to increase until 1975. Subsequently membership has been static and density levels have declined steadily.

Labor activity was initially encouraged by the abolition of oppressive laws including the notorious Peace Keeping Law, as well as by the formation of new labor laws that were introduced under the auspices of the Occupation Army. Union density increased as the unions codified unwritten practices arbitrarily managed by employers into universally applied collective agreements that were concluded between individual enterprises and enterprise-based unions.

Many of the newly emergent enterprise-based unions were militant, often led by leftist leaders. The Japanese economy was in a deep crisis and was struggling to recover from the massive destruction caused by the war. Workers had little union experience but were eager to "democratize the enterprises" which meant abolishing autocratic (called "feudalistic") practices within companies. As part of this democratization process, a symbolic demand to pay blue-collar workers monthly salaries and thus equalize the status of blue- and white-collar employees within firms was advanced. Although the communist-led *Sanbetsu* (CIO), which played a dominant role in early postwar years, lost ground and became powerless as a result of government and military repression and internal strife in 1949 and 1950, the reorganized labor movement led by left-wing social democrats also expressed a combative attitude toward management and the government.

The single most important issue in these years was employment security. Threatened by potential mass dismissals which were likely to follow the demobilization of manufacturing and other sectors, labor unions adamantly opposed any attempt to fire workers. Mass strikes at Hitachi and Toshiba in 1949 and 1950 and bloody and emotional battles against *Kubikiri* ("head-cutting" in direct translation) took place during this period—a period of transition when Japan's inflationary postwar economy supported by price control, government subsidies, and a nonrestrictive monetary policy was replaced by the tighter monetary and free market policies of Joseph Dodge. These policies were strictly implemented by both the Occupation Army and the Japanese government in 1949 (Kosai 1981). Massive discharges and the resultant violent conflicts left a tragic legacy not only for workers but also for management (Dore 1973).

During the 1950s when the Japanese economy was pursuing manufacturing-led growth, modernization of equipment and managerial practices (called "rationalization") was key. A leading advocate of the modernization effort, the Japan Productivity Center (JPC), was established in 1955 by organized business, the government, and some right-wing labor unions. The JPC called for cooperation between labor and management in order to achieve higher productivity and the equitable distribution of the benefits reaped by productivity gains. At first, the JPC was not very successful because its policy implied a "sacrifice now, share later" policy under acute economic conditions and great employment insecurity.

At the same time, the labor movement popularized the term *kanzen koyo*, which means "full employment" or rather "perfect employment," to express its desire for employment security within a firm. Management shared the antidismissals sentiment but preferred concepts such as *kazokushugi* or "company as a family" which entails the unilateral benevolence of management. A reason that the new concept of *shushin koyo*, or "lifetime employment," drawn from Abbeglen's book, was so widely accepted by management as well as by labor was in part because the concept successfully captured the sense of an implied exchange or social contract between employees, who would not resign from company management unless it seriously mistreated them, and a firm, which would not fire workers unless they committed a serious malpractice or the firm faced a real threat to its survival.

The bloody strike at the Miike Coal Mine in 1959 and 1960 reinforced the belief that conflicts caused by outright dismissals were too costly. Moreover, with the high growth rates characteristic of the Japanese economy after 1955, employers became more confident about the future of their business, and the JPC idea of cooperation for productivity increases and fair sharing gradually gained credibility among workers and labor leaders, who had experienced rapid economic growth driven by extremely high levels of capital investment.

Among the factors that enabled this rapid economic growth were the extensive importation of new technology, high rates of capital investment, ample supplies of well-educated young workers, easier access to growing international markets and an expanded domestic market based on postwar reforms, such as land reform. Another intangible but important factor was changes in management/ work practices. Quality control and industrial engineering were introduced by U.S. experts like Deming and Juran, and many managers, engineers, and even union leaders visited the United States to learn how America achieved its superior productivity and prosperity.

Foremen/group leader reform was an important element of the rationalization of management/work practices. Management was acutely aware that existing foremen/group leaders were not capable of promoting the revolutionary workplace changes required. They had not been selected strictly on their abilities to supervise and lead. Their authority and responsibility were not clearly defined. Technological change and the union movement had hollowed out their traditional leadership role, which was based on knowledge of their job and their senior status within a work group. The United States provided a widely cited model for the reform of supervision. TWI (training within industry), a thirty-hour training course for supervisors, first developed by the U.S. National Defense Advisory Commission during World War II, was introduced by the Occupation Army and the Ministry of Labor in 1950 and was enthusiastically embraced by a wide range of companies (Okamoto 1966). Alongside various organizational reforms at the workplace a new type of foreman/group leader, who had been through a rigorous selection and training process, emerged in the early 1960s. Although these new group leaders were, in theory, supposed to be able to climb the company hierarchy and become plant managers, they generally stayed within the union as regular members. This was a radical departure from the U.S. practices. It was these new foremen who apparently played a key role in the transformation of management/work practices in 1960s when QC circles and the ZD movement were introduced.

Thus it seems reasonable to suggest that the basic structure of employment practices described as lifetime employment and seniority-based wages were established in the late 1950s to early 1960s when prototypical forms of work organization and skill formation schemes were also being developed.

At the time some were skeptical about the viability of lifetime employment and seniority-based wages as the basic tenets of employment practice. First, it was argued that employers would be hard-pressed to keep their commitment to lifetime employment during a recession. Second, some believed that if management accommodated workers' requests for wage increases strictly based on seniority or age, performance would suffer. Reliance on arbitrary merit ratings by management might also cause serious discontent among workers. Finally, lifetime employment and seniority-based wages (and promotion) were essentially perceived to be contradictory practices since management would not be able or willing to resist the temptation to replace highly paid senior workers with lower paid younger ones (Fujita 1960). However, during the golden years of 1960s, many companies experienced spectacular growth and thus never had to confront either the first or the third kind of challenge. As for the second argument, management successfully developed the ability-based evaluation method (*noryoku shugi kanri*) in the 1960s. Thus those dismal predictions did not materialize during the era of rapid and sustained economic growth.

Everything changed, however, after the first oil crisis of 1973. To cope with the jump in the oil prices, companies were forced to raise product prices, lower production costs, and scale down the size of their operations. In addition to reducing their financial expenses and conserving resources and energy, companies sought to reduce labor costs. In the process, companies pushed ahead with employment adjustments. Dependence on imports for the majority of raw materials and spiraling prices meant that a significant amount of national income was being transferred overseas, so it became necessary to increase exports.

These two elements pushed Japanese companies into producing high-quality but low-priced goods which were in line with rapidly changing market needs. Flexible production and procurement systems based on microelectronics technology and the just-in-time delivery techniques—originally developed by Toyota—were widely introduced in many sectors of the Japanese economy. Many companies also tried to downsize by separating supplementary or support divisions into subsidiary firms. All of these changes created many challenges to established patterns of employment relations.

Through restructuring and adjustment, the Japanese economy was able to overcome the oil shocks but became increasingly dependent on export markets. This generated its own problems, especially visible after 1985, when trade frictions came to the fore in international relations and the value of yen rose sharply. Japanese export industries responded by boldly increasing overseas direct investment. While shifting their production strategies toward the international division of labor, they retained a significant part of their research, development and marketing functions, and the production of value added goods in Japan. Trade friction, internationalization, and the shift in production toward value-added goods in turn created many new issues for labor-management relations. Let us now turn to the changes in key employment practices that were observed after the mid-1970s.

Work Organization and Skill Formation

Several studies on work organization in the mid-1970s indicated that job rotation or job movement within a workplace was being carried out on a regular basis. Koike (1977) carried out the most thorough research through a series of highly detailed case studies in the iron and steel, chemical, and mechanical engineering (including automobile) industries. These studies revealed that almost all workplaces had adopted job rotation or intraworkplace job movement practices. Research by Yoneyama (1978), Inagami (1981), and Kawakita (1989) corroborated this trend in the iron and steel industry, while Takezawa et al. (1979) and MITI (1981) found similar practices in the automobile industry.

The important theoretical contribution of these studies was not that they identified incidents of job rotation at workplaces but rather that they revealed the following points (Koike 1977): First, job rotation/ movement decisions seemed to be left up to worker groups at the workplace. They did not result either from negotiations between the unions and management nor from policies emanating from personnel departments, but rather from the initiative of supervisors and group leaders. This did not mean, however, that these supervisors implemented job rotation in an arbitrary way. Rather, they gave careful consideration to the expectations of their group members. In this sense job rotation/ movement was carried out as a part of shop floor custom and practice. Second, wide-ranging rotation/movement enhanced the adaptability of workers. A worker could respond flexibly to small changes in production quantity or slight changes in worker composition at the workplace, which may have been caused by worker absence, a new recruit, or resignation/retirement. Third, workers could gain a better understanding of their machinery and equipment when they experience a wide range of jobs. The latter two factors explain how skill formation based on on-the-job training (OJT) relates to flexible job rotation.

In his study of the iron and steel industry, Inagami (1981) found that technological innovation and job rotation had prompted workers to lend a hand and advise their fellow workers, thus heightening the need for teamwork. By the early 1970s some machinery and equipment maintenance tasks had been incorporated into the duties of those who operated them (Kawakita 1989).

The issue of work organization and skill formation came to the fore following the microelectronic revolution. In the early 1980s there was concern that the rapid introduction of microelectronic technologies could cause polarization of the work force: A small number of workers would be engaged in highly intellectual jobs, while the majority would be confined to simple and less skilled jobs. It turned out, however, that quite a different path was taken by some major private corporations.

MITI (1984) researched the introduction of microelectronic technologies through a questionnaire survey and various case studies of the electrical machinery, automobile, aircraft, and machine tool industries. It reached the following conclusions:

1. Shop floor workers participated in the trial stage of the new technology and helped to stabilize operations by conveying their skills and knowledge to the production engineers who played a pivotal role in the process.

2. At the same time these workers obtained technical knowledge through OJT under the supervision of production engineers. Once the technology was fully operational, workers were ready to use the acquired knowledge to improve operations.

3. Through these steps, programming tasks were gradually entrusted to foremen/group leaders and then to workers. Once operations were stabilized, some new tasks were delegated to workers to develop and revise operational procedures.

4. As the waiting time between operations for each machine increased, parallel operation became a standard and two or more machines were assigned to each worker.

5. The maintenance tasks needed to keep the expensive microelectronics equipment running smoothly were added to the list of duties of shop floor workers.

Similar conclusions were reached by NIVER (1983) and Ito (1988). Contrary to theories that predict the increased polarization of workers along skill lines as the result of new technologies, it seems that workers in Japan were required to acquire more knowledge and to participate increasingly in decision-making processes. These findings about the evolution of work organization and skill formation resulting from new technologies lead us to the theoretically interesting question of whether or not and, if so, how work organization in Japanese industries departs from Taylor's "separation of planning and execution" principle.

The studies on the development of QC circles in Japan approach the point from a different angle. Juran (1967), who attended a national convention of QC circles in 1966, noted with surprise that they reflected a radically different perspective from the Taylorist principle, which is based on the notion that problems with production quality are caused by workers' failure to maintain standards set by management.

The now famous QC circles are problem-solving groups formed by workers to improve work methods, equipment, and quality control at the workplace. A small group activity, QC circles arose from a proposal by JUSE (Union of Japanese Scientists and Engineers) at the beginning of the 1960s (see Ishikawa 1984; Kogure 1988) and spread rapidly. Several descriptive studies on QC circles and other small group activities documented how effectively these activities involved workers and could be integrated into production and quality management (characterized as TQM). Takezawa et al. (1978, 1979) described the state of QC circles in the 1970s and 1980s in the electric machinery industry (1978) and in the automobile industry (1979) based on case studies, while NIEVR (1986) brought together case studies in the iron and steel industry, automobile industry, electric machinery industry, precision machine and tool industry, and chemical industry. Interestingly all of these studies suggest that these QC activities have spread widely, especially after the oil crises.

Based on observations in the steel industry, Nitta (1978) offered an analytical explanation for this phenomenal success. QC circles spread and took root because of the significant QWL benefits that they generated, notwithstanding the fact that QC circles were primarily introduced and promoted by production and quality managers to improve quality and reduce costs. These benefits include the following:

1. Better communication among workers through small group activities on the shop floor.

2. Unintended job enlargement and job enrichment since some production control tasks have been entrusted to shop floor workers in the diffusion of QC circles.

3. An opportunity for OJT in production and quality control techniques as well as in specific production know-how through skills sharing.

4. An opportunity for workers to make their work easier and less burdensome.

Nitta (1978) argued that QC circles should not be looked upon just as a unilateral control mechanism employed by management. Rather, they should be understood as a kind of coordination and negotiation process involving management and shop floor workers, with supervisors/group leaders as facilitators. According to this view QC circles could not function effectively unless worker groups could influence how the activities are organized and operated, ensuring that excess management control is kept in check and that the four QWL benefits described above remain meaningful.

Examining the formation of QC circles in a leading steel plant in the early 1960s, Nakamura (1992) presented supportive historical evidence for this argument. A group of workers in Kawasaki Works of NKK formed a QC circle following a management request in 1963. The group, however, was largely inactive until the introduction of self-inspection at the plant. With the transfer of the inspection function and personnel from the inspection and shipping sections to the production units, groups of workers started to explore how they could resolve quality problems and improve work methods by themselves. At that stage these work group efforts came to be referred to as QC circles.

Today in many Japanese workplaces workers are given greater responsibility in production control, so it has become normal for them to carry out work that requires intellectual judgment. Koike and Inoki (1987) were the first to point this out in detail. Based on detailed case studies in the cement, food and chemical, beer brewing, battery manufacturing, and machinery industry, they revealed that in addition to job rotation, workers in all areas were carrying out "unusual operations," dealing with changes and abnormalities. Changes included the introduction of new products, new product mixes, shifts in production methods and production runs, and changes in the composition of the work force. Being able to deal with these changes successfully is now an essential skill. Abnormalities included product defects, and to deal with this, workers acquired the additional skills helpful in identifying defects, diagnosing causes, and carrying out the necessary corrective actions.

In the automobile industry, production workers take part in process design with production technicians off line, and undertake quality control tasks while production is running smoothly (JIL 1992). The need for these intellectual skills grew as companies sought to overcome stagnation in mass consumer markets. Since the mid-1970s firms have begun to implement a production system that facilitates their prompt response to the changing needs of consumers (Ujihara 1989b).

In reviewing past research on work organization and skill formation in Japan, the following points have been discussed and are supported by some case study evidence: First, in major Japanese corporations the principles of work organization are substantially different from strict application of Taylor's "separation of planning and execution" principle. Workers on the shop floor are widely entrusted with responsibility for certain aspects of planning. Contrary to the technological deskilling hypotheses this sharing of responsibility seems to have been gaining momentum over the past twenty years. As a result we can now call those workers' skills "intellectual skills." Second, these skills have been acquired through on-the-job training, job rotation, and increased interactions with production engineers and technicians.

Third, given that the content of jobs, career patterns, and the allocation of planning tasks between shop floor workers and other groups of employees can vary significantly from company to company, the intellectual skills are acquired primarily through on-the-job training and actual work experience. Consequently the level of firm-specific skills may be higher in large Japanese corporations than in other internal labor market settings (Doeringer and Piore 1971; Koike and Inoki 1987).

Fourth, quasi-autonomous work groups led by foremen/group leaders play subtle but essential roles in the organization of work and skill formation. Job rotation/movement, QC circles, and the skills to deal with changes and abnormalities are not just the result of design and implementation efforts by management. Rather, these practices evolve as worker groups respond, learn, and innovate. Kondo (1986) suggests that team-based work organization implemented under the sociotechnical systems approach in the United States is to some extent similar to work organization in Japan. But consultants and engineers play a more important role in initiating and formulating work organization reform in America, while work organization changes in Japan have been a more or less encompassing and responsive process. To understand the process, one needs to explain how and under what conditions foremen/group leaders have played and can play a dual role as first-line supervisors and opinion leaders/voice agents. Overall, individual job-centered worker participation, or employee involvement in workplace management, has significantly advanced over the past twenty years.

Employment and Compensation Systems

The adjustment of employment levels to reduced economic growth was the primary issue in Japanese IR following the first oil crisis in late 1973. For the first time since the war, GNP declined in 1974. Both manufacturing and mining production indices fell in 1974 and 1975. Although the total number of people employed (excluding self-employment) continued to grow following 1974, employment declined for six consecutive years in the manufacturing sector. A sharply lower quit rate, double-digit wage hikes in early 1970s, and a strict anti-inflationary fiscal policy, all combined to increase the pressure on companies to reduce employment levels.

Faced with these overwhelming pressures, the manufacturing sector reduced its work force, although less quickly than was the case in the United States (Shimada 1976; Shinozuka 1989). The slower pace reflects the preference of Japanese companies to reduce their work force through attrition rather than outright discharge. However, attrition was not enough to cope with the extraordinary pressure. Based on a large-scale survey conducted by Ministry of Labor, Koike (1988) revealed that the most common methods of employment adjustment in large companies (with 1,000 employees or more) were cutting overtime and transfers. These two measures were not as common among smaller firms (both 30–99, 100–299 employees), 30 percent of which laid off workers at some time between 1973 and 1979. During the same period only 20 percent of the larger firms surveyed—precisely those firms that are expected to be the strongest adherents to lifetime employment practices—actually encouraged dismissals (i.e., voluntary severance or outright discharge). This suggests that large firms that have adopted the internal promotion system endeavor to minimize the number of redundancies.

Redundancy tends to be concentrated among workers aged over forty-five years. Larger firms relied almost entirely on voluntary severance, while smaller firms resorted to the more drastic measure of outright discharge. In a typical voluntary severance case, severance and retirement allowances were increased significantly to encourage workers to volunteer. However, in a number of cases, many high-paid older employees were pressed to take the offer through "patting on the shoulder" by management or subtle psychological pressure from colleagues (Ujihara 1989c), thus blurring the distinction between these two methods.

Despite the significant impact of the second oil shock in 1978 on the trade balance, production was not reduced on a large scale, and there was limited adjustment to employment levels. Instead, the shock seems to have been absorbed by wage restraint and a decline of real wages. This provoked interest in wage flexibility and macro economic performance in Japan (Gordon 1982; Yoshikawa 1992).

On the other hand, the third external shock caused by the sudden rise in the value of the yen (called *yen-daka*) caused a contraction of production in 1986 and a significant decline in employment in manu-facturing in 1986 and 1987. Hardest hit were marginally competitive export industries like shipbuilding which resorted to large-scale vol-untary severance and other measures (NIEVR/Koyo Chosei Mondai Kenkyu Iinkai, 1988).

The large-scale dismissals or employment adjustments seemed to support the skeptical views expressed earlier about the three-pillar model. Some speculated that the right-wing leadership of many unions and cooperative labor-management relationships at most firms would collapse. However, the development of more confronta-tional industrial relations practices never materialized. Various fac-tors can be cited to explain the lack of militance. First, adjustments were perceived as the direct consequences of unusual external shocks which neither companies nor government in Japan could control. As a result events were perceived to be exceptional and unavoidable. Sec-ond, within two years the Japanese economy had returned to fairly steady growth rate of 3 to 5 percent, which seemed to support the view that recent events were somehow exceptional or anomalous.

The efforts of many companies, unions, and the government to maintain employment were also important. Large-scale intrafirm transfers, temporary and permanent transfers to affiliated firms and even to nonaffiliated firms (e.g., from steel to automobile) were essen-tial elements of this strategy. Based on this experience, companies later established structures which enabled them to transfer workers more frequently, mainly within establishments, in an effort to respond flexibly to short- and long-term changes in production volumes (MITI 1981; Kawakita 1989). Moreover, partly motivated by the desire to widen the employment base for their employees, firms began expanding their diversification efforts (Nitta 1991). As a result lifetime employment as an ideology survived, and may even have been strengthened.

A notable development as a result of this process was increasing union involvement in employment and staffing decisions. From a theoretical perspective, if worker skills in the major private corporations in Japan are formed through OJT, and if these skills are highly firm specific, it would be quite natural for workers to pursue an active role in their own employment status (Koike 1983). Dismissals, promotions, and transfers are areas where workers want to have voices. It is obvious that these are areas where worker organizations that go beyond worker groups at the shop floor level must become actively involved. In Japan these issues are dealt with through consultations and negotiations between enterprise-based unions and management. In over 70 percent of large firms and 60 percent of smaller firms (100–299 employees) management policy on plant and equipment investment, new product development, and the firm's current financial position are the subjects of union-management consultations, although not necessarily negotiations (Koike 1988).

Whether or not workers and their representatives actually put forward their views is a different matter. Management does not always look at an issue in the same light as workers. For example, during the employment adjustments that followed the first oil crisis in 1973 it was absolutely essential for workers to participate in these business decisions. Although workers generally accepted the notion of wide-ranging transfers as a means to secure their jobs within a firm or group of firms, certain types of transfer could create an unbearable burden for specific groups of workers who may eventually be forced to choose voluntary severance.

Drawing primarily on research conducted before the mid-1970s, Koike (1977) found that (1) unions are generally involved in manning level changes which closely relate to transfers and other staffing measures, (2) some unions have a say regarding the number of workers transferred and the workplaces where they are transferred from, while others do not, and (3) no unions have a say in the selection of transferees—this is the responsibility of supervisors and managers. Inagami

(1981) and Yamamoto (1983) argued that in the iron and steel industry, unions and management communicate closely regarding production plans, temporary transfers, and overtime, which affect manning levels and staffing arrangements at both the establishment and workplace levels.

Based on case studies in the steel industry, Nitta (1988) concluded that in union-management discussions and negotiations on manning level changes and large-scale transfers (1) unions, in principle, do not oppose manning changes caused by restructuring, technological changes or large-scale transfers from, say, blast furnace shops to maintenance departments, declaring that workers and management must cooperate in rationalizing operations, (2) unions give voice to workers' concern for the effects of those rationalization measures (e.g., in a mass-transfer case the union proposed a full-scale retraining program, the criteria and method of selection, and measures to compensate for income reductions likely to follow the transfer), and (3) prior consultation is a key to smooth negotiations, and mutual trust is essential for the consultation process to remain peaceful and effective.

According to a most detailed and interesting study based on a comparison of two major companies in the automobile industry (Totsuka and Hyodo 1991), the agenda for consultation discussions between unions and management regarding monthly production plans, staffing plans, and temporary and permanent transfers varies by company. In one company the union, representing the views of its members, played an active role in the decision-making process, including personnel selection for transfers. In another, the union was merely given a briefing of the various plans. Studies of other auto companies by Inagami (1983) and Koshiro and Nagano (1985) document patterns of union involvement in staffing/employment issues similar to those found in the second case.

In short, the levels of voice actually exercised by unions with regard to employment/staffing decisions vary from company to company. A survey by Sato and Umezawa (1983) on union voice found that almost 30 percent of the unions that responded only became involved in decision-making processes regarding manning and transfers after decisions had been made by management, or were not involved at all. It should also be noted that not all unions and management succeeded in solving these issues without conflict. Even among major private corporations there were cases of industrial dispute over voluntary severance and other employment adjustment measures (Kawakita 1989; Kamiya 1983; Nitta 1992). This indicates that the Japanese industrial relations system is not automatically endowed with peaceful and effective functioning in dealing with employment/staffing but that positive and creative efforts on the part of unions and management are required.

Overall, the following points need to be stressed on changes in employment/staffing practices in the past two decades. First, frequent and large-scale intra- and interfirm transfers and other measures of employment adjustment in the latter half of 1970s and 1980s were some of the most important factors that kept alive and legitimated the concept of lifetime employment both as a shared expectation and as an ideology, despite the massive waves of voluntary severance and discharges. Second, the large-scale employment adjustments after the first oil crisis and throughout the 1980s helped to increase and deepen union involvement in employment/staffing decisions. Third, both the levels of union voice in employment/staffing decisions and the way employment adjustment issues were resolved by unions and management varied significantly from company to company. Choices and creative efforts by IR actors were essential to determine the process and outcome of negotiations or discussions.

An important condition for flexible intrafirm transfers and job rotation is a flexible wage system. Flexible staffing and wide-ranging job assignments, including unusual operational and planning work, would be extremely difficult under a system in which wages are narrowly linked to tasks or functions. Although the basic characteristics of Japan's wage system have not changed to a great extent over the past twenty years, the changes described below have taken place.

The postwar history of wage system policies in Japan is full of experimentation and of trial and error in figuring out the balance between employee expectations for seniority-based wage increases, incentives to maintain and enhance individual performance, and employer needs for flexibility with respect to the wage/task relationship. According to Ishida (1990), the most influential reform idea in Japanese wage systems took place in the latter half of the 1950s when the American-style job-evaluation-based wage practices were introduced by employer groups. There was active debate over the desirability and the feasibility of the introduction of these practices in Japan and several leading firms tried to adopt the system. However, these experiments were generally not successful due to the inherent inertia of the system, employee expectations for "traditional" systems, and the ever-increasing need for flexibility, partly necessitated by the establishment of lifetime employment (if workers can not be easily dismissed, companies must fully utilize them through flexible assignments).

One should not interpret these experiences as implying that Japanese companies were not concerned with linking wages and work performance. In the mid-1960s a system emerged in which wages were linked to work-related capability of individual employees instead of to specific jobs. Since work-related capability tends to increase with job experience, the new system was able to accommodate the pressure for seniority-based wage promotion. It also did not disturb flexible work assignment and transfer/rotation and gave employees strong incentives to upgrade their capabilities/skills through OJT and other training.

Following the shift in managerial beliefs about wage systems and personnel management as a whole (*noryoku shugi kanri*, "capability-based management") which took place around 1970, and pressured by market shifts after the oil crisis, companies started introducing full-scale capability-based wage systems from the mid-1970s (Ishida, 1990). Changes in work organization and employment/staffing arrangements that were discussed above lay behind this shift. As skills became more intellectual in character, differences in individual capabilities became more pronounced.

An important point here is that the capability-based wage system was not introduced unilaterally by management. Unions naturally have tried to limit the differences in their members' wages, stressing equity as opposed to performance and contribution to an organization, and they have succeeded in setting the minimum wage for each age/seniority group. Yet this does not mean that unions were opposed in principle to the wage system. Ishida suggests that both unions and the majority of their members believe that the capability-based wage systems were designed and are operated fairly despite the fact that management retains a certain range of discretion in evaluating capability.

The capability-based pay/skills formula works better for firms when they are growing in the business areas in which worker skills/capability can be utilized effectively. If the growth rate declines or becomes negative and/or if firms diversify into business areas in which accumulated skills/capability can contribute little to the new business, the past human resource investment can become redundant and/or obsolete in the same way an investment in equipment eventually becomes obsolete. Firms that operate in mature or maturing businesses have already confronted this issue. The typical response of large mainstream firms has been to diversify into technically related business areas to utilize human resources developed in the past as fully as possible (Nitta 1991).

If flexible work organization, the formation of intellectual skills, employee involvement and union-management cooperation in productivity enhancement are keys to better business performance, workers and unions are increasingly able to demand fair distribution. As noted earlier, the cooperation strategy to increase productivity advocated by the Japan Productivity Center had to be supplemented by fair distribution practices. The biannual bonus fits this notion of fair distribution. However, the most important form of fair distribution is the annual wage hike determined by the spring wage offensive (*shunto*). Bonuses are in large part determined on the basis of monthly wages/salaries and negotiations center on how many months salary are to be paid as a bonus.

According to Kenkyukai (1989), the way in which wages are determined changed considerably after the 1974 *shunto*. Before then the formula used by the unions in calculating their wage demand was the increase in the previous year plus something. This roughly resulted in their achieving the equivalent of the rise in labor productivity over the preceding year. During the severe inflation and serious employment crisis that followed the first oil shock, the aim of the unions shifted to the maintenance of real wages and they had to change this formula to the rise in the consumer price index (CPI) plus something. This shift has been the subject of much debate, but it seems clear that it was a key to Japan's success in weathering the second oil shock.

In the mid-1980s, however, employer organizations had achieved their goal of keeping nominal wage increase rates at or below the equivalent of the real GNP growth rate minus the rate of employment growth (productivity standard principle). In other words, wage increases were set at or below the level proposed by the management side, resulting in a debate over whether fair distribution had been achieved (Nitta 1989).

Two important factors lay behind employers' push for the new wage determination formula. First, major corporations in export industries such as steel and shipbuilding, which had historically led the way in wage pattern setting, were facing increasingly severe competition internationally and domestically and an uncertain macroeconomic environment owing to the surge in the value of the yen in 1985. Second, it was easier for companies that operate in sectors not subject to such intense competition to shift the cost of higher wages onto the price of their products and services. Therefore, if the highly productive export industries were to offer large wage increases based on productivity increases in the sector, that level would be extended to less productive sectors through the nationally linked wage determination scheme. This would then cause "productivity gap inflation" and would affect real wages. If we look at wage determination in the *shunto* system in this light, fair distribution can not be achieved only by wage increases. What is required is the reform of Japan's socioeconomic structure itself (Shimada 1989).

In summary, the following are the most important points regarding changes to the wage system after the first oil crisis. First, although there have been no drastic changes to the basic characteristic of Japan's compensation system, capability-based schemes have been widely adopted since the mid-1970s. This corresponds to the workplace changes mentioned earlier. Second, these changes in the wage system have been embraced by the majority of unions and their members. Third, combined with heavy investment in skills formation, the system works effectively when firms grow in technically related business areas. Fourth, the distribution of the fruits of productivity increases has become an issue of debate, particularly since the mid-1980s. Fifth, the issue cannot be fully dealt with within the industrial relations framework. Rather, it is deeply related to the reform of Japan's overall socioeconomic structure.

11.2   Corporate Governance and Participation in Strategic Business Decisions

A high level of enterprise-specific skills and employment practices that strongly favor longer tenure imbue workers with a deep interest in the business decisions that will affect corporate growth and well-being. As a group, the employees of a firm share management's view that corporate growth and prosperity are essential conditions for their career progression and well-being. Since it is widely believed that their input is critical for corporate success and many workers have the intellectual capability to understand and contribute to business decisions, workers and their representatives naturally feel that they are entitled to a say in strategic decision making which is normally reserved for top management (Koike 1983; Ujihara 1989d). This argument merely points out that participation in strategic decisions is necessary from a workers' point of view. However, there is no guarantee that management will accept this position.

The severe employment adjustment immediately after the first oil crisis was a powerful impetus for a more active union voice in business decisions. Most unions had already developed schemes for information sharing and consultation on business decisions. Case studies by Inagami (1983) in automobiles, Yamamoto (1983) in steel, and Kamiya (1983) in the electric machinery industry, revealed that union participation in business decisions (called "business policy activities") became widespread only when companies were forced to take on drastic restructuring measures to cope with the business downturn that followed the oil shock.

Nitta (1988) describes a case in which a union in the steel industry actively participated in a restructuring program which included large-scale plant shutdowns. Although the union was unsuccessful in attempts to persuade management to withdraw or significantly revise the program, management accepted the union's request to include them in future business planning, including decisions over future capital investment for those plants that were to be severely affected by the restructuring.

Sato and Umezawa (1983) conducted a questionnaire survey which revealed that the frequency of discussion (60.1 percent increased vs. 1.5 percent decreased and 1.8 percent not applicable), the amount of information provided to unions (60.4 percent increased vs. 1.2 percent decreased and 1.7 percent not applicable), and the way in which unions participated in the discussion (65.5 percent more positive vs. 2.6 percent more passive and 2.0 percent not applicable) all dramatically increased at the corporate level after the first oil crisis.

While the survey found that 36.3 percent of respondents indicated that their unions only received explanation of business plans *ex post* or were not involved at all, 63.2 percent stated that prior notification, consultation, or union consent was required. Thus the extent of union participation in business decisions varies significantly between companies.

Rapid technological change such as microelectronization in the 1980s further promoted union participation in business issues. "The Memorandum on the Introduction of New Technology," drawn up by an auto company and a union in 1983, played an important symbolic

role in this regard. It guaranteed prior consultation on the introduction of new technologies and declared that workers should not be sac-
rificed because of the introduction of new technologies. Other unions
in major industries followed the line proposed in the memorandum.

The 1980s not only saw union progress in organizational, power-
centered participation but also a new kind of union campaign to promote individual, job-centered participation in management by their
members. Unions realized that as the composition and attitudes of
workers grew increasingly diverse, it would be difficult for them to
secure their commitment if they left their traditional campaign styles
unchanged. Interestingly, borrowing the corporate identity concept,
the new campaign was labeled "Union Identity." Based on case studies, Inagami and Kawakita (1988) described how the campaign was
carried out, while Kawakita and Sato (1991) and Sato and Fujimura
(1991) added insight on the state of the campaign from interviews and
extensive observations. While symbolic changes included altering the
color of union flags from red to blue, more important was the emphasis placed on participation in business decisions. Some unions set up
their own suggestion programs for their members (Koike 1985).

But why does management accept union participation in critical
business decisions? One reason is that union cooperation is absolutely
critical when a company faces a business crisis. However, if one
considers the diversity of responses in similar situations in other
countries, it seems that the governance structure of Japan's major
companies is important.

By examining the characteristics of major shareholders of Japan's
large private corporations, Nishiyama (1980) discovered two patterns. One involves reciprocal shareholding among major corporations, while the other involves shareholding by banks, life insurance
companies, and other financial institutions. In the first case, companies are unable to exercise control over the other companies whose
shares they hold because this would invite immediate retaliation from
the others. In the latter case, since banks have little equity capital, relying basically on deposits, and the funds of life insurance companies
(many of which are mutual companies, not joint stock corporations)
come from the premiums of general policyholders, very few capital-
ists, either judicial persons or natural persons, are able to exercise
control over major private companies using their own capital. Who
then does control those corporations? And how do they exercise control? Nishiyama (1980) concluded that controlling power is basically

held by executive managers, and the basis for their power is status or ownership, not appointment by stock owners.

If one accepts the line of argument proposed by Nishiyama, union participation in strategic decisions is more likely to be accepted by management of major Japanese corporations because the interests of shareholders are not preeminent. From a worker and union perspective, Japanese management has more discretion to trade voice for commitment by offering safer employment and a fairer distribution of profits.

But even the executives that control major companies through status or ownership are bound by certain restrictions. First, because they borrow heavily from financial institutions, especially banks, major companies in the private sector normally have quite a low net worth ratio. Therefore, since a drastic deterioration of business conditions of a company would make loan recovery difficult, banks, as creditors, must constantly monitor the behavior of management. Major banks are usually long-term stockholders of borrower companies and use this status to monitor performance. Second, despite the fact that the main purpose of reciprocal shareholding is to secure control and remove the threat of disturbance from corporate raiders, companies that own the stocks of other companies have benefited from the huge capital gains following the stock market surge after the World War II. If the stock market reverses its course, as is the case today, reciprocal shareholding and holdings by financial institutions may not be sustainable. In this context shareholders need to be able to monitor the behavior of management.

Considering the pressures from financial markets as well as employee groups as stakeholders, Aoki (1988) analyzed behavioral patterns of Japanese executives in a more sophisticated way. According to Aoki's model, executives are supposed to act as arbitrators between investor and employee groups. As discussed previously, the employees of major Japanese corporations acquire skills/capabilities on the job and deal with changes and abnormalities through transfers and horizontal communications with workers, such as production technicians, in other divisions. These skills/capabilities are built up within worker groups as network-specific assets. With these assets employee groups are able to operate efficiently even when the market changes constantly. Management needs the cooperation of these workers to fully utilize their assets. Consequently, executives must strike a balance between the interest of investor groups and the interest of worker groups when formulating and executing business policies.

Based on the Aoki model, union participation in business decisions can be conceptualized as a management tool to take employee interests more broadly into account, since participation is not confined to decisions which directly relate to employment and remuneration matters.

Although the model contributes many interesting points to our theoretical understanding of industrial relations in Japan, we do not know much about how the system evolved. Nishiyama (1983) suggests that for the large *zaibatsu* (family-owned conglomerates) changes in the stockholding structure occurred in the postwar period as a result of the *zaibatsu* dissolution policy of the Occupation Army. For other types of firms, it occurred during the hypergrowth era when expansion was financed by borrowed capital. The employment practices established in the early days of hypergrowth might have been another impetus for the establishment of the control structure. If highly skilled/capable human resources must be found within the ranks of existing employees, those executives who possess a deep understanding of the skills, capabilities, interests, and sentiment of their employees can secure a strategically strong position in the negotiation games of corporate control. In raided companies the unions are often the strongest opponent of any kind of change in corporate control.

11.3   Union Voice on Social and Economic Policies: The Emergence of Neocorporatism in Japan

The overall advance of worker participation at the workplace, functional, and strategic levels of the corporation after the first oil crisis eventually led to a movement toward an expanded union voice in social and economic policy formation at national level. An important turning point for the labor movement was the formation of the Trade Union Conference for Policy Promotion by the leading industrial federations of private sector unions in 1976.

Devastated by high inflation after the first oil crisis in 1973 and the deep employment crisis that followed, private sector unions started mobilizing their membership to secure greater social influence and a more favorable and timely macroeconomic policy, policies aimed at employment security for private sector workers, consumer price stabilization, and a less burdensome and fairer tax system. The TUCPP later expanded their agenda to include policies concerning pension and health insurance, land use and housing, natural resource and energy, promotion of women's welfare and status, administration reform, and industrial policy. High on their agenda were policy changes to the corporate standard of mandatory severance at the age of fifty-five, to secure employment for elderly workers, to reform the Labor Standard Law to shorten maximum work hours, and a large increase in the legal minimum wage to catch up with inflation.

It is clear that the momentum toward policy participation ignited by the TUCPP has been one of the most powerful driving forces for the unification of the labor movement. This eventually led to the formation of the 8,000,000-member Japanese Trade Union Confederation and the disbanding of four rival national union centers which had emerged originally in the 1950s. A rationale widely cited by supporters of this historic change in the Japanese labor movement was that a united and powerful national federation is a prerequisite for effective policy participation.

It is noteworthy that these changes have been initiated and vigorously promoted by unions that organize in the private sector, particularly in the major export industries. This is largely because these unions have suffered most from business fluctuations and drastic changes in international economic relations as opposed to the public sector unions and unions organizing purely domestic sectors such as private railways and utilities, which have been more protected from these changes in market conditions.

A feud over the enactment of the Employment Insurance Law, which replaced the Unemployment Insurance Law in 1974, was instrumental in mobilizing private sector unions to form a coalition to participate in policy formulation. Private sector unions were enthusiastic about the new law because it followed the German model, establishing an Employment Stabilization Fund to help private sector employers avoid layoffs by subsidizing those employers who take measures to retain redundant workers. However, Sohyo, the largest national confederation at the time, with membership concentrated in the influential public sector and sheltered industries, opposed the law because it included a number of measures aimed at restricting unemployment benefits, curbing abuse and reducing the financial burden. The bill was killed by Parliament but later, through political maneuvering, became law.

As their participation in policy progressed, organized labor realized that piecemeal policy changes like tax reductions were not sufficient and that a more fundamental reform of Japan's society and the economy was necessary. The rapid rise of yen after the Plaza Accord in 1985 provided a strong impetus for the emergence of a new vision. As Shimada (1989) argues, if employers, workers, and unions in the export sectors had tried to cope with rapid currency changes by jointly applying rationalization measures to cut costs, as they have in the past, the value of exports would still not decline, and as a result the trade imbalance would persist and the further appreciation of the yen would become inevitable. In order to move out of this vicious cycle, structural reform of Japanese economy and society was called for. A key element of the reforms entailed the rationalization of inefficient sectors such as retail and agriculture which had been sheltered from international and domestic competition by policy measures, social customs and the holding of astronomically priced land. This kind of reform is expected to bring down domestic consumer prices and increase the purchasing power of workers as consumers.

JTUC now uses various channels or vehicles for policy participation including (1) regular consultations with those political parties that cooperate with the JTUC (particularly the Japan Socialist party and Democratic Socialist party), (2) "policy demands and proposals" prepared annually for discussions with the government and political parties, (3) regular consultations with ministries such as Labor and International Trade and Industry, (4) participation in consultative councils for ministries, (5) consultation with employer organizations, (6) mass demonstrations and various public relations activities.

A major difference between JTUC and its predecessors lies in the JTUC's recognition of the important role of Japanese bureaucrats in policy formation and the heavy reliance it places on seeking to influence policy development at the ministry level before a bill or policy is discussed in the Parliament. Particularly, JTUC has pursued an enhanced role in government consultative councils. The councils related to the Ministry of Labor have already been organized on a tripartite principle, and representatives of employer organizations and labor unions are equally represented. Neutrals, who are supposed to represent public interest, play the role of mediator. Essentially, it is very difficult for the Ministry of Labor to develop and propose a new policy initiative unless labor unions, represented by the JTUC, agree or show at least passive acceptance in these councils. Union representation in the councils of other ministries is more limited and the JTUC is seeking to expand its presence in them.

Union federations at the industry level also contribute to industrial policy formulation by participating in government councils and holding discussions with opposition parties. Some of the more powerful federations hold labor-management conferences with employers' organizations in the industry concerned (Shinoda 1991; JPTUC 1989).

To summarize the above, national and industrial federations of enterprise-based unions have played an active role in the formulation of social economic policies since the first oil crisis. It is difficult to gauge how much has been achieved but it is worth noting that government-labor-management consultation channels were established during this period. This represents the emergence of neocorporatism in Japan. The need for labor's participation in policy formulation became apparent when unions realized that industrial relations mechanisms within industries could not solve certain problems. Policy participation was a natural extension of union and worker experience in advancing participation at other levels within firms and industries.

We should note that some are skeptical about how much impact policy participation can have and how far unions are prepared to go. Export sector unions, which represent about a third or more of membership of JTUC, and public sector and quasi-public sector unions and domestic private sector unions have diverse interests and different views. As a strictly consensus-based organization the JTUC may find it difficult to promote coherent and radical policy changes. Policy participation relying heavily on the communication channels with ministries may inhibit radical reform since ministries help to maintain the existing socioeconomic structure of Japanese society. In order to establish itself as a change agent in politics, the JTUC will have to solve the difficult question of its relationships with political parties.

However, it is undeniable that the Japanese labor movement has stepped forward to policy participation. How the emerging neocorporatist pattern proceeds in Japan will largely determine not only the future of industrial relations but also of the Japanese economy and society as a whole.

11.4 Conclusion and Remaining Issues

Wide-ranging and significant changes to the Japanese IR/HR system and a variety of changes in Japanese IR/HR have taken place in recent years, especially after the oil shocks of the 1970s. But these changes were essentially adjustments to, and extensions of, the basic framework established in late 1950s and early 1960s. In this sense we have not observed fundamental change or transformation in Japanese industrial relations and human resource systems over the past twenty years.

However, we have stressed that the adjustment process was by no means automatic. Rather, there are internal tensions and contradictions which have brought about a variety of problems. Industrial relations actors have played a key role in detecting problems, finding solutions through the re-interpretation of past practices and through creative formulation of new practices and by negotiating at various levels in various forms. Although the behavior of the Japanese actors might have been somewhat unique when compared with other countries, we have shown that it is necessary to consider the expectations and assumptions of these actors as well as the dominant ideologies as the basis for analyzing recent adjustments.

It is particularly important to understand the role of unions in this process. The Japanese labor movement behaved as a pro-active partner rather than the passive and faceless follower popularly portrayed in industrial relations literature.

References

Abbeglen, James C. 1958. *The Japanese Factory*. Glencoe, IL: Free Press. (*Nihon no Keiei*, trans. by Kuniyoshi Urabe. Tokyo: Daiyamondo Sha, 1958.)

Aoki, Masahiko. 1984. *Gendai no Kigyo*. Tokyo: Iwanami Shoten. (*The Cooperative Theory of the Firm*. Oxford: Oxford University Press, 1984.)

Aoki, Masahiko. 1988. *Information, Incentive, and Bargaining in the Japanese Economy*. Cambridge: Cambridge University Press.

Doeringer, B. Peter, and Michael J. Piore. 1971. *Internal Labor Markets and Manpower Analysis*. Lexington, MA: D.C.Heath.

Dore, Ronald. 1973. *British Factory-Japanese Factory*. London: George Allen and Unwin.

Gordon, Andrew. 1985. *The Evolution of Labor Relations in Japan*. Council on East Asian Studies, Harvard University, Cambridge.

Gordon, Robert J. 1982. Why U.S. wages and employment behavior differs from that in Britain and Japan. *Economic Journal* 92:13–44.

Hyodo, Tsutomu. 1971. *Nihon ni okeru Roshi Kankei no Tenkai* (Evolution of Labor Relations in Tokyo: Japan. Tokyo Daigaku Shuppankai (University of Tokyo Press).

Inagami, Takeshi. 1981. *Roshi Kankei no Shakaigaku* (Sociology of Industrial Relations). Tokyo: Tokyo Daigaku Shuppankai (University of Tokyo Press).

Inagami, Takeshi. 1983. Pai no zodai to rodo kumiai no taio (Enlargement of a pie and union policies). In Japan Institute of Labor, *80 Nendai no Roshi Kankei* (Industrial Relations in 1980s). Tokyo: JIL.

Inagami, Takeshi, and Takashi Kawakita. 1988. *Yunion Aidentiti* (Union Identity). Tokyo: JIL.

Ishida, Mitsuo. 1990. *Chingin no Shakai Kagaku* (Social Science of Wages). Tokyo: Chuo Keizai Sha.

Ishikawa, Kaoru. 1984. *Nihonteki Hinshitsu Kanri* (Japanese-Type Quality Control). 2d ed. Tokyo: Nikkagiren (JUSE).

Ito, Minoru. 1988. *Gijutsu Kakushin to Hyuuman Nettowaak gata Soshiki* (Technological Change and Human Network Organization). Tokyo: JIL.

Japan Institute of Labor (JIL). 1983. *80 Nendai no Roshi Kankei* (Industrial Relations in 1980s). Tokyo: JIL.

Japan Institute of Labor (JIL). 1985. *Gijutsu Kakushin to Roshi Kankei* (Technological Changes and Industrial Relations). Tokyo: JIL.

Japan Institute of Labor (JIL). 1989. Searching for a new system in industrial *relations*. *Proceedings of the 30th Anniversary International Symposium*. Tokyo: JIL.

Japan Institute of Labor (JIL). 1992. *Seisan Bungyo Kozo to Rodo Shijo no Kaisosei* (Production and Work Organizations and Hierarchy in Labor Markets). Tokyo: JIL.

Japan Private Sector Trade Union Confederation (JPTUC). 1989. *Sangyo betsu Soshiki no Genjo Chosa Hokokusho* (Report on Functions of Industrial Union Organizations). Tokyo: JPTUC.

Juran, J.M. 1967. The QC circle phenomenon. *Industrial Quality Control* 23 (7).

Kamiya, Takuhei. 1983. Keiei kiki ni okeru roshi no tenkan (Industrial relations changes at a time of business crisis). In Japan Institute of Labor, *80 Nendai no Roshi Kankei* (Industrial Relations in 1980s). Tokyo: JIL.

Kawakita, Takashi. 1989. *Sangyo Hendo to Romu Kanri* (Industrial Changes and Personnel Management). Tokyo: JIL.

Kawakita, Takashi, and Hiroki Sato. 1991. *Yunion Aidentiti* Daisakusen (Campaigning for Union Identity). Tokyo: Sogo Rodo Kenkyujo.

Kogure, Masao. 1988. *Nihon no TQC* (TQC in Japan). Tokyo: Nikkagiren (JUSE).

Koike, Kazuo. 1977. *Shokuba no Rodo Kumiai to Sanka* (Worker Participation and Labor Unions at Workplace Level). Tokyo: Toyo Keizai Shinpo Sha.

Koike, Kazuo. 1983. Howaito karaaka kumiai moderu (White-collarized union model). In Japan Institute of Labor, *80 Nendai no Roshi Kankei* (Industrial Relations in 1980s). Tokyo: JIL.

Koike, Kazuo. 1985. "Denki sangyo A. (A case of electric machinery company A.). In Japan Institute of Labor, *Gijutsu Kakushin to Roshi Kankei* (Technological Changes and Industrial Relations). Tokyo: JIL.

Koike, Kazuo. 1986. Nihon no off-JT (Off-the-job training in Japan). In Kazuo Koike, ed., *Gendai no Jinzai Keisei* (Contemporary Human Resources Development). Kyoto: Mineruva Shobo.

Koike, Kazuo, and Takenori Inoki, eds. 1987. *Jinzai Keisei no Kokusai Hikaku*. Tokyo: Toyo Keizai Shinpo Sha. (*Skill Formation in Japan and Southeast Asia*. Tokyo: University of Tokyo Press, 1990.)

Koike, Kazuo. 1988. *Understanding Industrial Relations in Modern Japan*. New York: St. Martin's Press.

Koike, Kazuo. 1991. Kaiko to shitsugyo (Dismissals and unemployment). In Kazuo Koike, *Shigoto no Keizaigaku* (Economics of Work). Tokyo: Toyo Keizai Shinpo Sha.

Kondo, Takao. 1986. Kokusai hikaku kara mita Nihon no shokumu (A comparative look at job structures in Japan). In Hosei Daigaku Ohara Kenkyujo, ed., *Rodo no Ningenka* (Humanization of Work). Tokyo: Sogo Rodo Kenkyujo.

Kosai, Yutaka. 1981. *Kodo Seicho no Jidai* (The Hyper Economic Growth Era). Tokyo: Nihon Hyoron Sha.

Koshiro, Kazutoshi. 1983. *Nihon no Roshi Kankei* (Industrial Relations in Japan). Tokyo: Yuhikaku.

Koshiro, Kazutoshi, and Hitoshi Nagano. 1985. Jidosha sangyo (The case of automobile industry). In Japan Institute of Labor, *Gijutsu Kakushin to Roshi Kankei* (Technological Changes and Industrial Relations). Tokyo: JIL.

Kochan, Thomas A., Harry C. Katz, and Robert B. McKersie. 1986. *The Transformation of American Industrial Relations.* New York: Basic Books.

Kuwahara, Y. 1993. Industrial relations in Japan. In G. J. Bamber and R. D. Lansbury, eds., *International and Comparative Industrial Relations: A Study of Industrialised Market Economies.* 2d ed. New York: Routledge.

Ministry of International Trade and Industry (MITI). 1981. *Nihonteki Koyo Kanko no Yukue* (Where Will the Japanese Employment Practices Go)? Tokyo: Sangyo Noritsu Daigaku Shuppanbu.

Ministry of International Trade and Industry (MITI). 1984. *FA ga Kojo wo Do Kaeruka* (How Will Automation Change Factories)? Tokyo: Nihon Noritsu Kyokai.

Nakamura, Keisuke. 1992. Nihon Kokan ni okeru QC saakuru no seisei katei (Evolution of quality circles in NKK). Working Paper 23. Sangyo Joho Senta (Center for Business and Industrial Research). Hosei University, Tokyo.

Nakamura, Keisuke, Hiroki Sato, and Takuhei Kamiya. 1988. *Rodo Kumiai wa Honto ni Yaku ni Tatte Irunoka* (Are Unions Really Useful?). Tokyo: Sogo Rodo Kenkyujo.

National Institute of Employment and Vocational Research (NIEVR). 1983. *Maikuro Erekutoronikusu no Koyo ni Oyobosu Shitsuteki Eikyo ni Kansuru Kenkyu Hokokusho* (Report on the Qualitative Impact of Microelectronics on Employment). Tokyo: NIEVR.

National Institute of Employment and Vocational Research (NIEVR). 1986. *ME kara IT e* (From Microelectronics to Information Technology). Tokyo: JIL.

National Institute of Employment and Vocational Research (NIEVR). 1986. *Nihon ni okeru Shoshudan Katsudo no Jittai to sono Tenkai Joken ni Kansuru Jirei Kenkyu Hokokusho* (A Case Study on Small Group Activities and the Backgrounds of Their Diffusion). Tokyo: NIEVR.

National Institute of Employment and Vocational Research (NIEVR), Koyo Chosei Mondai Kenkyu Iinkai. 1988. *Koyo Chosei ni Tomonau Shokugyo Tenkan to Ido ni kansuru Chosa Kenkyu Hokokusho* (Report on Occupational and Location Changes Following Employment Adjustment). Tokyo: NIEVR.

Nishiyama, Tadanori. 1980. *Shihai Kozo Ron* (Corporate Governance Structure). Tokyo: Bunshindo.

Nishiyama, Tadanori. 1983. *Datsu Shihonshugi Bunseki* (Analysis of Postcapitalism). Tokyo: Bunshindo.

Nitta, Michio. 1978. Tekkogyo no "Jishukanri Katsudo" (JK Activity in the Steel Industry)." *Nihon Rodo Kyokai Zasshi* 234:13–33.

Nitta, Michio. 1988. *Nihon no Rodosha Sanka* (Worker Participation in Japan). Tokyo: Tokyo Daigaku Shuppankai (University of Tokyo Press).

Nitta, Michio. 1989. Structural Changes and Enterprise-Based Unionism in Japan. In Japan Institute of Labor, *Proceedings of the 30th Anniversary International Symposium*. Tokyo: JIL.

.Nitta, Michio. 1991. Business diversification and human resource management strategy in the Japanese chemical textile industry. Occasional Paper. University of Tokyo, Institute of Social Science.

Nitta, Michio. 1992. When the lifetime employment strategy fails. Occasional Paper. University of Tokyo, Institute of Social Science.

Nitta, Michio. 1993. Chusho kigyo ni okeru kigyo nai komyunikeeshon (Intrafirm communication in small- and medium-sized firms). *Musashi Daigaku Ronshu* (Journal of Musashi University) 40:81–100.

Okamoto, Hideaki. 1966. *Kogyoka to Genba Kantokusha* (Industrialization and Supervisors). Tokyo: JIL.

Organization for Economic Cooperation and Development (OECD). 1973. *Manpower Policy in Japan*. Paris: OECD.

Omi, Naoto. 1989. "Rengo" Jidai no roshi kankei no tenbo (An overview of industrial relations in the JTUC era). *Nihon Rodo Kyokai Zasshi* 363 (December).

Osterman, Paul. 1988. *Employment Futures*. Oxford: Oxford University Press.

Piore, Michael J., and Charles F. Sabel. 1984. *The Second Industrial Divide*. New York: Basic Books.

Showa Dojinkai. 1960. *Wagakuni Chingin Kozo no Shiteki Kosatsu* (A Historical Study of Wage Structures in Japan). Tokyo: Shiseido.

Shunto Kenkyukai, *Shunto Kawarunoka* (Will the Spring Labor Offensive Change)? Tokyo: JIL.

Sato, Hiroki, and Takashi Umezawa. 1983. Rodo kumiai no hatsugen to kumiai ruikei (Types and voice of unions). In Japan Institute of Labor, *80 Nendai no Roshi Kankei* (Industrial Relations in 1980s). Tokyo: JIL.

Sato, Hirioki, and Hiroyuki Fujimura, eds. 1991. *Ekuserento Yunion* (Excellent Unions). Tokyo: Daiichi Shorin.

Shimada, Haruo. 1976. Kajo koyo wo kangaeru (Thinking about overemployment). *Nihon Keizai Shinbun*, April 11 and 12.

Shimada, Haruo. 1989. Japan's industrial culture and labor-management relations. In Japan Institute of Labor, *Proceedings of the 30th Anniversary International Symposium*. Tokyo: JIL.

Shinoda, Toru. 1991. "Rengo" Jidai ni okeru "seisaku sanka" no gtenjo to kadai (Challenges for policy participation in the JTUC era). *Nihon Rodo Kenkyu Zasshi* 379:48–60.

Shinozuka, Eiko. 1989. *Nihon no Koyo Chosei* (Employment Adjustment In Japan). Tokyo: Toyo Keizai Shinpo Sha.

Taira, Koji, and Solomon B. Levine. 1985. Japan's industrial relations: A social compact emerges. In Industrial Relations Research Association, *Industrial Relations in a Decade of Change*, Madison, WI: IRRA.

Takezawa, Shin-ichi, et al. 1978. Denki sangyo ni okeru rodo seikatsu no shitsuteki kaizen no doko (Developments in quality of working life in electric machinery industry). *Nihon Rodo Kyokai Zasshi* 236:67–87.

Takezawa, Shin-ichi, et al. 1979. Jid osha sangyo ni okeru rodo seikatsu no shitsuteki kaizen no doko (Developments in quality of working life in automobile industry). *Nihon Rodo Kyokai Zasshi* 240:53–69.

Totsuka, Hideo, and Tsutomu Hyodo, eds. 1991. *Roshi Kankei no Tenkan to Sentaku* (Changes and Choices in Industrial Relations). Tokyo: Nihon Hyoron Sha.

Ujihara, Shojiro, Wakao Fujita, and Naomichi Funahashi. 1960. *Nihongata Rodo Kumiai to Nenko Seido* (Japanese Unionism and Seniority-Based Employment Systems). Tokyo: Toyo Keizai Shinpo Sha.

Ujihara, Shojiro. 1989a. Nenko chingin, shogai koyo, kigyobetsu kumiai wa sanmi ittai ka (Are seniority-based pay, lifetime employment and enterprise-based unionism the trinity in employment relations in Japan? In Shojiro Ujihara, *Nihon no Roshi Kankei to Rodo Seisaku* (Industrial Relations and Labor Policy in Japan). Tokyo: Tokyo Daigaku Shuppankai.

Ujihara, Shojiro. 1989b. Daiichiji sekiyu kiki igo no rodoryoku jukyu kozo no henka (Changes in labor demand and supply structures after the first oil crisis). In Shojiro Ujihara, *Nihonkeizai to Koyo Seisaku* (Japanese Economy and Employment Policy). Tokyo: Tokyo Daigaku Shuppankai (University of Tokyo Press).

Ujihara, Shojiro. 1989c. Chukonen rodosha no koyo fuan to jinken (Employment insecurity and human rights of middle-aged and senior workers). In Shojiro Ujihara, *Nihonkeizai to Koyo Seisaku* (Japanese Economy and Employment Policy). Tokyo: Tokyo Daigaku Shuppankai (University of Tokyo Press).

Ujihara, Shojiro. 1989d. Dantai kosho to roshi kyogi (Collective bargaining and joint consultation in Japan). In Shojiro Ujihara, *Nihon no Roshi Kankei to Rodo Seisaku* (Industrial Relations and Labor Policy in Japan). Tokyo: Tokyo Daigaku Shuppankai.

White, Michael, and Malcolm Trevor. 1983. *Under Japanese Management*. London: Heinemann.

Womack, James P., Daniel T. Jones, Daniel Roos, and Donna Sammons Carpenter. 1990. *The Machine That Changed the World*. New York: Rawson Associates.

Yamamoto, Ikuro. 1983. Keiei sanka to rodo kumiai no hatsugen (Workers' participation in management and union voice). In Japan Institute of Labor, *80 Nendai no Roshi Kankei* (Industrial Relations in 1980s). Tokyo: JIL.

Yamazaki, Kiyoshi 1989. *Nihon no Taishokukin Seido* (Severance Allowance Systems in Japan). Tokyo: JIL.

Yoneyama, Kikuji. 1978. *Gijutsu Kakushin to Shokuba Kanri* (Technological Changes and Shop-floor Management). Tokyo: Bokutakusha.

Yoshikawa, Hiroshi. 1992. *Nihon Keizai to Makuro Keizaigaku* (Japanese Economy and Macro Economics). Tokyo: Toyo Keizai Shinpo Sha.

12

Conclusion: The Transformation of Industrial Relations? A Cross-National Review of the Evidence

Richard Locke
Thomas Kochan

The evidence presented in the previous chapters documents how many individual firms and even entire industries in different countries are adapting their employment practices to the new terms of international competition. Yet this process of adaptation is neither universal nor uniform. In some firms the new competitive strategies build on a variety of industrial relations and human resource practices that enhance the skill base and flexibility of the workplace and promote greater communication, trust, and coordination among the firm's stakeholders. Yet other firms have sought to adjust to increased competition by subcontracting work to lower-wage workers and firms, downsizing, and seeking to compete on the traditional bases of cost and price competition. In other words, although a new approach to employment relations has emerged in all the advanced industrial nations included in our research, the particular forms it has taken and the extent to which it has diffused vary considerably, both across countries with different institutional arrangements and historical traditions and within nations, across firms, industries, and regions.

In the face of these contrasting developments, unions, employer associations, and national governments are attempting to adapt to greater international competition and increased diversity of practices within their orbits of responsibility. But here too we see much variety. While in some countries, institutions like national and/or industry-level bargaining arrangements have been weakened in recent years as individual firms seek to gain greater flexibility to make employment decisions on their own, elsewhere institutions that extend beyond the boundaries of individual firms are beginning to play new roles, including the support of innovative employment practices.

This chapter seeks to make sense of these contrasting developments documented in the various country chapters by first describing and then explaining the extent and modality of recent changes in employment relations in the advanced industrial states. The chapter is divided into three sections. The first section describes in what forms, and to what extent, the new patterns of employment relations are emerging in the eleven advanced industrial nations covered in this book. Are the pace, scope, and nature of changes observed in these countries sufficient to argue that employment relations have been transformed in some fundamental way that requires a new interpretive model? Or, are these changes better described as incremental adjustments to, or extensions of, historical practices that are adequately captured in existing theories and explanations?

The second section then seeks to explain variations observed in new employment patterns both within and across the different nations covered here. Why, for instance, have flexible work organizations been more widely diffused in Germany, Japan, and Italy than in the United States or the United Kingdom? Conversely, why have more flexible work hours and employment arrangements (contingent, part-time) become so pervasive in Spain and Japan but are resisted in France and Norway? To understand these differences, we seek to assess the different meanings or valences various new employment practices may have in different national contexts as well as the role different national institutional arrangements may play in facilitating (or hindering) the development and diffusion of new employment patterns within the respective states.

Finally, in the third section we generalize from the individual country studies to consider what our findings may imply for the future of industrial relations and human resource management practices, policies, and research. Given the incremental, ad hoc, and often internally contradictory nature of the changes underway, does it still make sense to view industrial relations as a "system" in which the various policies, procedures, and institutions fit together and mutually reinforce each other? Or, should we instead reconceptualize national employment arrangements as composites of different human resource patterns that coexist (often uneasily) within the same national territory? Moreover, given the incremental nature of the changes underway, as well as the highly differentiated consequences (in terms of job security, wages, training and career opportunities, etc.) of these changes for different groups of workers, what role (if any) should public policy play in promoting certain changes, hindering others, and maintaining national standards?

12.1   A Transformation in Industrial Relations? Reviewing the Evidence

Common Patterns

The evidence provided in the various country chapters suggest that several general patterns are indeed emerging across the advanced industrial states.

An Enterprise Focus
In all the countries covered in this study, the individual enterprise has emerged as an increasingly important locus of human resource and industrial relations decision making and strategy. This in turn implies that managers (sometimes in collaboration with local unions or works councils) have been the driving force for introducing changes in employment practices in recent years. This was not always the case. In the past, in most European countries as well as in Australia, national or industry level union-management bargaining or even tripartite negotiations with government established the basic wage benefits and conditions of employment. Even in the United States with its highly decentralized industrial relations system, industrywide pattern bargaining arrangements in industries such as coal, steel, rubber tire, and transportation existed for much of the postwar era. Both in these sectors and in others where these arrangements did not exist, labor unions were the driving force behind improvements in wages and benefits while management reacted to (or sought to insulate itself from) union initiatives. All of this has changed in recent years.

Sweden represents the most visible case in point. There employers have led efforts to break out of national- and even industry-level collective bargaining structures in order to allow individual firms to negotiate the terms and conditions of employment that best fit their particular circumstances. Australia's highly centralized system of national arbitration awards has also been reformed in order to promote enterprise bargaining and wage adjustments in return for efficiency enhancing changes in work practices. Individual employers must now take the lead in proposing the specific changes necessary to improve productivity in their operations in order to justify wage increases. Similar decentralizing trends are visible in Italy, where the national wage escalator (*scala mobile*) was recently abolished and where a reconfiguration of bargaining arrangements toward the local level is taking place, and in Japan, where a debate is beginning to emerge over whether the national spring wage offensive is still workable, given the pressures on labor costs resulting from the fallen yen/dollar ratio. More subtle but comparable signs of decentralization are visible in Germany where it is reported that works councils are taking on a greater role vis-à-vis industrywide collective bargaining as the "qualitative issues" related to training, new technology, work organization, and employment adjustment grow in importance. Decentralization occurred throughout the 1980s in the United States with the decline of industrywide pattern bargaining and was also reinforced in the United Kingdom through various government policies (i.e., privatization) and managerial strategies.

Increased Flexibility

Decentralization was accompanied by the search for greater flexibility in how work is organized and labor is deployed. In just about every country covered in this study, various government regulations and norms governing hiring, firing, layoffs, and the use of labor have been relaxed or modified so as to give individual employers greater discretion. For example, in Italy regulations requiring that employers seeking new hires give priority to workers who have waited longest on the government unemployment agency's lists have been modified so that employers can hire the specific individuals they want. In Germany, the CDU-led government also promoted a limited deregulation of the labor market, which permitted temporary work contracts and simplified the regulation of part-time jobs. Similar modifications took place throughout the advanced industrial nations. As a result youth, part-time, and/or temporary employment contracts exploded in number in Italy, Spain, Norway, the United Kingdom, the United States, Germany, and Japan. Swedish employers are pushing for analogous changes in their country's regulatory framework.

Linked to these changes in external labor market practices are a series of related efforts on the shop floor and in the internal labor markets of firms. The essence of these initiatives is to draw out the discretionary effort and creative potential of workers at all levels of the organization by providing work arrangements that delegate decision-making authority to the source of the problem, encourage teamwork, promote problem identification and resolution, and enhance coordination across functional boundaries. In the United States, for example, Paul Osterman has reported that 64 percent of the establishments covered in his nationally representative survey have introduced innovations such as employee problem solving groups, work teams, total quality management, and job rotation. In a survey of industrial enterprises in Lombardia, Italy's most industrial region, 56 percent of the companies claimed to have introduced new job rotation arrangements. Flexible work hours were reported to be even more widespread. Job rotation, flexible job arrangements, quality circles, and small group activity are reported to be widely diffused in a number of Japanese industries, including the iron and steel, automobile, chemical, and machinery industries. Even in the United Kingdom, the Third Workplace Industrial Relations Survey reported that 20 percent of all large enterprises covered in the study had problem solving groups and/or quality circles.

Growing Importance of Skill Development
Another common pattern we are observing across these countries is the premium that the labor market places on skills of the work force. Since the pressures for continual improvements in productivity and quality are intensifying, and since effective use of new technologies require increased analytical and behavioral skills, both firms and governments in most of the advanced industrial nations covered in this study are increasing their investments in training and skill development. For example, the federal government of Canada has sought to support training efforts by earmarking $800 million a year to finance these efforts. The Australian and French governments have both established compulsory levies on companies in order to fund expanded training programs. The British, Spanish, Norwegian and Swedish governments have all promoted a series of major institutional reforms aimed at enhancing the quality of vocational training in their respective states. The reform of the apprenticeship and vocational training systems are hotly debated issues in the United States and Italy as well.

Associated with the greater attention to skill development and training is an increase in performance- and/or skill-related pay systems. Thirty-nine percent of Australian workplaces with five or more employees have performance-related compensation schemes. The 1992 Workplace Industrial Relations Survey in Britain reported that 20 percent of both skilled manual and nonmanual workers received some form of merit pay and a recent survey of company-level negotiations in Italy found that between 1984 and 1989, 130 agreements covering 700,000 employees had introduced different forms of performance-based pay arrangements. Similar developments were reported in the United States and Japan.

Union Membership Declines
A fourth common finding is that unions are experiencing major challenges in all countries as the pace of restructuring intensifies, the work force becomes more diverse, and as the average size of enterprises declines. In an era of rapid organizational and industrial restructuring, the ability to recruit new members or retain existing members when they move across jobs, organizations, or in and out of employed status becomes crucial for unions. Managerial ideology and the degree of legitimacy unions enjoy in the broader society also influence the ability of unions to adapt to the changes underway. Thus countries in which unions have a difficult time recruiting or retaining members and/or where the role of unions in society or in specific enterprises meets with the strongest ideological resistance from business and/or government leaders, experienced the largest losses in union membership and the greatest challenges to shift their basic role and patterns of worker representation. Not surprisingly, unions in the United States, Britain, and France experienced especially difficult times and steep membership declines over the course of the past decade. But similar (although less pronounced) declines in union membership are visible in Japan, Australia, Italy, and in the private sector in Canada. Moreover in several countries—namely Italy, the United Kingdom, and Norway—new kinds of unions or employee associations have emerged to challenge the organizational dominance of the more established unions.

As this quick survey of common trends suggests, it appears that a general process of change or transformation of employment relations is indeed taking place throughout the advanced industrial world. Everywhere unions are in decline and management is resurgent. In all counties we can identify firms engaged in new forms of work organization and more flexible use of labor. And a greater appreciation for, and investment in, skill formation and training is manifest in all the countries covered in this study. Yet common trends can sometimes be deceiving given that not all countries began at the same starting point and that seemingly similar practices and arrangements can have significantly different meanings in different national contexts. For example, employer efforts to reorganize work on the shop floor are sometimes strongly resisted by unions in the United States, since they undermine narrow job definitions with their related wage, seniority, and security provisions -practices that represent the institutional anchors for American labor's rights within the firm. In Germany, however, where employment security and union strength are not dependent upon shop floor practices like job control, workers and their unions have welcomed similar changes that upgrade their skills and enhance their autonomy. Conversely, American employers have traditionally enjoyed substantial flexibility both in the determination of wages and in the hiring, firing, and laying off of workers. But the drive for employment flexibility in Germany and for wage flexibility in Sweden have produced major new conflicts between labor and management since the late 1970s.

The point is that while employers' "search for flexibility" (Boyer 1988) may be a general phenomenon emanating from international pressures that are common to all the advanced industrial nations, different institutional arrangements filter these common pressures differently so that the valence of particular issues and changes in practices are quite varied in the different national contexts. Thus equally interesting to analyze are the variations in patterns of adaptation observed across different nation states. We now turn to a discussion of these issues.

12.2   Cross-National and Cross-Firm Variations

Work Organization

As noted above, flexibility in work organization is becoming a key source of competitive advantage for firms across all the advanced industrialized nations we are studying. Experiments with greater teamwork, employee participation in problem solving and productivity improvements, quality circles and the use of total quality management tools, were documented in all the country chapters. But diffusion of these practices remains uneven. In some countries, such as Japan and Germany, these flexible and team-oriented work systems were relatively common already, while in others, they represent such fundamental changes in culture and practice that they tend to be adopted slowly and meet with strong resistance from supervisors, managers, and in some cases union leaders. For example, in the United Kingdom, no more than 2 percent of all establishments with more than twenty-five workers have quality circles or problem-solving groups. Team work and major alterations in job content are even more rare. In the United states recent survey research suggests that no more than one-third of American workplaces have introduced more flexible work systems covering a majority of their employees. And the majority of these were introduced within the past five years and therefore remain subject to the challenge of skeptics that they are just another management fad that will not withstand the test of time. Canada appears to have experienced only a handful of cases (predominantly in large companies) where large-scale innovations in work organization have taken place.

In contrast, quality circles, team-based work, job rotation, and flexible jobs appear to be extensive and diffuse throughout Japanese industry. Research by the SOFI Institute of Göttingen also suggests that new forms of work organization are also widespread in the German automobile, machine tool, and chemical industries. The diffusion of new forms of work based on more flexible and autonomous teams of workers was also documented in several case studies on the Italian petrochemical, telecommunications, personal computer, machine tool, and automobile industries (Regini and Sabel 1989). Elsewhere, in Spain, Norway, and Sweden, for example, work reorganization has also taken place but primarily within large, "leading edge" firms, or in the case of Spain, within multinational, companies.

These observed differences in patterns of work reorganization suggest that those countries that come from a tradition of job control—the United States, Australia, Britain, and Canada—in which work was traditionally organized along more rigid Taylorist lines, have experienced the greatest pressures to transform their work organization arrangements. In contrast, those national systems of industrial relations that were never completely Taylorist and/or where they already had workplace practices that promote flexibility and communication such as Japan, Germany, and to some degree Italy, seem to have been able to accommodate more easily the need for these new workplace practices through incremental adaptations of their existing arrangements.

Interestingly enough, systematic patterns in who adopts flexible forms of work organization exists not only across but also within most of the countries covered in this study. Within all of these countries, even the ones which appear to be most advanced in new forms of work organization, the most profound departures from traditional practices are manifest in settings where (1) a new "greenfield" plant or worksite was established (e.g., Volvo's Kalmar and Udevalla plants, Opel's Mosel plant and Volkswagon's Eisenach facility in eastern Germany); (2) major technological changes were introduced and employees or their representatives have some voice in that process (e.g., many of the large Japanese firms in the automobile, steel, and electronics industries); (3) in industries such as autos, steel, electronics, and related high technology sectors where the pressures of international competition have been strongest; and (4) in settings where new union-management partnerships were created such as in the Japanese transplants in the United Kingdom or Saturn Corporation in the United States. In Germany, for instance, where new forms of work organization are reported to be widespread, differences in the extent and modalities of workplace change nonetheless exist across sectors, or between new and older plants within the same industry. As one indicator of this variation, take for example the emergence of new kinds of more broadly trained/highly skilled workers. Recent research by the SOFI Institute of Göttingen revealed that these so-called system regulators made up only 5 percent of the total work force in the automobile industry but 33 percent of the chemical industry's labor force. Likewise, in Japan, tremendous variation in the use of teams, quality circles, and job enrichment programs exists between large and small enterprises within the same industries. In short, even within countries there appears to be significant variation in the extent and modality of change, and these differences seem to be linked to the particular characteristics of individual firms and industries and not merely the institutional environment in which they are embedded.

Clearly many of these workplace innovations remain in a fragile or vulnerable state, and face a number of obstacles that limit their sustainability and diffusion. Among these obstacles, the most serious appear to be the lack of an adequate rate of economic growth needed to absorb the jobs lost to increases in productivity. This reinforces the already strong pressures to downsize or "reengineer" organizations in ways that produce short-term cost savings but that, in the long run, may destroy the trust and mutual commitment needed to sustain work organization innovations and flexibility.

Some countries also suffer from a lack of strong government support for innovation. With the possible exception of Australia, there are no national institutions that approach the significance of the Japan Productivity Center for sharing information and promoting adoption of ideas and practices that promise long-term gains to firms and their employees. Some countries also continue to suffer from highly adversarial labor-management relations, and declining membership, power, and security of unions. This makes it difficult to develop sustained partnerships between labor and management at the macro level of these economies or at the industry level that are needed to provide a supportive institutional umbrella for labor-management cooperation and innovation in specific enterprises and workplaces. Although the relative importance of these obstacles vary across these countries, our prediction is that those countries that are able to overcome them will be the ones where innovations in work organization are likely to diffuse most widely in the future.

Job Mobility, Staffing, and Employment Security

One of the most widely accepted propositions in our field is that innovations in work practices or other forms of worker-management cooperation or productivity improvement are not likely to be sustained over time when workers fear that by increasing productivity they will work themselves out of their jobs. Unfortunately, the past decade has been a time when the demand for change and innovation has been strong while job security generally declined in nearly all of the countries included in our study. But again there has been tremendous variation among countries. In the United Kingdom, for example, one-half of all workplaces in manufacturing and one-third in private services resorted to compulsory redundancy as a means of reducing the size of their work forces. In Canada, only about 20 percent of workers employed in large establishments enjoyed any kind of employment and/or income guarantees. The situation was even more precarious for workers in smaller firms. Even in Japan, many companies promoted voluntary severance (de facto forced layoffs with severance pay) as a way of drastically reducing their labor forces. In contrast, in Norway and Sweden, a combination of laws and collective bargaining agreements provided relatively high job security for workers, while in Italy, laid-off workers received income maintenance payments and benefits until they were either hired back by their employers or paid a severance bonus. German workers also enjoyed considerable employment security and extensive benefits during layoffs, as did Spanish workers fortunate enough to be employed in the primary labor market.

A quick review of these differences illustrates clearly the important role strong and legitimate institutional arrangements play in providing workers with various forms of job and/or income security. Notwithstanding various efforts to roll back state intervention in the Italian, French, and German economies or the setbacks Social Democratic regimes in northern Europe have suffered in recent years, most of these countries continue to possess an array of institutional arrangements (retraining programs, *cassa integrazione guadagni*, active labor market policies, etc.) aimed at protecting workers from the consequences of job loss. Yet here too we see significant variation within countries as well. For example, employees in small Japanese and Italian companies do not enjoy the same kinds of benefits, security, and possibilities for transfer as workers in larger establishments. Likewise, in the United Kingdom, employment security (insecurity) is as much a sectoral and status issue as a national phenomenon. Although manual workers in the private sector enjoy little if any job security—they can be dismissed with a week's notice—in the public sector, both manual and nonmanual workers are so well protected that they enjoy de facto lifelong employment.

Nonetheless, the problem of job security is one that all parties who seek to promote innovations must face. Unfortunately, there are no easy answers to this dilemma. As recent experiences by leading high-tech firms in the United States or large manufacturing companies in Japan have illustrated, few, if any, individual firms can credibly guarantee lifetime employment security. Negotiating or offering job transfers, early retirements, severance payments, and other adjustment assistance is and has been used as part of the way out of this dilemma. But in the longer run perhaps the greatest employment security a firm can offer is to provide employees continual training and development opportunities while employed so that if and when the time comes for employees to reenter the external labor market, they will possess the skills necessary to secure another job.

Unfortunately, it is not clear that many firms are thinking this way at the moment. Instead, there has been an explosion in the use of part-time and temporary employees or short-term employment contracts in many countries. This builds on a trend that was first introduced with "guest workers" in Germany and other northern European countries during periods of labor shortages in the 1960s and 1970s. These contingent or flexible employment relationships pose difficult problems for managers, public policy officials, and unions, since the traditional lines of authority and responsibility for management often get blurred and the training, benefits, and other human resource practices needed to promote a highly skilled, committed, and productive work force are less likely to be found in contingent employment relationships. Sometimes mixing regular and contingent workers also introduces new social tensions in the workplace and in the larger society. Women, minorities, and immigrants are particularly vulnerable and over-represented in these situations. The United States, for example, has experienced major debates and conflicts between labor and management over the increasing trend to "contract out" work that was previously performed by full-time career employees. In Japan, the role of immigrant workers has become a significant political and social issue as well. Clearly a major development in recent years has been the increase in the diversity of the labor force and the types of employment relationships found within these economies. Whether these are managed in ways that promote mutual gains through new opportunities for new classes of workers or whether they degenerate into two classes of employment—a small and shrinking core of well-paid and secure employees surrounded by a large number of lower-paid, less secure, less loyal, and less well-trained employees—remains to be seen.

Japan faces an especially acute employment adjustment crisis, particularly in the service sector of its economy. Pressures from U.S. trade negotiators to open Japanese markets to foreign competitors are likely to uncover considerable overstaffing and inefficiencies in this sector. Some of our colleagues in Japan are now openly questioning whether the lifetime employment system commonly found in large firms will survive.

Compensation

The worldwide slowdown in economic growth and productivity along with the recessions of the early 1980s and again in the early 1990s held back real wage growth in most advanced industrialized countries of the world. Real wages were most stagnant in the United States, however, and grew moderately in Japan, Germany, and several other European countries. Inequality in income also grew within most of the countries included in this study but, again, to the greatest extent in the United States. In contrast, income inequality remained stable or grew only slightly in Germany, Norway, and Japan (Freeman and Katz 1994). In these countries their centralized wage setting structures and traditions continued to hold down expansion of wage differentials, while in Italy and Sweden the long-standing solidaristic wage policies that followed through most of the 1970s gave way somewhat as business pushed hard to decentralize bargaining structures and lower labor costs. Once again we see that in countries lacking strong national or sectoral bargaining arrangements (e.g., the United States and United Kingdom), wage differentials and income were greatest. Nonetheless, in all countries there was a resurgence of inequalities, either in income or employment opportunities. This threatens not only to polarize these societies into "haves" and "have nots" but also to undermine the solidaristic principles around which labor movements have traditionally organized.

These varying wage developments are closely related to other features of the employment relationships examined in this book. For example, the growth in inequality is in part a function of the increased demand for skilled blue-collar, technical, and professional workers with advanced analytical and problem solving skills needed to effectively use new technologies. In the United States where training institutions that other countries use to produce new employees with these skills are relatively weak and where the unions that traditionally supported development of these skills have declined precipitously, the supply of workers with the requisite skills also declined. This combination of shifting supply and demand accompanied by the institutional differences in wage setting helps explain why the United States appears to be such a deviant case (Freeman and Katz 1994).

Human Resources and Firm Governance

Some believe that a strategy for adjusting to the changing environment of employment relations that achieve mutual gains for firms and their employees will only be chosen and sustained over time if employee interests and human resource considerations are strongly represented in the top strategic level and governance processes of corporations. This representation might be direct and formal—through worker representatives on supervisory or corporate boards of directors—or indirect and/or informal through the role of the top human resource management professionals and/or union-management consultations and information sharing. Yet we observe wide variation in the extent to which human resources has gained this strategic position in corporations around the world.

Although we have seen a good deal of debate and some experimentation with new ways to engage human resource issues in corporate strategy and governance processes, the general view from our country teams is that relatively little has changed over the course of the past decade. Those countries that had strong formal institutional arrangements, such as Germany and Norway, continued them or strengthened them in marginal ways. As noted earlier, in Germany the evidence suggests that the role of works councils increased relative to the role of unions as the "qualitative" issues such as the introduction of new technologies, training, and work reorganization gained in importance. In Japan informal labor-management consultation continued and perhaps was strengthened somewhat as firms and union representatives sought to cope with the aftermath of the two oil shocks of the 1970s. There have also been a variety of experiments with greater information sharing, union-management consultation, and worker representation on corporate boards in the United States, Britain, and Australia, but these experiences have so far been quite limited.

12.3   Current Tensions and Future Research in Employment Relations

The development of this research network and project was motivated by the proposition that changes in employment practices were occurring in such diverse settings that they called into question the prevailing theoretical frameworks in the field of industrial relations. From early on it was clear that answering the question of whether a new framework is needed, and if so, how to conceptualize it, would require a long-term, multiple-phased research project. This book reports only on the first phase—national studies of the evolution of employment practices. More thorough answers to this question must await the results of the next phase of work—intensive cross-national comparisons of developments within specific industries. Nevertheless, even at this stage of our work, a number of interesting tensions can be identified that deserve further investigation as our comparative work progresses. Several of these tensions are discussed in this final section.

The Coexistence of Cost-Based and Value-Added Strategies

Within all the countries we studied we see the uneasy coexistence of cost-based and differentiation high value added competitive strategies. These two polar opposites do not divide up along national lines, although the distribution of the two may vary within different countries. The essence of the strategic choice perspective associated with the MIT research team suggests that the nature of employment practices and relationships derives from an interaction of changing environmental conditions and the strategies of business, labor, and government actors. For business the key strategic choice is viewed as the competitive strategies adopted to respond to increased competition in product markets and new technological possibilities. Value-added-based strategies are expected to lead to the most fundamental transformations in employment relations and have the best chance of producing outcomes of mutual benefit to firms and their employees. Cost-based strategies, on the other hand, are expected to lead to a downward spiral of wages, working conditions, and labor standards and to reinforce adversarial relations at the workplace. Given the values we hold for industrial relations, a strong preference is expressed for the value-added strategies. Therefore in the more normative work based on this school of thought, we explore ways in which institutions, practices, and the strategies of business, labor, and government decision-makers can be moved to support this general choice.

The data provided in the national reports suggest that firms are indeed struggling with these choices, but few firms can be clearly identified as pure adopters of either option. Instead, we observe most firms engaging in both strategies, sometimes simultaneously but often sequentially. The dramatic changes in Fiat's strategy over the course of the 1980s and early 1990s illustrate the point most vividly. After an intensive period of labor conflict initiated by the company's decision to restructure and lay off 20,000 workers in the early 1980s in order to reduce its costs and weaken the unions, Fiat has engaged in a gradual process of rebuilding its relationships with its work force and unions in order to pursue its current strategy of rapid product development, extensive use of state-of-the-art technologies, and production of high-quality products (Locke 1995; Camuffo and Volpato 1994). Countless similar examples can be found in the United States where the initial round of concession bargaining of the early 1980s in industries as varied as airlines, autos, steel, and paper (Cappelli 1983) were followed by efforts to engage employees and their union representatives in partnerships to improve quality, productivity, and labor-management relations. The case of AT&T in telecommunications is especially instructive, since this company and its union representatives experienced a tumultuous decade of continual downsizing and restructuring in the face of emerging new competition. Yet even as the downsizing continued, by the 1990s this company and its union were developing one of the more advanced models of labor-management partnership and employee participation found in the United States today (e.g., the "Workplace of the Future"). A number of the high-technology firms long known for their commitment to state of the art human resource practices such as IBM and Digital Equipment Corporation have taken the reverse path in the 1990s as markets for their hardware products declined forcing them to downsize and cut labor costs dramatically. Volvo in Sweden presents another example of the reverse scenario. After developing one of the world's boldest efforts to reorganize work in its Kalmar and Udevalla auto assembly plants, the company decided to restructure by closing these innovative operations in favor of its larger and more traditionally organized facilities in Gottenham. In Britain the mixture of traditional and new human resource practices observed in many industries has led to a debate over whether or not anything was changing at all.

The low-cost response to market pressures and changes appears to be most frequent in countries with weak institutions, low levels of unionization, decentralized bargaining structures, and a limited government role in labor market affairs. Again the United States is the extreme case, followed closely by Britain. Cost-based strategies may give firms a comparative advantage over value-added firms in the short run. However, they exert a perverse externality on the society by making it riskier for competing firms to make the long-term investments needed to upgrade skills and change their organizational practices to get the benefits of these investments. Thus, to the extent that cost-based strategies dominate in a country, the nation risks getting caught in a low-wage—low-skill equilibrium. Nations that lack strong institutions that constrain the choice of the low-wage option are particularly vulnerable to this problem. The United States may be suffering from this phenomenon at the moment.

Although there is less flexibility for individual firms to choose the low-cost option in countries such as Germany, Japan, Sweden, and Norway, even in these countries firms have experienced increasing pressures to restructure in ways that reduce their labor cost disadvantages. Thus, while strong industrial relations institutions can moderate the tendency of firms to adjust by controlling labor costs, firms working within these institutional contexts nonetheless experience increasing pressures from competitors in other countries. Whether negotiated adjustments will occur through traditional institutional mechanisms or whether we observe a general weakening of these previously strong institutional arrangements is an issue that needs to be followed closely by future comparative research. An equally important question is whether a negotiated or gradual adjustment strategy involving worker representation produces outcomes that better balance the interests of all the stakeholders involved than the now unilateral management driven approach observed in countries with weaker and more decentralized unions and industrial relations institutions. A good experiment to watch carefully on this point is the "managed decentralization" strategy described in the Australian chapter.

The Flexibility/Polarization Nexus

A second tension that appears to be arising from the drive for increased flexibility in work organization, and the related employment practices discussed in the previous chapters is the potential for polarization of employment opportunities between those with access to jobs with innovative practices and those without. Inequality in income, temporary or other forms of contingent work, differential access to training and career opportunities that build the human capital necessary to be competitive in external labor markets—all of these are the product of the type of partial diffusion of the workplace innovations discussed in the previous chapters. This not only makes it more difficult to sustain commitment to value-added strategies at the micro level but also exacerbates the divisions among different groups within society. The potential for polarization is again the greatest in situations where the decisions about how to structure employment relations are left to individual employers unmediated by strong institutions that represent the interests of workers. Yet strong institutions alone are not enough. The evidence suggests that worker representatives and/or government regulatory agencies need to have strategies of their own that both support the innovative efforts of individual firms and *complement* these strategies by extending access to these innovations and their benefits to those work groups in which individual firms have no self-interest in investing. In contrast, strong worker institutions that lack this type of complementary strategy are likely to simply resist these innovations for fear of undermining their traditional roles and approaches to representing or protecting workers. In this case the result is increased conflict over the innovations themselves that further limits their diffusion.

Again, the United States provides the clearest example. The U.S. chapter made reference to the growth in contract workers in the petrochemical industry in recent years as firms in that industry have sought to increase their flexibility, lower their labor costs, and substitute unionized workers with non-union contract employees (Kochan et al. 1994). One of the consequences of this development is that the influx of less experienced and less trained workers has led to increased rates of accidents and personal injuries among those doing the most high-risk work in this industry. Despite the vocal opposition of the unions representing petrochemical workers, and despite the understanding of these trends and their effects by the government agencies responsible for enforcing safety regulations, little has yet been done to deal with the consequences of this search for flexibility by individual employers. Only recently have some local unions and employers, and some local employer associations acting on their own, begun to address these issues by forming regional partnerships to train the contract workers and upgrade the labor standards under which these employees work.

Examples of this same phenomenon can be observed in other countries as well. In Europe the general debate over "insiders" versus "outsiders" in the labor market is a macro level manifestation of this issue. In Japan the general exclusion of women from the lifetime employment system and the debates about whether those working in the smaller subcontracting firms that lie outside the interlocking networks of large firms enjoy benefits and labor standards similar to those inside these networks are likewise manifestations of this issue.

Variations in wages, working conditions, and labor market outcomes will be found in any employment relations system reflecting differences in individual human capital and a host of other well-documented organizational and institutional factors. Thus it should not be surprising that a gap exists on these dimensions between those with access to workplace innovations and those left out. The question that begs for more micro-level research is whether this gap is larger or smaller than these found in traditional employment systems. If it is found to be larger, the question then might well turn to what institutional responses on the part of unions, industry-level associations, and government can best cope with the consequences of this disparity by extending access to these innovations rather than by policies that seek to return to the more traditional modes of employment relations and regulation.

Voice versus the Decline of Traditional Unions

It is ironic that just as unions in many countries around the world have been declining in influence and membership the need for a strong role for employee voice in corporate decision making, industry-level interactions, and national policymaking is growing. Yet the country chapters also found little evidence that human resource issues have gained increased influence in corporate decision making. Even in Germany where the law institutionalizes employee representation in corporate governance through establishment-level works councils and codetermination, unions now appear on the defensive. Moreover the decentralizing trend observed in most countries is leading to a weakening of industry-level bargaining and other forms of union-management interaction in some countries. In other countries national-level tripartite or corporatist structures have been in decline for a number of years (Swenson 1989).

Yet, as the above discussion of polarization suggests, a simple reconstruction of union membership and union power exerted around traditional strategies is not only unlikely to occur in many countries, but also, given the forces that have led to union decline, such a mirror image rebound would not effectively serve the interests of workers in coping with the forces affecting their vital interests in an international economy. The question therefore is, What new or modified voice mechanisms can effectively represent worker interests in the current environment?

Several examples from the country studies suggest some tentative answers or hypotheses that need to be tested in future micro-level analyses. The German study reported that works councils are becoming increasingly important because they deal with "qualitative" issues such as training, new technology, work organization, and adjustments to restructuring. Moreover they do so by representing all of the workers in an establishment, not just union members or blue-collar workers. Works councils also represent workers while operating under a "peace obligation." By their design, works councils are expected to be integrative rather than distributive institutions. Likewise IG Metall has initiated its own strategy for promoting "group work," its version of the type of teamwork employers in the automobile and many other manufacturing industries are seeking as part of their agenda for workplace innovation and transformation. It is not surprising therefore that there is growing interest and debate over how to achieve the functional equivalent of the German works council system in the United States and Canada (Adams 1985; Freeman and Rogers 1993; Rogers and Streeck 1994; Kochan and McKersie 1988; Weiler 1990).

The Australian case illustrates an effort to reform national institutions and to decentralize industrial relations decision making to the enterprise while attending to some of the potential negative side effects of decentralization and work reform within individual enterprises. The Australian national report described this approach as "managed decentralism," a strategy that evolved in part out of policy debates initiated by the labor movement and the labor government. Included in the decentralizing program in Australia are efforts to restructure the trade union movement along industry lines and to promote industrywide training and occupational standards. In the auto industry, a Trade Union Training Authority (TUTA) helps oversee these standards and supports training on an industrywide basis. Although it is too early to tell whether this managed decentralism strategy will obtain the changes in employment practices and institutions needed to improve the competitiveness of Australian industry while simultaneously safeguarding employment standards, it does provide an interesting model for other countries to observe, and one that needs to be tested in future research.

The Bottom Line: Is There a Transformation Underway?

What does the weight of the evidence presented in these chapters tell us about the question of whether or not a transformation in employment practices is occurring around the world? Is there enough change to require a new theoretical model of industrial relations? Our tentative answer is that there is indeed a transformation underway, albeit it does not conform neatly to the predictions of either the strategic choice model or the institutional school of thought. Instead the common trends and varied patterns reviewed above suggest that explaining the current and future distribution of employment practices will require a model that (1) integrates institutional and strategic actions or choices into a single predictive framework and (2) gives greater attention to the historical factors that create different "starting points" or baseline conditions for change. Consider, for example, the experience of two polar cases, the United States and Australia.

U.S. industrial relations practices are changing in dramatically divergent directions precisely because the United States historically had weak labor institutions and decentralized structures, which were then further weakened by the employer-led changes of the past fifteen years. In the absence of strong legal or industrywide structures and in the face of a weakening and declining labor movement, firms have gained increasing discretion over which way to adjust—through higher-value-added or low-cost strategies. The logical prediction is that these divergent trends will continue in the United States unless, or until, a political backlash from the labor force gives rise to a new government policy or a resurgence of labor. Thus the strategic choice, enterprise-based model fits not only countries like the United States but firms in similar settings that have sufficient discretion to initiate change.

The propositions presented in chapter 2 (see the appendix to that chapter) by Keith Sisson serve as useful starting points for predicting the direction of changes that micro- and firm-level employment practices will take in environments where employers are not constrained by industry or national structures, laws, or powereful labor organizations. The propositions all emphasize management as the initiator of action. Whether employers choose to move toward more value-added or cost-driven strategy then depends on the institutional constraints and the response of labor and government actors. This approach recognizes that the forces for change are universal but the direction and nature of the responses are not random nor completely determined by a singular market or technological imperative. Instead they can be predicted only by having sufficient detailed knowledge of the historical factors that produce the baseline or starting point for change, the institutional constraints, and the power and strategic responses of labor and government.

Alternatively, consider the experience of Australia, a country with a long history of centralized institutions and a strong militant labor movement. The transformation underway in Australia did not flow out of a natural adaptation of its existing institutions toward a more decentralized system and greater flexibility in work practices. Nor did employers serve as the driving force for change, at least in its initial stages. Employer actions were limited by both the power of the labor movement and the constraints imposed by the centralized system of arbitration. Change was clearly motivated by economic pressures but launched by the labor movement's strategic actions based on its consideration of alternative models from other countries. Once opened up, employers took up the cause, urging greater decentralization, flexibility, and changes in work practices.

Clearly institutional constraints limited the options available for introducing change in Australian employment relations; it took strategic actions on the part of labor and government first and employers second to open up the prior system to the fundamental restructuring now underway. Thus history, institutions, and choice are all important considerations in explaining the nature and extent of change underway in Australia.

Do National Industrial Relations Systems Still Exist?

Given the tensions, contradictions, and variations within, and not simply across, the different nation-states covered in this volume, does it still make sense to speak about national industrial relations systems, or should we think of national employment arrangements as composites of different subnational (sectoral or strategy-based patterns)? Clearly an understanding of employment relations as a system in which all the pieces fit together and reinforce one another is something that does not capture well the mix of practices described in the various chapters in this book. Perhaps Germany was the lone exception in this study, but even in that country pressures to restructure and adjust are mounting as well. Elsewhere Locke (1992) has argued that the new terms of international competition and technological innovation challenges industrial relations theory as much as it challenges unions and management. Variations in industrial relations practices resulting from the productivity coalitions emerging in many plants (and the absence of such coalitions in other forms and plants) leads to the end of distinctive national systems of industrial relations. Does it still make sense to speak of a distinctive Italian or American industrial relations system if there is wider variation within each of these countries in terms of employment relations than there is between the practices characteristic of each country? Every chapter in this book has made clear that these subnational patterns are worthy of study and should not be so quickly discussed as outliers or exceptions to the dominant (national) model. Nonetheless, this question is impossible to answer in the abstract. Indeed this is precisely the type of issue that can only be answered conclusively by applying the common analytical framework used to guide the national reports to comparisons of industries across countries as well as within national-states across industries and types of firms. This is precisely the type of research we hope to see developed in the second phase of our research project.

12.4   Lessons and Next Steps

This phase of our work has opened the debate over the appropriate analytical framework for interpreting and guiding the study of contemporary employment relations. We have done more to elaborate than to answer questions over the adequacy of models inherited from a prior generation of scholars or the ones offered as alternatives. This debate must go on, and will do so as the reports of different industry-level comparative studies now underway become available. Projects are moving forward in the telecommunications, auto, steel, and banking industries. A parallel project is underway in Asia where research teams from the newly industrializing countries are addressing the issues raised in this volume with a common analytical framework modified to fit developing countries in that part of the world.

We are heartened by the growing interest in international and comparative research that seems to be occurring in the field of industrial relations. While it is too early to label it a renaissance, several lessons learned from this project suggest how a renaissance might be achieved.

The first lesson is that description void of an analytical model or theoretical argument has lost its value for moving our understanding ahead or providing the information and perspective for action needed by professionals who shape employment practices. This project started with several theoretical propositions derived from the work of the MIT research team. These were subjected to lively debate and critique by some of the chapter authors and country teams included in this volume. As a result we now have sharpened and elaborated the questions that need to be answered to resolve whether the strategic choices of employers, labor organizations, and government actors or the institutional structures that link these parties are the dominant determinants of change and patterns of practice observed in different settings.

Second, we hope this work has begun the overdue process of challenging the neoliberal models of market economies and economic restructuring that have dominated political discourse and macro policymaking in recent years. The variations in employment practices and outcomes documented in the country chapters demonstrate that there is not a single natural response to increased market competition. Nor are the variations observed simply random deviations from a single market-determined result. Instead, employment relations are shaped in systematic and predictable ways by institutions that filter these external pressures and by the strategies of the key actors. Adjustment patterns in countries that have a history of strong centralized industrial relations institutions tend to follow a more incremental, negotiated adjustment pattern and aim to achieve results that balance the interests of different social groups and economic interests. When guided by a strategy for adjustment that can gain and maintain a general political consensus, significant change can and does occur, as we are seeing in Australia. Germany, Japan, and Norway are likely to serve as the next test cases. In the United States and Great Britain, adjustment has been more unilateral with unions and their traditional institutional supports and political allies put on the defensive. Even in these countries, debate has recently begun to turn toward how to cope with some of the consequences of an adjustment path that is driven by market deregulation and managerial action. The social strains of increased wage inequality, and the increased gap between those who benefit from and those left behind by the new economy and new employment practices are leading to efforts to find a new role for government policy, and for labor unions or alternative institutions for representing worker interests at the workplace, in enterprise decision making, and in industrial and economic policymaking.

This places new intellectual demands on professionals in our field. We can no longer afford to sit on the sidelines while advocates of neoliberal policies advise national governments or international agencies on how to best restructure economies and develop free-market systems. But joining the fray also requires that we have clear models of the types of institutions, strategies, and workplace practices that can effectively balance the interests of workers, employers, and societies today. Moreover we must be ready and able to translate these models into concrete policies and actions that deliver their promised results. This was one of the distinguishing features of prior generations of industrial relations scholars who translated their values and theoretical ideas into practices that made collective bargaining, dispute resolution, and labor standards administration work effectively in their respective societies. This is the standard and the tradition that contemporary students of employment relations must uphold.

A third lesson is the need for micro research. This is essential for both the theoretical model building and the more activist policy roles called for above. Note that both the propositions underlying new models of industrial relations and the arguments for new policies and strategies for adjustment were generated from studies of what was happening to traditional practices in the workplaces that served as first movers in response to changing conditions. Out of these micro experiments evolved an understanding of both the strengths and weaknesses of traditional practices and the ability to conceive of new approaches that, if more widely adopted and accepted, hold the promise of benefits to the macro economy and society. Moreover the variations within each country studied demonstrate the new comparative employment relations research must move away from efforts to conceptualize and compare national systems in order to explain why common patterns and systematic variations are visible both within and across nations.

The rich and well-informed case studies provided in the chapters of this book demonstrates this type of micro research is best conducted by individuals and research teams with deep knowledge of their local cultures but with a broad knowledge of comparable developments or functionally equivalent practices and institutions found in different parts of the world. Explaining why flexible work systems and various forms of teamwork are appearing with frequency in internationally competitive industries such as autos, steel, and telecommunication can only be done by examining enterprise and workplace practices in some detail in different countries. Moreover understanding the subtle but critical differences in what teamwork means in these different settings, and how local customs, union traditions and strategies, and social norms shape the emergent team systems, requires the cultural knowledge that only local country experts hold.

But too much local knowledge, unchallenged by a global perspective, can blind one to an understanding of current developments or to considering alternative ways to structure employment practices. This then is the real value of an international network for structuring comparative research and analysis. We can have the best of both worlds—detailed studies grounded in local knowledge and the means for comparing and debating comparable work from other countries.

Finally, we hope this volume puts to rest the old debate over convergence or lack of convergence of employment systems around the world. In its place should be an active search for both common patterns that reflect the growing interdependence of national economies, the ease of transfer of technologies, information, and organizational innovations, and systematic variations that can be explained by differences in local history, the strength of institutions, and the values and strategic choices of key actors. Such analysis could produce the renaissance in the comparative studies of work and employment relations that we seek.

Index

Absenteeism, and Swedish model, 267, 268
Affirmative action (employment equity), in Canada, 97, 121–22
Aix-en-Provence group, xiii–xiv
America. *See* United States, industrial relations in
Analytical model, need for, 381
Annual improvement factor (AIF), in U.S. automobile industry, xvi, 12
Apprenticeship, 363
  in Britain, 42–43
  in Germany, 247
  in Italy, 143, 152
  in Norway, 310–11
  in U.S., 10
Australian industrial relations and human resource policies, 59–60, 85–88, 378
  adjustment patterns of, 382
  compensation, 76–78, 363
  and corporate governance, 80–83, 372
  data gathering in, 70–71
  distinctive features of, 60–67
  employment security and staffing, 72, 78–80
  enterprise focus in, 361
  and predictions of change, 379–80
  proposals for change in, 67–70
  skill formation, 74–76, 87
  stability or change factors in, 83–86
  training, 74–75, 363
  unions, 60–61, 364, 378 (*see also under* Unions)
  work organization, 71–74, 77, 87, 366
Automobile industry
  in Canada, 118, 119, 120

in Germany, 242–43, 246, 367
in Japan, 338, 342
in Spain, 181–82
in Sweden, 267, 270, 272–73, 374
in U.S., xvi, 11, 12, 18–19

Banks, and Japanese corporations, 349
British (United Kingdom) industrial relations, 33–34
  adjustment patterns of, 382
  change in, 38, 47–48
  compensation, 44–45, 363, 371
  and corporate governance, 48–51, 372
  distinctive features of, 34–38
  employment security, 45–47, 368, 369
  pay as important in, 157
  policy implications of, 52
  research propositions from, 52–53
  skill formation and development, 41–44
  training, 42–44, 363
  unions, 33, 35, 37, 41, 47, 51, 364
  work organization, 39–41, 365–66, 367, 374
  and work organization (flexible), 360, 362, 363
Business unionism, in U.S., 2, 3

Canada, industrial relations and human resource practices in, 91–93, 123–26
  collective agreements, 107–108, 109
  and demographic composition of labor force, 106
  and economy, 93–94
  employment and income guarantees, 119–20, 368
  Employment Standards legislation, 97
  fairness and equity in, 121–22

Canada (cont.)
and German works council system, 378
and government, 98–99
and international competitiveness, 98, 126
labor legislation, 95–96
and management, 99–100
and political parties, 94–95
and productivity lag, 106–107
and recessions/unemployment, 106
research and policy issues from, 125–26
social-security legislation, 96–97
training, 122–23, 363
unions in, 92, 94, 100–105, 107, 110–11, 124, 125–26, 364 (see also under Unions)
wage incentives, 120–21
work organization, 117–19, 366
workplace governance, 108, 110–17
workplace regulations, 97–98
Canada-U.S. Free Trade Agreement (FTA) (1989), 94, 107, 115, 124, 126
Capability-based wage systems, in Japan, 344–45, 346
Capitalism, institutional framework of, x
Cassels, Sir John, 48
Casual workers, in Australia, 80
Centralization
in Australian system, 60, 86
in German firms, 245–46, 257
in Norwegian bargaining system, 321
of Swedish wage bargaining, 274–75, 278
Clinton administration, 26–27
Clothing industry, in U.S., 21
Codetermination
in Germany, 232, 234, 235, 249, 259
and Italian Protocollo, 156
in Norway, 309
Collective bargaining. See also Enterprise bargaining; Unions; Wage bargaining
in Australia, 60
in Britain, 34, 35–37, 38, 51
in Canada, 91, 92, 96, 108, 110
enterprise focus in, 361–62
in France, 204, 206, 213, 218–19
in Germany, 237, 244–45, 248, 252, 255–56, 257, 260
in Italy, 132, 135, 154
and new labor relations model, xviii–xix
in Norway, 300
in Spain, 169, 170, 175–79, 184–85, 192

in Sweden, 267, 269, 291, 292, 293
in U.S., xvi, xvii, 2, 3, 9
Communication Workers of America (CWA), 20, 105
"Company as family" ideology, in Japan, 329, 331
Comparable worth (pay equity), in Canada, 97, 121
Compensation
in Australia, 76–78, 363
in Britain, 44–45, 363, 371
in Canada, 120–21
in France, 218–20
in Germany, 370, 371
in Italy, 147–51, 371
in Japan, 325–26, 339–46, 370, 371
in Norway, 303, 313–16, 371
performance-related, 363–64
in Spain, 175–79, 192
in Sweden, 274–82, 371
in U.S., 12–15, 19, 370, 371
variations in, 370–71
Competitive strategies, cost-based and value-added, 373–75, 379
Computer industry, in U.S., 19–20
Concertation
in Italy, 158
in Quebec, 116
in Spain, 192
Contingent workers, 360. See also Contract work; Part-time work; Temporary work
in Britain, 46–47
in U.S., 16, 17
Contract work. See also Contingent workers
in Australia, 80
and corporate culture, 246
in France, 222
and German union organization, 251
increase in use of, 369–70
in Spain, 173–74, 188
in Sweden, 287–88
in U.S., 17–18, 370, 376
Convergence debate, 384
Core-periphery model, xix
in Britain, 46–47
in future, 370
of Japanese IR/HR systems, 327
and Spanish unions' claims, 179
Corporate culture
in Germany, 246
in Spain, 184, 186–87

Corporate governance, xx–xxi
  in Australia, 80–83, 372
  in Britain, 48–51, 372
  in Japan, 346–50
  in Norway, 317–20
  in U.S., 19, 372
  variations in, 371–72
Corporatism, 171–72, 280. *See also*
  Neocorporatism
Cost-based strategies, 373–75, 379
Cost of living adjustment (COLA)
  in Italy, 147
  in U.S. automobile industry, xvi, 12
Craft unions
  and Britain, 36
  in U.S., xvii

Decentralization
  and Australian system, 59, 67–70, 86,
    375, 378, 379–80
  in collective bargaining, 361–62
  in collective bargaining (Britain), 38,
    51
  and corporate culture, 246
  in Germany, 245–46, 256, 257, 362
  in Norwegian bargaining system, 321
  of Swedish human resource
    management, 290
  of Swedish wage bargaining, 274–75,
    278, 280, 281, 282
  trend toward, 377
Demographic composition of labor force,
  in Canada, 106
Deregulation, xi, xvii, 14, 59, 382
Description, analytical model needed
  with, 381
Distribution or redistribution of income
  in Australia, 76
  in France, 210–12
  and German system, 257–58, 260
  growth in inequality of, 371
  Japanese method of, 345–46
  in Norway, 298–99, 316
  and Swedish wage compression,
    275–76
  in U.S., 15, 18
Dodge, Joseph, 330
Donovan Commission, 35
Dore, Ronald, xiii
Downsizing, corporate
  in Spain, 175
  in U.S., 16, 17

Dual system of industrial relations, and
  Britain, 36
Dunlop, John, xii, xiii, xiv, xxi

Economic policy participation, in Japan,
  350–53
Economics, vs. politics (France), 227
Economic theory, and creation of market
  systems, x
Education. *See also* Training; Vocational
  training
  in Britain, 42
  in Germany, 247
  in Italy, 143–43
  return on (U.S.), 15
  in Sweden, 282–84
  in U.S., 26
Employee buy-out, by United
  Steelworkers of America, 121
Employee participation
  in Australia, 73–74, 81
  in Canada, 108
  in France, 215
  in Japan, 348
  in Sweden, 269
  in U.S., 4, 6, 8–9
Employee stock ownership plans
  (ESOPs), in U.S., xix, 13–14
Employment equity (affirmative action),
  in Canada, 97, 121–22
Employment and income guarantees, in
  Canada, 119–20
Employment levels, in Japan, 339–46. *See
  also* Staffing
Employment policies
  and enterprise-level strategies, xx
  and surrounding systems, xix–xx
Employment practices, xxii
  research and analysis of, 383–84
  variations in, 382
Employment relations. *See also* Industrial
  relations
  analytical framework for, 381
  current tensions and future research in,
    372–81
  as national systems, 380
  new approach to, 359–60, 364–65
  transformation in, 378–80
Employment security, xxii. *See also*
  Staffing
  in Australia, 72, 78–80
  in Britain, 45–47, 368, 369

Employment security (cont.)
in Germany, 368
in Italy, 151–55, 368, 369
in Japan, 330
in Japan (Employment Stabilization
Fund), 351
in Norway, 316–17, 368
in Spain, 171–75, 180
in Sweden, 286–89, 368
in U.S., 15–18, 26
variations in, 368–70
Employment systems, convergence or
lack of convergence of, 384
Enterprise bargaining, in Australia, 65–66,
68–69, 70, 87, 88
Enterprise focus for industrial relations,
361–62
Enterprise unionism
in Japan, 326, 330, 341, 353
and Swedish model, 281
Equity, and Canadian system, 121–22
Europe
alternative human resource practices in,
25
economic integration in (West), xi
and German model, 259
vs. U.S. training practices, 11
Ex-employed population, in Spain,
188–89

Factory councils, in Italy, 134. See also
Works councils
Fairness, and Canadian system, 121–22
Fiat, 138, 373
Financial services industry, in U.S.,
21–22
Firm, U.S. notion of, 3
Firm-specific skills, of Japanese workers,
338, 341
Flexibility, employers search for, 365
Flexibility/polarization nexus, 375–77
Flexible specialization, xviii
Flexible wage system, in Japan, 343–44
Flexible working time
and German bargaining, 248, 252
in Italy, 140
Flexible work organizations, 360, 365
explanation of, 383
in Japan, 366
in U.S., xviii
Ford Foundation interuniversity study,
xiii, xi-xii

Fordism, 201. See also Mass production;
Taylorism
and Britain, 39
and career advancement, 142
and French system, 198, 201, 202
and German model, 238, 242, 250
and Italy, 137, 152
transition away from, 165
Foremen, in Japan, 332
France, industrial relations (IR) in,
197–98
changes in, 212–13
employers, 206–208
and employment crisis, 198–201
and flexible employment arrangements,
360
levels of, 208–209
management and supervision methods,
223–25
managerial thought, 202–203
negotiated agreement, 209–10
and productions systems shift, 201–202
redistribution, 210–12
research questions in, 226–28
and social welfare, 220–23
state role, 205–206, 211, 214
training, 201, 210–12, 215–18, 363
unions, 203–205, 207, 220, 221, 225–26,
364
wages and income from work, 218–20
work organization, 213–15
Free Trade Agreement (FTA), Canada–
U.S. (1989), 94, 107, 115, 124, 126
Functional mobility, in Spain, 179–83

German industrial relations, 231–32
adjustment patterns of, 382
changes in, 239, 249–53
compensation, 370, 371
corporate governance, 377
decentralization in, 245–46, 256, 257, 362
and decision-making restructuring,
245–46, 257
and distributional issues, 257–58, 260
employer federations, 236–37
employment security, 368
enterprise-level representation
emphasized, 248–49
guest workers in, 369
human resources development, 246–48,
372
and national system, 380

new approaches to collective bargaining, 244–45
new organizational forms, 241–44
skill formation, 157
struggle over working hours, 240
supervisory boards, 232–34
training, 243, 247–48, 254
and uncertainties of 1990s, 253–60
and unemployment, 239–40, 250, 260
unions, 235, 236, 237–39, 250, 251, 255, 258, 365 (*see also under* Unions)
work organization, 365, 366, 367, 374
work organization (flexible), 360, 362
works councils, 231, 234–39, 241, 243, 248, 249, 257, 362, 372, 377–78
Governance, corporate. *See* Corporate governance
Governance, workplace. *See* Workplace governance
Governance structure, of U.S. firms, 26
Government (state)
and Canadian IR/HR system, 98–99
and French industrial relations, 205–206, 211
in German industrial relations, 237
and Italian labor-management relations, 136
and Norwegian employment relations, 314, 315
and U.S. industrial relations, 27–28
Gramsci, Antonio, 132
Great Britain. *See* British industrial relations
Greenfield plants or worksites, 6, 24, 124, 367
Guest workers, in Germany, 369

Harbison, Fredrick, xii, xiii
Harvey-Jones, Sir John, 52
Health care costs, in U.S., 14–15
Health care industry or system
in Britain, 35
in Canada, 92
in U.S., 22
High-technology firms, in U.S., 4
Human resource development, commitment to (U.S.), 11, 21
Human resource management
in Britain, 47, 48
in Germany, 246–48
and globalization of markets, xi
variations in, 371–72

Human resource policy, xix
and corporate decision making, 377
Human resource practices
clustering of (U.S.), 23
future issues of, 360
and new competitive strategies, 359
Human resource systems
and blue-collar job security (U.S.), 16
and work organization, 5

IBM, 16, 20–21, 123, 374
IBM Germany, 255
Immigrants
as Italian workers, 152
in Spanish four-cornered game, 189
and U.S. clothing industry, 21
Income guarantees, in Canada, 119–20
Income from work, in France, 218–20
Industrial democracy
in Australia, 81
in U.S., 3
Industrialism and *Industrial Man* (Kerr, Dunlop, Harbison, Myers), xii
Industrial policy, French, 206
Industrial relations, ix. *See also* Employment relations; *specific nations*
future issues of, 360
growing importance of skill development in, 363–64
increased flexibility in, 362–63
international and comparative dimension of, x–xi
as national systems, 380–81
new approach to, 361–65
and new competitive strategies, 359
question of new framework for, 372
recent scholarship on, xi–xiv
variations in (cross-national and cross-firm), 365–72, 383
Industrial relations scholars, 382–83
Industrial Relations Systems (Dunlop), xii
Industry developments, in U.S., 18–24
Inequality of income, 15, 375. *See also* Distribution or redistribution of income
Inflation
in Australia, 62
and Italian wage increases, 147–48
in Japan, 350
and Rehn-Meidner model (Sweden), 265
in Spain, 167, 168, 171, 175, 180, 193
in Sweden, 265

Information technologies
  and downsizing, 17
  and white-collar jobs, 7
Innovations
  in Canada, 92, 110–11, 115
  and insiders vs. outsiders, 376–77
  in Italy, 132
  and polarization, 375
  technological, 165, 334–36 (*see also*
    Technology)
  in U.S., 6–7, 16, 24–25
  at Volvo, 270, 272–73
  vulnerability of, 367
  worker resistance to, 376
Intellectual skills, of Japanese workers,
  326, 338, 344, 345
International competition
  and Australian future, 84
  and Canada, 98, 126
  and cooperative relationships (Italy), 159
  employment practices adapted to, 359
Internationalization of economic activity,
  xviii
International labor standards, emergent
  debate about, xi
Investment fund, of Quebec Federation of
  Labor, 116
Italy, industrial relations and human
  resource practices in, 131–37, 157–59
  compensation, 147–51, 371
  employment security and staffing,
    151–55, 368, 369
  enterprise focus in, 361–62
  Fiat strategy, 373
  and international competition, 159
  skill formation and development, 141–47
  unions, 132, 133–34, 135–37, 150–51, 159,
    364 (*see also under* Unions)
  work organization, 137–41, 366
  work organization (flexible), 360, 362,
    363
  workplace governance, 134–35, 155–57

Japan, industrial relations and human-
  resource practices in, 325–28, 353–54
  adjustment patterns of, 382
  alternative human resource practices, 25
  vs. American model, xiii, 11
  compensation, 325–26, 339–46, 370, 371
  corporate governance and participation
    in strategic decisions, 346–50
  decentralization in, 362

employment and compensation, 330,
    339–46, 368, 369
  and employment crisis, 370
  evolution of, 328–46
  and flexible employment arrangements,
    360
  immigrant workers in, 370
  "insiders" vs. "outsiders" in, 376
  labor-management consultation, 372
  and lifetime employment, 325, 326–27,
    332, 341, 343, 344, 370
  neocorporatism, 328, 350–53
  and new labor relations models, xviii
  and oil crisis (1973), 328, 333, 341, 343,
    345, 350, 372
  and oil crisis (1978), 340, 345, 372
  and overall socioeconomic structure,
    346, 351–52
  skill formation, 334–39
  unions, 326, 328, 329–30, 350–53, 364 (*see
    also under* Unions)
  as U.S. competitor, 18, 24
  work organization, 327, 334–39, 365, 366,
    374
  work organization (flexible), 360, 362
Japan Productivity Center, 331, 345,
    367–68
Job classification
  in Sweden, 281
  in U.S., 5, 6
Job control unionism, 2, 6
  in Canada, 108
  in Norway, 301
  in U.S., 3
Job definitions, and U.S. labor relations
  system, xvi, xvii
Job mobility, xxii
  variations in, 368–70
Job redesign, and Swedish model, 291, 292
Job security. *See* Employment security
Joint consultation
  in Australia, 81
  in Japan, 327
  in Sweden, 269
Joint governance, in Canada, 111–13

Katz, Harry, xv
Kerr, Clark, xii, xiii
Kochan, Thomas, xv

Labor disputes, social functions of, 227–28
Labor and human resource policy, xix

Labor legislation, in Canada, 95–96
Labor movement, current-apprehension
  over, x
Labor policy, U.S., 27
Labor unions. *See* Unions
Layoff, protection from. *See* Employment
  security
Layoffs
  and retraining (Italy), 144
  "voluntary severance" as (Japan), 325
Lindbeck Commission (Sweden), 288
"Low-skills equilibrium," Britain in, 43

McKersie, Robert, xv–xvi
Management
  and Canadian IR/HR system, 99–100
  of French firms, 223–26
  as initiator of action, 379
  Japanese corporations controlled by, 349
  research propositions on, 52–53
  resurgence of, 364
  short-termism of (Britain), 49–50, 52
Management compensation, in Spain,
  177–78
Managerial prerogative, in U.S., 2, 3
Marxian scholarship, and labor studies,
  xii
Mass production. *See also* Fordism;
  Taylorism
  vs. atypical employment (Italy), 152
  in Germany, 238, 256
  in Italy, 137
  and New Deal industrial relations, 3
  and U.S. labor relations system, xvii
Micro research, need for, 383
Middle-level managers, and holistic
  systemic changes (U.S.), 25
Multi-skilling, in Australia, 72
Myers, Charles, xii, xiii

National Labor Relations Act (NLRA)
  (1935), 1–2
National Longitudinal Survey of young
  people, 10
Neocorporatism, in Japan, 328, 350–53
Neoliberalism, ix–x, xi, 382
New Deal industrial relations system, 2,
  3–4, 12
New Factories project (Sweden), 268
Nonwage compensation, in U.S., 14–15
North America, economic integration in,
  xi

North American Free Trade Agreement, 94
Norwegian employment relations, 297,
  320–22
  adjustment patterns of, 382
  compensation, 303, 313–16, 371
  corporate governance, 317–20
  employment security and staffing,
    316–17, 368
  and flexible employment arrangements,
    360
  and human resource engagement, 372
  and "labor market parties," 299–306
  and North Sea oil drilling, 308, 321–22
  skill formation and development, 310–13
  and social democratic order, 297–99
  training, 312, 363
  unions, 299–306, 312–13, 320, 321, 364
  wage bargaining, 303
  work organization, 306–309, 366, 374
  work organization (flexible), 362

Organization of work. *See* Work
  organization
Osterman, Paul, xvi, 6, 8, 10, 24, 362–63

Para-professionalization, of white-collar
  jobs, 7, 17, 22
Part-time work, 360. *See also* Contingent
  workers
  in Australia, 80
  in Britain, 46–47
  increase in use of, 369–70
  in Italy, 153
  in Norway, 314
  in Sweden, 288
  in U.S., 17
Paternalism
  in France, 202, 214, 216
  in Spain, 185
Pay equity, in Canada, 97, 121
Piece-rates, in Sweden, 277
Piore, Michael, xv
Poland, organized labor in, x
Polarization of employment
  opportunities, 375–77
Policy participation, in Japan, 350–53
Political parties, Canadian, 94–95
Politics
  vs. economics (France), 227
  and Spanish industrial relations, 166–67
Production systems shift, in France,
  201–202

Productive flexibility, in France, 213–15
Productivity
  Australia's slowdown in, 83–84
  in Britain, 41
  and Canadian IR system, 93, 106–107
  for Japan (JPC), 331, 345, 367–68
  in Norway, 307–308
  and Spanish industrial relations, 171
  and workplace innovations, 367
Productivity pact, in Germany, 237
Profit-sharing
  in Australia, 78
  in Canada, 120
  in U.S., 13
Public education. *See also* Education;
  Training; Vocational training
  in Italy, 143
  in Sweden, 282–84
  in U.S., 26

Quality circles
  in Australia, 73, 81
  in Britain, 40–41, 47–48, 365–66
  in France, 215
  in Italy, 140–41, 159
  in Japan, 332, 336–37, 338, 366
  and Spain, 181–82
  in U.S., 8
Quality of working life (QWL)
  and QC circles (Japan), 336, 337
  in U.S., 4, 18

Rationalization
  in German economy, 241–44, 248
  in Japanese economy, 331, 332, 352
  in Swedish economy, 269
Reagan, Ronald, ix
Redistribution of income. *See*
  Distribution or redistribution
  of income
Redundancy programs, in Australia,
  79–80, 87
Rehn-Meidner (RM) model, 265, 278, 284,
  285

Sabel, Charles, xv
Scheduling of work, xxii
Scientific management, 202
Second Industrial Divide, The (Piore), xv
Self-employed workers
  in Britain, 46–47
  in Italy, 152

Severance allowance, in Japan, 325, 329,
  340
Sexual harassment, provisions against
  (Canada), 122
Short-termism
  in Britain, 49–50, 52
  in Spain, 180, 192
Skill formation and development, xxii
  in Australia, 74–76, 87
  in Britain, 41–44
  growing importance of, 363–64
  increased appreciation of, 364
  in Italy, 141–47
  in Japan, 334–39
  in Norway, 310–13
  in Spain, 183–84, 190, 363
  in Sweden, 282–86
  in U.S., 9–12
  and wages, 371
Social conflict, and work relationships,
  228
Social contract(s)
  in Canada, 114, 116
  in Spain, 171
Social insurance
  in Germany, 237, 241
  in Sweden, 289
Social policy participation, in Japan,
  350–53
Social security
  in Britain, 35
  in Canada, 96
  and contract workers (Spain), 188
  in Germany, 252
  in Italy, 135–36
  in U.S., xiv
Social unionism, of CAW, 120
Social welfare
  in France, 220–23
  in Italy, 157
  of Swedish model, 263–66
Solidaristic work or wage policy
  in Norway, 300
  as Swedish strategy, 265, 274, 275, 276,
  278, 291
South Africa, organized labor in, x
Spanish human resource and industrial
  relations practices and policies, 165–66,
  169–71, 184–86, 187–93
  compensation, 175–79, 192
  and corporate culture, 184, 186–87
  and economy, 167–69, 193

employment security, 171–75, 180
and flexible employment arrangements, 360
and flexible work organization, 362
as "four-cornered game," 189, 191, 193
and Franco's victory in civil war, 172
and political conditions, 166–67
regulation of employment or staffing, 157
skill formation and training, 183–84, 192, 363
unions, 169–70, 180, 186, 187, 190–91, 192 (*see also under* Unions)
work organization and functional mobility, 179–83, 190, 192, 366
Specialization, flexible, xviii
Staffing, xxii. *See also* Employment levels; Employment security
in Australia, 78–80
in Italy, 151–55
in Japan, 341–43
in Norway, 316–17
in U.S., 15–18
variations in, 368–70
State. *See* Government
Storey, John, 47
Strategic choice, cost-based vs. value-added, 373–75, 379
Strategic participation, in Japan, 346–50
Strike(s)
in Canada, 92, 106
civil servants' right to (Canada), 95
by German metalworkers' union, 240–41
in Japan, 326, 329, 330, 331
replacement workers banned (Canada), 96
right to (Canada), 91, 96
right to (Italy), 133
Spain's decriminalization of, 169
Supervisors
and holistic systemic changes (U.S.), 25
role of (Australia), 72–73
Supervisory boards, in Germany, 232–34
Swedish model, 263–66
employment security, 286–89, 368
enterprise focus, 361
flexible wages, 365
future vision(s) of, 289–93
labor legislation, 270, 288–89
skill formation and development, 282–86
and Taylorism, 266–68, 269, 277
training, 284–86, 291, 292, 363

unions, 263, 268–70, 275, 279, 282
wage bargaining and compensation, 274–82, 290, 371
work organization, 266–74, 281, 286, 291–92, 362, 366, 374
System regulator (worker), in Germany, 242, 367

Taylorism, 179, 202, 366. *See also* Mass production
and Britain, 39
and career advancement, 142
in France, 202, 213–14, 225
in Germany, 238, 242
and Italy, 137, 142
modernized, 242
Ontario Shell plant reverses, 117
planning and execution separated in, 336, 338
vs. Quality Circles, 336
in Spain, 179
and Swedish model, 266–68, 269, 277
Team briefing, in Britain, 40, 41, 48
Teamwork
in Australia, 73
in Canada, 117
explanation of, 383
in Germany, 378
in Japan, 366
as rare, 366
in U.S., 338
Technology. *See also* Innovations
in Britain, 41
and Japanese work organization, 334–36
and production-system transition, 165
Telecommunications industries, in U.S., 19–20
Temporary work. *See also* Contract work
in Australia, 80
in Britain, 46–47
increase in use of, 369–70
and innovation, 375
in Italy, 152–53
in Spain, 174, 187, 188, 189, 190
in Sweden, 287
in U.S., 17–18
Thatcher, Margaret, ix
Total quality management (TQM), 363
in Britain, 43
in U.S., 6, 7, 19
"Toyotism," 181

Trade unions. *See* Unions
Training, xxii. *See also* Vocational
    training
  in Australia, 74–75, 363
  in Britain, 42–44, 363
  in Canada, 122–23, 363
  as employment security, 369
  in France, 201, 210–12, 215–18, 363
  in Germany, 243, 247–48, 254
  increased appreciation of, 364
  and internal labor markets, 142
  in Italy, 142–46
  and Norwegian employment relations,
    312, 363
  in Spain, 183–84, 192, 363
  for supervisors (Japan), 332
  in Sweden, 284–86, 291, 292, 363
  vs. Taylorism, 202
  in U.S., 10–12, 363
Transfers within firm, in Japan, 340–41,
    343
*Transformation of American Industrial
    Relations, The* (Kochan, Katz, McKersie),
    xv–xvi
Turnover, and Swedish model, 267, 268

Underground economy
  in Spain, 171, 172–73, 176, 187, 188, 189,
    190, 191
  in Sweden, 288
Unemployment
  in Australia, 62, 76
  and Australian redundancy programs,
    79–80, 87
  in Canada, 106
  in France, 198–201, 213, 224
  in Germany, 239–40, 250, 260
  in Norway, 307, 311, 314, 317
  in Spain, 168, 172–73, 176, 179, 189–90
  in Sweden, 265, 266, 286–87
Unemployment benefits
  in Canada, 96–97
  in Spain, 174, 176–77, 188
  in Sweden, 289
Union avoidance
  in Canada, 124
  in U.S., 4
Unions, 377–78. *See also* Collective
    bargaining
  in Australia, 60–61, 62, 81–82, 86–87, 364,
    378
  in Britain, 33, 35, 37, 41, 47, 51, 364

  in Canada, 92, 94, 95, 99, 100–105, 106,
    107, 110–11, 118, 124, 125–26, 364
  and core-periphery model, xix
  decline in membership of, 364–65
  enterprise unionism, 281, 326, 330, 341,
    353
  in France, 203–205, 207, 220, 221, 225–26,
    364
  in Germany, 235, 236, 237–39, 240–41,
    241n.1, 247–48, 249, 250, 251, 252, 255,
    257, 258, 365
  in Italy, 132, 133–34, 135–37, 140, 141,
    142, 143, 144, 147, 150–51, 154, 156–57,
    159, 364
  in Japan, 326, 328, 329–30, 340, 341–42,
    344, 346, 347–49, 350–53, 354, 364
  job control unionism, 2, 3, 6, 108, 301
  in new labor relations model, xix
  in Norway, 299–306, 312–13, 320, 321,
    364
  in recent years, ix
  in Spain, 167, 169–70, 172, 173–74,
    174n.4, 179, 180, 184, 186, 187, 190–91,
    192
  in Sweden, 263, 268–70, 275, 279, 282
  and training (U.S.), 11–12
  in U.S., xvi, xvvii, 1–3, 20, 21, 22, 125,
    365, 376
United Automobile Workers (UAW), 18,
    94, 120
United Kingdom. *See* British industrial
    relations
United States, industrial relations in,
    xvi–xvii, 1–5
  adjustment patterns of, 382
  basic strategies of, xx
  Canadian compared with, 92, 118, 124
  clustering of, 23
  compensation, 12–15, 19, 370, 371
  and contract work, 17–18, 370, 376
  and corporate governance, 19, 372
  diffusion of new IR/HR practices, 5,
    24–27
  diversity within, 4
  employment security and staffing
    arrangements, 15–18, 26
  and German works council system, 378
  implications of for IR/HR theory, 27–28
  industry developments, 18–24
  labor-management relations, 373–74
  new model in, xviii–xix, 361
  and predictions of change, 379

and skill formation or development,
  9–12
training, 10–12, 363
unions, 1–3, 125, 365 (*see also under*
  Unions)
work organization, 5–9, 366, 367
work organization (flexible), 360, 362
United Steelworkers of America, 100, 105,
  107, 110–11, 113, 119, 121

Value-added strategies, 373–75, 379
Vocational training, 363. *See also* Training
  in Britain, 42
  in Germany, 246–48, 310
  in Italy, 142–43, 363
  in Spain, 183–84, 190
Voluntarism
  in Britain, 35, 36–37, 41–42, 50–51
  in Canada, 91
  in France, 209
  in Italy, 132–33, 137, 146
Voluntary severance, in Japan, 325,
  327–28, 339–40, 343, 368

Wage bargaining. *See also* Collective
  bargaining; Enterprise bargaining
  in Norway, 303, 314–16, 321
  in Sweden, 269, 274–82, 290
Wage compression, as Swedish union
  demand, 275–76
Wage determination
  in Australia, 62–65, 67, 86, 87
  in Italy, 147–48
  in Japan, 327, 345–46
  in Norway, 316
Wage drift, 186, 275–76
Wage incentives, in Canada, 120–21
Wages. *See also* Compensation
  in France, 218–20
  in Japan, 343–46
War Labor Board, 4
Western Europe. *See* Europe
White-collar employees and jobs
  compensation for (U.S.), 13
  in Germany, 246, 251
  internal labor markets for, 15–16, 17
  in Norway, 314
  para-professionalization of, 7, 17, 22
  and skill formation (U.S.), 9–10
  in Sweden, 274, 275, 281, 284, 286, 290,
    290–91
  and work organization (U.S.), 7–8

Work Environment Act (Norway), 318–20
Working time, in Italy, 157. *See also*
  Flexible working time
Work organization, xxii
  in Australia, 71–74, 77, 87, 366
  in Britain, 39–41, 365–66, 367, 374
  in Canada, 117–19, 366
  in France, 213–15
  increased flexibility in, 362–63
  in Italy, 137–41, 366
  in Japan, 327, 334–39, 365, 366, 367
  in Norway, 306–309, 366, 374
  and production-system transition, 165
  in Spain, 179–83, 190, 192, 366
  in Sweden, 266–74, 281, 286, 291–92, 362,
    366, 374
  in U.S., 5–9, 366, 367
  variations in, 365–68
Workplace, social function of, 227–28
"Workplace of the Future," 20, 374
Workplace governance
  in Canada, 108, 110–17
  in Italy, 134–35, 155–57
Work redesign, in U.S., 6, 7
Works councils
  in France, 210, 225
  in Germany, 231, 234–39, 241, 243, 248,
    249, 257, 362, 372, 377–78
  in Italy, 156
  in Spain, 170, 174n.4, 184, 185
World Trade Organization (WTO), xi

Zaibatsu, 350